Teaching Music through Performance in Beginning Band

Grade 1

G-5337

Teaching Music through Performance in Beginning Band

Grade 1

Thomas Dvorak
Larry Blocher
Scott Emmons
Bruce Pearson
Darhyl S. Ramsey
Marguerite Wilder

Compiled and Edited by Richard Miles and Thomas Dvorak

GIA Publications, Inc.
Chicago

G-5337

Copyright © 2001 GIA Publications, Inc.
7404 S. Mason Ave., Chicago, IL 60638
www.giamusic.com
ISBN: 1-57999-107-6
Printed in the United States of America.

Table of Contents

PART II: Teacher Resource Guides

ACKNOWLEDGEMENTS

The following research associates are gratefully acknowledged for outstanding scholarly contributions to the "Teacher Resource Guides":

John Bleuel
University of West Georgia • Carrollton, Georgia

C. Kevin Bowen
Wake Forest University • Winston-Salem, North Carolina

Gordon R. Brock
University of North Dakota • Grand Forks, North Dakota

John C. Carmichael
Western Kentucky University • Bowling Green, Kentucky

Scott Carter
East Carolina University • Greenville, North Carolina

Rod M. Chesnutt
Mississippi State University • Mississippi State, Mississippi

Lynn G. Cooper
Asbury College • Wilmore, Kentucky

Susan Creasap
Morehead State University • Morehead, Kentucky

Maxon Day
University of Wisconsin–Milwaukee • Milwaukee, Wisconsin

Wayne F. Dorothy
Kansas State University • Manhattan, Kansas

Patrick Dunnigan
Florida State University • Tallahassee, Florida

Bradley P. Ethington
Syracuse University • Syracuse, New York

Mark Fonder
Ithaca College • Ithaca, New York

Thomas George Caracas Garcia
University of West Georgia • Carrollton, Georgia

William A. Gora
Appalachian State University • Boone, North Carolina

Richard Greenwood
University of Central Florida • Orlando, Florida

Brian Harris
University of Texas at San Antonio • San Antonio, Texas

L. Kevin Kastens
University of Iowa • Iowa City, Iowa

Roy M. King
Louisiana State University • Baton Rouge, Louisiana

Daryl W. Kinney
Ohio State University • Columbus, Ohio

Jeremy S. Lane
Louisiana State University • Baton Rouge, Louisiana

John M. Laverty
Syracuse University • Syracuse, New York

Matthew Mailman
Oklahoma City University • Oklahoma City, Oklahoma

Andy McMahan
Nicolet High School • Glendale, Wisconsin

Charles T. Menghini
VanderCook College of Music • Chicago, Illinois

Linda R. Moorhouse
Louisiana State University • Baton Rouge, Louisiana

Steven J. Morrison
University of Washington • Seattle, Washington

Richard Anthony Murphy
Middle Tennessee State University • Murfreesboro, Tennessee

Rodney C. Schueller
Western Illinois University • Macomb, Illinois

Matthew J. Seifert
Louisiana State University • Baton Rouge, Louisiana

Deborah A. Sheldon
University of Illinois at Urbana-Champaign • Urbana, Illinois

Frederick Speck
University of Louisville • Louisville, Kentucky

Robert Spradling
Western Michigan University • Kalamazoo, Michigan

John Villella
West Chester University • West Chester, Pennsylvania

Christopher Werner
University of Wisconsin–Milwaukee • Milwaukee, Wisconsin

PART I

THE TEACHING
OF MUSIC

CHAPTER 1

Beginning with the End in Mind: A Personal Perspective for Teaching Music through Performance in Band

Larry R. Blocher

On most days, I have the best job in the world because I not only get to make music with students in band, but I also get to work with students who are preparing to teach other students to make music in band. What a deal—on most days. There are, however, those *other* days. Those are the days when, as I drive home from school listening to the tape of the day's rehearsal, I find myself thinking that there must be an assistant manager position available somewhere at a local mini-mart and…(you may have had similar thoughts). Usually, however, before I have had time to give that idea any real consideration, my mind is back "in the rehearsal," making plans for the next one and hoping that Annie was right: tomorrow, tomorrow….

In our Introduction to Music Education class at the university, we spend time giving students the opportunity to think about why anyone should know and be able to do anything special with music in general and/or in performing groups. We start this process by asking students to think about what got them "hooked" on music in the first place. Most responses are variations on the following theme: making music with a special music teacher. That was (and maybe still is) the "hook" for many of us.

This introductory chapter is intended to provide a starting point for making a personal decision about the importance of teaching music through performance in young band. I will begin by telling you some of the most important aspects of my early involvement with band. As you progress through the chapter, others will share their experiences and ideas. During your reading, I challenge you to think about your early band experiences, especially those that may have been pivotal points in your own music education. It is my hope that an honest self-analysis of your personal journey into music will not only cause you to think about the value of teaching music through

performance in band but also allow you to revisit your own personal philosophy of music teaching.

Being in the Band "Then"

I always wanted to be in the band. I never really thought about not being in the band. My mom had been in band. My brother had been in the band. My sister was in the band at the same time I was in band. Band was just something that you were in.

Now, I admit that I grew up in a small town in Ohio that had a strong band tradition. My hometown even had a band shell in the park. This outdoor "auditorium" was home to community band concerts every Sunday night during the summer. Actually, as I look back now, there might not have been a whole lot more to do in my hometown other than to be "in the band" and/or "on the team" and/or work "on the farm." Since I didn't live on a farm and since I spent several hours keeping the bench warm at a variety of sporting events very early in my "athletic" career, the choice to be in the band was an obvious one for me.

In the Beginning

To be perfectly honest, I do not remember much about my own beginning band experience. I do remember my silver Martin alto saxophone, the same one that my mom had played when she was in the high school band. I remember that it had a white, plastic mouthpiece. I remember that the handle of the case was held on with duct tape (I wish I had invented that stuff!). I remember that I polished that saxophone quite often. I also took it apart once, but that is another story.

I remember that my first beginning band concert was delayed while I ran back to my fifth grade classroom to get my *Belwin Band Builder* book. No one had told me to bring music to the concert, which perhaps was intentional. Anyway, I also remember that my grandfather used to turn his hearing aid off just before the start of the concert. I often wondered at the time why he smiled quite often during the concert. I now understand.

I remember playing that alto saxophone a lot. I'm not sure that what I did with it could be called *practice*. I just played it. I remember playing whatever came to mind, and I remember thinking that it (I) was wonderful. I often wondered why my dad asked me to play in the garage, especially since the garage was not attached to the house. Now that I have a sixth grade son who plays alto saxophone (my parents always told me there was justice in the world), I have a better understanding of that playing "arrangement." Anyway, the dog and I (she was just old enough that her hearing was not the best) enjoyed our playing sessions together, even in the winter in Ohio (the garage wasn't heated). For me, the first hook was "in."

The Next Big Step

While there have been many hooks for me (and probably for you), I remember that in eighth grade I was given the opportunity to play fourth tenor saxophone in the high school stage band (it was called a stage band back then). Since my brother had played tenor saxophone through high school, I now had a "new" instrument: his old one. My dog, who was by now totally deaf (this was not my fault, by the way), was in for a whole new set of practice experiences.

The stage band met two times a week at night, very cool for an eighth grade student in the 1960s. The band conductor was also a professional trumpet player with his own dance band. His dance band worked a lot, and the musicians got paid to play. What a concept! I was convinced that life as a music teacher, who was also a professional musician with his own dance band, just could not get any better than that.

I remember that on one particular occasion, the first tenor saxophonist was not at stage band rehearsal. That night the band was rehearsing Henry Mancini's *Pink Panther*. Now, you may recall that the *Pink Panther* tune has a tenor saxophone solo in it. In fact, that entire arrangement was built around the tenor saxophone. With only one tenor saxophonist at rehearsal that night, my chances of getting to play that solo on that particular night were greatly improved.

To be honest, I don't remember how well the solo went. I do remember standing up, and I know that I must have played something. I also know that even though the "real" tenor saxophonist returned the next rehearsal, I practiced—yes, *practiced*—that solo every night for a long time. For me, the musical hook was in for good.

Seeing Ourselves "in Context"

The above reminiscence is not intended to be just a trip down my own personal memory lane (remember the challenge to think about personal pivotal moments from your musical past). If we are to consider the value of a band music experience in a young person's life, then we must do so in context.

Several years ago, Dr. James Croft gave a presentation at the Midwest International Band and Orchestra Clinic, which he called "Seeing Ourselves as Others See Us." I remember that he started this session by talking about an informal research project that he had conducted for several years while traveling in and out of the Atlanta airport. His research methodology went

something like this: He would sit down beside a stranger in the Atlanta airport, turn to him/her and ask, "What's a band?" While he was quick to point out that many people when asked the question quickly and quietly stood up and walked away, several "subjects" did respond. The results of this informal survey, based on the comments of 400 respondents, suggested that a band was one of the following: a marching band, a rock band, or a big band. The public perception of the term "band," when taken out of the context of a real band experience, was somewhat different than he had expected.

Borrowing the "if you want to know the answer to something, then ask" technique from Dr. Croft, I decided to ask current band students "in context" some questions about their participation in young band. Additionally, I asked current band conductors some questions about the purpose of young band.

I divided my student subjects into three groups: young band students (fifth through eighth grade), high school students (ninth through twelfth grade), and university band students (freshmen through graduate students). My band conductor sample included teachers who taught students in each individual area listed above.

I asked the young band students the following questions:

1. Why are you in band?
2. What do you learn in band?
3. What is the best thing about band?

I asked the older students the following questions:

1. What is the purpose of young band (beginning/middle school)?
2. What did you learn in young band?
3. What was the best thing about young band?

Finally, I asked the band conductors the following questions:

1. What is the purpose of young band?
2. What do you teach in young band?
3. What is the best thing about teaching young band?

Demographic data were collected detailing each student's/conductor's year in school or level taught, number of years in band or number of years of teaching experience, and instrument played (students only).

Young Band Participation

More than 300 students and their band conductors completed the survey as part of a regular band rehearsal during the fall of 1999. All students in each ensemble were given the opportunity to respond. While detailed data analyses

are beyond the scope of this chapter, selected student and conductor responses follow. Generalizations should be made with caution.

Being in the Band "Now"

At the time the survey was completed, the fifth grade students had only been part of the band for a few weeks. When asked why they were in band, common fifth grade responses included:

- My brothers (sisters) were in band, and I liked the sound of their instruments.
- I wanted to learn to play an instrument.
- Because it is cool.
- I think it is fun.
- Because I love to play music.
- Because I wanted to learn something new.
- Because I wanted to be.

For sixth grade students, the most common reasons for participating in band included:

- Because I like to play my instrument and I love music.
- Because of my teacher.
- I enjoy playing music in front of people.
- I like to play loud (these answers were from trumpet players).

The most common seventh and eighth grade reasons included:

- I love music and being part of a whole.
- I think it's fun to create such wonderful music.
- I love making music with other people. It's really rewarding.
- I love my band teacher.

Looking back through their own experiences, upper-level students suggested that younger students are often more willing to try new things and that if they don't get the "hunger" for music early on, that hunger may never come. My favorite response came from a ninth grade flute student who said, "I believe that the purpose of young band is to teach children at a young age to love music, and to understand how to perform it and how it is put together." When asked what they learned in young band, student responses were similar for all levels of respondents. Most answers included various aspects of learning how to play an instrument and/or learning about music while performing. Less common answers included learning that practice is important, learning how to cooperate, learning not to quit, and learning that "playing is

not just about learning fingerings and playing the right notes. It is also about learning how to express yourself."

The "Good Stuff" for Students

Responses to the question concerning the best thing about young band included:

- Being exposed to something I wouldn't otherwise be exposed to.
- Getting to the level where I could actually play songs.
- It's what you remember forever.
- It was my life, and band still is today.

For students, choosing to be in the band when choices are all around suggests that music may still be powerful "stuff" and that band conductors are still important people to students.

The "Good Stuff" for Band Conductors

Teaching experience for band conductors included in the study ranged from two to twenty-five years. Most band conductor responses about the purpose of young band and what was taught focused on the need to give attention to the basics of playing, teaching concepts (elements) of music, and building a love for music. Several band conductors indicated that both student attitude and desire were at the highest levels with beginning students. The idea that young band should be more than a "feeder program" for high school band programs was a common theme. Many band conductors stated that young band students should not just be "trained" for high school band. Rather, these young students should be educated musically through their band rehearsal/performance experiences. The idea that band students should receive a music education through their performance experiences in band is the philosophy of the *Teaching Music* series.

The "Philosophical" and the "Practical"

Providing a music education for students through performance in band requires band conductors to make decisions about *what* to teach, *how* to teach, how to know *if* students understood the "it" that they were trying to teach and, perhaps most importantly, *why* band students should know or be able to do anything special with music (why they should study music through performance in the first place). For many band conductors, once the *why* of music teaching is "in place," the *what*, *how*, and *if* questions related to music teaching fall into place as well. Providing answers to these primary questions may be an important starting point for developing or revisiting a personal philosophy of music teaching.

The word *philosophy* elicits various responses from band conductors. According to David Elliott in his book, *Music Matters*, "some dismiss philosophy as ivory-tower conjecture on the far side of an unbridgeable gulf from classroom practice. As one suspicious colleague put it: 'Philosophy is like a pigeon: it's something to admire as long as it isn't directly over your head.'"[1]

Madsen and Madsen in *Experimental Research in Music*, state that "one often hears the phrase, 'I don't have time to think about it, I have too much to do.'" For Madsen and Madsen, "those who contrast 'philosophical' and 'practical' show their lack of understanding."[2] Bennett Reimer in *A Philosophy of Music Education* suggests that "everything music educators [band conductors] do in their jobs carries out in practice their beliefs about their subject. Every time a choice is made a belief is applied."[3] When a philosophy of music teaching is viewed, at least in part, as a basis for thoughtful, practical decision-making regarding the music education of real music students, the relationship between the philosophical and the practical becomes clear.

In *Music Matters*, David Elliott states that "a philosophy is both the engine that drives a person's commitment to educating and the rails that guide the way."[4] At the same time, Elliott is careful to point out that no single philosophy can be perfectly applicable to all situations.[5]

Product and Process

In *Vision 2020: The Housewright Symposium on the Future of Music Education*, Judith Jellison states that "the success of education is based on deciding what is important to learn and structuring frequent opportunities for practice and learning to occur over time."[6] Band conductors at all educational levels spend a great deal of time preparing ensembles for public performance. Consequently, for students in these ensembles, opportunities for practicing and learning what is important occur during band rehearsals. In the same *Vision 2020* document cited above, Bennett Reimer states that "the values of music education for students of any age, but especially for young people, lie primarily in learning how to be more skilled when they are engaged in musical processes." Reimer is quick to point out, however, that "there is a danger in forgetting that, in music, process cannot be separated from product."[7]

Teaching for musical understanding and knowledge while teaching the performance skills needed to play not only "the music" but also music in general requires a *balanced* approach. If the band does not sound good, then the band does not sound good, regardless of the age of its members.

The idea of comprehensive musicianship—teaching both the skills and knowledge needed for practical music making—is not new to young band.

Many of today's young band materials have the words "comprehensive method" included in their titles. What may be "new," however, is that teaching the music and teaching about music in a young band performance setting does not have to be an "either-or" proposition. We can do both well at the same time in the same rehearsal. We must, however, be willing to teach musical concepts—the big ideas in music—as a part of our daily rehearsals.

Beginning with the End in Mind

In *Process of Education*, Jerome Bruner suggested that we could teach anything to anyone at any age in some "intellectually honest" way.[8] Whether we apply that statement to music students in younger bands or "older" bands, one of our primary objectives as music teachers—band conductors—must be to teach music through performance in band. Starting where the students are, regardless of level, and taking them over the time that we have them with us to where we want them to be may be the key. Dr. Robert Duke uses the phrase *beginning with the end in mind* to describe this process.

Not every student who starts a young band program in public school will play for a lifetime, or be in the high school band, or be in the middle school band, or make it past the second day of beginning band or, for that matter, find the classroom on the first day of band. While that is sometimes difficult for us to understand and more difficult to not take personally, it is a reality of teaching instrumental music. Everyone may not choose to participate for the "long haul." What seems important for all band students, however, is that while we have those students with us in band, we teach them not only the skills and knowledge needed to "do band," but also help them make connections to music through performance. When we *begin with the end in mind* as a music teaching philosophy, the young band experience has the potential to be much more for students than a waiting period where they spend time getting ready to get ready for some future moment when they get to be "real musicians."

The good news for all of us is that today, more than ever before, there are many wonderful techniques and materials available to assist us as band conductors in providing opportunities for even the youngest band students to get to the *good stuff* in music that real musicians get to on a regular basis. Many of these techniques and materials are described in detail in the following chapters.

[Editor's note: In exploring the musical repertoire in both the Teacher Resource Guides and in the accompanying CDs, one will quickly see a musical repertoire of aesthetic depth for young players performing at the Grade 1 level. For the very young, there does exist a music that can excite and satisfy musically. There is no need to wait until a later time for that excitement; the time to teach a musical repertoire based on solid philosophical grounds is now...it is with our young.]

1   Elliott, David J. *Music Matters*. New York: Oxford University Press, 1995, 9.

2   Madsen, Clifford, and Charles Madsen, Jr. *Experimental Research in Music*. Raleigh, NC: Contemporary Publishing, 1978, 12-13.

3   Reimer, Bennett. A *Philosophy of Music Education*. New Jersey: Prentice Hall, 1989, 7.

4   Elliott, 11.

5   Ibid, 10.

6   Madsen, Clifford K., ed. *Vision 2020*. Reston, VA: MENC, 2000, 134.

7   Ibid, 39.

8   Bruner, Jerome S. *The Process of Education*. Cambridge, MA: Harvard University Press, 1960, 33.

CHAPTER 2

Beginning Band—Goals and Objectives: Teaching Music through Performance in Band— Beginning Band

Darhyl S. Ramsey

Perhaps the most important time in the development of good band students and programs is the first year of instruction. So many basics are introduced to young instrumentalists, and so many of the habits that shape their entire career are established during the time that students first learn their instrument. Practice procedures, instrument skills, and virtually all aspects of playing throughout the life of the band student are developed, becoming habits during the first year of instruction.

If a goal of music education is to train lifelong skill in and enjoyment of music, it becomes imperative that music educators focus their greatest attention and teaching expertise on this crucial developmental period.

There are an overwhelming number of goals that must be addressed during the first year of instruction. These goals seem to fall into five categories: 1) tone quality, 2) technical training of basic playing fundamentals for an individual's instrument, 3) development of skills to participate in music making activities, 4) development of skills in experiencing music and making discriminating choices in music, and 5) instilling values, knowledge, and skills that enable students to pursue musical experiences throughout their lives.

Addressing each of these categories at the beginning level and continuing throughout the students' instrumental instruction should develop good musical and technical skills necessary to be independent musicians. Each of these goals will help encourage students to become active participants in music beyond the performance venue. It is hoped that students who participate and graduate from a comprehensive program of musical instruction would be able to continue to play throughout their adult life if they so choose; if the students are not inclined to continue playing, they will have received proper instruction to become good audience members and advocates for band and music programs in the communities in which they reside.

It is important for teachers of beginning band to understand that each of the five goals of instruction that will be discussed have both a *cognitive* and *psychomotor* component. For students to be truly good musicians and bring good musical skills to the rehearsal, they must not only understand the musical concepts as they are presented on the written page, but they must also be able to hear the concepts and be able to reproduce them on their instruments. For example, to understand and recognize a staccato marking in the music and be able to call it "staccato" is important, but students must also be able to produce a staccato note and aurally recognize when a note is or is not being played with the correct articulation.

Many students can go through their career and develop a great deal of cognitive music reading knowledge, but they are unable to aurally recognize that knowledge when it is realized by an ensemble or especially when they are participants in the ensemble. Without the ability to aurally recognize, discriminate, and reproduce many of the cognitive concepts introduced in beginning band programs, students become dependent on others to tell them how something must be played and how something should sound. More importantly, these students fail to become independent musicians who contribute to the musical performance of the ensembles in which they participate or knowledgeable and discriminating listeners who enjoy attending band concerts throughout their lives.

With the various alternative scheduling options available to school administrators today, band conductors may have to make choices at the beginning levels. It should be noted, however, that sacrifices must *not* be made in the content or presence of any of the objectives. Any adjustments in the curriculum must be made in the depth or scope of the goals and objectives, not merely eliminating or glossing over some of the goals. Teachers of beginning band who see their students five days a week should be able to teach with depth in each goal; teachers who meet their students two or three times a week may have to reduce some of the practice and drill components in order to cover material in each of the goals.

Tone Quality

Perhaps the most important single focus of teachers of instrumental music students should be the development of a good characteristic tone in both the individual's instrument and the ensemble as a whole. Presenting good aural models, either by the teacher or through the use of recordings, is the primary means of establishing a characteristic sound. After the aural sound has been presented, beginning instrumentalists must implement several physical factors to begin the process of producing the appropriate sound.

Posture and Body Position — It is very important that students understand and know the importance of good posture and practice playing with good posture from the very beginning of their playing career. Not only does good posture help in allowing the body to produce the best possible sound, but it also aids in good breathing.

Breathing — From the very beginning of the instructional process, beginning students must inhale and exhale properly to produce a characteristic sound correctly on their instrument. Even when students are making their first sounds or singing pitches prior to playing, they must inhale a large amount of air and exhale with proper support to produce a full, robust sound. Lecture is not the most effective means of teaching these concepts and skills. Students seem to react to and understand imagery better, therefore making a better sound without having to think about the mechanics of breathing too much. An example of this imagery might be to have the students focus their sound toward the back of the room or to imagine inflating a balloon located on the bell of their instruments when they play.

Embouchure — To establish and develop a characteristic sound on their instrument, students must be capable of forming a proper embouchure. Combined with air support to provide the energy for the sound, the embouchure must be developed to have the firmness needed for good anchoring and flexibility (softness) to produce a characteristic sound. In addition, students must develop control to be able to play the music performed in the beginning band ensemble and to increase the technical ability necessary for the full extent of their playing experience. Care must be taken with students to establish the most appropriate embouchure early in their playing experience and to continually monitor the embouchure to make sure the student's small, individual differences do not adversely affect the proper tone quality of the instrument. How to form and refine each instrument embouchure is beyond the scope of this chapter, but the topic must be addressed for each instrument and for each student.

Tone Production — Putting together all of the aspects mentioned to this point occurs when the students must produce and maintain the proper sound on their instruments. Many students will have difficulty performing this multiple-task activity at first; teachers must be patient and encouraging as students try to remember all of the cognitive and motor skills that must be performed simultaneously to produce a sound on a musical instrument.

Tone Quality (individual instrument and ensemble) — Proper breath, posture, and embouchure must work together to enable the students to produce a characteristic sound on their instruments. The teacher must work with the students to help them understand the technical aspects of producing a good sound and establishing a good aural concept of what an appropriate sound is on each individual instrument. The teacher can aid the students in making the transfer from

what they hear as a good sound to producing that sound on their instrument. Constant monitoring of the sound with appropriate feedback by the teacher is essential! Students must be exposed to numerous recordings of good ensembles so that they establish, in their ears, an appropriate ensemble sound. The teacher must insist on these characteristic sounds so that students constantly address and evaluate the quality of sounds produced. It is also important that teachers guard against losing their perspective of a professional sound.

Technical Training of Basic Playing Fundamentals
of the Individual's Instrument

One of the most obvious goals of beginning band instruction is technical training of basic playing fundamentals, enabling the students to make appropriate sounds and produce music on their instruments. Without the basic fundamentals of instrument playing, students will not develop in the proper manner. Constant monitoring of these fundamentals by the teacher is necessary so that students do not slip into bad habits as the complexities of instrument playing increase; new challenges can often overshadow those basics that have already been addressed.

Care and Maintenance of Instruments — Because each student is responsible for his or her personal instrument, it is imperative that teachers spend sufficient time near the beginning of instruction, addressing the importance of care and maintenance of an instrument. This will be the only instrument many students will own, so they must treat it with respect and take the time to perform the regular maintenance that is required. From correct assembly of the instrument to placing the instrument into the case after playing, the responsibility of explaining the procedures belongs to the teacher; the responsibility of doing proper care and maintenance rests with the student.

Holding the Instrument — Proper hand position is very important for a beginning player. Without the correct habits of holding the instrument, students can experience many problems in their playing experience. Teachers must spend time demonstrating correct prototypical instrument position and helping students develop the position that is most comfortable for them, while not compromising the future demands that will be placed on the hands as technical demands become greater. It is also important to note that teachers should be aware of the potential for orthopedic problems caused by improper holding techniques; students should be encouraged to use devices like straps, where appropriate, to relieve some of the weight of the instrument while allowing the student to have control of the instrument.

Ear Training — From the first day of beginning band, teachers should be developing good listening and aural skills. This objective should be the center of instruction because it is through aural training that students will be able to play in tune, in time, and with good musical style. Aural training should begin with vocally matching pitches (perhaps this can be a part of the beginning lessons before the student is actually playing the instrument). Next, have students sing phrases and familiar folk songs to help them establish their ability to match pitch. This can be followed by having students play familiar songs on their instruments; play these songs in several keys by changing the starting pitch. Also, have the students "echo sing" and "echo clap." This also will help develop their ability to hear and reproduce music without being bound to the written page; it will help in the development of their tonal memory as well.

Articulation — Students must begin to learn very quickly, the proper manner to articulate sounds on their instruments. Proper articulation involves both the beginning and the ending of notes; the teacher must address both of these factors. How the tone is started will impact the initial sound, while the release will involve both sound and length of note. Articulation and length of note will ultimately lead to correct performance of different musical styles.

Fingerings/Stickings — As students begin to play their instruments, many songs can be played without formal knowledge of note reading. Associating specific note names with particular fingerings for the given notes is not necessary for students to play songs on their instruments. Singing of musical lines and playing rote songs can be used to train pitch matching skill. In addition, rote playing of songs by following the demonstration of the teacher can help students begin to listen to their sound and play "music." Students can experience, from the first rehearsal, the ability to play simple melodies on their instruments with good basic fundamentals without the complication of staff and note reading. As the students develop a good characteristic sound, good embouchures, and correct instrument position, the teacher must begin the process of associating notes read from the staff to particular fingerings and muscular feel. It goes without saying that fingerings are important, but because fingerings introduce a new level of task to the players, they must come after the students have established good playing skills with the embouchure and breath. Percussionists similarly must become familiar with the basics of sticking to meet the demands of playing each of the instruments in the percussion inventory, be it snare drum, keyboards, or timpani.

Note Reading — Learning to read musical notation is a very necessary skill for the beginning band student. Every student who participates in the beginning band program must be able to recognize the lines and spaces, and the note and rest symbols for each clef and each meter signature. However, the teacher should not spend inordinate amounts of time in the initial lessons teaching music reading. Students attend band to play music and make sounds; learning to read music must follow good tone development and basic musicianship, or students may lose motivation. Many basic skills of playing can be developed and much music made without complicating the process with yet another layer of knowledge for beginners. Playing songs by rote and by ear can

be just as effective for learning the fundamentals of good playing and developing talents that will be beneficial to the students in future lessons. Reading activities without the instruments can be incorporated into the lessons before playing and reading are combined. When the combination of playing and reading does enter into the playing equation, the teacher should build on previous knowledge of music reading developed during earlier elementary general music classes. If the school does not have elementary music, or if instruction in music reading was not addressed, then a very structured, sequential approach should be taken, building upon the rote and ear training developed earlier.

Signs and Symbols of Music Reading — Along with learning to read the actual notation (lines and spaces, note and rest symbols, etc.), it also is very important that beginners learn the signs and symbols that signify form, style, and musical interpretation. These markings must be taught both from the cognitive and the psychomotor perspectives. Cognitive learning includes learning to recognize each symbol at sight, being able to identify and give a definition of the symbol and what it does. It is also important that beginners are able to employ their psychomotor and listening skills to make their instruments perform the symbol in an appropriate manner.

Counting and Rhythm Work (steady beat, subdivisions, and odd meters) — This objective is closely aligned with the ear training skill, in that students must practice keeping a steady beat both with and without the aid of a metronome. The ability to keep internal time is crucial for successful playing throughout their playing experience. Steady feel for pulse must be developed early in their experience. Students must continue to practice and increase the difficulty of steady beat at different tempi and in a variety of meters. A segment of the steady beat training must include working with the underlying beat in both duple and triple metric subdivisions. Students must be able to recognize stress points in order to function in duple, triple, and odd meters; function means being able to sing, play, and clap even before reading and reproducing the written notation. Students can experience more complex rhythms and subdivisions even if they are not yet ready to read them. This can be accomplished through rhythmic "echo" patterns.

Vibrato — Vibrato is an aspect of playing that the teacher may choose to address early on for instruments that use this technique. As soon as good habits for consistency of sound are developed on the instrument, the students could be introduced to the basics of vibrato. If taught, the students should learn how to control the vibrato so that it can be used or not used depending on the situation. In developing the proper sound for the instrument, the students must be introduced to the proper way of producing a vibrato rather than allowing the students to attempt to produce a vibrato in ways that may be much more difficult to change later if the technique is incorrect.

Practicing — An objective of the beginning band program that is often overlooked is that of teaching students how to practice effectively. This includes the most efficient use of time and, most importantly, recognizing when something is being practiced incorrectly so that bad habits are not rehearsed. Students need to understand that motor skill is best developed slowly, methodically, and on a daily basis. Students cannot practice long amounts of time on weekends, not practice during the week, and expect proper development and achievement. Likewise, beginning band students need to be taught that merely putting in a specified amount of time without concentration is not going to make them play better. It is the teacher's responsibility to help the students know how to practice and what to practice before the students are sent away to develop and practice on their own.

Development of Skills to Participate in Music Making Activities

Scales, Arpeggios, Slurs — In the beginning band experience, it is necessary to begin the rudimentary work on scales, arpeggios, and lip slurs (for brass instruments). All three of these technical skills will continue to develop throughout a student's playing experience, but it is necessary that the basic fundamentals of each of these musical skills be introduced and developed as much as possible. The first step is to introduce the skills by sound so that all students can aurally recognize scales, arpeggios, and lip slurs. The teacher might begin this process by introducing tetrachords rather than full scales; as students develop greater skill, these tetrachords can be combined to form scales. Because so much of the practice time spent by beginning band students is away from the teacher, each student must be able to discriminate aurally between a correctly played scale (tetrachord) and/or arpeggio and one that contains errors. Next, the student should be introduced to the knowledge of fingerings and scale interval patterns necessary to physically play the scales and arpeggios. Finally, the student must perform the skills correctly both from memory and from notation. By the conclusion of the first year, each student should be able to play several scales followed by the tonic arpeggio; subdominant and dominant arpeggios should be introduced gradually as students grasp the concepts and skills necessary to produce the scale and tonic arpeggio. The range of these skills should be determined by the individual player's ability, but a strong effort should also be made to expand the student's range. In addition to being able to play the scales and arpeggios, brass players must also be taught how to change pitch on a given valve combination by using the embouchure and air stream.

Phrasing — Students must be taught the sound of cadences so they can determine the existence of phrases in music. Cadences provide the aural cues

necessary to make intelligent decisions about breathing and "lifting" to make musical phrases. Even in simple exercises and song material found in beginning instructional books, there is an implied (if not direct) harmony that indicates to students an appropriate place to break the musical line and take a breath. Only after students have begun to recognize these phrase points should phrase markings be introduced. Because phrasing is often the function of editors, it is equally important that students be able to hear the breaks rather than merely read them.

Tuning/Intonation — Tuning and intonation are two factors that seem to "torment" band conductors at all levels. A prerequisite for good tuning and intonation must be the production of a good sound, because tone quality is essential to playing in tune. Teaching pitch matching and listening must begin at the earliest level. As soon as students have achieved some degree of control of the sound of their instruments, they should begin to match pitch between the instrument and an external sound source (another instrument, a voice, or an electronically reproduced tone from a tuner). Prior to this time and continuing throughout their playing experience, students should practice singing pitches or exercises before playing them. The act of singing will help internalize the pitch and force the students to listen very carefully to their sound (vocal or instrumental) as compared with some external sound. In addition, the practice of singing will help the students play intervals in tune more readily; this should enhance their ability to play all notes of a phrase in tune with other players playing the unison lines.

Ensemble Tone Quality — It is never too early to stress to students the importance of their individual role in the total ensemble experience. Too often students do not listen to anything but their own part; they often fail to understand that their part is but a portion of the whole ensemble experience. Introducing the terms "balance" and "blend" is appropriate at this time as long as teachers insist that students put into musical practice the dictionary definitions of the terms. Balance and blend then become an ensemble listening skill, which must be addressed along with other ear-training activities. Students can be reminded to listen for the melody line or harmonic treatment and determine how their own part fits into the musical performance.

Interpretation — Musical interpretation is an aspect of musical development that should be introduced during the beginning instrumental experience and developed more fully as students progress. Students should be allowed the opportunity to experiment with interpreting melodic lines, phrases, and dynamic contrast. The teacher's role here is to facilitate the experimentation with interpretation and to question the students on the appropriateness of an interpretation. If students are to be expressive themselves through music, teachers must provide the freedom for students to make some interpretative decisions. Of course, this must be done at a time when the ensemble is not preparing for a performance, when a common interpretation is necessary.

However, teachers could try to implement some of the appropriate student interpretive decisions in the performance decisions; students will then share in the performance.

Sight-reading — Sight-reading is an indication of a student's ability to perform independently. For this reason, it is imperative that this skill be introduced, developed, and practiced early in the learning process. Rather than giving students answers, the teacher should quiz the students on musical information, allowing them to think about the musical experience and implement musical skills individually. Allowing students to do this in the first year of study will help them become less dependent on others, allowing them to make musical decisions for themselves.

Development of Skills in Experiencing Music and Making Discriminating Choices in Music

Literature for the beginning band (playing) and "Standard Repertoire" for band (listening) — As students become more proficient on their instruments, they need to begin playing quality literature. The beginning band is the time to start this process. Teachers should help students perceive those attributes that make each musical selection "quality." In addition, the conductor should provide a vocabulary the students can use to conceptualize and describe the music they are hearing. A student's ability to comprehend the aural complexities utilizing the appropriate vocabulary will be far greater than his or her psychomotor ability to perform the music—students can hear more in the music than they can physically perform. As a result, instruction should address these two competency levels. Students should perform music in the class that motivates and challenges their psychomotor skills and expands music reading skills. In addition, recordings of outstanding wind bands playing "standards" of the wind literature should be included in the beginning band rehearsal to expand listening and analysis skills as well as develop concepts of sound. Listening helps the students in their playing and provides them good role models for ensemble tone quality and ensemble playing. In addition, this type of activity helps establish a standard repertoire for the wind band that students can experience for their entire lives. In the same manner that students experience characteristic instrument tone quality, they must also experience characteristic wind band sounds.

Listening and Describing Music — Many references have been made in this chapter to providing listening experiences for beginning band students. Coupled with this must be the development of a vocabulary that students can use to describe the listening event. It is this vocabulary that will enable listeners to better comprehend and gain deeper enjoyment of all music throughout their lives. Teachers must be diligent in introducing listening

examples with the correct vocabulary and insist that students use that vocabulary in their everyday discussion of music. Students must be required to use the correct terminology when asking and answering questions in band rehearsals. For example, when students express like or dislike of a particular musical selection, they should be able to address the specific musical elements that contribute to their preferential decision.

Determination and Discrimination of Musical Forms (primarily aural but also visual) — Another important way teachers need to help students organize music is through the perception of form. Often, students are not aware of the overall formal organization of music. Repetition of an exact (or a very similar) passage is not recognized as such and is not performed in a similar manner. (Recognition of this simple fact will make for a much more efficient rehearsal because less time has to be spent rehearsing the repeated section.) Also, in an attempt to develop lifelong skills in music, students must be able to perceive formal elements aurally. Therefore, teachers must provide opportunities where students are forced to recognize form by listening rather than by analyzing the written music. One way to implement this might be to question students about the degree of repetition or contrast in a section of the music they are rehearsing, as well as whether it is appropriate for the music to be played similarly to the first time or whether changes might be appropriate. With increased listening skill, teachers might also ask students what changes they would suggest.

Aural Discrimination of Different Styles of Music and Playing — Through listening, performing, and demonstrating, the beginning band class should be introduced to a number of different styles and types of music. Exposure to new types of music in both the playing and listening venues is important for students. An individual's preferences for music change, especially if presenting new challenges and opportunities in music expands his or her horizons. As students mature, they comprehend music on new levels and desire new experiences. This can be crucial to beginning instruction because band starts about the time these new ways of thinking develop, and quite often band becomes the sole formal musical instructional setting for these students.

Composition (playing of student compositions) — A part of beginning band instruction that is often seen as unnecessary, and consequently is often omitted, is composition. Band conductors who teach beginners must allow, encourage, or even require students to experiment with composing music for their instruments. The process of writing music for an instrument will provide students with creative outlets and strong motivational impetus, but more importantly, much valuable information about their instrument can be developed. Students gain a greater working knowledge of the musical staff, the inner workings of music, fingerings and finger patterns, and limitations of range of their instruments by writing music that can be performed. Composition in the beginning band class can consist of short excerpts, between two and eight measures; students should not be expected to compose lengthy works at this time. After this, students should have the opportunity to perform their compositions in the classroom either during a lesson or during the full ensemble. More inquisitive and adventurous students will be able to begin writing for small ensembles or even full band. We often justify music by highlighting its ability to provide self-expression. However, in reality, little opportunity for self-expression exists in the beginning band class other than through playing; composition provides another avenue of self-expression.

Improvisation — Improvisation work is similar to the composition described previously. At this level of development, very simple, guided improvisation activities of short duration are appropriate. Traditionally, improvisation has been associated with the playing of jazz; however, the underlying musical benefits of improvisation should be nurtured by every teacher for every student. The ability to hear harmonic changes and to be creative in melodic treatment above these harmonic changes are skills that can improve a student's overall musical ability. Much of the instruction that occurs in the beginning band is focused on reading music from the written page and reproducing music from the published parts. All students deserve the opportunity to play music by ear and compose in their minds through improvisation. Providing students with the opportunity to expand or change a written melody provides a chance for students to increase their listening skills and to develop the freedom to play by ear on their instruments, unencumbered by written notation, hopefully providing motivation for greater achievement. As cognitive skills of chords and harmonic structure are developed, a student's improvisation skill can be expanded to include playing over a series of chord changes. Students who bring these increased skills to the band rehearsal become better ensemble members and consequently improve the quality of the ensemble.

Evaluation — Teaching students to make educated choices about their musical experiences needs to be a goal of every instrumental music teacher. While it is hoped that learning a musical instrument and having the experience of playing in an ensemble will enable the students to make musically intelligent decisions, this transfer often does not occur. Whether the students are not trained in the correct ways to listen or they simply do not see the connection between quality learned in the playing environment and quality in the music they consume, it seems that many students do not apply good evaluative skills when it comes to musical choices. One of the goals of the beginning band program should be to acquaint students with musical choices available to them and the tools they should use to critique music in making personal choices about musical consumption. Teachers should provide a vocabulary of musical terminology and appropriate criteria for making evaluative judgments that the students can use to conceptualize and describe the music they are hearing. In addition, teachers should encourage and give

guidance to students in preparing a checklist of listening objectives and applying these standards to musical compositions or performances. This should not be an indoctrination experience about one or two types of music but a chance to provide students the opportunity to transfer knowledge from their band instruction to their lifelong musical experience.

Instilling Values, Knowledge, and Skills that Enable Students to Pursue Musical Experiences Throughout Their Lives

Playing music should be a main focus of the instruction that takes place in beginning band rehearsal. However, development of knowledge and skill that can be used throughout a student's life is another crucial element of the beginning band program. This knowledge can be helpful in the students' contributions and involvement in the band rehearsal and can also be taken from the formal instructional setting into their everyday lives. The information must be presented in age-appropriate scope and at an age-appropriate level. The basic groundwork is established at the beginning band level; students can develop greater insight, knowledge, and understanding throughout the remainder of their lives.

History of Musical Instruments — It is important that students know the history of the instruments they are playing as well as other instruments in the ensemble. This information can be helpful in forming a concept of the appropriate sounds for an instrument and the correct style for playing certain passages. This goal is one that can be accomplished early in the beginning band experience and later expanded upon as musical demands make further information appropriate.

Differing Styles of Music (both in contemporary and historical settings) — Beginning band rehearsal is an ideal time to make students aware of different stylistic characteristics of composers and eras of music history. Students should be made aware of similarities in the music of the composers who write for beginning band. It is the existence of these similarities that become the cornerstone for developing expectations in music based on the common features of every composer. Likewise, through listening and playing activities, students will be introduced to different styles from music historical periods and composers.

Changes in Instrumentation (both in contemporary and historical settings) — As early as possible in the beginning band experience, students should be introduced to small ensembles and solo performance. This can be a good introduction to changes in instrumentation depending on the ensemble or the historical style period. Students also need to be made aware of the original intent of the composer when transcriptions are being introduced to the students. A short excerpt of the original composition performed on modern or historically correct instruments can be played while students are rehearsing a transcribed melody or portion of a larger work.

Understanding Music in Relation to History and Cultures — Another relationship between music and history that should be discussed with students is the importance of music's role in influencing certain historical and cultural events. (For example, the band has developed from a military role into a legitimate concert ensemble throughout the years.) Tracing the impact band music has had on both American and world history is important because it gives a perspective to both disciplines. Not only has music influenced history, but music has also been influenced by history. World events provide the impetus for composers to write music with the event in mind. The compositional devices used by these composers should be discussed as a means of expanding personal expression in young players. The complex relationship between music and history is often left to discovery; quite often that discovery is not made by students and an important influence of music is lost.

Music of the American Culture and Other Cultures of the World — This goal is very easily accomplished in the band. Because much of the repertoire of the band/wind ensemble has been written by American composers, the opportunity to discuss American contributions to music is easily available. Likewise, the material used by many American composers reflects the cosmopolitan nature of American music. Incorporation of music from other cultures has become a mainstay of the wind band composers. Many pieces in standard band literature reflect the influence of cultures of other worlds as well as the American culture. The music addressed in this publication and in the accompanying recordings is a good example of a broad-based curriculum that incorporates music from America and from many other cultures.

Relationship of Music and Other Arts and Disciplines Outside the Arts — As a component of the "Fine Arts," music must be taught in relation to the other arts. The common elements of visual and dramatic arts should be explored as should the use of music and dance in their strong relationship. The exposure to the other arts and their relationship to music (and music's relationship to them) is something the band conductor must develop in coordination with teachers of the other arts. Quite often music is justified by saying that it is capable of teaching things like math and science. While we must be very careful in making those types of claims, there does seem to be a strong connection between the skills developed in the musical experience and other disciplines.

Conclusion

The goals for beginning band must be broad and far-reaching. Beginning band is a transitional time from the general music instruction in elementary school to the performance-based program in both the middle school and high school. While this is a time for building fundamental groundwork and

establishing the basic vocabulary for many skills that will be developed later, it is also a time for the development of good musical knowledge, understanding, and skills for lifelong musical learning and enjoyment. The beginning band teacher must strive to include musical independence, musical sensitivity, and musical literacy in the beginning band program. The beginning band often becomes the only formal instruction in music available to students beyond the elementary experience, so it behooves each teacher to develop a comprehensive program that includes technical skill development on the individual instruments, concepts for good ensemble growth, and knowledge and attitudes that students can keep with them as they become musical consumers throughout their lives.

CHAPTER 3

Starting from the Beginning: The Recruitment Program in the Elementary School

Thomas Dvorak

...music making is a unique and major way of gaining self-growth, self-knowledge, and optimal experience, both now and in the future. And to the extent that these values are achieved in and through the development of musicianship, musicing is also a unique and major way of developing self-esteem. For these reasons, music making is something worth learning to do well by all students.[1]

··· David J. Elliot ···

The purpose of this chapter is to share some thoughts about recruiting young students to play a band instrument. Recruiting students to play an instrument may well be the most important aspect of a band conductor's job in the elementary or middle school. When recruiting is done well, the foundation for success in elementary school, middle school, and high school band programs will have been laid.

Early in my teaching career as a high school band conductor for the McFarland Public Schools in McFarland, Wisconsin, I was given the opportunity to teach the elementary band program as well. What good fortune it was for me; it was the perfect job! If the high school band were to be successful, it meant that the foundations for that success were going to be built in the elementary school band program. In my view, both the high school and elementary programs were equally important musical ensembles, both designed to educate students musically. I never viewed the beginning band program as a "feeder" for either middle school or high school, but rather as an ensemble/lesson experience geared towards the educational musical needs of younger musicians. Their musical knowledge, understanding, skills, and aesthetic experiences were as important to them and to me as were the overall

experiences for my high school students.

At the same time in my career, I had the good fortune to participate in a research program sponsored by the National Association of Band Instrument Manufacturers (NABIM) and spearheaded by James Froseth. The purpose of the two-year project was to determine the effects of experimental recruiting procedures on beginning band enrollments in our school and other selected schools in the project. The results of the NABIM project and the work that went into it were astounding, creating an enormous impact not only upon our beginning band program, but our entire music program and our music faculty as well. During the research phase, and subsequent to that, our band enrollments doubled, with approximately 77 percent of the elementary students becoming involved in the beginning band program. Over the next five years, both the middle school and high school band enrollments in our district increased considerably, creating the need for additional bands, supporting instructional budgets, and increased staffing. The NABIM recruiting procedures had worked for our school! Not only were we recruiting more youngsters, but we were retaining more of them in our band program. All of us on the teaching faculty in the McFarland Public Schools were becoming increasingly more sensitive to the individual needs and abilities of our students as well. We not only became better at recruiting students for instrumental music study, but we also became better teachers.

The outline for recruitment in this chapter is founded upon some of the objectives of the original NABIM research but also incorporates recent research into testing and other ideas currently utilized in many of our nation's finest school band programs. Our aim here is to establish objectives for developing a recruitment program and further identify some guiding principles and working procedures in reaching recruiting objectives.

Objectives of the Beginning Band Recruitment Program

1. Provide each child with the opportunity to study a band instrument. This means that, regardless of any preconceived notions of ability, interest, socio-economic background, family history, or other factors, the study of a band instrument is open to and available to all children. A recruitment plan should never discourage a child from taking part in the beginning band experience.

2. Identify each child's musical potential and individual musical differences, providing them, their parents, teachers, and school administrators with information that can be effectively utilized in the recruiting process, and later in the teaching process.

3. Identify and actively recruit those children who display excellent potential in music. Many children in a given population will exhibit strong potential for learning music. It could well be that children who exhibit qualities like strong musical aptitude, interest in music, and good academic achievement skills stand a higher probability for success in learning how to play a band instrument. These children should be strongly encouraged to study an instrument, for it is these children in all likelihood who will become successful in playing.

4. Evaluate each child's instrument preference and compatibility in an attempt to give the child the instrument of his or her choice. However, be ever watchful that when more than one choice is possible, every attempt should be made to persuade children to play less popular instruments, such as oboe, bassoon, horn, trombone, or tuba, so that a balanced instrumentation can be possible. A balanced instrumentation should be a primary focus of recruiting.

In meeting these recruiting objectives, the teacher's role becomes one of serving as a catalyst. Each band conductor is ultimately responsible for initiating, coordinating, communicating, collecting data, and implementing every aspect of the recruitment program.

Guiding Principles for Achieving Objectives

Our first aim is to outline some guiding principles upon which our recruiting objectives can be met. In doing so, we want to establish the importance of systematically collecting data on each child. Gathering information about students, such as their musical aptitude test scores, instrument preference ratings, academic achievement scores, physical characteristics evaluation, music interest, and the like, will provide invaluable information in the recruiting process. This data allows us options and alternatives in recruiting. In outlining these "Guiding Principles," everyone is urged to keep an open mind, to re-examine older, perhaps preconceived ideas about recruiting. This is particularly important regarding the value and use of testing for musical aptitude, musical instrument preference, and academic achievement.

Principle #1

Develop a recruitment program based upon a knowledge and understanding of students' music aptitude.

As musicians, and as teachers, we are affected by music aptitude. We are affected by our own music aptitude and the music aptitudes of our students. When we conduct and teach our ensembles, we are certainly aware of the differing levels of musicianship among our players; we understand that some students play with greater degrees of musical sensitivity than others; some play with greater rhythmic precision, while others play with less; some play with a greater sense of pitch, exhibiting higher levels of aural awareness. Certainly many of the individual differences in performance achievement among players can be contributed to factors like practice, home environment, teaching, and the such, but achievement levels are equally affected by various degrees and levels of musical aptitude found within individuals. In his book, *Introduction to Research and the Psychology of Music*, Edwin Gordon, the famed music psychologist and learning theorist, believes that music aptitude "interacts with all aspects of our professional development and pursuits."[2] His definition is that "music aptitude represents a students' potential to learn, whereas music achievement represents what a student has learned."[3] He further suggests that "when music aptitude and music achievement are believed to be the same, the pedagogical process of music education is less effective than it should be, because without specific knowledge of students' music aptitude, a teacher is not able to offer precise instruction that takes musical differences among students into consideration."[4]

In developing a recruiting plan, it is important to understand that music aptitude does exist among students and that some aspects of music aptitude as we know it can be measured and evaluated through reliable and valid music aptitude tests.

Principle #2

Test for music aptitude.

There are differing viewpoints and ideas concerning the usefulness of tests, whether test results can be trusted, or if time should be taken from the school day to test. Whatever one's reasoning or persuasion, if we are to understand more about aptitude for our recruiting and teaching purposes, a valid music aptitude test is necessary in helping us better understand the description and measurement of music aptitude.

With the research of Edwin Gordon and his publication of the *Musical Aptitude Profile*, *Primary Measures of Music Audiation*, and *Intermediate Measures of Music Audiation*, we have tests specifically designed to identify children's music aptitudes. In his test manual for the *Primary Measures of Music Audiation* and the *Intermediate Measures of Music Audiation*, Gordon suggests that "when used with judgment and wisdom, scores on the *Primary Measures of Music Audiation* and the *Intermediate Measures of Music Audiation* can serve the following three purposes:

1. Periodically to evaluate the comparative tonal and rhythm aptitudes of each young child.
2. Periodically to identify young children who can profit from the opportunity to participate in additional group study and special private instruction in and out of school.

3. Periodically to evaluate the tonal and rhythm aptitudes of each young child as compared with the tonal and rhythm aptitudes of other children of similar age."[5]

Purposes 1 and 2 are especially useful in the beginning band recruitment program because it serves as an aid in achieving recruiting objectives 2 and 3 listed earlier.

To summarize, testing for music aptitude with reliable and valid aptitude batteries such as those developed by Edwin Gordon should be the first prerequisite in developing a recruitment program. *Never should these tests be utilized to eliminate children from studying a band instrument, for every child can profit from playing.* All youngsters should be tested in a given grade. When the tests are scored, raw scores should be converted to percentile rank norms for both tonal and rhythm tests. The percentile rank norms for both the tonal and rhythm tests, plus a composite percentile rank norm, should be recorded on the Recruiting Profile Form, Appendix A. These test results are important data and can serve as primary indicators in recruiting students to study a band instrument.

For our purposes, the *Intermediate Measures of Music Audiation* battery by Edwin Gordon, available from GIA Publications, Inc., Chicago, Illinois, is recommended. The test comes complete with a manual, giving explicit directions for administering, scoring, and interpreting the test; it is complete with cassette recordings, answer sheets, scoring masks, a Profile Card for each child, and finally a Class Record Sheet for each group or class of students.

Note: A thorough discussion of the nature of music aptitude can be found in the following books: Edwin E. Gordon, *The Nature, Description, Measurement, and Evaluation of Music Aptitudes* (Chicago: GIA Publications, Inc., 1987) and Edwin E. Gordon, *Introduction to Research and the Psychology of Music* (Chicago: GIA Publications, Inc., 1998).

Principle #3
Test for instrument timbre preference.

Edwin Gordon developed the *Instrument Timbre Preference Test* solely to aid both teachers and parents in helping youngsters choose an appropriate woodwind or brass instrument for study. There are no correct or incorrect answers to the questions found on this test; rather, it is a test designed to indicate a student's preference to synthesized timbres of melodies performed on a Moog Opus 3 synthesizer. As Gordon suggests, "Each of the derived seven synthesized timbres is intended to represent the timbres of one or more woodwind or brass instruments. The first timbre [A] represents the flute; the second, [B] clarinet; the third, [C] saxophone and French horn; the fourth, [D] oboe, English horn, and bassoon; the fifth, [E] trumpet and cornet; the sixth,

[F] trombone, baritone, and French horn; and the seventh, [G] tuba...."[6] The test tape is approximately twenty-two minutes and should require no more than thirty minutes to administer.

Gordon's research into music timbre preference is indeed enlightening and should be considered as a necessary part of the recruiting process. Based upon his very extensive research with timbre preference, Gordon believes that "the timbre of the music instrument a student plays is second only to his music aptitude as an important factor in his success in instrumental music. A student becomes highly motivated and successful if he learns to perform with good tone quality on a music instrument that has a timbre which he likes."[7] He furthermore suggests that "students who learn to play music instruments associated with their timbre preferences demonstrate higher levels of music achievement than do students who learn to play music instruments for which they do not have timbre preferences...a student without a timbre preference who wants to study a percussion instrument should be encouraged to study a keyboard instrument as well as a percussion instrument."[8] In his test manual, Gordon states that when students' *Instrument Timbre Preference Test* results are combined with their scores on a valid music aptitude test, as much as sixty-five percent of the reason or reasons for their success in instrumental music can be predicted after they have received only one year of instruction."[9] Instrument timbre preference results, when coupled with a student's physical characteristics evaluation, can really be helpful in selecting an instrument also. The skillful use of these two evaluations can offer students a choice and furthermore help the teacher in trying to balance the instrumentation of the beginning band.

In summary, Gordon's research into instrument timbre preference testing allows us to utilize valuable information in helping guide a student's choice in selecting an instrument to study. It provides the band conductor with useful information, ultimately helping in the pursuit of our recruiting objectives. Scores on the *Instrument Timbre Preference Test* should be recorded under each heading (A, B, C, D, E, F, or G) and should be recorded on the Instrument Timbre Preference and Physical Characteristics Evaluation Form, Appendix B.

The *Instrument Timbre Preference Test* by Edwin E. Gordon is available from GIA Publications, Inc., Chicago, Illinois. Test materials include a manual, which gives directions for administration of the test, a cassette recording, answer sheets, scoring masks, and a Class Record Sheet for each class of students tested. We strongly recommend that either the *Musical Aptitude Profile* or the *Intermediate Measures of Music Audiation* be administered in conjunction with the *Instrument Timbre Preference Test*.

Note: For a detailed description of the purpose, rationale, content, and design of the *Instrument Timbre Preference Test*, see Edwin E. Gordon's test manual.

Principle #4

Utilize academic achievement test results.

Standardized academic achievement percentile scores were an integral aspect of the NABIM recruiting plan described in the earlier part of this chapter. Evidence in the NABIM research supported substantial positive relationships between students' academic achievement and band instrument achievement. Gordon's position on academic achievement supports this relationship also…"with regard to music, there is a known positive correlation between a student's membership in a school band and the student's overall academic achievement…."[10]

Many school districts utilize academic achievement results in recruiting. Prevailing thoughts among instrumental teachers tend to support the idea that students who are good academic achievers will most likely become good achievers on their instruments. Good academic students have excellent study habits, positive attitudes toward school work, and good motivation, and they possess the necessary organizational skills needed to accomplish their school work; consequently, they react to practicing and achieving on an instrument in much the same manner as they do in their school achievement.

Standardized test batteries, such as the *Iowa Tests of Basic Skills* or *Terra Nova* to name a few, provide national percentile norms and are extremely useful in recruiting. Percentile rank norms from these tests can be obtained from school counselors. Total composite percentile rankings should be recorded for every student in each classroom; these scores also become part of the recruiting data assembled for each student. These scores, along with scores from music aptitude tests and instrument preference rankings can be entered on the Recruiting Profile Form, Appendix A. Students who receive high academic achievement scores in either the upper half or upper quartile in all likelihood will be good candidates for instrumental music study. However, as Froseth emphasized in the NABIM research, "academic achievement should be viewed as only a secondary factor for predicting success in instrumental music."[11] Music aptitude is the single most important contributing factor for success in music learning.

Principle #5

Utilize music interest.

Music interest has long been an integral aspect of the beginning instrumental recruitment program. In many school districts today, it remains the major factor in recruiting. When school districts have excellent achievement histories with their bands, interest in joining the band can be overwhelmingly positive. However, when recruiting largely on music interest, without considering music aptitude and academic achievement factors, much can be lost!

Interest played a role in the NABIM recruitment program, albeit much less of a factor than either music aptitude or academic achievement. Froseth

acknowledged the problems associated with interest in the NABIM research stating that, "...interests of students fluctuate with the passage of time and are influenced greatly by specific experiences and events. For example, motion pictures, school assemblies, TV shows, and the like can cause heightened interest in musical activities. Then again, regular contact with a hostile music teacher can "turn off" an entire school population to music. Since interest is easy to influence, recruiting efforts frequently attempt to "soften up the kids." Unfortunately, many music teachers fail to consider that efforts to heighten one type of interest may actually influence quite a different type of interest."[12]

Our position here is that interest is an important factor in recruiting. However, because there is no valid or precise way to measure music interest, as there is with both music aptitude and academic achievement, interest in music learning and playing a band instrument is more suspect and should not be the only factor in recruiting. To evaluate interest, teachers usually have to ask students if they are interested. We suggest that this be accomplished through a recruitment letter sent to all parents in the grade(s) in which recruiting takes place. The recruitment interest letter should be mailed to parents after recruiting activities (like instrument demonstration, school concerts, and instrument tryouts) are held in school so students become well acquainted with the various instruments available. (A sample recruitment interest letter can be found in Appendix C.) Once the responses are collected from such a letter, interest response becomes part of each student's data. Responses to the interest letter should be recorded on the Recruiting Profile Form, Appendix A.

Principle #6

Evaluate physical characteristics.

Evaluating each child's physical characteristics and compatibility to a band instrument is also an important aspect of the recruitment program; this evaluation should be done by the band conductor as part of the data gathering process. Time must be taken in school to evaluate each student's compatibility by having the student produce sounds on flute head joints, double reeds, and various mouthpieces for both woodwinds and brass. Students interested in percussion can be given a variety of sticks to evaluate their dexterity and kinesthetic responses. Keyboard background should also be a part of the percussion evaluation since keyboard mallet should be an important aspect of total percussion performance.

All students should receive a physical characteristics evaluation regardless of their level of interest because some students who may not be interested may show outstanding potential on this evaluation; if all children are given the opportunity to try out, it will help them learn more about each instrument, adding to their knowledge and understanding of the instruments available. In the NABIM recruitment program, we were oftentimes able to convince students with strong music potential to study such instruments as oboe, bassoon, horn, or trombone, provided they were physically compatible to the instrument. We were often able to justify the use of school-owned instruments for these students as well; we learned, in many instances, that what appeared to be a lack of interest on the part of children and their parents was, more often than not, a matter of financial constraints in either renting or purchasing an instrument. When this happened, it became the perfect fit for both the student and our school-owned instruments!

The Physical Characteristics Evaluation Form is found in Appendix B. Results of the physical characteristics evaluation should be considered along with results from the *Instrument Timbre Preference Test*; these two indicators can help a student decide which instrument to choose. Both evaluations are helpful to band conductors in balancing instrumentation. In such cases as flute, saxophone, and percussion (where interest in these instruments is often too high), several choices for an instrument can be suggested to students, hopefully giving them options so that a balanced instrumentation can become a reality. Recruiting a balanced instrumentation is one of the most important goals in recruiting! The overall musical, aesthetic experience of students will be affected by instrumentation balance!

Activities and Suggestions for Organizing the Recruitment Program

Recruiting is communicating—two-way communication. The band conductor's job is to *convey* to administrators, classroom teachers, other music colleagues, music dealers, parents, and students the various steps of the recruitment process. Then, the conductor must *listen* to the students so that their needs can be addressed. Once this two-way communication begins, a dialogue must begin so everyone understands what needs to be accomplished if the goals of the recruitment program are to be met.

The following activities are offered by way of suggestion in organizing recruiting efforts:

1. *Communication with school administrators*
   Each band conductor's personal philosophy of beginning instrumental music, including the need for music aptitude and musical preference testing, data collection of students' academic achievement scores, and physical characteristics evaluations, must be communicated to school administrators, including the superintendent, building principals, and music coordinators/supervisors. Recruiting goals and the process for achieving those goals need to be articulated in a manner that can be understood. Once school administrators understand the recruitment program, give their support, and provide the time and resources

necessary for the various recruiting activities, systematic steps can be taken to ensure that the recruitment program gets underway.

First, order the music aptitude and instrument preference tests. Next, meet with classroom teachers and seek their help in administering the tests in their classroom settings. Children feel more comfortable in their own classroom settings, and it is important that they feel comfortable taking these test batteries. Once the tests are completed, make provisions for scoring them (either through professional machine scoring or hand scoring). Plans for ordering the testing materials as well as the actual testing, scoring, and recording of the results should be done at least three months prior to any other recruiting efforts. Time for both the administration and scoring of these tests needs to be taken well in advance of any other type of recruiting activity. Once the scoring is complete, record the results from both the music aptitude and instrument preference tests on the Recruiting Profile Form, Appendix A.

Next, secure the help of the academic classroom teachers or school counselors by asking them to record each student's academic achievement percentile ranking on the Recruiting Profile Form, Appendix A. When complete with data entries, this recruiting form becomes the most important part of each band conductor's recruiting file; it provides valuable information for building a recruiting strategy.

2. *Communication with all students*
   Communicating with all of the students in the recruitment grade(s) is obviously a large part of the recruiting plan. All students need to know that beginning instrumental study is available to them. Following the testing for both music aptitude and musical instrument preference, activities like concerts performed by either the middle or high school band, films, recordings, Internet access, or individual instrument demonstrations should be given so students have the opportunity to learn about the instruments and the band. Arranging individual tryouts of the available instruments is another worthwhile activity, providing the understanding as to how each instrument works from a physical standpoint. When individual tryouts on the instruments are given, note the physical compatibility and physical characteristics of each student on the Instrument Timbre Preference and Physical Characteristics Evaluation Form, Appendix B. These results, along with the results gained from the *Instrument Timbre Preference Test* serve as the basis for helping children and their parents choose an instrument for study.

3. *Communication with all parents*
   Communication with parents should be done through a letter sent by

the school to *all* parents and their children in the grade(s) being recruited. By communicating to all parents in writing, the band conductor will have fulfilled an important aspect of a solid teaching philosophy, that of offering band instruction to all children and not being selective for only a chosen few. The recruitment letter should include either a self-addressed postcard or a "tear-off" response so information such as level of interest can be obtained.

If parents return a response card saying that their child is not interested in playing a band instrument, it provides immediate information about the level of interest. However, a less-than-positive interest response from parents should always be weighed against a child's music aptitude and academic achievement data. For example, a child who expresses no interest but exhibits outstanding music aptitude test results should be heavily recruited! Conversely, a child who expresses no interest and exhibits rather low music aptitude potential may not be a child who should be heavily recruited.

Responses from the recruitment interest letter should be recorded on the Recruiting Profile Form, Appendix A. This, along with data on the music aptitude and academic achievement, becomes part of the overall information for each student. (A sample recruitment letter can be found in Appendix C.)

When communicating with students and their parents, it is important that the band conductor, along with the school district, makes the opportunity available to *all* students; this is an educationally sound policy and the only defendable educational position a district can take in offering curricular music instruction to its students.

4. *Recruiting through telephone communication*
   As we have said previously, one of the most crucial aspects of a well-organized and productive recruitment program is the recruitment of students who exhibit strong musical potential but indicate little, if any, interest in learning to play a band instrument. Once the Recruitment Profile Forms are complete, conductors need to review the forms, becoming especially watchful for promising students who did not return the recruitment interest "tear-off" or, if in returning the "tear-off," indicated no interest. These students, if convinced to try an instrument, are often some of the finest students in band. We quickly discovered in the NABIM research that students who we were able to recruit in this manner became some of our finest players. Once their achievement levels became a positive experience for them, their interest in music increased. Oftentimes, we were able to suggest instruments to these students and their parents that were needed to balance the instrumentation. Just think of the joy of recruiting an outstanding

young student who had strong music aptitude, a high academic achievement profile, and whose very physical compatibility to, say, the oboe, bassoon, or French horn made them a natural fit!

Although much of the telephone recruiting needs to be accomplished in the evening when parents are home, the rewards of doing this successfully far outweigh any consideration of not doing it. Simply put, to have an outstanding program, one must have outstanding players! A band program cannot be as successful as it could be if many of our schools' most musically promising students are sitting in either the academic classroom or study hall when the band is rehearsing!

5. *Teacher-Parent-Student conferences*
Scheduling a conference with each child and his or her parents is a necessary part of the recruiting process. Conferences should be held during the school day or immediately following the conclusion of the school day in much the same manner as other academic conferences are held with parents during the school year. The conferences can be held either prior to or subsequent to the recruiting night explained in number 6, which follows.

During this time, parents and children can be given a variety of valuable information about a child's involvement in the beginning band. It is an excellent opportunity to reassess the physical characteristics of the students by having them try out their instrument choice and the instrument(s) they showed the strongest compatibility for in the earlier instrument tryout evaluation. Results from the *Instrument Timbre Preference Test* along with the physical characteristic evaluations should be used in guiding the child's choice of an instrument at this time. When this is done with the parents present, it can strengthen the appropriate choice of an instrument.

Other issues, such as securing an instrument, availability of school-owned instruments, method book purchases, the role of the parents in regular home practice and concert attendance, lesson schedules, band rehearsals, and the like, can all be dealt with during conference times. The most important goal during conferences is to place students on an instrument compatible to their interest, music aptitude, and physical characteristics and to make certain that at the conclusion of the conference, the parents, the children, and the band conductor understand first and foremost that the children are participating in band with the appropriate instrument choice. The conductor must track the instrumentation during conferences and, based on the information at hand, try to secure a balanced instrumentation.

6. *Organizing a recruiting night*
Many school districts include a recruiting night as part of the recruitment

program. The purpose is usually twofold: first, to present an overview of the beginning band program and to answer questions parents may have concerning the program; and second, to have music dealers present, displaying instruments that are available for acquisition or rental. The evening is really a convenience for parents in making decisions about instrument rental. The meeting should be a time to secure an instrument. However, all instruments should be delivered to the band conductor prior to the first lesson and not given to the students on the evening of the meeting. In this way, many unfortunate experiences can be avoided when students try to learn how to play on their own. The first contact with an instrument, including its maintenance and care, assembly, instrument position, posture, embouchure, and the like, can only be addressed properly by the band conductor during those early lessons.

If the teacher-parent-student conferences have been held prior to the recruiting night, then questions about securing an instrument from a music dealer have been answered. The recruiting night, or parent conferences, will then serve as the final step in the recruitment activities.

7. *Involvement of music dealers*

Music dealers are an integral and extremely important part of the recruitment program. In the NABIM research, Froseth felt very strongly that it was appropriate and advisable for school administrators and boards of education to authorize music dealers that best met the criteria for fulfilling the needs of the band program. He felt that the endorsement of a music dealer should be a policy set forth by the school administration and board of education. In this way, it was school board policy that would protect the interests of students, parents, and teachers. We strongly support this notion as well, for it places the burden of school vendors directly in the hands of the people who are responsible for making vendor choices: the administration and the board of education.

Froseth's criteria in the NABIM research dealt with issues of a dealer's quality of products including instruments, acquisition and rental plans, instrument repair and general service (such as school calls, adequate accessories, and availability of competitive bids on school purchases).

The music industry continues to play an important role in the success of our nation's band programs today, and it is imperative in developing a successful beginning band program that a reliable music dealer exhibiting qualities of trust and good business service be asked to help in the job of providing business services to students, their parents, and band conductors. Music dealers should never be asked, however, to do the job of teachers, for only

teachers are responsible for the ultimate job of recruiting, teaching, conducting and program building.

Conclusion

By way of conclusion, the recruitment program outlined in this chapter, utilized in *whole* or in *part*, will hopefully lead young musicians, their parents, and band conductors to a clearer understanding of an individual's musical differences and interest in learning to play a band instrument. The philosophy, objectives, principles, and activities outlined here were done in a manner to hopefully help in guiding the energies of band conductors entrusted with the awesome responsibility of teaching band at the elementary level.

1 Elliott, David J. *Music Matters* (New York: Oxford University Press, 1995), 122.

2 Gordon, Edwin E. *Introduction to Research and the Psychology of Music* (Chicago: GIA Publications, 1998), 2.

3 Ibid.

4 Ibid, 3.

5 Gordon, Edwin E. *Primary Measures of Music Audiation and Intermediate Measures of Music Audiation* (Chicago: GIA Publications, 1986), 1-2.

6 Gordon, Edwin E. *Manual for the Instrument Timbre Preference Test* (Chicago: GIA Publications, 1984), 1.

7 Ibid, 5.

8 Ibid.

9 Ibid.

10 *Introduction to Research and the Psychology of Music*, 216.

11 Froseth, James O. *NABIM Recruiting Manual* (Chicago: GIA Publications, 1974), 15.

12 Ibid.

Appendix A
Recruiting Profile Form

Name of School _____   Academic Classroom Teacher _____

Name of Student	Music Aptitude Test (IMMA)			Academic Achievement (percentile)	Attend Meeting (Yes or No)	Interested (Yes or No)	Telephone Call Needed (Yes or No)	Telephone Number
	Tonal (percentile)	Rhythm (percentile)	Composite (percentile)					
1.								
2.								
3.								
4.								
5.								
6.								
7.								
8.								
9.								
10.								
11.								
12.								
13.								
14.								
15.								
16.								

Appendix B
Instrument Timbre Preference
and Physical Characteristics Evaluation Form

Name of Student _____ Grade _____

Academic Classroom Teacher_____

Instrument Timbre Test Results:

A	B	C	D	E	F	G

Enter the seven scores in the appropriate column.
Scores of 10 and higher indicate a strong preference.

Physical Characteristics Evaluation Results:

Enter the following numerical ranking with the instrument evaluated (5 = excellent, 4 = very good, 3 = good, 2 = fair, 1 = poor). Factors such as teeth, lips, size of hands/ fingers, etc., should be evaluated.

_____ Flute   _____ Oboe   _____ Bassoon   _____ Clarinet

_____ Alto saxophone   _____ Tenor saxophone   _____ Trumpet   _____ Horn

_____ Trombone   _____ Baritone (euphonium)   _____ Tuba   _____ Percussion (sticks)

Comments:
(keyboard experience, guitar, stringed instruments, etc.)
_____
_____
_____
_____

Final Instrument Choice: _____

Appendix C
Sample Recruitment Letter

Dear Jonesville School Parent(s):

We are writing to inform you that beginning band instruction will soon be offered to all fifth grade students in the Jonesville Elementary School. We would like you to consider having your child participate in the program.

Our music faculty has been meeting with all fifth grade students to acquaint them with the band and the various instruments available. We would like you to discuss these activities with your child. It may help in determining your child's interest in joining the beginning band.

Your involvement with your child in the beginning band program is extremely important. To help you better understand the program, we are hosting a **beginning band recruiting night** in the auditorium of Jonesville Elementary School on Wednesday, September 20, at 7:00 p.m. During this meeting, the music faculty will review all aspects of the instructional program. We will also have music store representatives present to answer questions regarding instrument rental and acquisition.

So that we can begin to evaluate the level of interest among our fifth grade class, we ask that you take a moment to return the form below by September 10 in the self-addressed envelope. Save the upper portion of this letter for your reference. Should you have questions that need to be answered prior to this meeting, do not hesitate to call the school and we will return the call as soon as possible.

Thank you in advance for your cooperation. We look forward to seeing you on September 20.

Sincerely,

Instrumental Music Faculty and
Mr. Edward Jones, Principal

- -

Jonesville Elementary School Beginning Band Questionnaire
(Please return to: Mr. Andrew Smith, Director of Bands)

____ I am interested, and my child and I will attend the recruiting night.
____ I am interested, but we cannot attend the recruiting night.
     Please call me at (h) _____ *or (w)* _____ *to arrange a conference.*
____ My child is not interested in participating in the beginning band program.

Child's Name _____ Parent's Name _____

My child is interested in playing the following instruments:

First choice _____ Second choice _____ Third choice _____

Parent's Signature: _____

Comments:

CHAPTER 4

Selecting Music for the Young Band

Bruce Pearson

Without a doubt, one of the band conductor's most important responsibilities is the selection of music for their ensemble. Over the decades, the quantity of pieces being published each year for school bands has grown dramatically. While this has given teachers many more choices, it has also made the task of selecting just the right music for their ensembles more difficult. When teachers consider their curriculum requirements, programming needs, technical limitations of the ensemble, and musical possibilities, selecting music for band can be a daunting task.

One of my fondest memories of being a young band conductor was the Saturday morning "mentoring sessions." For me, Saturday mornings were a time when band conductors of all ages and years of experience would meet at the local music store to have a cup of coffee together and talk about repertoire. These "shop talk-mentoring sessions" gave me tremendous help in selecting music for my ensemble. I recall that when a colleague suggested a piece of music, we would pull that score from the shelf and study it as if it were a rare treasure. We each looked at it from many perspectives. Was it playable with the ensemble I conducted? Where could it be placed on the concert program? What concepts could be taught using it? Did it meet my curriculum needs? Was it good music that was worth the time and energy to carefully prepare it? Was the musical maturity of the piece under consideration commensurate with the maturity level of the ensemble? After many sessions and over a period of years, I became more aware of what must be considered when selecting repertoire for young bands.

The first consideration should be the musicality of the piece. Is it a piece worth studying and preparing? Artists expressing themselves in all media and art critics alike have attempted to answer the question, What makes a work artistic? Musically, one should examine the following components of a composition in an effort to answer that question:

"Does the music have...
1. a well-conceived formal structure?
2. creative melodies and counterlines?
3. harmonic imagination?
4. rhythmic vitality?
5. contrast in all musical elements?
6. scoring that best represents the full potential of beautiful tone and timbre?
7. an emotional impact?"[1]

Much can be learned by examining state contest and festival lists and repertoire books on the subject to see what others think is good music. While this can provide extremely valuable assistance, band teachers should determine for themselves what good music is.

Band conductors must first be excited about the music before they can excite their students. An exciting performance is primarily the result of performing quality music with passion. If the conductor and/or ensemble is not passionate about a work, a lackluster performance will be the result. Teachers can broaden their musical tastes by listening to great live performances and inspiring performances on compact disc. Nothing can quiet a conductor's jangled nerves more quickly than listening to a fine performance. It feeds, nourishes, and rejuvenates a conductor's musical soul. Listening to artistic performances should be a priority in each teacher's daily regimen.

Prudent band conductors should temper their enthusiasm for the music with good judgment. Ultimately, the music that is selected for study and performance must ensure student success. A conductor may fall in love with *Lincolnshire Posy* (and who doesn't?), but that piece probably isn't suitable for bands comprised of 13-year-old students. Careful attention must be given to the technical limitations of every ensemble. A meaningful musical experience involves more than playing the right notes at the right time. Music should be selected at a level of difficulty that will enable students to develop technique as well as musical literacy and understanding. It is important to find the balance between challenging students and providing an attainable goal.

Over the years, I have observed that many bands routinely perform music beyond their technical limitations. As a result, the conductor and students are often frustrated. If the students and, ultimately, the ensemble are to express themselves through their instruments, they should not be burdened with a struggle to play only the right notes and correct rhythms.

All the pieces that an ensemble performs during a concert season should not be at the maximum performance level for the ensemble. Students should have some pieces that do not require every ounce of energy to perform them. Use the "easier" pieces to provide an opportunity to bring the ensemble to a new level of musicianship. Musicians deserve the opportunity to enjoy artistic

performances. This can only be achieved if the repertoire selected is well within the technical limitations of the ensemble.

There are many things to consider when assessing the technical limitations of an ensemble. A thoughtful decision regarding the playability of a work must consider such things as meter, rhythm, dexterity and facility, range, tessitura, melodic treatment, harmonic treatment, key, scoring, texture, musical maturity, and endurance.

Meters

In general, students initially have more success performing in duple meter than in triple meter. This is primarily due to the fact that most young musicians have had far more experience moving (marching, jumping, hopping, and skipping) to duple meter music (e.g., 2/4, 4/4) than to triple meter music (e.g., 3/4, 3/8, 6/8). A comprehensive music education should provide students with ample opportunity to experience both duple and triple meter activities. In addition to performing music, these activities should include movement to music.

The work of the famed music educator, Emile Jaques-Dalcroze, disclosed and stressed the importance of movement to music. Students must "feel" the meters and the rhythms before they can accurately execute them. While Dalcroze's activities often include marching, jumping, hopping, and skipping to the music, these activities are often difficult to perform in the typical band room. Even though space limitations in the band room may prohibit the large motor skill activities that Dalcroze suggests, band room activities may include simultaneous counting and clapping. This will help provide the students with the opportunity to feel the music and to develop a sense for "rhythmic flow." An effective strategy to teach the students to "feel" duple and triple meter may be a combination of thigh pats and hand claps (4/4: pat-clap-clap-clap; 2/4: pat-clap; 3/4: pat-clap-clap). Doing these exercises for a few minutes each day during the early stages of a student's music education will pay dividends later.

Listed below are the recommended meters for Grade 1, 2, and 3 music. Much of this material is from the Conductor's Score of the *Standard of Excellence Comprehensive Band Method*. It is used with permission of Neil A. Kjos Music Company.

GRADE 1:
2/4, 4/4, 3/4

Oftentimes, young students experience difficulty performing music that uses both duple and triple meter within the same selection. The first pieces that an ensemble experiences should be in duple meter only. Once the students experience success with music in duple meter, the teacher should then select music in triple meter. Only after students are confident performing duple and triple meter

music separately should they perform music with both duple and triple meter within the same piece.

More difficult Grade 1 pieces can include both duple and triple meter providing there is a definite stop in the music between the duple and triple meter. This stoppage will provide the students ample time to adjust their inner sense of "musical feel" between duple and triple meter. It should also be noted that young students find it easier to perform music that has a stronger pulse and a moderate tempo. Slow, sustained music often finds the students rushing the tempo at differing speeds, and the ensemble's precision suffers dramatically.

GRADE 2:
In addition to those used in Grade 1: 3/8, 6/8, 4/4, 2/2 (alla breve or cut time)

GRADE 3:
Same as Grades 1 and 2

Rhythms

One of the goals of a music program should be to have all students develop music reading skills, for music reading can unlock the door to a storehouse of musical treasures. Unfortunately for instrumental music teachers and students, learning to play an instrument and learning to read music are not necessarily synonymous.

Rhythmic accuracy is a combination of two elements: steadiness of pulse and accurate execution of rhythms within that pulse. Therefore, before beginning to actually play an instrument, it is critical that students first develop a good feel for a steady pulse. This can be achieved through large motor skill activities such as counting and clapping the rhythms.

Many problems encountered in a sectional or band rehearsal stem from the students' inability to count and feel rhythms. These interruptions can be minimized with daily attention to rhythm and the integration of a counting system. From day one, the use of a counting system encourages the development of rhythmic understanding and control of the rhythmic pulse, and helps to "catalog" the rhythms the body feels into student memory banks. Clapping and counting should be a regular part of all instrumental music classes. Listed below are the recommended rhythms for Grade 1, 2, and 3 band music:

GRADE 1:

GRADE 2:
In addition to those used in Grade 1:

GRADE 3:
In addition to those used in Grades 1 and 2:

Music needs to have elements of unity, repetition, and variety. Unity and repetition provide a sense of cohesion, while variety provides interest. Compositions written for beginning bands should have more unity and repetition than do works written for more experienced ensembles. Some time ago, I was commissioned to write a piece for a band comprised of 11-year-old students. While the band was rehearsing the piece in preparation for the premiere performance, I was routinely checking with the conductor to inquire how preparations were going. He told me that one measure, in particular, was giving the band much difficulty. He told me that they were continually playing that one measure like a similar measure that appeared earlier in the piece. The small variation I had made didn't make it a better composition, but it certainly made it more difficult for those young musicians to perform. I changed that one measure to make the two measures the same. By changing that one measure, I made life much more pleasant for the students and at the same time eliminated a lot of "hair pulling" on the part of the conductor. For beginning bands, rhythm patterns in particular must have more repetition than do pieces written for more experienced ensembles.

Another rhythmic element that must be considered is the "rhythmic flow" of a piece. Music written for less experienced ensembles should have a steady pulse going at all times. In Grade 1 and Grade 2 music, I like to write my compositions with a steady eighth note pulse. This subdivision of the beat promotes greater rhythmic accuracy and helps the students develop a sense of steady pulse.

ADDITIONAL GRADE 1 PERCUSSION RHYTHMS:

Certainly, the comments that were made earlier regarding the importance of repetitive rhythm patterns apply to the percussion section as well.

Another consideration that applies to the percussion section is how rolls are prepared and presented in music for the beginning band. In beginning band music, it is often very helpful to have each roll preceded by the primary strokes of that roll. For example:

Yet another consideration is to avoid having snare drum parts with successive alternating hand rolls such as five stroke (eighth note) roll, nine stroke (quarter note) roll, or seventeen stroke (half note) roll. While alternating hand rolls can be used in Grade 3 music, it should be avoided in Grade 1 and Grade 2 music.

Dexterity and Facility

Musical dexterity and facility, often called *technique*, are important skills that should be developed by individuals and ensembles alike. All too often performance errors, especially sluggish playing, are diagnosed as rhythm problems when, in fact, they are often the result of lack of breath support and poorly developed dexterity and facility skills. If individuals and ensembles are to develop their dexterity and technical facility, they must have command of their instruments. This can only be achieved through good breath support (fast air) and the mastery of scales (major and minor), thirds, arpeggios, chromatic scales throughout the entire range of the instrument, and finger patterns for wind players and rudiments for percussionists. Good technical facility cannot be achieved through repertoire alone. Prudent band conductors encourage their students to work on technique building skills during practice sessions and structure the rehearsal to provide for activities that develop the ensemble's technical skills.

Listed below are the technical facility limits that are recommended for Grade 1, 2, and 3 band music.

GRADE 1:

 at ♩ = 100

GRADE 2:

 at ♩ = 120

GRADE 3:

 at ♩ = 92

Ranges and Tessitura

From the beginning of my teaching career, I considered the ranges for the various instruments before selecting music for the ensemble I conducted. As I gained more experience, I learned that only considering the highest note and sometimes the lowest note was insufficient when examining playing ranges.

I once had, as a private student, a very promising young trumpet player. When he started studying with me, the student was twelve years old and had a beautiful tone. He was a diligent student, and we worked together on all the studies that would enhance his tone quality, develop his technical facility, and foster good musicianship. During his lessons with me, I began to notice that his tone quality was deteriorating and that the notes in his upper range were sounding more and more forced. For a while, I was mystified as to what was causing his tone quality and range to deteriorate. It wasn't until I looked at his band music that I found the answer. One of the selections his band was preparing required playing repeated top line Fs at a *fortissimo* volume. As the band rehearsed this piece day after day, this young and promising trumpet player's tone and range were being compromised. While it is relatively easy to examine a work's ranges for each instrument, it requires experience and good judgment to select music that will not compromise the development of young musicians.

Listed below are the recommended outside ranges for Grade 1, 2, and 3 band music.

GRADE 1:

GRADE 2:

GRADE 3:

Melodic Treatment

How well a composition is crafted often determines the playability of the piece. Sometimes a work that looks very difficult is more readily playable than one might expect; certainly the converse is true also. Composers who have a good understanding of the instruments they are writing for usually have better-crafted pieces that are more playable. All of the great composers in the field of band music have a good understanding of the instruments for which they were writing. This becomes especially apparent when examining the melodic treatment.

Listed below are recommendations for melodic treatment for Grade 1, 2, and 3 band music:

GRADE 1:
- *mostly steps and skips with larger leaps permissible in woodwinds*
  Larger leaps in the brass require a more developed musical ear and an understanding of intervals. This is especially true in the upper partials of the harmonic series for brass players.
- *very limited use of accidentals*
  Accidentals are used, of course, when the notes are outside of the key. Inexperienced musicians have more difficulty hearing pitches outside the key than they do pitches inside the key. Perfect, major, and minor intervals are more familiar and, consequently, easier for most musicians to hear than are augmented and diminished intervals.
- *mostly four- and eight-measure phrases with adequate opportunities for breathing*

GRADE 2:
- *steps, skips, and occasional leaps, within key, permissible in all instruments*
- *predictable use of accidentals*
- *occasional modal melodies*
- *primarily four- and eight-measure phrases*

GRADE 3:
- *steps, skips, and leaps, within key, permissible in all instruments*
- *moderate use of accidentals with mild atonality permissible*

- *some modal melodies*
- *primarily four- and eight-measure phrases; occasional odd-length phrases or motive-based melodic treatment*

Harmonic Treatment

In the process of teaching inexperienced musicians to play with good balance and blend, the harmonic treatment of a work plays an important role. Consequently, young musicians must learn to play consonant sounds with good balance, blend, and intonation before dissonant ones. Listed below are the recommended harmonic treatments for Grade 1, 2, and 3 band pieces.

GRADE 1:
- unisons, thirds, fourths (limited), fifths, sixths, and octaves
- triads

GRADE 2:
In addition to Grade 1:
- primarily consonant intervals; suspended triads and seventh chords

GRADE 3:
In addition to Grades 1 and 2:
- consonant and dissonant intervals; seventh chords, ninth chords, occasional carefully-scored eleventh or thirteenth chords; suspensions

Scoring and Texture

How a composer scores a piece can determine its playability. Great musical ideas can be squandered if scored inappropriately for the musical maturity of the members of the ensemble. Because inexperienced musicians often lack rhythmic independence, they need the security of all members within their section playing the same rhythms. For example, all the woodwinds should perform the same rhythms. The same is true, of course, for brass. As the musicians and ensembles become more mature and experienced, more rhythmic independence becomes permissible, first between sections (e.g., brass, woodwinds, and percussion), then within the woodwind section (e.g., flutes, double reeds, clarinets, and saxophones) and brass (e.g., trumpets, horns, low brass), and finally within individual instrument sections. Below are two examples of a piece scored in two ways: a Grade 1 scoring practice and a Grade 2 scoring practice.

GRADE 1 SCORING:

GRADE 2 SCORING:

OTHER SCORING AND TEXTURE CONSIDERATIONS FOR GRADE 1:
- melody for all instruments sometime during selection (helps to develop musicianship and maintain interest for all members of the ensemble)
- all parts doubled by at least one other instrument
- bass line in all low woodwind and brass instruments
- no more than two rhythmic ideas occurring simultaneously, exclusive of percussion
- two parts for flutes, clarinets, alto saxophones, and trumpets only
- inclusion of a short percussion *soli* acceptable
- scored as if oboe, bassoon, alto clarinet, French horn, baritone, and tuba were not present
- scored primarily in *tutti* style

OTHER SCORING AND TEXTURE CONSIDERATIONS FOR GRADE 2:
- melody for all instruments sometime during the selection
- all parts doubled by at least one other instrument
- bass line in all woodwind and brass instruments; trombones may deviate occasionally
- two parts for flute, clarinets, alto saxophones, and trumpets; two parts occasionally for trombones and horns
- inclusion of a short percussion solo permissible
- scored primarily in *tutti* style; some solos acceptable

OTHER SCORING AND TEXTURE CONSIDERATIONS FOR GRADE 3:
- melody for all instruments sometime during selection
- bass line in tuba and low woodwind instruments, with few exceptions
- two parts for flutes, alto saxophones, trombones, and horns; two parts occasionally for oboes
- three parts for clarinets and trumpets
- variety of textures may occur, from relatively transparent to *tutti*
- some solos acceptable, cued when occurring in instruments other than flute, clarinet, alto saxophone, or trumpet

Keys

It is generally thought that the keys of B-flat, E-flat, and F major are most suitable for beginning bands. Every key, however, has its own peculiar problems. This is particularly true when considering intonation. When taking intonation into account, many band conductors feel that E-flat major is the most in-tune key for beginning bands. This is because F major (tonic in the key of F major and the dominant in the key of B-flat) and C major (the dominant in the key of F) are two of the most difficult chords to play in tune for beginning bands.

When considering the key of F major, several problems exist:

- F concert is one of the most out-of-tune (sharp) notes for alto and baritone saxophone.

- The third of the F major chord (A) is often played very flat by valved brass instruments and young trombonists playing in second position.

- The dominant chord in F major is a C major chord. When this is played by valved brass instruments and young trombonists with short arms, it is usually played very sharp. The problem is exacerbated when one considers that the third of that chord (E) is often played flat by young musicians.

Many of the same problems exist when playing in B-flat concert, for once again, the dominant chord (F) is difficult to play in tune for the reasons mentioned above. E-flat major may be the most inherently in-tune key for beginning bands. E-flat major, however, has range limitations for young musicians.

Listed below are the keys most often associated with Grade 1, 2, and 3 band music:

GRADE 1:
- Concert B-flat, E-flat, and F major

GRADE 2:
- Concert B-flat, E-flat, F, and A-flat major
- Concert g and c minor

GRADE 3:
- Concert B-flat, E-flat, F, A-flat, C, and D-flat major
- Concert g, c, d, and f minor

Musical Maturity

When considering the musical maturity of a piece, the musical content as well as the musical nuances should be considered. Even though the piece under consideration may be very playable by the ensemble, the musical content must be at a level to which the ensemble can relate. When considering expressive qualities, less experienced musicians are, in general, less flexible and less malleable to musical nuances. To facilitate a fine performance, the following are suggested musical maturity guidelines for Grade 1, 2, and 3 bands:

GRADE 1:
- selections with a strong rhythmic pulse
- limited use of *ritardandos* (ending in *fermatas*); no *accelerandos*
- tempo changes only after *fermata*
- limited dynamic variation
- predictable arranging and orchestration
- considerable repetition in percussion with limited use of rolls (no snare drum rolls on *fermata* notes)
- predictable binary and ternary forms

GRADE 2:
- occasional meter and key changes
- limited use of *ritardandos* and *accelerandos*
- moderate dynamic variation
- predictable arranging and orchestration
- moderate use of repetition in percussion; moderate use of rolls
- primarily binary and ternary forms; moderate use of variation techniques

GRADE 3:
- moderate use of meter and key changes
- *ritardandos*, *accelerandos*, and *rubato*
- frequent dynamic variation
- use of varied, less predictable arranging and orchestra techniques

- frequent use of rolls in percussion (as appropriate); inclusion of multiple mallet percussion parts
- any basic formal structure permissible

Endurance

It is extremely important to consider the endurance factor when selecting music for beginning band. Most publishers today are providing the performance time of a selection in the conductor's score. While this is obviously a very important consideration, many other factors need to be evaluated. A piece can be relatively short, but if the tessitura and dynamics are extreme, the actual performance time may be less important. While rehearsing, the band conductor should be constantly aware of the endurance of the students. It is critical that the students are not being pushed beyond the limit of their endurance. When pushed beyond their limit, additional rehearsing becomes counterproductive and the students' musicianship and physical well-being may be compromised. As stated earlier, many factors need to be considered when assessing the endurance level of a piece of music.

Below you will see listed the time limit recommended for Grade 1, 2, and 3 band music.

GRADE 1:
- Performance time generally should not exceed two minutes and thirty seconds.

GRADE 2:
- Performance time generally should not exceed three minutes and thirty seconds, unless adequate resting time is provided.

GRADE 3:
- Performance time generally should not exceed five minutes and thirty seconds.

Curriculum

Early in my teaching career, one book captured my attention and literally changed how I would teach music for the remainder of my teaching career. That one book was *Teaching Musicianship in the High School Band* by Joseph A. Labuta (originally published by Parker Publishing Company in 1972 and revised and republished in 1996 by Meredith Music Publications). Labuta "presents a curriculum based on instructional content in which students learn more than performance skills."[2]

This approach was new to me, for prior to reading this book, I selected music with my only criteria being, Does it sound good and can the band play it? I gave little thought to what the students were actually learning. Selecting repertoire based on what the students could learn from a specific piece of music and then considering how that specific piece fit into a larger curriculum was a foreign but very exciting thought.

"One of the outstanding achievements of public school music during the twentieth century has been the phenomenal development of performing groups. As the performance grew in importance and was accepted by the public, the training of the music teacher became increasingly dominated by courses which were directly related to a performance-oriented music curriculum.

In more recent years, however, music educators have begun to evaluate the outcomes of music education and have expressed increasing concern with the fact that in spite of the high standards of performance in many schools, the large majority of high school students had no formal contact with music during any of their high school years. They also noted that even those students who were active in performance groups, though technically well-trained, were frequently deficient in understanding music as an art."[3]

The National Standards for Arts Education has addressed this concern and has identified what all American students "should know and be able to do in the arts." In many ways, the Standards have structured what music educators have for some time called *comprehensive musicianship.*

Comprehensive musicianship has often been defined as theory applied to practice and knowledge applied to practical music-making. In the band room, this takes the form of studying in-depth the band literature that is being prepared for performance. The music repertoire should be selected for its musical worth, stylistic validity, and teaching potential. Learning about the music being rehearsed in no way precludes a culminating performance. Concerts, after all, should be a logical outgrowth of classroom learning. It is prudent to perform what the ensemble has been studying rather than to study what the ensemble is about to perform.

There has been considerable concern expressed that teaching activities designed to achieve comprehensive musicianship may consume so much rehearsal time that performance skills may be compromised. On the contrary, students perform better because they understand what they are doing and why they are doing it.

Band conductors should understand their responsibility in making discretionary decisions regarding the balance of meeting the students' educational needs and the public's educational desires. To that end, an effective strategy is to select one composition to study in-depth for each concert season. Activities may include providing incidental information during rehearsals, distributing worksheets to the students regarding the music, providing program notes, out-of-class study, and/or utilizing class discussion.

The repertoire selected should be the source and model for activities that would include studies in tonality, rhythm, melody, music theory, phrasing, terms and symbols, ear training, composition, form, and multi-cultural and interdisciplinary studies. These elements can then be studied in the context of music history. By carefully selecting repertoire, students may examine how melody, for example, was treated in the Renaissance, Baroque, Classical, Romantic, and Twentieth Century periods. In this manner, the students will gain an understanding of the piece they are preparing for a performance while learning about melodic development.

When developing a curriculum for the teaching of comprehensive musicianship, band conductors must consider how many years a student has been in the program. Is it a two-year, three-year, or four-year program? This, along with the number of concert seasons, will determine how many and what concepts can and should be studied.

Concert Programming

Concerts afford band conductors the opportunity to share the band's musical experiences with the public. Each performance is but one aspect of the students' total musical experience. A concert that is fun to perform and enjoyable to listen to has musical interest and variety, and showcases the developing talents of the ensemble and individual players. The following program format will enable students to make the most of their performance:

Opener:
Establish a positive atmosphere and aura of confidence with an energetic piece that is not too difficult. This sets the proper mood for the rest of the concert and allows the students to become used to the surroundings and settle their concert jitters.

Major Work:
Display music of the highest quality. This selection should hold technical and musical demands for all sections and students. It is often advisable to have the *Major Work* include a 'big ending.'

Quiet Piece:
Contrast the rhythmic activity, loudness, dissonance, and texture of the major work. Display the development of students' sensitive musicianship.

Feature Tune:
Showcase an entire section, perhaps one whose parts have been less challenging or one that is particularly strong. Use an enjoyable piece that can be used to teach specific objectives.

Closer:
Finish with a powerful, upbeat selection—a piece that the students can play confidently. Make sure the audience leave with a positive feeling about the concert and the band program, in general.[4]

Unquestionably, the selection of music is one of the band conductor's most important and difficult responsibilities. Much time is required to find repertoire that is quality music, is within the technical limitations of the ensemble, supports the curriculum, and meets the ensemble's programming needs. Only after these have been considered in the selection of repertoire for an ensemble can band conductors be assured that they have provided their ensembles with the best music education experience possible.

1 Miles, Richard, edit. *Teaching Music through Performance in Band.* Chicago: GIA Publications, Inc., 1997, 8.

2 Ibid, 49.

3 Ernst, Karl D., and Charles L. Gary. *Music in General Education.* Washington, DC. Music Educators National Conference, 1965, v.

4 Pearson, Bruce. *Standard of Excellence Comprehensive Band Method.* San Diego: Neil A. Kjos Music Company, 1993, 573-574.

CHAPTER 5

A Comprehensive Approach to Teaching Grade 1 Band Music

Marguerite Wilder

The musical elements of rhythm, melody, harmony, and form in Grade 1 band literature are often challenging for beginning students. Moreover, some instrumental music teachers believe that once these students are "told" about the rhythm, melody, harmony, and form, the young musicians subsequently should be able to play the literature successfully.

Elizabeth Green, the famous music educator, once said, "Telling isn't teaching." In Webster's *New World Dictionary of the American Language,* the primary definition of the verb *to teach* is "to show, demonstrate." As a band conductor, when you prepare to teach a Grade 1 band piece, are you preparing *to show* or *demonstrate* the musical concepts and skills that students will need to understand, to perform and, ultimately, to "own" the piece?

An immediate goal for all music rehearsals is to teach musical understanding, with the long-term goal of transferring that understanding to other repertoire. With that in mind, how do beginning band students learn best? Consider this outline of "Principles of the Pestalozzian System of Music"[1] as a guideline for teaching and learning:

1. To teach sounds before signs and to make the child learn to sing before he learns the written notes or their names;
2. To lead him [the child] to observe by hearing and imitating sounds, their resemblances and differences, their agreeable and disagreeable effect, instead of explaining these things to him—in a word, to make active instead of passive in learning;
3. To teach but one thing at a time—rhythm, melody, and expression, which are to be taught and practiced separately, before the child is called to the difficult task of attending to all at once;
4. To make him [the child] practice each step of each of these divisions, until he is master of it, before passing to the next;

5. To give the principles and theory after the practice, and as induction from it;
6. To analyze and practice the elements of articulate sound in order to apply them to music; and
7. To have the names of the notes correspond to those used in instrumental music.

The Pestalozzian principles outlined here can be applied to *Chant and Celebration*, a Grade 1 band piece by Feldstein and O'Reilly (Alfred Publishing). As suggested earlier, many music teachers might introduce their students to such a piece by "talking down the score"—that is, by "telling." However, in the Pestalozzian system, the *experience* of this music should come before much, if any, *verbal information* is given about the piece itself.

To teach *Chant and Celebration* most effectively, the teacher should prepare "to be the music." This is best accomplished through *modeling*. In Webster's *New World Dictionary of the American Language*, the primary definition of the noun *model* is "a standard or example for imitation or comparison."

MODELING[2]

Modes for Modeling
- Teacher demonstration (vocal or instrumental)
- Student demonstration (vocal or instrumental)
- Media (photographs, audio recordings, video recordings)

Some Objectives for Musical Modeling
- To develop improved musical concepts
- To teach students to discriminate musical and technical differences in performance
- To define music learning objectives: It is! It isn't!
- To stimulate and motivate
- To save time and eliminate excessive teacher talk

Some Perceptual Qualities of an Instrumental Musical Model

- Posture
- Tone quality
- Rhythm
- Form
- Energy
- Instrument position
- Intonation
- Melody
- Phrasing
- Expressive nuance
- Hand position
- Articulation
- Harmony
- Style
- Attitude
- Embouchure
- Technique
- Dynamics
- Tempo
- Timbre

The most appropriate response to music teacher modeling is music student imitation of that model, as implied in Pestalozzi's Principle 2: "To lead him to observe by hearing and imitating sounds, their resemblances and differences, their agreeable and disagreeable effect, instead of explaining these things to him—in a word, to make active instead of passive in learning."

Consider Pestalozzi's Principle 3: "To teach but one thing at a time—rhythm, melody, and expression, which are to be taught and practiced separately, before the child is called to the difficult task of attending to all at once."

Rhythm

The following rhythm warm-up exercise for *Chant and Celebration* serves as an application of teacher modeling/student imitation and student association of modeled rhythmic patterns to rhythmic notation.

When planning and practicing this teaching assignment, teachers may wish to refer to the following outline of the music learning sequence:

A. SOUNDS LIKE   Rhythm syllables or sounds

"Read - y now, ech - o me" (on pitch)

Sing or Play rhythm on Concert D for Chant Rhythm Cards.
Sing or Play rhythm on Concert F for Celebration Rhythm Cards.

B. LOOKS LIKE   Rhythm syllables and flashcards

"Read - y now, ech - o me" (on pitch; card up on "ech - o me")

C. ASSESSMENT   Flashcards
(individual patterns)

"Read - y now, look - and play" (on pitch; card up on "look - and play")[3]

D. ASSESSMENT   Associating rhythmic flashcard patterns to the students' music in *Chant and Celebration*. (Example: Flashcard #6 corresponds to m. 9 in the flute, oboe, and clarinet parts.)

1. Rhythmic Flashcard Reading Options for the Chant Section (mm. 1–23) of *Chant and Celebration* are Flashcards 1 through 11. (See below.)

2. Suggested piece of music from *Music for Movement* compact disc. (Froseth, James O., and Albert Blaser; Chicago: GIA Publications, 1993) Selection 9. The pitch for this exercise is Concert D.[4]

3. Rhythmic Flashcards Reading Options for the Celebration Section (mm. 24 – 61) of *Chant and Celebration* are Flashcards 1, 3, 4, 5, 9, 11–25. (See below.)

4. Suggested piece of music from *Music for Movement* compact disc (Froseth, James O., and Albert Blaser; Chicago: GIA Publications, 1993) Selection 4. The pitch for this exercise is Concert F.[5]

Rhythmic Flashcards

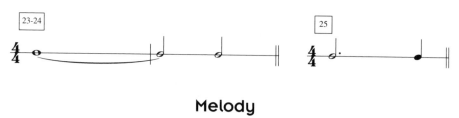

Melody

The following "by ear" warm-up exercise for *Chant and Celebration* serves as an application of teacher modeling/student imitation.

1. Tell students, "The starting pitch is B-flat concert. Echo me."

2. On an instrument of choice, play each melodic pattern in a sequence on the same starting pitch. If the starting pitch is to be changed, "build a bridge" to the new starting pitch and emphasize the change with a simple, repeated pitch pattern. Avoid abrupt transitions from easy to difficult patterns. Reduce complex patterns into simple sequences that build skills gradually.

3. When hearing a mistake, "retreat." Return to the last pattern the class performed correctly. Upon reaching the final exercise of the "by ear" chant warm-up, the teacher should be modeling the style, tempo, and articulation of the melody found in measures 1 and 2 of *Chant and Celebration*.[6]

4. Tell students, "The starting pitch is B-flat concert. Echo me."

5. Move through the examples, increasing the tempo. Upon reaching the final exercise of the celebration "by ear" warm-up, the teacher should be modeling the style, tempo, and articulation of the melody found in measures 24 through 27 of *Chant and Celebration*.

Teacher Modeling/Student Imitation Exercise
for Chant and Celebration

Flute: Demo/Echo Chant Melody Exercise

Trumpet: Demo/Echo Chant Melody Exercise

Teacher Modeling/Student Imitation Exercise
for Chant and Celebration

Flute: Demo/Echo Celebration Melody Exercise

Trumpet: Demo/Echo Celebration Melody Exercise

Musical Form

Young instrumentalists should have an understanding of the structure of the music. As students move from band method book music to full band arrangements, they are often uncertain as to what to listen for in the music. Most of the songs in band books are performed in a unison or duet format, while Grade 1 band literature offers melody, countermelody, bass, and percussion lines.

Full band literature requires that the students perform a single line of music while relating their line to the other components of the music. It is helpful for students to hear and see the other parts in the full band piece.

The use of a "lead" sheet for each instrument group shows melody, harmony, bass, and percussion lines. The lead sheet gives an understanding of the purpose of each component part and its relationship to other parts of the music; this enables the students to play the melody, harmony, rhythm, and bass lines found in the music. This comprehensive approach facilitates the achievement of balance and blend by the beginning students.

Balance and blend are often new concepts for beginning band students. Musical growth can be achieved when students acquire ownership of these concepts. Beyond reading and performing music, instrumentalists should gain an understanding of the importance of structure in music. Being able to recognize these components aurally and to describe this recognition verbally enhances students' overall musicianship. Knowledgeable performers, by understanding how music communicates, are then prepared to see and hear the individual lines as they relate to the full score.

Flute: Chant and Celebration

BASS LINE

HARMONY

Clarinet: Chant and Celebration

MELODY

BASS LINE

HARMONY

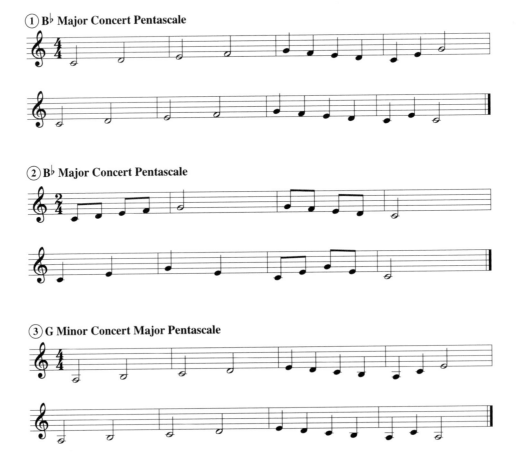

Warm-up Scales for B-flat Clarinet

The following are examples of major and minor scales that correlate with *Chant and Celebration*. Most of the scales are in five-note formats that are readily usable for beginning instrumentalists. There are also examples of rhythm scale exercises, which correlate to specific measures in the piece.

① B♭ Major Concert Pentascale

② B♭ Major Concert Pentascale

③ G Minor Concert Major Pentascale

④ **G Minor Concert Major Pentascale**

⑤ **G Minor Concert Scale Etude**

⑥ **B♭ Major Concert Scale Etude**

⑦ **Rhythm Measures 1-2**   **Concert B♭ Major**

⑧ **Rhythm Measures 9-10**   **Concert G Minor**

⑨ **Rhythm Measures 36-43**   **Concert B♭ Major**

⑩ **Rhythm Measures 36-43   Concert G Minor**

An example of a worksheet for *Chant and Celebration* is shown on the next page. This sample allows the students to "score study" their individual parts. Students will turn in the worksheet after several rehearsals of the music. A class discussion of the worksheet should offer an understanding of how a piece works.[7]

Musical understanding, as well as proficiency on an instrument is an immediate goal for all music rehearsals. An instructional sequence that provides both a melodic and rhythmic foundation teaches musical understanding, which transfers this understanding to other repertoire. Through the use of rhythmic patterns, "by ear" melody patterns, a variety of scale warm-ups, lead sheets with all the lines of the piece, and a worksheet, students should gain ownership and understanding in the music of *Chant and Celebration*.

Chant and Celebration Worksheet

Name _____ Date _____

1. Give the definition for *chant*.

2. Give the definition for *celebration*.

3. Name the composers of *Chant and Celebration*.

4. When was this piece composed?

5. Name the publishing company of *Chant and Celebration*.

6. List the dynamic markings in this piece.

7. Add a dynamic marking in measures 32 through 46. Why did you choose that dynamic marking?

8. How many tempo changes occur in this piece?

9. Give the definition for *andante*.

10. Give the definition for *allegro*.

11. Do you observe repeat signs in this piece? List the measures.

12. Do you observe first and second endings?

13. List the time signatures of this piece.

14. List the key signatures of this piece.

15. Give a musical description of the first four measures of this piece. Explain what is happening. Who is playing? How long are they playing?

16. Are measures 1 and 2 smooth and connected or detached and separated?

17. What is the musical term that describes this style of playing?

1   Abeles, Harold F., Charles R. Hoffer, and Robert H. Klotman. "History of Music Education." Chapter 1 in *Foundations of Music Education*, 2nd edition, 3-39. New York: Schirmer, 1994, 11.

2   Froseth, James O. Unpublished teaching materials, Ann Arbor, MI: University of Michigan, 1993-1999.

3   Weaver, Molly A. Unpublished teaching materials. Morgantown, WV: West Virginia University, 1993-1999.

4   Froseth, James O., Albert Blaser, and Phyllis Weikart. *Music for Movement*. Book and compact disc. Chicago: GIA Publications, 1981.

5   Ibid.

6   Froseth, James O., and Judith K. Delzell. *The Individualized Instructor Teaching Skills Workbook*. Chicago: GIA Publications, 1981.

7   Larry Blocher, Ray Cramer, Eugene Corporon, Tim Lautzenheiser, Edward S. Lisk, and Richard Miles. *Teaching Music through Performance in Band:* "The Quantum Conductor," Eugene Corporon, 20.

CHAPTER 6

Technology for Beginning Band

Scott Emmons

Throughout the history of music education, we see constant development and use of technology in music teaching. Thomas Rudolph reminds us in *Teaching Music with Technology* that the organ, the piano, and the valved trumpet were all the hot new technologies of their day.[1] Thinking about how the phonograph revolutionized music education in this country can give us a glimpse at how the state-of-the-art electronic technology of today (microcomputers, CD-ROM, electronic keyboards, worldwide web) will continue to revolutionize music education during our own careers as music educators.

Leaders from industry and education stress the need for increased use of technology in music. One of the suggestions from the publication, *A Nation at Risk*, was that educators embrace technology.[2] While developing the National Standards for the Arts (MENC, 1994), leaders of the music education profession listed technology use as a high priority. Advances in music computer technology, such as sequencing software, can help us solve many of the technical problems in learning music, such as the mechanics of musical notation.[3] Using technology to solve these problems enables teachers to focus more attention on teaching musicality and less on teaching mechanics, thus giving students more time for creative reflection and revision of their work.

All of us in recent times have witnessed the way computers, the worldwide web, and video games captivate the attention of children. Because computers are motivating, researchers have shown them to be appropriate instructional tools for teaching music. They concluded that students using computer training were more likely to express, refine, or revise ideas. Growth was also apparent in students' confidence and self-esteem, student-student interaction, teacher-student interaction, and classroom management.[4] Additionally, the researchers' findings indicate that development of independent and original thinking was fostered by the creative use of computers. Recent hardware and software developments that make music activities using computer technology both more effective and easier to use now make computer-assisted teaching appropriate and desirable for applications in music.

When using state-of-the-art technology to teach music, it is important to remember to use the technological tools in the same way any other teaching tool would be used, such as a blackboard or an overhead projector. Teachers must remember that their job is to focus on teaching music; the technology simply helps them achieve this goal.

Using Technology in Beginning Band

Band conductors teaching beginning students can address each of the nine National Standards[5] in music using computer-assisted instruction. I will address each of these standards as this chapter progresses. I will then address several practical uses of technology for band conductors to help with day-to-day chores.

Many music educators group the nine National Standards into three clusters. The first of these clusters is *performance*. This includes Standard 1 ("Singing, alone and with others, a varied repertoire of music") and Standard 2 ("Performing on instruments, alone and with others, a varied repertoire of music"). The second cluster, *creative standards*, includes Standard 3 ("Improvising melodies, harmonies and accompaniments") and Standard 4 ("Composing and arranging music within specified guidelines"). The last cluster of standards is made up of the *knowledge* standards: Standard 5 ("Reading and notating music"), Standard 6 ("Listening to, analyzing, and describing music"), Standard 7 ("Evaluating music and music performances"), Standard 8 ("Understanding relationships between music, the other arts, and disciplines outside the arts"), and Standard 9 ("Understanding music in relation to history and culture").

THE PERFORMING STANDARDS

Providing students with musically played performances of the literature they are performing is especially important in the early stages of learning. Band teachers today are fortunate to have new method materials for beginning band that include prerecorded solo and accompaniment tracks on CD. A teacher can play the recordings of the "book one" exercises the students are learning to help model concepts such as tone quality, intonation, and rhythm. Since most teachers of beginning students are not equally facile on every instrument, these recordings can be helpful in guiding students to the correct instrument sound.

When equipped with a computer and accompaniment program, such as Coda's *SmartMusic*, students can rehearse solo literature with an electronic accompanist that can substitute for the pianist, who is not always readily available for each practice session or rehearsal. Using a computer and keyboard with sequencing software (a digital recorder that records playing instructions rather than sounds), such as Mark of the Unicorn's *Performer*, it is also possible for a teacher to record all of the parts to duets, trios, quartets, etc. Because each line of the score can be turned off or on, the students are able to rehearse their parts with any combination of other voices of the piece, including or excluding their own part.

Because of scheduling and recruiting problems, it is not always possible to have a complete complement of parts for every band rehearsal. Although it is imperfect in sound, students and teachers can use an electronic keyboard to fill in important solos (e.g., a bassoon solo) during rehearsals.

More than teachers in other educational endeavors, music educators must know how to teach many different instruments and recognize the problems that occur in learning each of these. Diagnostic programs, such as Froseth's (1999) *Visual Diagnostic* CD-ROM package, can give both teachers and students an interactive way to visualize and hear proper playing techniques as well as the means for recognizing and correcting flaws in instrument performance.

THE CREATIVITY STANDARDS

The most neglected standards in a band curriculum are typically Standards 3 and 4, the improvisation and composition standards. Fortunately, band conductors can use technological tools when teaching these standards.

Teaching improvisation to students can be challenging, especially for teachers who have done very little improvisation themselves. The following lesson plans provide an approach for teaching improvisation using the "intelligent accompaniment computer program," *Band-in-a-Box*. *Band-in-a-Box* allows the user to simply type in the chord symbols desired and choose the tempo and style of the music. The program then generates a realistic-sounding accompaniment.

Improvisation Lesson 1:
Blues Improvisation

Objective:
- Students will improvise variations to *Sonnymoon for Two* (by Sonny Rollins).

Materials:
- Handout with the melody for *Sonnymoon for Two* transposed for all band members.
- B-flat blues rhythm background on *Band-in-a-Box*.

Prior Knowledge and Experiences:
- Students can perform a B-flat concert scale for a complete octave.
- Students have sung and played on their instruments the B-flat minor pentatonic scale (B-flat – D-flat – E-flat – F – A-flat).

- Students have been taught the melody to *Sonnymoon for Two*. The entire melody is composed from the minor pentatonic scale.

Procedures:
1. Perform the melody of *Sonnymoon for Two* as a group to the computer's rhythm background. (Percussionists should all use mallet instruments.)
2. Start the background track. With a good swing feel, model short "blues licks" (two to four notes, maximum length) for students using the notes concert B-flat and concert A-flat. Have students echo them back immediately in correct time to the background music.
3. Repeat Step 2 with a gradually expanding collection of notes. Add notes in this order: B-flat – A-flat – D-flat – F – E-flat.
4. Ask the students to improvise softly as a group to the background track using licks they learned in the previous steps.
5. Give students several chances to improvise solos to entire choruses when they feel comfortable.

Indicators of Success:
- Students will be successful at improvising short, melodic "licks."

Follow-up:
- Transfer the information learned to other pentatonic melodies.

Improvisation Lesson 2:
Accompaniment Improvisation

Materials:
- *Jump Right In Solo Book* or other appropriate collection of tunes
- Prerecorded rhythm track using *Band-in-a-Box*

Prior Knowledge and Experiences:
- Students have sung and played on their instruments several simple folk tunes.
- Students have practiced singing roots of chords to folk melodies.

Procedures:
1. Sing the folk melody to be used that day.
2. Play the folk melody on instruments by rote. Do this several times to make sure students are all performing the melody correctly.
3. Perform the melody with the accompaniment.
4. Ask half of the students to perform the melody on their instruments. Ask the other half to figure out and sing harmony lines by ear (chord roots and chord tones).

5. Repeat Step 4, except ask the group to play the chord roots on their instruments instead of singing them.
6. Switch roles and repeat Steps 4 and 5.

Indicators of Success:
- Students will be able to improvise harmony lines to the folk tunes used.

Follow-up:
- Transfer the information learned to other songs in different styles.
- Ask the students to improvise lines using any chord tone they hear.

Teaching students to compose provides another difficulty for beginning band conductors. Using a computer program for sequencing and notating music can provide the motivation needed for both the teacher and the students to succeed in this task. Two lesson plans follow that will provide ideas for creating lessons that integrate technology with the teaching of composition.

Composition Lesson 1:
Variation Technique

Students will sing *Frère Jacques*. They will then discuss with the teacher various ways composers can compose variations. Each student will compose a limited-note variation on *Frère Jacques*; the students will only be allowed to use the notes and rhythms from the theme in each corresponding measure of the variation. After performing the variations in small groups, the students will listen to and discuss Mahler's treatment of *Frère Jacques* in the third movement of his Symphony No. 1.

Materials Needed:
- Recording (Chicago Symphony Orchestra—Solti)
- *Frère Jacques* handout

Objectives:
At the conclusion of the lesson, the students will be able to:
- Perform *Frère Jacques* on their instruments.
- Compose a variation on Frère Jacques.
- Identify ways Mahler changed *Frère Jacques* in the third movement of his Symphony No. 1.

Procedures:
1. Sing and play *Frère Jacques* as a group.
2. Discuss variation technique.
3. Compose a variation by switching the order of pitches and rhythms in each measure.
4. Perform variations in small groups.
5. Listen to and discuss Mahler's *Frère Jacques*.

Indicators of Success:
- Evaluation will be based upon class discussion and performance of the variations.

Composition Lesson 2:
Melodic Composition with Student-Selected Backgrounds

Students will listen to several computer-sequenced (using *Performer, Master Tracks,* or *Band-in-a-Box*) like-chord examples of music. Each student will select his or her favorite background and compose melodies that he or she believes fit with the background.

Materials Needed:
- Sequenced accompaniment track
- Computer and keyboard
- Sample melodies (notated and sequenced)

Objectives:
At the conclusion of the lesson, the students will be able to:
- Compose a melody to correspond with given I, IV, V7 function accompaniment.
- Demonstrate ways of making melodies fit with chord functions.

Procedures:
1. Discuss given melodies and chords, and review chord function.
2. As a group, listen to sequenced background styles and then choose the background to be used in class.
3. Compose a melody that fits the background; revise the melody as desired.
4. Perform student melodies in small groups with the accompaniment.

Indicators of Success:
- Evaluation will be based upon class discussion and performance of the sequenced melodies.

THE KNOWLEDGE STANDARDS

With the explosion of the use of the worldwide web, opportunities for cognitive music growth through computer-assisted learning are limited only by a teacher's creativity and a student's curiosity.

Teachers need to develop assignments that complement the literature being performed by the ensemble. This will help the students better understand the music being performed. For example, if a beginning band is performing O'Reilly's *Simple Gifts*, a work based on the shaker tune (available on accompanying CD), the teacher may make a presentation using a computer connected to the worldwide web that will demonstrate web sites about shaker colonies and their arts. Students can then be assigned to do "scavenger hunts" to find their own web sites about these or related subjects. Using the web and other Internet resources, such as on-line encyclopedias, can be a helpful tool for teacher and student research on composers, style periods, or cultures being studied in literature being explored.

Band teachers are fortunate to have access to a wealth of CD-ROM packages, such as Voyager's *The Orchestra*, available for use with small and large group instruction. These multimedia programs use sound and video to give students added insight into the world of style periods, composers, and music of various cultures. CD-ROM packages give the benefit of almost instant access to information that requires much fast forwarding or rewinding to find on video or audio tapes.

Standard 5, "Reading and notating music," can be addressed using one of the many notation programs, such as Coda's *Finale* or Passport's *MusicTime*. For example, students might be asked to notate their compositions for the previous lessons using the computer and notation software. Providing students with scoring and transcription exercises gives students additional knowledge about their instruments and the rules for notating music.

Productivity for Band Conductors

Several day-to-day tasks for band conductors can be made more manageable with the use of technology. Database programs are essential in helping teachers to keep track of recruitment information. Data about parent information, pre-band test scores, instrument preference, and physical characteristics evaluations can be entered into a database program. Teachers can then use this data to help students choose the best instrument. Having good data will help ensure that fewer students with high potential are missed in the recruitment process.

After students are enrolled in a band program, band conductors must maintain parent/student data lists. It is important for them to have information such as address and phone numbers, as well as information regarding instrument and uniform, on a database at their fingertips. These lists can be used to generate

mailing labels when sending letters to parents about important events and concerts. Teachers can also use database programs to keep school instrument inventories.

Communication with parents and students can be further enhanced with band program web pages. Many school districts today are setting up district home pages with links to teacher and program web pages. Band conductors can use these pages to post event calendars, student and parent notices, and even information about student successes! Although many schools employ "web masters," programs such as FileMaker's *Home Page* make designing and maintaining your own web page relatively simple.

Band conductors typically have a broad range of interests and expertise. Anyone can design lesson strategies incorporating technology that will enhance student learning and enjoyment with music; all that is needed is a small amount of time and creativity. That is not to say that teachers should completely redesign their school curricula to fully incorporate all of the technological tools available to them. To start though, teachers can, and should, take their best lesson ideas and augment them with technology. Watch the way music and technology can work together to captivate and motivate students.

Recommended Reading

Booty, C. TIPS: *Technology for Music Educators*. Reston, VA: MENC, 1990.
Carpenter, R.A. *Technology in the Music Classroom*. Van Nuys, CA: Alfred Publishing, 1991.
Muro, D. *The Art of Sequencing*. Miami, FL: CPP/Belwin, Inc., 1993.
Otuska & Nakajima. *MIDI Basics*. New York: Amsco Publications, 1987.
Purse, B. *The Finale Primer*. San Francisco, CA: Miller Freeman Books, 1998.
Rudolph, T.E. *Teaching Music with Technology*. Chicago: GIA Publications, Inc., 1996.

1   Rudolph, T. *Teaching Music with Technology*. Chicago: GIA Publications, 1996.
2   National Commission on Excellence in Education. *A Nation at Risk: The Imperative for Educational Reform*. Washington, DC: U.S. Government Printing Office, 1983.
3   Reimer, B. "Music Education and Aesthetic Education: Toward the Future." *Music Educators Journal*, 75(7), 26-32, 1989.
4   Carmichael, H.W., J.D. Barnett, W.C. Higginson, B.G. Moore, and P.J. Pollard. *Computers, Children and Classrooms: A Multisite Evaluation of the Creative Use of Microcomputers by Elementary School Children*. Toronto: Ontario Ministry of Education, 1985.
5   Music Educators National Conference. *National Standards for Arts Education*, 101-102. Reston, VA: Author, 1994.

PART II

TEACHER RESOURCE GUIDES

Grade One

For a breakdown of the levels of difficulty of the above selections (entry, intermediate, or advanced Grade One), please refer to the index on page 393 of this book.

Teacher Resource Guide

African Festival

arranged by Quincy Hilliard (b. 1954),
Chuck Elledge (b. 1961),
Bruce Pearson (b. 1942)

Unit 1: Composer

Quincy Hilliard was born in Starkville, Mississippi, on September 22, 1954. Hilliard's compositions are distributed by several major music publishers and are performed throughout the world by wind bands with British-American instrumentation. His stature as a composer is apparent, as conductors frequently commission him for new compositions. He is a five-time recipient of the distinguished American Society for Composers, Authors, and Publishers (ASCAP) award, recognizing the numerous performances of his works. He was also chosen as one of a select group of composers to write a piece for the 1996 Olympics. Hilliard is an established conductor and educator who has been invited to all parts of the world to conduct, adjudicate festivals, and demonstrate teaching techniques.

Hilliard's extensive pedagogical publications include journal articles and books, such as *Selecting Music for the School Band* (Southern Music Company, San Antonio, Texas), *Skill Builders* Books 1 and 2 (with Andrew Balent as co-author), and *Theory Concepts* Books 1 and 2 published by Carl Fischer (New York) in the *Sounds Spectacular* series.

Hilliard is also a recognized scholar of the music of Aaron Copland. He serves as a consultant/clinician/conductor for music publishers Boosey and Hawkes and Carl Fischer. He is also the president of Hilliard Music Enterprises, Inc., a consulting firm that has a corporate board of distinguished music educators. He is currently associate professor of music theory and composition at the University of Southwestern Louisiana in Lafayette.

Chuck Elledge is a contributing editor and contributing composer of the *Standard of Excellence Band Method* as well as co-author of the *Standard of Excellence Music Theory & History Workbooks*. He currently holds positions as instrumental editor and staff writer at Neil A. Kjos Music Company. He has also collaborated with Bruce Pearson on the *Best in Class Performance Selections*, *A Best in Class Christmas*, and *A Best in Class Showcase* for concert band. Elledge has numerous concert band, full orchestra, and string orchestra works published by Neil A. Kjos Music Company. In addition, he serves as the in-stadium music coordinator for the National Football League's Minnesota Vikings. Elledge received his Bachelor of Music degree in Theory and Composition from the University of Minnesota.

Bruce Pearson, author of the *Standard of Excellence Comprehensive Band Method* and contributing editor of the *Standard of Excellence in Concert* series, is a world-renowned music educator, composer, and author. He is also author of the *Best in Class Comprehensive Band Method*, as well as numerous correlated materials for both *Standard of Excellence* and *Best in Class*. Pearson has over three decades of experience teaching music at all levels, having produced widely acclaimed and award-winning concert bands, small ensembles, and jazz ensembles. He received his Bachelor of Science degree in Music Education from St. Cloud State University, his Master of Arts degree in Music Education from the University of Northern Colorado, and has completed further graduate studies at the University of Minnesota.

Unit 2: Composition

Arranged in 1999, *African Festival* is a Grade 1.5 composition based on the African folk song titled *Siyahamba*, which was written when South Africa was governed by apartheid (1948–early 1990s). The lyrics of *Siyahamba* repeat, "…we are marching in the light of God."

African Festival is a one-movement work, approximately two minutes and thirty seconds in length. The piece correlates with the Neil A. Kjos publication, *Standard of Excellence Comprehensive Band Method*. Students who have progressed to page 26 in Book 1 (red book) have been introduced to the technical demands, rhythmic challenges, and musical terms used in *African Festival*. Included with the concert piece are worksheets, study guides, historical information, and listening guides. These materials designed by Wendy Barden, contributing editor to the *Standard of Excellence in Concert Series*, can be used to expand a student's knowledge of *African Festival* beyond mere performance.

Other compositions at a similar grade level in the *Standard of Excellence in Concert Series* include: *A Baroque Celebration*, arr. Chuck Elledge; *El Marinero*, arr. Mike Hannickel; *Grand March: The Australian Land*, Ralph Hultgren; *March of the Nightcrawlers*, Thomas Duffy; *Matterhorn Overture*, Chuck

Elledge; *Stanley River Overture*, Barrie Gott; and *Visions on an Old American Tune*, Wayne Pegram.

Unit 3: Historical Perspective

A substantial amount of wind band literature is derived from folk songs. One of the most notable and well-known compositions of this genre is Grainger's *Lincolnshire Posy*. *African Festival* is a contemporary composition of a folk song that is also relatively recent in the scope of musical history. Although the actual composition of the folk song *Siyahamba* is debated, it is known to have come from the latter half of the twentieth century. The text of the tune describes the plight against South African apartheid, which formally began in 1948. It is quite possible that this chant of *Siyahamba* accompanied individuals going to prison for revolts against apartheid. Much of African music is based on simple rhythms with chant-like melodies often accompanying work, allowing the time to pass quicker. Many of these chants are never written down; they are passed orally from generation to generation.

Unit 4: Technical Considerations

Written in E-flat major, the true mode for the selection is B-flat mixolydian. Included with the piece is a warm-up study that addresses the appropriate scale (E-flat major) but not the relative mode. The meter for the selection is 4/4, it never varies, and the tempo is marked "Joyfully" at quarter note = 112. There are no *ritardandos*, *accelerandos*, or other tempo considerations.

Instrument ranges are accessible for first-year band students: clarinets below the break; first trumpet to C, third space; and remaining instruments in very idiomatic ranges. *African Festival* requires a minimum of seven percussionists; to maximize the desired percussion timbres and rhythmic continuity, seven should be utilized. The percussion parts for this selection could easily be expanded, provided the conductor stays within the ideas of "African" music. Expanded mallets (marimba) and additional drums (congas) could increase the impact and add to the historical importance of the drums and their role in African music. The supplemental activities use the rhythms in *African Festival* to create a percussion ensemble that is comprised of an iron bell, shaker, stomping stick, and conga drum.

Unit 5: Stylistic Considerations

Tempo is very important in this piece; every effort should be made to play the marked tempo of 112 and continue the style of "joyfully." Slower performance tempos will certainly be less effective and less stylistically accurate. A fine balance between *marcato* and *legato* should prevail considering no articulation instructions are given at the onset of this piece. Terraced dynamics are used in that there are no *crescendos* and/or *decrescendos* in the piece. In keeping with the African history of this selection, the ensemble must perform the terraced dynamics effectively to obtain the chant-like characteristics. Phrase markings are also indicated throughout the score and should be followed closely.

Unit 6: Musical Elements

MELODY:

Every instrument (aside from some non-melodic percussion) eventually receives the melody, or a fragment thereof. An effective warm-up strategy might be to have everyone in the ensemble perform the melody together. On the reverse side of the student parts is a warm-up activity sheet. Selection number 4 gives every instrument the melody. This would be an effective warm-up so that all students could hear the melody with the differing sounds. Simultaneously, conductors can work on melodic phrasing with the ensemble using this activity. Practicing the melodic modes of B-flat and C mixolydian would also be worthwhile since the melody is written using these scales.

HARMONY:

On the aforementioned warm-up sheet is a scale study example (number 2). This example shows the complete layout for the E-flat major scale. Since the work uses this key signature and the underlying harmonic structure is in this key, practicing this scale would be an effective warm-up. It would also be effective to devise a warm-up or introduction that includes work on the B-flat mixolydian mode since the melody is based on this scale. An easy way to accomplish this is to use the same key signature but start on the fifth note of the E-flat scale. In explaining this mode, it would be best to write it for each instrument. Hopefully, after a few rehearsals, the ensemble may have a better aural concept of mixolydian mode.

There is an implied modulation to the key of F major from measure 61 to the end of this piece. Use of the F major scale would be beneficial for the correct performance of the final bars. Chord structure throughout *African Festival* utilizes triadic harmony. Chords are built using bass voices on tonic throughout the entire piece. Beat three of measure 60 takes the listener and ensemble from B-flat mixolydian (E-flat major) to C mixolydian (F major). Within the eight-measure phrase, the chord structure is I, I, I, V, I, I, IV–V, I. Students playing accompanying voices need to change at the appropriate time to make the harmonic movement effective. Warm-ups such as short chorales in the key of E-flat would acquaint each performer with the I–IV–V–I chord progressions found in *African Festival*.

RHYTHM:

The meter of the piece is 4/4, the beat is slower than traditional march tempo, and eighth note steadiness and subdivision is of utmost importance. After repeated rehearsals, students may begin to rush the easier eighth note passages. Rhythmic complexity is apparent in passages involving the eighth note. There are a few passages in both the melody and accompaniment that have syncopation. *Standard of Excellence Comprehensive Band Method* (Neil A. Kjos) formally introduces the concept of syncopation in Book 2 (blue book) on page 5. It will be important for the conductor to have a strategy established for the instruction of syncopation since this piece introduces syncopation prior to its introduction in the corresponding text. Dotted-quarter note and eighth note rhythms are used frequently in the accompaniment (see measure 21). The emphasis of the eighth note is important; however, it should not dominate. Implied syncopation could likely be a challenge to first-year players. Strategies to count the dotted-quarter note and eighth note passage should be devised. Warm-up strategies included with the piece (number 3) can be used to introduce the different rhythms in *African Festival*.

Section A describes the dotted-quarter note and eighth note challenge. Section B overviews the syncopation into tied notes. Sections C, D, and E are all variations of Section B. After students master this warm-up, the conductor should be creative and devise additional warm-ups to combine elements of harmony (scales/modes) with rhythm. For example, play the B-flat mixolydian mode using the rhythm of Section A. Writing rhythms on a dry-erase board, overhead projector, and/or study sheets, and having students fill in the counts is also an effective exercise. Counting and clapping as an ensemble, a section, or an individual might also prove to be worthwhile, allowing students to better assimilate what they are learning.

TIMBRE:

Lower voices (tuba, baritone, trombone, low reeds) should be the foundation for each chord and phrase, while other voices should balance in relationship to the bass. The percussionists should be of importance throughout the work, for they are the link between Western and African music. The dynamics throughout the percussion ensemble are terraced. Seven players are needed to cover all parts. Expansion could be used if personnel warrants. However, it is not recommended to add snare drum or crash cymbals since those instruments have little to do with African timbres. Percussion should never dominate but can truly add to the composition if the parts are played tastefully. Each voice is important; however, a good blend from all voices will give listeners a true chorale style.

Unit 7: Form and Structure

FORM	MEASURES	KEY	EVENT AND SCORING
Introduction	1	B-flat mixolydian	Percussion introduction (*p*)
A	5	B-flat mixolydian (melody)	Clarinet and alto saxophone on melody; percussion continues introduction material (*p*)

FORM	MEASURES	KEY	EVENT AND SCORING
B	13	E-flat major	Low brass and low reeds (*f*) on melody; upper winds and upper brass (*f*) on accompaniment; percussion changes rhythms (*f*)
C	21	E-flat major (accompaniment) B-flat mixolydian (melody)	*Tutti* ensemble: high brass, high reeds (*f*) on melody; low brass, low winds, and percussion (*f*) on accompaniment
B´	29	E-flat major (accompaniment) B-flat mixolydian (melody)	Trumpets on melody (*p*); low brass and low reeds (*p*) on accompaniment
A´	37	B-flat mixolydian	Flute, oboe, and saxophone (*p*) on melody; one trumpet (*p*) on accompaniment; percussion (except bongos) tacet
B´´	45	E-flat major (accompaniment) B-flat mixolydian (melody)	Melodic fragmentation (call/response): similar to B´ section in instrumentation
C´	53	E-flat major (accompaniment) B-flat mixolydian (melody)	*Tutti* ensemble: high brass, high reeds, saxophones (*f*) on melody; low brass, low winds, and percussion (*f*) on accompaniment
D (new key) similar to C, C´	61	Modulation: F major (accompaniment) C mixolydian (melody)	*Tutti* ensemble: high brass, high reeds, saxophones (*f*) on melody; low brass, low winds, and percussion (*f*) on accompaniment
Coda	68	F major (accompaniment) C mixolydian (melody)	Continues as before; incorporates some call and response, similar to m. 45; final chord on F major (*f*)

Unit 8: Suggested Listening

Wind band literature:

Jim Curnow, *African Sketches*

Quincy Hilliard, *Spirituals!*

Quincy Hilliard/arr. Charlie Hill and Chuck Elledge, *Variations on an African Hymnsong*

Paul Jennings, *African Road*

Robert W. Smith, *Africa: Ceremony, Song and Ritual*

Other literature:

Hans Zimmer, *The Power of One* (movie soundtrack)
Music by: *Ladysmith Black Mombazo*

Paul Simon:
Graceland
Diamonds on the Soles of Her Shoes

Unit 9: Additional References and Resources

Dvorak, Thomas L., and Cynthia Crump Taggart. *Best Music for Young Band.* New York, NY: Manhattan Beach Publishing, 1987.

Hilliard, Quincy, et al. *African Festival.* San Diego, CA: Neil A. Kjos Music Company, 1999.

Miles, Richard, ed. *Teaching Music through Performance in Band.* Volume 3. Chicago, IL: GIA Publications, 2000.

Pearson, Bruce. *Standard of Excellence Comprehensive Band Method.* Neil A. Kjos Music Company.

Randel, Don, ed. *The New Harvard Dictionary of Music.* Cambridge, MA: The Belknap Press of Harvard University, 1986.

Rehrig, William. *The Heritage Encyclopedia of Band Music.* Edited by Paul E. Bierley. Westerville, OH: Integrity Press, 1991.

White, John D. *The Analysis of Music.* Englewood Cliffs, NJ: Prentice-Hall, Inc., 1976.

Web site,
http://www.shs.starkville.k12.ms.us/mswm/MSWriterAndMusicians/musicians/Hilliard.html

Contributed by:

Christopher Werner
Graduate Conducting Associate
University Bands
University of Wisconsin–Milwaukee
Milwaukee, Wisconsin

Teacher Resource Guide

African Folk Trilogy

Anne McGinty
(b. 1945)

Unit 1: Composer

Anne McGinty (b. 1945), a native of Findlay, Ohio, received her Bachelor of Music and Master of Music degrees from Duquesne University with emphases in flute performance and composition. McGinty is a well-known composer and arranger of music for young bands and has been active throughout her career as a teacher and clinician. She has composed over 160 works for band ranging from levels one through five. Along with her husband, John Edmondson, McGinty operates Queenwood Publications, a music publisher specializing in music for young musicians. Along with *African Folk Trilogy, Bartok: Folk Song and Dance, English Folk Trilogy, Japanese Folk Trilogy,* and *Kum Ba Yah.*

Unit 2: Composition

Composed in 1997, *African Folk Trilogy* features three authentic children's songs with traditional accompaniment. The first song, "Banuwa," is from West Africa and means "Don't cry little girl." The second song, "Ditho tsa mmele," is a South African game song that teaches children the words for head, shoulders, etc., by pointing during the song. The third song is a playground song from Ghana, "Sansa Kroma," and also a singing game. *Trilogy* is scored for flute, oboe, two clarinets, alto saxophone, tenor saxophone, two cornets, horn, a low brass and woodwind line in octaves, bells, claves, cabasa, cowbell, and snare drum. The oboe, tenor saxophone, horn, and bass line in octaves are all optional in this beginning band series. McGinty encourages the use of traditional African percussion instruments such as the ndungu, ngoma, igbin, and ganda, if available, though they are not essential. The performance time is approximately two minutes.

Unit 3: Historical Perspective

Folk music has historically been an important part of African tribal life. Folk songs and dances are traditionally performed for births, marriages, and other festive celebrations. In addition, folk music can reflect the events of daily tribal life, such as hunting, building, and learning activities. The authentic children's songs and accompaniment patterns were suggested to McGinty by Bryan Burton, Associate Professor of Music Education, West Chester University, West Chester, Pennsylvania, an expert in the field of multicultural music.

Unit 4: Technical Considerations

The composition presents the first two folk songs in the key of B-flat major and concludes with the third in E-flat major. The first and third songs have an indicated tempo of quarter note = 152-160 beats per minute. This is contrasted by a slightly slower second song with an indicated tempo of quarter note = 120 beats per minute. All tempo changes are *subito* and will require close attention by the entire ensemble. Five separate percussion parts, including bells, snare drum, claves, cabasa, and cowbell, are important to the rhythmic continuity of the work. Rhythmic syncopation is present in the claves, bells, and cowbell parts. Dotted-quarter and eighth note patterns are prevalent throughout the third song in straight articulated and tied syncopated forms.

Unit 5: Stylistic Considerations

African Folk Trilogy is built upon short, repeated melodic and rhythmic patterns which, along with variations and improvisations, are characteristic of African music. To capture the quality of this style, it is important to avoid playing the simple melodies and harmonies too heavily. Maintaining a light *mezzo forte* throughout and giving special attention to the detachment or spacing of notes, particularly in repeated patterns, will allow the rhythmic interplay to complement the melodic voices. Attending to the tone quality of rhythmic foot stomps will accentuate the stylistic flavor of the work.

Unit 6: Musical Elements

MELODY:

In the first song, "Banuwa," the four-measure quarter note and half note melody is presented eight times. Beginning with the third statement and continuing with each successive statement, new voices are added to the melody, which fill out the harmonies and provide a short, chant motif to complement the melody. This format provides the conductor an opportunity to expand students' awareness of other parts and how they interact with each other. In addition, it provides another way to teach the adjustment of balance and blend as voices are added to the mixture. All of the melodic movement is stepwise or incorporates intervals of a third in the key of B-flat major.

The tempo slows slightly for "Ditho tsa mmele" as the melodic line incorporates a quarter note/eighth note pattern. Articulation becomes an issue, as some groups of four eighth notes occur in a slur two/tongue two pattern and others are all tongued. McGinty often writes repeated, tongued notes for beginners to develop the concept of blowing through the notes, thereby giving them direction or forward motion. Since beginning musicians tend to make repeated notes sound isolated and separate from the musical line, the conductor will want to give particular attention to using these patterns in the students' development of musical direction. While overall only twelve measures in length, this four-measure, stepwise theme is presented once by the flutes and oboes before being treated canonically over the following eight measures in the cornets, alto saxophones, bells, clarinets, oboes, and flutes.

The key changes from B-flat major to E-flat major with the introduction of the third song, "Sansa Kroma." The initial tempo returns and the eight-measure melody is presented twice, with the brass playing the arpeggiated opening figure and the woodwinds responding with a stepwise, descending line.

HARMONY:

The simplicity of these children's songs is also reflected in the homophonic character of the harmonies. The chords for all three tunes are built upon the first, fourth, and fifth scale steps. In "Banuwa," the repeated chordal progression of I–IV–I–V–I in B-flat becomes clearer with the addition of each new voice. As is typical in much of the African tribal music, the thirds and fifths of the chords are often heard in the upper voices above the melodic line. The short "Ditho tsa mmele" incorporates only the I–V–I chord progression in B-flat, which makes the canonic treatment of the melody function well. The tonal center moves up a fourth to E-flat for "Sansa Kroma" and returns to the I–IV–I–V–I progression found in the first tune. In discussing the key change, it should be pointed out that the "Banuwa" theme returns as a coda at measure 61 in the key of E-flat rather than the original B-flat. A short discussion of the coda term will expand students' musical vocabulary and provide an opportunity to show how composers often bring back familiar material from earlier in the composition to, as in this case, bring the *Trilogy* to its strong conclusion.

RHYTHM:

The rhythmic element of this music is highlighted from the beginning with foot stomps provided by the band members. With the addition of each percussion voice in the first tune comes a new rhythmic pattern. Creating a rhythm worksheet for the band that incorporates all of the percussion parts would provide an opportunity for all of the ensemble members to learn to clap and count these rhythms along with the percussion section. Not only does this exercise provide everyone with a valuable counting experience, but it also provides the conductor the opportunity to introduce the concept of internalizing subdivisions. Tied rhythms and syncopation occur in percussion or wind parts in each of the three folk songs. The importance of solidifying students' understanding of these concepts as well as their ability to clap and count the rhythms cannot be overstated.

TIMBRE:

As mentioned previously, much of the "tonal color" of this work is a result of the various percussion instruments called for in the score. Attaining proper balance between brass, woodwind, and percussion voices as they are added in "Banuwa" will allow the intensity to build without losing any of the individual parts. It will be important to emphasize both the balance and lightness of the quarter note chords that accompany the melody on the opening of "Ditho tsa mmele." This characteristic lightness must be carried into the canon at measure 37, with emphasis placed upon the spacing and articulation of notes. The blend and balance of octaves combined with the spacing of the syncopated rhythm played by the cornets, low brass, and low woodwinds will set the style for the opening of the final folk tune. Once again, it is the light, joyful quality of this music that the timbre ensembles must present to their audiences.

Unit 7: Form and Structure

African Folk Trilogy may best be described as a medley of three songs each of which has a short, repeated theme with variations. In a more extended format, we might expect to see extensive improvisation as well as many different rhythmic and textural variations as the melodic and harmonic sequence is repeated.

MEASURES	TONAL CENTER	THEME/VARIATION ACTIVITY
"Banuwa"		
(tempo: quarter note = 152-160 beats per minute)		
1-4	B-flat	Theme stated in cornet with foot stomps and *ostinato* cowbell
5-8		Mm. 1-4 repeated
9-12		Clarinet harmony and claves syncopation added
13-16		Alto saxophone harmony added
17-20		Clarinets divide to carry melody and harmony with alto saxophones; cornets begin chant figure; add cabasa rhythm
21-24		Cornets divide to harmonize chant; flute and oboe join chant figure

MEASURES	TONAL CENTER	THEME/VARIATION ACTIVITY
25-28		Flute and oboe divide to harmonize chant; add horn and tenor saxophone to clarinet and alto saxophone harmonic line; add bass line; add rhythmic variations in the bells and snare drum
29-32		Repeat mm. 25-28

"Ditho tsa mmele"
(tempo: quarter note = 120 beats per minute)

33-36	B-flat	Melody in flute, oboe, and bells; eighth note *ostinato* rhythm in the cabasa
37-40		Canonic treatment of the melody in cornet, flute, oboe, bells, clarinet, and saxophone; snare drum rhythm added
41-44		Canonic treatment of the melody continues; add claves' syncopated rhythm

"Sansa Kroma"
(tempo: quarter note = 152-160 beats per minute)

45-52	E-flat	"Question and answer" melody initiated by cornet, horn, low brass, and low woodwinds; answered by the upper woodwinds and bells; snare drum, cabasa, and cowbell provide rhythmic *ostinato*
53-60		Repeat of mm. 45-52 with the addition of claves to rhythmic *ostinato*

Coda
(tempo: quarter note = 152-160 beats per minute)

61-68		Reprise of mm. 25-32 in E-flat with a foot stomp conclusion

Unit 8: Suggested Listening

Heskel Brisman, *Uganda Lullaby*
John Barnes Chance, *Incantation and Dance*
James Curnow, *African Sketches*
Martin M. Greene, *Tina Singu*
Robert W. Smith, *Africa: Ceremony, Song and Ritual*

Unit 9: Additional References and Resources

"Anne McGinty, *The Red Balloon." Teaching Music through Performance in Band.* Compiled and edited by Richard Miles. Chicago, IL: GIA Publications, Inc., 1997.

Apel, Willi, ed. *Harvard Dictionary of Music*, 2nd edition. Cambridge, MA: Belknap Press, 1972.

Dvorak, Thomas L. *Best Music for Young Band.* Brooklyn, NY: Manhattan Beach Music, 1986.

Kreines, Joseph. *Music for Concert Band.* Tampa, FL: Florida Music Service, 1989.

Miles, Richard, ed. *Teaching Music through Performance in Band*, Volume 2. Chicago, IL: GIA Publications, Inc., 1998.

Randel, Don Michael. *The New Harvard Dictionary of Music.* Cambridge, MA: Harvard University, 1986.

Rasmussen, Richard Michael. *Recorded Concert Band Music, 1950-1987.* Jefferson, NC: McFarland Press, 1988.

Rehrig, William H. *The Heritage Encyclopedia of Band Music.* Westerville, OH: Integrity Press, 1991.

Smith, Norman, and Albert Stoutamire. *Band Music Notes.* Lake Charles, LA: Program Note Press, 1989.

Contributed by:

Robert Spradling
Director of Bands, Professor of Music
Western Michigan University
Kalamazoo, Michigan

Teacher Resource Guide

African Sketches
James Curnow
(b. 1943)

Unit 1: Composer

James Curnow was born in Port Huron, Michigan, and raised in Royal Oak, Michigan. He is a graduate of Wayne State University (Detroit, Michigan) and Michigan State University (East Lansing, Michigan). He lives in Nicholasville, Kentucky, where he is president, composer, and educational consultant for Curnow Music Press, Inc. He also serves as Composer-in-Residence on the faculty of Asbury College in Wilmore, Kentucky.

Curnow has taught at all age levels of instrumental music and is a member of many professional organizations. His work as a composer, educator, and conductor has achieved worldwide acclaim. He has won several awards for band composition including the ASBDA/Volkwein Award in 1977 (*Symphonic Triptych*) and 1979 (*Collage for Band*), the ABA/Ostwald Award in 1980 (*Mutanza*) and 1984 (*Symphonic Variants for Euphonium and Band*), the 1994 Coup de Vents Composition Contest of Le Havre, France (*Lochinvar*), and he has received annual ASCAP standard awards since 1979.

With well over 400 published works, Curnow has become one of the world's most prolific writers for concert band, brass band, and orchestra.

Unit 2: Composition

African Sketches is based on three African folk songs. The first folk song (Oteng' teng') is a dance song of the Luo tribe from Kenya, the second (Mwana wange) is a Buganda lullaby from Uganda, and the third song (Zira! Zira!) is an Ethiopian war song. *African Sketches* was published in 1992 and correlated with the *Essential Elements Band Series* (book 2, page 14). It is approximately two minutes and forty-five seconds in length.

Unit 3: Historical Perspective

This piece helps fill a significant void in African music available for band. *African Sketches* provides teachers with an opportunity to lead students to meaningful discoveries about the music of another culture. The three folk songs used in this piece provide an overview of some of the great diversity of music on the African continent.

Unit 4: Technical Considerations

African Sketches uses the scales of B-flat major and F Mixolydian (F major with a flatted seventh). Accidentals are found in the flute, oboe, and first clarinet parts in two measures of the second folk song and, for most instruments, in the third folk song to produce the needed flatted seventh. In addition to basic rhythmic groupings (using whole, half, quarter, and eighth notes), ties across bar lines, eighth note/eighth rest groups, dotted-quarter/eighth note groups, and eighth/quarter/eighth note syncopations are utilized in this piece. It is suggested that these two scales be reviewed with the students using the rhythmic patterns found in the piece.

As with most music by Curnow, a variety of percussion instruments are required: shaker or maracas, tambourine, triangle, suspended cymbal, snare drum, bass drum, bells, chimes (optional), xylophone, and timpani. Clear performance instructions are given for percussion instruments, including mallet choices and a coin-scrape on suspended cymbal. Students are asked to produce a dynamic range of *mezzo piano* through *fortissimo*. All instruments will enjoy the opportunity to play a melody at some point in the piece.

Unit 5: Stylistic Considerations

The music calls for accented, *legato*, and *marcato* styles of playing. Students should be able to perform in those styles and define their meanings. Many ties across bar lines and slurs of up to four measures (in 3/4 at dotted-half note = 92 mm) will require players to achieve good breath control. Students will need to be reminded to retain a fine tone when playing the war song accented and *fortissimo*. The stylistically accurate percussion parts are essential to the performance of this work. Three meters (2/4, 3/4, and 4/4) are used in the piece with appropriate transitions.

Suggested teaching strategies include singing each of the three African folk songs in their original format with the English or original text. Accompaniment for singing should include the use of authentic African percussion instruments. Students would also benefit from designing appropriate dance movement for each song. "Oteng' teng'" (the Creeper) is traditionally a long-line dance that weaves its way around the room. A slow, graceful dance would be appropriate for "Mwana Wange" (the Lullaby), and an exaggerated, march-like dance would portray "Zira! Zira!" (the War Song).

Unit 6: Musical Elements

MELODY:

"Oteng' teng'" is a dance song with a range of only a fifth. The original melody has two seven-measure phrases that are identical except for the last measure of each phrase. Curnow extended the end of each phrase to achieve eight-measure phrases.

"Mwana wange" is a fairly complex, seven-phrase folk song with some phrases being repeated. Curnow omitted the third and fifth phrases, which seems to provide a more consistent melodic line. This lullaby uses a range of only a sixth.

The war song, "Zira! Zira!," has three phrases of unequal length (four, five, and four measures). Curnow adds several repeats while shortening the middle phrase structure to achieve phrases of eight, six, and eight measures in length. This war song uses a range of a sixth.

HARMONY:

The folk songs are generally harmonized with open fifth sonorities although the third is sometimes lightly scored. The use of pedal notes and long-note countermelodies produces some additional harmonic interest.

RHYTHM:

The selection of three folk songs in different meters allows the teacher to increase student understanding of these meters (2/4, 3/4, and 4/4) and provides the opportunity for young students to learn to transition from one meter to another during a piece. Curnow's practice of writing a harmony part and a countermelody for these folk songs requires young musicians to develop musical independence.

TIMBRE:

Curnow uses all of the instruments in a variety of interesting and effective groupings. His percussion writing is particularly effective and inventive.

Unit 7: Form and Structure

MEASURES	EVENT AND SCORING
Section 1 (in 2/4): "Oteng' teng'"	
1-4	Introduction
5-20	The melody is presented in unison trumpet; accompaniment of full percussion section and long notes in the winds
21-35	A second presentation of the melody in flute, oboe, and alto and tenor saxophone; accompaniment in all other winds and timpani is an eighth note/eighth rest, eighth note/eighth rest pattern

MEASURES	EVENT AND SCORING
36-38	Transition

Section 2 (in 3/4): "Mwana wange"

39-40	A two-measure introduction
41-48	The first two sections of the melody are presented in trombone, baritone, baritone saxophone, bassoon, and alto clarinet; accompaniment is triads in horn, clarinet, and alto and tenor saxophone; the third phrase of the original tune is omitted
49-52	The fourth section of the tune is presented twice by trumpets over a pedal D in low voices; two original countermelodies are in the flute, oboe, and first clarinet group and in a horn and alto and tenor saxophone group; the fifth phrase of the original tune is omitted
53-56	The sixth phrase is presented twice by flute, oboe, and first clarinet over a pedal D in bassoon, second alto saxophone, tenor saxophone, and horn; an original countermelody is in the first alto saxophone part
57-60	The seventh phrase is played by first alto saxophone and first trumpet over a pedal D in bassoon, bass clarinet, baritone saxophone, baritone, and tuba; another original countermelody is played by alto clarinet, second alto saxophone, tenor saxophone, second trumpet, and horn

Section 3 (in 4/4): "Zira! Zira!"

61-64	Transition
65-76	This three-part melody (in F Mixolydian) is presented by various sections over an open fifth rhythmic accompaniment pattern
77-82	Coda; built on the middle section of the last folk song

Unit 8: Suggested Listening

Heskel Brisman, *Uganda Lullaby*
James Curnow, *Stonehenge Overture*
Albert Oliver Davis, *Songs of Nyasaland*
Martin M. Greene, *Tina Singu*
John Higgins, *South African Suite*
William Himes, *Kenya Contrasts*
Anne McGinty, *African Folk Trilogy*

Unit 9: Additional References and Resources

Dvorak, Thomas L., Cynthia Crump Taggart, and Peter Schmalz. *Best Music for Young Band.* Edited by Bob Margolis. Brooklyn, NY: Manhattan Beach Music, 1986.

Kofi, Francis, Paul Neeley, and Richard Levan (ed.). *Traditional Dance Rhythms of Ghana.* Everett, PA: HoneyRock Publishing, 1997.

Kreines, Joseph. *Music for Concert Band.* Tampa, FL: Florida Music Service, 1989.

National Band Association Selective Music List for Bands, 4th edition. Nashville, TN: National Band Association, 1997.

Contributed by:

Lynn G. Cooper
Director of Bands
Asbury College
Wilmore, Kentucky

Teacher Resource Guide

Ahrirang

arranged by Robert Garofalo (b. 1939), Garwood Whaley (b. 1942)

Unit 1: Composer/Arranger

Robert J. Garofalo was born on January 25, 1939, in Scranton, Pennsylvania. He received his B.S. in Music Education at Mansfield University and his M.M. and Ph.D. from The Catholic University of America. Garofalo is Professor of Music and Director of Graduate Programs in Instrumental Music at the Benjamin T. Rome School of Music of The Catholic University of America in Washington, DC. From 1978 to 1988, he was conductor of Heritage Americana, a recreated Civil War-era brass band, which was featured in the video series, *The History of Bands in America*, and heard on the sound track of Ken Burn's television documentary, *The Civil War*. A prolific writer and composer, Garofalo has authored nine books, including *Guides to Band Masterworks* and *Guide to Score Study* (co-authored with Frank Battisti), as well as numerous journal articles and music publications. His works for young band include *Chinese Folk Song Medley* (1999) and *Hungarian Folk Round* (1981, arranged in collaboration with Garwood Whaley).

Garwood Whaley was born on November 21, 1942, in Dobbs Ferry, New York. He received his artist diploma from the Juilliard School of Music and his M.M. and D.M.A. degrees at The Catholic University of America. Whaley is the director of the Bishop Ireton Symphonic Wind Ensemble in Alexandria, Virginia; Adjunct Professor of Music at The Catholic University of America; and President of Meredith Music Publications. He is the author of more than twenty highly acclaimed percussion method books, co-author of two supplementary band methods, and composer of numerous solos and ensembles.

Unit 2: Composition

Based on the simple, yet beautiful Korean folk melody used by John Barnes Chance in his *Variations on a Korean Folk Song*, this percussion feature with band is well suited for young bands with at least one year of playing experience. In the foreword to the score, the arrangers suggest additional activities for stimulating creativity. Optional vocal parts for children's voices (soprano and alto) are included and can be performed by members of the ensemble, the school chorus, or a general music class. A glossary of terms and the transposed pentatonic scale upon which this work is based is printed on each of the instrument parts. The approximate length of this work is three minutes. Originally published by Heritage Music Press, *Ahrirang* is currently published by Meredith Music Publications.

Unit 3: Historical Perspective

Traditional folk tunes are frequently used by composers as a basis for their works. For the performers and the audience, folk songs can provide a cultural sampling of the country of origin.

Korea has a rich musical heritage, influenced centuries ago by Chinese music and instruments. *Ahrirang* is named after a scenic hill located in the Kangwon Province in South Korea. The song tells of a man about to take a long journey without the company of his girl:

Walking over the peak at Ahrirang you left me behind.
You will be tired before you reach one mile.
Walking over the peak at Ahrirang the sorrows in my heart
    are as many as the stars in the sky.

Unit 4: Technical Considerations

The instrumentation calls for a single part for each wind instrument except for clarinet and cornet (two parts each). Ranges are appropriate for this Grade 2 piece, as are the rhythmic demands. The percussion writing is divided into two separate parts. Part I is scored for triangle, suspended cymbal, finger cymbals, and optional metal wind chimes. Part II is scored for woodblock, snare drum, bass drum, and optional wood chimes. An optional bells part is also included. The arrangers encourage the substitution of traditional, Orff-Schulwerk or homemade percussion instruments for those listed in the score. At least six percussionists are needed to comfortably cover all of the parts.

The meter is 3/4 throughout. The printed key signature is E-flat concert, but the work is based on the pentatonic scale beginning on B-flat (B-flat–C–E-flat–F–G).

The text for the optional vocal parts is sung on the syllable "lu." The soprano part is always doubled by the flutes in unison or octaves; the alto part is always doubled by the clarinets in unison or octaves.

A brief *ritardando* prior to the last measure completes the arrangement.

Unit 5: Stylistic Considerations

The brass and woodwind parts remain lyrical throughout the piece. Care must be given to the accurate articulation of the slurs in the upper woodwind/upper brass parts. The countermelody, when present, must be sustained and lightly articulated. The plentiful percussion parts provide a constant, forward-moving, rhythmic motion. Although the printed dynamic range is limited (*mf–f*), the conductor is encouraged to extend the dynamics according to the ability of the ensemble. Dynamic contrasts are primarily achieved in this arrangement by the use of *soli* and *tutti* instrumentation.

Unit 6: Musical Elements

The lyrical nature of this work provides an excellent opportunity to review and apply proper breath control techniques. The conductor must carefully consider the phrasing of this particular melodic line. Four-measure phrases work well if the players have the ability to do so and best accommodates the original Korean lyrics. Nearly every presentation of the melody ends with a *decrescendo*. The wind players will need to be reminded not to clip off the last note under each slur.

The melody is not harmonized in this arrangement. The only contrasting line is the sustained countermelody presented in the low brass and low woodwind parts. The piece concludes on the root (E-flat) and the fifth (B-flat) in unison/octaves.

The percussion *ostinato* always contains an instrument playing on each downbeat. The players must provide a constant, even pulse and avoid the temptation to rush. The percussion parts are grouped according to timbre (metallic and wood/skin) and should be rehearsed separately for accurate balances.

After the percussion interlude midway through the arrangement, the canonic treatment of the melody at measure 35 must be equally balanced between the two instrument groupings (flute/soprano voice and clarinet/alto voice). Due to the *tutti* scoring at measure 55, the balance between the canonic treatment of the melody, the sustained countermelody, and the percussion must be carefully evaluated.

Unit 7: Form and Structure

MEASURES	EVENT AND SCORING
1-4	Introduction; metallic percussion *ostinato*
5-12	First phrase of the melody stated in upper woodwinds
13-20	First phrase of the melody repeated in cornet and horn; sustained trombone countermelody added (cued in baritone and low woodwinds)
21-28	Second phrase of melody; *tutti*
29-32	Percussion interlude; can be repeated and expanded as desired
33-50	*Soli* flute with optional soprano voices; m. 35, *soli* clarinet enters with optional alto voices in a canonic treatment of the melody
50-52	Percussion *soli*
53-70	Upper woodwinds begin melody accompanied by a sustained low brass countermelody (doubled in the low woodwinds); m. 55, cornet and horn enter with canonic treatment of melody

Unit 8: Suggested Listening

John Barnes Chance, *Variations on a Korean Folk Song*
Ray Cramer, *Fantasy on "Sakura, Sakura"*
James Curnow, *Korean Folk Rhapsody*
Robert J. Garofalo, *Chinese Folk Song Medley*
James D. Ployhar, *Korean Folk Song Medley*

Unit 9: Additional References and Resources

"The Basic Band Curriculum: Grades I, II, III." *BD Guide*, September/October 1989, 2-6.

Garofalo, Robert J. *Instructional Designs for Middle/Junior High School Band*. Fort Lauderdale, FL: Meredith Music Publications, 1995.

Kinyon, John. "Choosing Music for Young Bands," *BD Guide*, January/February 1992, 18.

Miles, Richard, ed. *Teaching Music through Performance in Band*. Chicago, IL: GIA Publications, Inc., 1997.

Miles, Richard, ed. *Teaching Music through Performance in Band*. Volume 2. Chicago, IL: GIA Publications, Inc., 1998.

Strange, Richard E. "Band Music Reviews," *School Musician*, LIII December 1981, 22.

Contributed by:
L. Kevin Kastens
Assistant Director of Bands
University of Iowa
Iowa City, Iowa

Teacher Resource Guide

Air and Dance

John Kinyon
(b. 1918)

Unit 1: Composer

One of the most active composers of band music, John Kinyon has been productive throughout his life as a teacher, arranger, conductor, and composer. He has hundreds of published compositions to his credit and has received several awards from ASCAP for prestigious compositions. He has also written articles for *The Music Journal* and *The Instrumentalist*. Kinyon received his education from the Eastman School of Music and Ithaca College. He served in various capacities as a public school music educator and was Professor of Music Education at the University of Miami. Other works by Kinyon include *Wildwind Overture*, *Chanson*, *Shenandoah Valley*, and *Blue Ridge Rhapsody*.

Unit 2: Composition

Air and Dance is a two-part composition that introduces young musicians to the contrasting styles of *staccato*, *marcato*, and *legato*. The piece is not technically difficult, and it is accessible to first-year players. Published in 1982, the work is scored for standard concert band. Percussion scoring calls for bells, snare drum, bass drum, and crash cymbals. The piece is approximately three minutes and thirty seconds in duration, played as one continuous movement.

Unit 3: Historical Perspective

"Air" is a fairly generic term to describe a lengthy, flowing melody; however, the air has taken a number of forms throughout the course of music's history. "Ayres" were a type of English madrigal popular during the Renaissance; the term evolved to include arias, which are long, melodic operatic passages, usually in ABA form. Dance has been integrated with music from the earliest of times, and there are countless styles and genres of the art form. Examples of dance-influenced music for winds include Grainger's *Shepherd's Hey*, Arnold's *Four Scottish Dances* and two sets of *English Dances*, and John Barnes Chance's *Incantation and Dance*.

Unit 4: Technical Considerations

The technical demands of this piece are well within the range of first-year players. Rhythms are simple combinations of whole, half, quarter, and eighth note patterns. There is no use of syncopated rhythms in any of the woodwind parts, and there are no dotted rhythms. The meter and key both change once, but the transition is easily negotiable by young players. There is minimal use of accidentals throughout; the melodies used in both movements are scalar and very tuneful. The major technical concern is with the length of the piece, which may present some endurance difficulties.

Unit 5: Stylistic Considerations

The "Air" is marked full *legato* and should be played in a smooth, singing style. Proper air support and tone quality is a must for this movement. The "Dance" is marked considerably lighter; students will need to be able to perform *staccato* and *marcato* styles. Dynamics are terraced by marking, but there is room for conductors and players to explore variations of dynamics and tempi.

Unit 6: Musical Elements

This entire composition is based on short motives that are repeated several times, almost in a minimalistic fashion. The main themes are not manipulated; contrast is provided by changes in textures, dynamics, and accompanying material. The motives are not scalar but are based on skips of thirds or fourths. There are several instances of call-and-response patterns between groups of instruments.

This piece is an excellent choice for the spring concerts of the first year. The simplicity of the work allows for transfer and reinforcement of concepts taught during the beginning months of playing. It allows conductors to stress fundamental aspects of playing, such as tone production and the need to play correct notes and rhythms, while at the same time introducing basic concepts of dynamics, balance, and phrasing.

Unit 7: Form and Structure

SECTION	MEASURES	EVENT AND SCORING
"Air"	**1-48**	
A	1-8	Clarinet and bells only
B	9-16	Saxophone, cornet, low brass, and woodwinds
A	17-24	Clarinet and bells as at m. 1; flute answers
A/B 2	5-32	Combination of A and B themes
Transition	33-40	Clarinet, low brass, and woodwinds
Coda	41-48	Clarinet and bells as in m. 1
"Dance"	**49-96**	
A	49-56	Cornet and percussion only
A	57-64	Cornet and percussion as before; clarinet accompaniment
A	65-72	Add low voices to a third presentation of the A theme
B	73-84	Call and answer between woodwinds and brass; *tutti* mm. 81-84
A	85-90	Fourth presentation of A theme; *fermata* in m. 90
Coda	91-96	Cornet; all others accompany

Unit 8: Suggested Listening

Malcomb Arnold, *Four Scottish Dances* and two sets of *English Dances*
J.S. Bach, *Air on a G String*
John Barnes Chance, *Incantation and Dance*
John Dowland, various ayres for voices and lute
Percy Grainger, *Shepherd's Hey*

Unit 9: Additional References and Resources

Dvorak, Thomas, Cynthia Crump Taggart, and Peter Schmalz. *Best Music for Young Band.* Brooklyn, NY: Manhattan Beach Music, 1986.

Kennedy, Michael, ed. *The Concise Oxford Dictionary of Music*, 3rd edition. Oxford: Oxford University Press, 1980.

Lane, Jeremy. *Teaching Music Through Performance in Band and Texas U.I.L. Grade I Prescribe Music List for Band.* Graduate project. Waco, TX: Baylor University, 1998.

Miles, Richard, ed. *Teaching Music through Performance in Band.* Chicago, IL: GIA Publications, Inc., 1997.

Miles, Richard, ed. *Teaching Music through Performance in Band*, Volume 2. Chicago, IL: GIA Publications, Inc., 1998.

Smith, N., and A. Stoutamire. *Band Music Notes*, revised edition. Lake Charles, LA: Program Note Press, 1979.

Contributed by:

Jeremy S. Lane
Doctoral Graduate Assistant, Music Education
Louisiana State University
Baton Rouge, Louisiana

Teacher Resource Guide

All Ye Young Sailors
Pierre La Plante
(b. 1943)

Unit 1: Composer

Pierre La Plante was born in September 1943 in Milwaukee, Wisconsin. He attended the University of Wisconsin at Madison where he earned Bachelor of Music Education and Master of Music degrees, and he studied arranging with Jim Christensen. La Plante currently resides in Oregon, Wisconsin, and teaches K-6 general music and beginning band in the Pecatonica Area School District. He is a former bassoonist with the Beloit-Janesville Symphony Orchestra. He has composed numerous works for wind band, including *Overture on a Minstrel Tune* (1978), *Prospect* (1978), *Lakeland Portrait* (1987), *March on the King's Highway* (1988), *American Riversongs* (1990), *Barn Dance Saturday Night* (1993), *Nordic Sketches* (1994), *Come to the Fair* (1995), *English Country Settings* (1997), *Prairie Songs* (1998), and *In The Garden of the King* (in press).

Unit 2: Composition

Based on the traditional sea chanty, *Blow the Man Down*, La Plante composed *All Ye Young Sailors* in 1988. It serves as a rousing and spirited introduction to compound meter for beginning students and is an excellent example of advanced compositional techniques used in a work of reduced difficulty. The piece begins with a short (four measures) introduction based on a fragment of the main theme. This is followed by two fairly straightforward statements of the theme in its entirety. La Plante sustains interest throughout these two statements by varying the orchestration and dynamic markings. No single instrument or section provides a complete rendition of the main theme, but rather the composer divides the theme into two-measure segments passed between various sections in unique combinations. By using this technique, La Plante retains the call-and-response character of the original material. *Subito* dynamic effects (e.g., *mezzo piano* for two measures followed by *forte* for two measures) add to the challenge and general musical interest. These initial statements are followed by a "development" section featuring the theme in augmentation (performed by first trumpet). During this section, the xylophone provides a "pedal point" (on concert F) against the theme. The augmentation technique continues as the flutes and oboes join the trumpets, while the low brass and low woodwind chords in eighth notes punctuate the approaching dominant chord. This powerful cadence is followed by a surprising two-measure woodwind statement of another melodic fragment featuring a flute melody at a much slower tempo. (These two measures are the only deviation from the suggested tempo of 72–80 beats per minute.) A short canonic section precedes the *fortissimo* closing.

Unit 3: Historical Perspective

This arrangement of *All Ye Young Sailors* is based on a traditional sea chanty popularly known as *Blow the Man Down*. The Harvard Dictionary of Music defines a *chanty* (also "shanty" or "chantey") as a work song sung by sailors, especially one that coordinates strenuous effort. Typically these work songs were sung in alternation (call and response) between a leader (or shantyman) and a chorus of sailors. Good shantymen were often recognized for their ability to increase productivity and were often paid more than the common sailor. Sea chanties are associated with merchant ships (as opposed to the military) and are classified by the type of work performed. *Blow the Man Down* is a member of the classification "halyard chanty," which means it was most often sung when hoisting sails into position. Of particular importance is the word "blow," during which a coordinated pull of the ropes was executed by those working on the task at hand. As is typical with folk songs, slight variations in the melody and text are associated with regional differences.

Unit 4: Technical Considerations

In keeping with the Grade 1 designation, ranges for most instruments have been controlled by the composer. There are unison parts for all sections except the divided trumpet and clarinet parts and the occasional *divisi* in alto saxophone. The highest note for first trumpet is written C (third space, treble clef). Both clarinet parts are written below the "break" with the highest note being A (second space, treble clef). The low brass and woodwind instruments (trombone, baritone, baritone saxophone, bass clarinet, and bassoon) share the same part to enhance player security and the overall bass sonority of the beginner ensemble. The tuba part doubles most of this same bass material an octave lower. Optional notes are indicated for bass clarinet and baritone saxophone. The French horn and alto saxophone parts are functionally

independent, although important material is doubled or cued across other sections. The piece is limited to the notes of the B-flat scale except for one measure that contains a concert B-natural accidental in second clarinet, second alto saxophone, and tenor saxophone. Six percussion instruments are required: snare drum, bass drum, crash cymbals, orchestra bells, triangle, and xylophone. The xylophone part plays an important harmonic role (see Unit 7) and should not be eliminated. The indicated tempo of 72-80 beats per minute may seem conservative to some conductors, and while a slightly faster tempo is possible, the composer warns against this in the score. A piano reduction is provided in the full score allowing a qualified pianist to perform with ensembles of incomplete instrumentation.

Unit 5: Stylistic Considerations

Beginning students will require considerable training in 6/8 meter to perform the work accurately, as it undoubtedly will be an early experience in compound meter. Conceptual preparation is imperative for a stylistically correct performance. Students must become sensitive to the inherent "pulse" of the compound meter, i.e., slightly stressing the first eighth note then noticeably not stressing the following two eighth notes in each dotted-quarter combination. It is highly recommended that this technique be practiced using unison notes and/or scales before introducing the piece.

Conductors should note the rhythm in measures 37 through 39, as the performers are required to execute a quarter note/eighth note combination followed by a rest. Young students may tend to rush the quarter note or otherwise struggle with the precise placement of the notes. It is suggested that this rhythm (quarter note/eighth note/dotted-quarter rest) be incorporated into the warm-up procedure using familiar scales until rhythmic stability is achieved.

Unit 6: Musical Elements

There are numerous musical elements that serve to introduce (or reinforce) important concepts to the beginner ensemble. These include time signature (6/8, compound meter), key signature (B-flat major), written dynamics (*piano*, *mezzo piano*, *mezzo forte*, and *forte*), articulations (various combinations of slurs, accents, *staccatos*, and *tenutos*), performance markings (*fermata*), phrase markings (breath mark), terminology (*legato*, *a tempo*, *crescendo*), and the graphic representation for *crescendo* (expanding lines). Numerous compositional devices (fragmentation, augmentation, and canon) are also employed.

Unit 7: Form and Structure

SECTION	MEASURES	EVENT AND SCORING
Introduction	1-2	Fragment of theme in unison
	3-4	*Tutti* cadence to V chord
Theme	5-12	Letter A; first complete statement of melody fragmented across various sections; progressive layering of instruments across phrase; texture increases from clarinet, horn, and triangle (mm. 5-6) to full band (mm. 11-12)
Theme	13-20	Letter B; second complete statement of melody; mostly *tutti* scoring; musical interest derived from alternation of subito dynamic effects (*mezzo piano* to *forte*); important alto saxophone melody cued in trumpet parts
Development	21-22	Letter C; two-measure fragment of theme performed by *soli* flute accompanied by triangle
	23-28	Augmentation of theme with melody in first trumpet; *piano* dynamic; *legato* style throughout
	29-30	Letter D; two-measure *crescendo* for the entire ensemble
	31-34	Cadence to V chord brings augmented melody to a close; low brass and woodwind chords used to punctuate
	35-36	Letter E; *much slower*; woodwinds only; flutes perform variation of a melodic fragment
	37-39	A *tempo*; imitation (unison melodic fragments passed from section to section, first as two beats, then as one beat)
	40	Percussion solo
Coda	41-44	Letter F; two-measure canon begins with flute, oboe, and trumpet; subsequent entrances begin with alto saxophone, then bass woodwinds and brass, and finally clarinet and orchestra bells

SECTION	MEASURES	EVENT AND SCORING
	45-46	*Tutti*; two-measure cadence to dominant chord
	47-50	Ending; tonic chord in upper brass and upper woodwinds; fragment of melody in low brass and low woodwinds; ends on unison concert B-flat

Unit 8: Suggested Listening

Percy Grainger, *Lincolnshire Posy*, Movements I and IV
Clare Grundman, *Fantasy on American Sailing Songs*
Thomas Knox, *Sea Songs*
Pierre La Plante, *American Riversongs*
Ralph Vaughan Williams, *Sea Songs*

The Library of Congress has produced numerous recordings of American folk music. *Blow the Man Down* may be found on *American Sea Songs and Shanties (II)*, edited by Duncan Emrich. This vinyl LP recording is part of the *Folk Music of the United States* series and was recorded in 1952. It may be found in some school libraries; otherwise, check with the Library of Congress for item number AAFS L27.

Unit 9: Additional References and Resources

Harlow, F.P. *Chanteying Aboard American Ships*. Barre, MA: Barre Gazette, 1962.

Hugill, S. *Shanties and Sailors' Songs*. New York, NY: Frederick A. Praeger Publishers, 1969.

Shay, F. *American Sea Songs and Chanteys from the Days of Iron Men and Wooden Ships*. New York, NY: W.W. Norton & Company, 1948.

Contributed by:

Patrick Dunnigan
Florida State University
Tallahassee, Florida

Teacher Resource Guide

Amazing Grace
John Edmondson
(b. 1933)

Unit 1: Composer

John Edmondson is one of the most respected composers of educational music for young bands. He received his education at the University of Florida and the University of Kentucky. His primary composition teachers were Kenneth Wright and R. Bernard Fitzgerald. He has experience as a teacher, editor, performer, and conductor, and he has hundreds of published compositions to his credit (all for band). A member of ASCAP, Edmondson has received several annual awards from that organization. He and his wife, Anne McGinty, operate Queenwood Publications, devoted to publishing quality music for bands. Other works by Edmondson include *Three English Folk Songs* and *Three Scottish Folk Songs*.

Unit 2: Composition

Amazing Grace is a setting of the well-known hymn. There are three presentations of this melody: the first and third are direct setting, while the middle section is a variation of the tune in 4/4 time. Edmondson has scored the work to feature the two large wind choirs in a band: brass and woodwinds. The counterpoint is more fully developed than in most Grade 1 pieces; there are more separate lines that need to be heard. The piece was originally written in 1970 and was re-edited and re-published in 1990. It is approximately two minutes and fifty seconds in duration.

124

Unit 3: Historical Perspective

Settings of hymntunes are common throughout music's history. During the Renaissance, plainchants (the hymntunes of the era) were used extensively in motets and masses; this practice continued throughout the Baroque and Classical periods. Chorale preludes, as used by Bach and other composers, were another common form of hymntune settings. During the Romantic era, composers expanded the hymntune settings into larger forms, such as Brahms's *Variation on a Theme of Haydn*, which is a setting of the "St. Anthony's Chorale." The practice has continued into the twentieth century in a variety of forms: Copland's setting of "Simple Gifts" from *Appalachian Spring* and Stravinsky's setting of "A Mighty Fortress Is Our God" in *L'histoire du Soldat* are two contrasting examples. Famous settings of hymntunes for band include the series of chorale preludes by Vincent Persichetti, a number of settings of Bach hymns by Alfred Reed, and William Schumans's *Chester Overture*.

Unit 4: Technical Considerations

This piece is an advanced Grade 1. The ranges are suitable for second-year students (flutes play D above the staff; clarinets play C above the staff). The instrumentation is full; there are three clarinet parts, two cornet parts, two horn parts, and two trombone parts. With the exception of the bells, percussion parts are only active eight measures of the entire piece. There are two key changes and two meter changes. There is considerable use of accidentals in most parts. Dynamics are extended, with *crescendos* and *decrescendos* building over four- or eight-measure phrases. Rhythmically the piece is simple; however, there are some instances of quarter notes tied across a bar line. The students must be able to count independently, as there are three or more layers of rhythms at any given time.

Unit 5: Stylistic Considerations

This setting is designed to teach young musicians how to play *legato* style. There are no instances of *staccato* or *marcato* note lengths. Balance is an important issue; there are usually two separate parts accompanying the melody, so care must be taken that the melody can be heard at all times. Dynamics must be carefully observed; otherwise, the piece could become stale and uninteresting. There is ample opportunity for the conductor and students to experiment with *rubato* phrasing. This is an excellent piece to help young musicians develop a sense of musicality.

Unit 6: Musical Elements

The melody of this piece is very well known, and this melody is varied only slightly in the 4/4 section. Rhythmically, the work is not difficult: simple combinations of whole, dotted-half, dotted-quarter, quarter, and eighth notes. The students will need to be able to play independently of each other; there are

numerous entrances and releases that are not in line with the melody. Harmonically, the piece begins in F major, modulates to B-flat major, and ends in E-flat major. There is some use of non-harmonic tones; otherwise, the harmonic motion is traditional.

For a successful performance of this work, students must be taught ways to make slow music interesting. Students should be made aware that if the style, dynamic, and tempo markings on the page were strictly observed without thought, a stale, uninteresting performance would result. However, if students were taught to listen for the melody and support it at all times, to exaggerate dynamics, to follow the conductor in tempo nuances, a study and performance of this work could prove very rewarding. Fortunately for the conductor, the technical demands are not severe. While there are issues of tuning chords and balance that will need to be addressed, the conductor should have plenty of time to work towards developing musicianship and listening skills.

Unit 7: Form and Structure

SECTION	MEASURES	EVENT AND SCORING
Introduction	1-8	*Tutti* scoring; cadence in F major
Melodic Statement I	9-24	Brass choir: cornet I with melody; all other brass harmonize
Melodic Statement II	25-40	Woodwind choir: flute, oboe, clarinet I, and bells with melody; all other woodwinds harmonize (horn and tuba also harmonize); change of key to B-flat major; variation of melody in 4/4 time
Melodic Statement III	41-56	*Tutti* scoring; change of key to E-flat major; meter change to 3/4 time; *fermata* and break-pause in m. 56
Coda	57-60	*Tutti* scoring; *mp* and *p* dynamics; cadence in E-flat major

Unit 8: Suggested Listening

Aaron Copland:
  Emblems
  Old American Songs, Simple Gifts
Antonin Dvorak, *Symphony No. 9* ("New World"), Movement II
Frank Ticheli, *Amazing Grace*

Unit 9: Additional References and Resources

Dvorak, Thomas, Cynthia Crump Taggart, and Peter Schmalz. *Best Music for Young Band*. Brooklyn, NY: Manhattan Beach Music, 1986.

Kennedy, Michael, ed. *The Concise Oxford Dictionary of Music*, 3rd edition. Oxford: Oxford University Press, 1980.

Lane, Jeremy. *Teaching Music Through Performance in Band and Texas U.I.L. Grade I Prescribe Music List for Band*. Graduate project. Waco, TX: Baylor University, 1998.

Miles, Richard, ed. *Teaching Music through Performance in Band*. Chicago, IL: GIA Publications, Inc., 1997.

Miles, Richard, ed. *Teaching Music through Performance in Band*, Volume 2. Chicago, IL: GIA Publications, Inc., 1998.

Smith, N., and A. Stoutamire. *Band Music Notes*, revised edition. Lake Charles, LA: Program Note Press, 1979.

Information and recordings of Kinyon's music are available on-line at www.queenwood.com

Contributed by:

Jeremy S. Lane
Doctoral Graduate Assistant, Music Education
Louisiana State University
Baton Rouge, Louisiana

Teacher Resource Guide

Anasazi

John Edmondson
(b. 1933)

Unit 1: Composer

John Baldwin Edmondson was born in Toledo, Ohio, and grew up in Culpepper, Virginia. He gained his early musical training as a trumpeter in his family's dance band and received degrees from the University of Florida (Bachelor of Arts) and the University of Kentucky (Master of Music in Composition). For ten years, Edmondson taught music in the public schools of Kentucky, where his compositional talents were used extensively for his own students. Eventually he was engaged as staff arranger for a number of university marching bands. He became affiliated with several major music publishing houses and was elected into the American Society of Composers, Authors, and Publishers (ASCAP) as a result of his compositional success. Edmondson, whose works appear in the catalogs of thirteen different publishers, has written extensively for school bands, with hundreds of publications to his credit. He is well known as a guest conductor, clinician, and lecturer. And along with his wife, Anne McGinty (who is also a composer), Edmondson owns and operates Queenwood Publications.

Unit 2: Composition

This composition was written for the 1986–87 Anasazi (pronounced "on-uh-SAH-zee") Elementary School Band and its conductor, Mark Alexander. The school is located just blocks from the composer's Scottsdale, Arizona home.

This Grade 1 band work is fifty-six measures in length and approximately three minutes in duration. The word *Anasazi* is translated from the Navajo meaning "ancient people" or "ancient enemies." The Anasazi lived in the "four corners" area (New Mexico, Arizona, Utah, Colorado) of the United States from about 1 A.D. to 1300. These Native Americans were cliff dwellers, building their homes in canyon walls and under rock overhangs. Due to a variety of circumstances, including incursions by the Navajo and Apache tribes and a prolonged drought, the Anasazi population declined and eventually disappeared. The modern day Hopi nation claims the Anasazi as ancestors.

Unit 3: Historical Perspective

Although an original composition, *Anasazi* shares elements often associated with Native American music, such as rhythmic and bass line *ostinati*. The use of the Dorian mode further reinforces its association with folk-like music. This piece provides tremendous potential for team-teaching or interdisciplinary study with social studies and history.

Unit 4: Technical Considerations

As with many Grade 1 elementary band compositions, *Anasazi* works with variable instrumentation. The composer has scored the bass clarinet, baritone saxophone, bassoon, trombone, baritone, and tuba in unison or octave unison stating, "Any one or more of these instruments will provide an adequate bass part." Tenor saxophone, oboe, and horn parts are optional. Cornet and clarinet parts are divided into two parts.

Instrument ranges are modest. Clarinet parts never cross the break. The first cornet range is an octave: C below the staff to middle C. The other brass and alto saxophones have ranges less than an octave. Percussion parts (including bells) can be performed by as few as three players, although splitting up the woodblock and tambourine parts allows for a fourth player while still not doubling voicings.

The rhythmic challenges are minimal because of the tempo (*slowly*, quarter note = 72) and predominantly block scoring. Mainly, quarter and half notes with some basic eighth note rhythms characterize the selection. The bass voices employ only quarter, half, and whole notes but not eighth notes.

The key is G minor, primarily in the Dorian mode. Players read some easy accidentals.

Unit 5: Stylistic Considerations

The composer calls the style "subdued and mysterioso" offering a fine opportunity to develop sustained, *legato* lines at softer dynamics. Since the selection is a composer's characterization rather than a direct quote of Anasazi or Native American music, look to slower, expressive minor folk songs for performance exemplars. In band literature, movement two of *Three Hungarian Songs* by Bela Bartok (arranged by Philip Gordon) is similar in style.

Unit 6: Musical Elements

MELODY:

The melody might be approached most expressively by following the axiom "as the melody gets higher, play louder; as the melody goes lower, play softer." This practice works especially well in the middle section of the piece. Also, even though all notes are held for full value, every whole note should be approached with some kind of shaping strategy. If the whole note is at the end of the phrase, it can be tapered to a softer dynamic. If it is located mid-phrase, it can increase in volume.

HARMONY:

The B section of *Anasazi* is canonic in parallel thirds. Players can listen to determine if both voices are balanced. The concepts of minor tonality and the Dorian mode can be introduced by defining where the major and minor second intervals occur.

RHYTHM:

The term *ostinato*, defined as a phrase that is repeated persistently (from the Italian word for "obstinate"), characterizes the rhythm in the percussion and the bass line. The rhythms should be performed with a steady, controlled beat. Subdivision of the quarter notes to the eighth note rhythm will help prevent rushing the beat.

TIMBRE:

Since rhythmic and range challenges are so minimal, there are developmental opportunities for teaching the fundamentals of blend and balance. This piece would be an effective choice for a band capable of playing Grade 2 or 3 music to review ensemble tone production and color. Players should control individual tones and "play into" the tone produced by the group-at-large. There are opportunities for the woodwind and brass (plus saxophone) choirs to blend their sections independently and then eventually with the bass line.

Unit 7: Form and Structure

Anasazi is composed in an arch form (ABCBA with an introduction and coda).

SECTION	MEASURES	EVENT AND SCORING
Introduction	1-2	Bass line/percussion *ostinato*
A	3-10	*Tutti*; 4+4 phrasing
B	11-18	Canon; 4+4 phrasing
C	19-34	Percussion *ostinato* stops; brass choir 4+4 phrasing; woodwind choir 4+4 phrasing
B	35-42	Identical to first B section

SECTION	MEASURES	EVENT AND SCORING
A´	43-52	*Tutti* with canonic flute part; percussion *ostinato* returns
Coda	53-56	Bass line/percussion *ostinato*

Unit 8: Suggested Listening

Various recordings of Native Americans of the Southwest are available from
Canyon Records and Indian Arts, 4143 North Sixteenth Street, Phoenix,
AZ 85016.

Bela Bartok, *Mikrokosmos*

Unit 9: Additional References and Resources

Anasazi: Pueblo Dwellers of the Southwest (website). Site address:
http://raysweb.net/canyonlands/pages/anasazi.html

Anderson, William M., and Patricia Shehan Campbell, eds. *Multicultural Perspectives in Music Education*, 2nd edition. Reston, VA: Music Educators National Conference, 1996.

Brody, J.J. *Anasazi and Pueblo Painting*, 1st edition. Albuquerque, NM: University of New Mexico Press, 1991.

Kvet, Edward J., ed. *Instructional Literature for Middle-Level Band*. Reston, VA: Music Educators National Conference, 1996.

Kvet, Edward J., and Janet M. Tweed, eds. *Strategies for Teaching Beginning and Intermediate Band*. Reston, VA: Music Educators National Conference, 1997.

MacDonald, Margaret Read. *Peace tales: world folktales to talk about*. Hamden, CT: Linnet Books, 1992.

Rehrig, William H. *The Heritage Encyclopedia of Band Music*. Westerville, OH: Integrity Press, 1991.

"The Natives of the Southwest" from *The Native Americans*. #3218 (videotape). Atlanta, GA: Turner Home Entertainment.

Contributed by:

Mark Fonder
Chair, Music Education Department
James J. Whalen Center for Music
Ithaca College
Ithaca, New York

Teacher Resource Guide

Arioso

John Visconti
(b. 1938)

Unit 1: Composer

John Visconti is a pen name for the award-winning ASCAP composer, Elliot Del Borgo. Born in Port Chester, New York, on October 27, 1938, Del Borgo earned a Bachelor of Science degree from Temple University in Philadelphia and a Master of Music degree from the Philadelphia Conservatory, where he studied composition with Vincent Persichetti. He taught instrumental music in the Philadelphia public schools early in his career, and since 1965, he has been associated with the State University of New York in Potsdam, where he served as a teacher and administrator. He currently holds the title of Professor Emeritus. In addition to writing over 300 works for band, he has composed material for orchestra, chorus, chamber groups, and method books. Del Borgo wrote music for the 1980 Winter Olympics in Lake Placid, New York, and is presently involved with his own company, Cape Music Enterprises. In addition, he is active as a clinician, conductor, and consultant. Another band composition under the pen name of John Visconti is *Space Echoes*, published by Warner Brothers Music.

Unit 2: Composition

An original work for band, *Arioso* is composed in a lyrical style with a time signature of 4/4 and a tempo marking of quarter note = 70. This piece has no written key signature and is set primarily in the D Aeolian mode (D-natural minor); it ends on a quiet D major triad (Picardy third). The work uses an instrumentation of one part per section and requires basic percussion instruments (bells, triangle, and suspended cymbal).

Arioso is both homophonic (one melodic line over chords or secondary material) and polyphonic (two or more significant melodic lines appearing together). There are few exposed lines. *Arioso* was published in 1995 by Belwin-Mills Publishing Corporation, a division of Warner Brothers Music, as part of the company's beginning band series. The composition is 44 measures in length and approximately two minutes and thirty seconds in duration. Previously out of print, *Arioso* is once again available and is a "must have" for young band libraries.

Unit 3: Historical Perspective

In opera there are generally two ways performers communicate the text to the audience and between each other: 1) through an *aria* and 2) through *recitative*. The term *arioso* (lyrical recitative) is an Italian word derived from the word *aria* (song) and describes a type of *recitative* (sung narration) that is more song-like than speech-like. *Recitative* refers to a style of singing that more closely resembles dramatic speech than song. With relatively little change in pitch, the rhythm is dictated largely by the rhythm of the text. Most recitatives are accompanied by an instrument (usually harpsichord or organ) playing simple chords. Recitatives are used to tell the basic circumstances of the plot, while the characters' thoughts and feelings are expressed in the arias. *Ariosos* are commonly regarded as being more lyrical and expressive than unadorned recitatives. The shift from *recitative* to *arioso* is common in the works of Johann Sebastian Bach, who used the term *arioso* to describe a work wholly in this style.

In present day pop culture, what we refer to as "rap music" could be considered a form of recitative. "Rap" is another word for talk; hence, "talk-music" can be thought of as sung narration, or *recitative*.

Unit 4: Technical Considerations

Instrumental ranges in *Arioso* are accessible to young players with little experience; clarinets do not cross the break, and the highest note in the trumpets is third space C. Even though the work is written with one part per instrument, the flute part has a few *divisi* measures. The absence of divided parts will give students a sense of confidence. There is a great deal of doubling at the unison and octave in the low brass and low woodwind lines, and the French horn part offers a choice of octaves in a couple of measures. With all of the unison playing, the composer suggests students seek a "centered tone" (good characteristic sound, played "in tune").

Musical interest is created through polyphony. Rhythms are uncomplicated combinations of whole, half, dotted-half, quarter, dotted-quarter, and eighth notes. The horizontal alignment of the rhythms requires individual and section rhythmic independence and stability. There are no meter changes, and the use of tied notes across the bar line is seen occasionally. The counting of rests may prove challenging to some (trumpets have fourteen measures of rests at one point). With no written key signature, accidentals occur in all of the parts. Low brass, flute, and oboe players will need to know how to finger concert D-flat.

Unit 5: Stylistic Considerations

Ariosos are defined as expressive in musical quality. Expressive music is characterized by its ability to communicate through nuances of phrasing, tempo, articulation, dynamics, style, and sound. Young musicians easily become bored with slow music and will "plod" from note to note when they do not comprehend the contour or shape of the musical phrase. The "ebb and flow" of the phrasing is critical to the students' understanding of expression. Because composers leave many interpretive decisions up to conductors, there are a few basic rules of musical expression that can be followed. Repeated notes should *crescendo* or *decrescendo*, all phrases should have some type of dynamic contour, and long notes should sound into rests. (Correct breathing should leave the note sounding while taking a breath.) Students should be discouraged from breathing collectively at the ends of measures, or bar lines, unless at the end of a phrase. "Stagger breathing" should be encouraged whenever possible. This is critical for both melodic and supportive material in slow tempi.

As the title refers to a type of song, the composer appropriately asks for *cantabile* ("singing style") playing. Both long and short notes should be held for their full durations, and students should be persuaded to play in a connected style as if they were indeed *singing* the passage (both primary and secondary material). Tonguing should be accomplished in a light manner using a "du" or "da" tongue stroke.

Unit 6: Musical Elements

MELODY:
Phrase lengths in *Arioso* are generally four to eight measures. The challenge for students will be to sustain and be expressive with all melodic and harmonic lines at the suggested tempo (quarter note = 70). To prompt students to play long phrases, the conductor will want to mark the appropriate measures in which to take a breath.

The composer recommends the use of *rubato* (slight *accelerandos* or *ritardandos*) to make the music more engaging. In addition, the conductor may choose to add expressive markings, such as *crescendos* and/or *diminuendos*, for phrases that have none. In slow music, bar lines tend to act as visual barriers for students. For *crescendos* occurring across a bar line, tell students to pretend they are "pushing the bar line down with their air so it falls to the right."

The mood of the work is calm and reflective, and the dynamic range is mostly in the *mezzo* levels. The conductor and students will need to understand the hierarchy of balance so that secondary material is always subordinate to the melody. This is especially true when secondary material is in the same register as the melody. Remind students about the genesis of the term *arioso* (lyrical recitative) and how very few instruments would be used to accompany *recitative* passages.

Eighth note passages should be played evenly, such as the opening flute passage in measures 2 through 4, or the arpeggiated clarinet passage in measures 9 through 13. To avoid rushing, have students think about the inner part of the beat (the "and" of the beat). It is important to connect each of the eighth notes at this tempo.

HARMONY:

The work is modal in nature. While students have no set key signatures in their music, all instruments encounter some type of accidental, from one flat and one sharp (clarinet) to four flats (flute).

For centuries, much of western music has been based on church modes. Modes are directly related to what we refer to as *scales*. Three of the seven basic church modes correspond to major scales and four correspond to minor scales. Two of the seven basic modes are identical to our descriptions of the major scale (Ionian) and the natural minor scale (Aeolian). Modes can begin on any pitch and are defined by the sequence of their individual whole- and half-step patterns.

Using only the white keys on the piano as an example, the seven basic modes and their whole- and half-step sequences would appear as follows:

C-C = Ionian (whole step, whole step, half step, whole step, whole step, whole step, half step)

D-D = Dorian (whole step, half step, whole step, whole step, whole step, half step, whole step)

E-E = Phrygian (half step, whole step, whole step, whole step, half step, whole step, whole step)

F-F = Lydian (whole step, whole step, whole step, half step, whole step, whole step, half step)

G-G = Mixolydian (whole step, whole step, half step, whole step, whole step, half step, whole step)

A-A = Aeolian (whole step, half step, whole step, whole step, half step, whole step, whole step)

B-B = Locrian (half step, whole step, whole step, half step, whole step, whole step, whole step)

The Mixolydian, Dorian, Ionian, and Aeolian modes are the most common. Modes are determined by their linear structure (melodic material) more so than their vertical structure (harmony).

Arioso is constructed in the D Aeolian mode (D–E–F–G–A–B-flat–C–D), or D-natural minor scale. In the Aeolian mode, half steps occur between the second and third scale degrees (2-3) and the fifth and sixth scale degrees (5-6). The Aeolian mode corresponds to the scale constructed from the sixth degree of any major scale. For example, if you take an E-flat major scale (three flats) and find the sixth scale degree (C), you can build the Aeolian mode using the next seven tones in that key (C–D–E-flat–F–G–A-flat–B-flat–C). The half steps occur between the D and E-flat (2-3) and the G and A-flat (5-6).

Teaching strategy — Distribute staff paper to the students. Using a chalkboard or dry erase board, draw four staffs. Also, you will need a large picture of a piano keyboard. Discuss the relationship of the white and black keys on the piano (half steps and whole steps). Next, have students write their respective clefs on their staff paper for four separate lines/staffs. On the first staff, have students build a C major scale (C Ionian) one octave up and down in half notes, starting on middle C and repeating the upper note (C–D–E–F–G–A–B–C–C–B–A–G–F–E–D–C). Tell students to mark the pitches where the half steps occur (3-4, 7-8, 8-7, 4-3). Then, have students transpose the mode for their instrument on the second staff.

On the third staff, have students build a C Aeolian scale (C-natural minor) one octave up and down in half notes, again starting on middle C and repeating the upper note (C–D–E-flat–F–G–A-flat–B-flat–C–C–B-flat–A-flat–G–F–E-flat–D–C). Tell students to mark the pitches where the half steps occur (2-3, 5-6, 6-5, 3-2). Have students transpose the mode for their instrument on the fourth staff.

Once this is done, you can play and sing each scale/mode. Divide the band into sections, then have half of the band play and half sing. Discuss the relationship of modes and tonal centers; how are they different and similar?

The unexpected final chord of *Arioso* utilizes what historians call a "Picardy third." Until the sixteenth century, most chords had no thirds; and it wasn't until the sixteenth century that it became commonplace to end a work with a major third in the last chord, regardless of mode.

RHYTHM:
With no tempo changes and the meter in 4/4 throughout, *Ariosi* is not complex rhythmically. The challenge will be to maintain a steady subdivision at the slow tempo. Consider using a metronome set at the eighth note pulse in the early learning stages (eighth note = 140 or close to it). Encourage students to work for rhythmic subdivision and alignment. Once students have established a good sense of internal pulse, disregard the metronome and add *rubato* to elicit an "ebb and flow" in the music. Encourage students to listen for lines different from their own. They should always know where the melody is located and how their part fits into the total structure. In time, this makes for a more challenging and rewarding performance atmosphere.

TIMBRE:

In those young bands we recognize as "exceptional," students have acquired a basic understanding of quality tone production. In addition, they perceive the mechanics of pitch matching (a continual decision-making process), and they know how to blend or fuse sounds together when required. These skills require students to be discriminating listeners: to themselves, to those close at hand, and to those across the ensemble.

Teaching strategy — Developing an excellent characteristic sound in all dynamic levels should be a priority. Over the years, long-tone studies have been a necessary exercise for many teachers. Tone studies will be limited without proper breathing technique. Here is an exercise that teaches students to breathe deeply and focus their air speed.

1. Have students stand and then sit down in their chairs with both feet on the floor. Their torso should still be "standing up."

2. Have students exhale the air from their lungs *through* their horns. Embouchures should be *very* relaxed. The only sound being made is air traveling through the horn. It may take a few times for brass players to get used to this.

3. With the horns pulled slightly away from their faces, tell students to slowly take air into their lungs, breathing "down" verses "in" for four counts. They should take air in however they were taught (through the corners of the mouth, jaw dropped, etc.). The goal is to fill up the lower rib cage in four counts.

4. Now, have the students put the horn back to their face and exhale the air through the horn in a count of four. Ideally, you should be able to hear a huge volume of air from the ensemble. Initially students will not "push" a lot of air through the horn. Ask for more air sound. You should hear quite a dramatic change. If students become dizzy, this is a good sign. They are beginning to breathe deeply. Repeat this a few times.

5. Stop and relax. Tell the students that when they inhale the air, their shoulders should not move and their necks should be relaxed and "open." The column of air traveling through their body should be quite large. When they exhale, they should say "hoe" and not "who." Keep asking for more air speed and warm air.

6. Begin the exercise again, starting with the posture sequence if needed.

7. After two or three times using a four-count sequence, decrease to a three-count sequence (with repeats), then a two-count sequence (with repeats), then a one-count sequence. Ideally, the one-count sequence

should be the type of breath you want the students to take on any initial preparatory gesture.

It is amazing how this exercise changes the timbre of an ensemble. It is good to use at the beginning of the rehearsal as it accomplishes two goals: 1) it forces everyone to stop what they are doing and focus, and 2) it begins or continues to "warm up" the horns.

Professional singers strive for full sounds, clear diction, beauty of tone and, when desired, blend of tone. The same holds true for outstanding wind players at any level. Many teachers use professional musicians (recordings or live) to serve as models for tone and technical development. This is the basis of the famous Suzuki method: teacher demonstrates, student replicates teacher, repeat, repeat, repeat. As an outside creative project, students might be asked to assemble a catalog of their own favorite "role models" for their instrument by finding information through the Internet, musical societies, magazines, recordings, private teachers, etc.

Unit 7: Form and Structure

MEASURES	EVENT AND SCORING
1-7	D Aeolian clarinet melody; simple accompaniment; open texture; *mf, mp*
8-15	Melody in flute and oboe; secondary passage in clarinet; sustained harmony in all other voices; full texture; *mp*
16-23	Full block *tutti* melody; secondary ideas in flute, oboe, and clarinet; modal shifting; *mf*
24-26	Transitional material; modal shifting; *fp, mp*
27-32	Upper woodwind homophonic melody; followed by transitional material in clarinet, alto saxophone, trumpet, horn, trombone; *mf, mp*
33-35	D Phrygian melody in flute and bells; D Aeolian transitional line in clarinet, French horn, trumpet; *mp, mf*
36-44	Contrapuntal, full scoring; loudest phrase of the work; basically D Aeolian; *decrescendos* and *ritardandos*; cadence on a D major chord; *f, mf, mp*, implied *piano*

ERRATA:
Conductor's score
| m. 19 | Add a flat to the E-natural in the bell part |

Unit 8: Suggested Listening

Samuel Barber, *Adagio for Strings*

Elliot Del Borgo, *Adagio for Winds*

Percy Grainger/arr. Cliff Bainum, *Australian Up-Country Tune*

Percy Grainger:
> *Colonial Song*
> *Sussex Mummers' Christmas Carol*

William Latham, *Three Chorale Preludes*

Vincent Persichetti, *Symphony No. 6 for Band*, Movement II,
"Around Me Falls the Night"

H. Owen Reed, *La Fiesta Mexicana*, Movement II, "Mass"

Randall Thompson/ed. Lewis Buckley, *Alleluia*

Ralph Vaughan Williams, *Folk Song Suite*, Movement II, "Intermezzo"

Unit 9: Additional References and Resources

Apel, Willi. *The Harvard Dictionary of Music*, 2nd edition. Cambridge, MA: The Belknap Press of Harvard University Press, 1970.

Blum, David. *Casals and the Art of Interpretation*. Berkley, Los Angeles, CA: University of California Press, 1977.

Dallin, Leon. *Twentieth Century Composition*, 3rd edition. Dubuque, IA: William C. Brown Company Publishers, 1974.

Del Borgo, Elliot. Telephone conversation, April 17, 2000.

Dvorak, Thomas L., Peter Schmalz, and Cynthia Crump Taggart. *Best Music for Young Band*. Brooklyn, NY: Manhattan Beach Music, 1986.

Grout, Donald Jay. *A History of Western Music*, 3rd edition. New York, NY: W.W. Norton & Company, 1980.

Lisk, Edward. *The Creative Director: Intangibles of Musical Performance*. Ft. Lauderdale, FL: Meredith Music Publications, 1996.

Miller, William. *Band Director Secrets of Success*. Edited by N. Alan Clark. Lakeland, FL: Aiton Publishing, 1997.

Rehrig, William H. *The Heritage Encyclopedia of Band Music*. Edited by Paul Bierley. Westerville, OH: Integrity Press, 1991.

Thurmond, James. *Note Grouping*. Detroit, MI: Harlo Press, 1982.

Vandercook, H.A. *Expression in Music*, revised edition. Chicago, IL: Rubank, Inc., 1962.

Westrup, Jack Allan. *The New College Encyclopedia of Music*, revised edition. New York, NY: W.W. Norton & Company, Inc., 1976.

Contributed by:

Linda R. Moorhouse
Associate Director of Bands
Louisiana State University
Baton Rouge, Louisiana

Teacher Resource Guide

Ayre and Dance
Bruce Pearson
(b. 1942)

Unit 1: Composer

Bruce Pearson is a world-renowned music educator, composer, and author. He is the author of the best-selling *Standard of Excellence Comprehensive Band Method*, which is regarded as an important contribution to the band music field. In addition, he is the author of *Best in Class* and *Encore!*, supplemental band study series. He is co-author of the *Standard of Excellence Jazz Method* with Dean Sorenson. Pearson is an active composer and arranger, with numerous published works for beginning and intermediate band.

Pearson received his Bachelor of Science degree in Music Education from St. Cloud State University and his Master of Arts degree in Music Education from the University of Northern Colorado. He has over three decades of teaching experience at the elementary, junior high, high school, and college levels. During his 22-year tenure in Elk River, Minnesota, Pearson received numerous honors, including the Wenger's "Most Outstanding in the Field of Music Education" award for the state of Minnesota and two nominations for the prestigious "Excellence in Education" award. He has also served as Director of Bands and Coordinator of Instrumental Studies at Northwestern College in St. Paul, Minnesota.

In addition to his work in the classroom, Pearson is a respected guest conductor, speaker, and adjudicator, having made appearances in Australia, Canada, Finland, Great Britain, Holland, Hong Kong, Japan, Korea, Mexico, Norway, Singapore, Taiwan, and every state in the United States.

Pearson and his wife, Dee, currently live in Elk River, Minnesota, a part of the Minneapolis-St. Paul metropolitan area. A father of three with five

grandchildren, he enjoys sports and outdoor activities of all types. He is also an active participant in local school, church, and community affairs.

Unit 2: Composition

This original composition is one that utilizes the ancient form ayre and dance. The two-part work correlates with the *Standard of Excellence* comprehensive band method, book 1, page 18, also authored by the composer. The chant-like quality of the *Ayre* is reminiscent of ancient times, and the *Dance* is light-hearted in style. Pearson writes:

> I wanted to provide students with the opportunity to see and hear great contrasts. The contrasts are displayed, not only in the styles but also between the ancient and contemporary treatment of the musical elements.

The use of major seventh chords and deceptive cadences are examples of contemporary harmonies.

Unit 3: Historical Perspective

The idea of presenting a slow-moving main dance followed by a lively dance in combination is found in music from both the fifteenth and sixteenth centuries. The Italian bassadanza-saltarello and the Franco-Burgundian bassedanse-pas de breban are examples of such pairs. Dances were viewed as both courtly entertainment and an art form. A large variety of dance music was written for the lute, keyboard, and other ensembles.

Unit 4: Technical Considerations

The *Ayre* is written in C minor with its melody based on the Aeolian mode. The limited range of the melody, a perfect fifth, allows clarinet to stay below the break and trumpet to play only in the staff and no higher than A. French horn is written on fourth line D in the staff. Four percussionists are required to play bells, timpani, suspended cymbal, triangle, tambourine, snare drum, and bass drum. Chimes are included but optional. From a rhythmic standpoint, only whole notes, half notes, and quarter notes are used.

The *Dance* is written in E-flat major and is to be performed at MM = 108 to the quarter note. A light, separated articulation is required. The range of the melody is a perfect fourth. Both the melody and accompaniment have simple rhythmic structures.

Unit 5: Stylistic Considerations

The style for the *Ayre* is smooth and connected, requiring students to master the concept of a consistent air stream. Each note should be sustained for its full value. The bass line should have clear articulation by using a harder "du" or "dah" sound but with a *tenuto* feel for each note.

The *Dance* is to be performed with a light, separated articulation.

Unit 6: Musical Elements

C minor is used to create a haunting atmosphere in the *Ayre*. The melody is first in octaves and repeated in thirds. The third time the melody is heard, an *obligato* is added.

The *Dance* features a short, ternary melody. The ABA melodic form is heard twice through. The second includes an *obligato*.

Unit 7: Form and Structure

MEASURES	EVENT AND SCORING
1-2	*Ayre*; *Andante*; introduction
3-10	Unison, chant-like melody
11-18	Harmonized melody
19-26	Harmonized melody with *obligato*
27-28	Extension
29-32	Augmented extension
33-40	*Dance*; *Allegro*; A section of melody
41-48	B section of melody
49-56	A section of melody
57-64	A section of melody with *obligato*
65-72	B section of melody
73-80	A section of melody with *obligato*
81-84	Augmented extension

Unit 8: Suggested Listening

Robert Russell Bennett, *Suite of Old American Dances*
Timothy Broege, *Three Pieces for American Band*, Set 2
John Kinyon, *Air and Dance*

Unit 9: Additional References and Resources

Apel, Willi. *Harvard Dictionary of Music*, 2nd edition. Cambridge, MA: The Belknap Press of Harvard University Press, 1970.

Garafolo, Robert. *Instructional Designs for Middle/Junior High School Band*, Unit I. Fort Lauderdale, FL: Meredith Music Publications, 1995.

Grout, Donald J. *A History of Western Music*, 3rd edition. New York, NY: W.W. Norton & Company, 1980.

A specially prepared "Teacher Resource Guide" is included with the score and parts. Warm-ups are offered along with exercises and lesson plans that address the National Standards.

Contributed by:

Richard Greenwood
Director of Bands
University of Central Florida
Orlando, Florida

Teacher Resource Guide

Barn Dance Saturday Night
Pierre La Plante
(b. 1943)

Unit 1: Composer

Pierre La Plante was born in September 1943 in Milwaukee, Wisconsin. He attended the University of Wisconsin at Madison, where he earned Bachelor of Music Education and Master of Music degrees. As an undergraduate student, he studied arranging with Jim Christensen. La Plante currently resides in Oregon, Wisconsin, and teaches K-6 general music and beginning band in the Pecatonica Area School District. He is a former bassoonist with the Beloit-Janesville Symphony Orchestra. He has composed numerous works for wind band, including *Overture on a Minstrel Tune* (1978), *Prospect* (1978), *Lakeland Portrait* (1987), *March on the King's Highway* (1988), *All Ye Young Sailors* (1988), *American Riversongs* (1990), *Nordic Sketches* (1994), *Come to the Fair* (1995), *English Country Settings* (1997), *Prairie Songs* (1998), and *In the Garden of the King* (in press).

Unit 2: Composition

La Plante composed *Barn Dance Saturday Night* in 1993 basing it on melodies associated with the American folk music tradition of the great westward expansion. It is an exciting and appropriate introduction to American folk music for beginning band students. The title evokes images associated with the American square dance movement, but La Plante notes that the piece has more in common with African-American spirituals and the play-party tradition (see Unit 3).

La Plante uses numerous compositional techniques to capture the free-wheeling, celebratory style associated with this tradition. The piece begins with a hand clap/foot stomp sequence invoking the spirit of a large crowd of American pioneers eagerly anticipating an evening of song, dance, and revelry. This is followed by statements of two quasi-original themes based on borrowed material from play-party tunes. La Plante continues the festive character of the piece by utilizing colorful percussion instruments (cowbell and woodblocks) suggesting a barnyard atmosphere. As the range of notes is intentionally restricted, musical challenges are provided in the form of numerous dynamic changes that are somewhat atypical for a piece designed exclusively for beginning students. Near the end of the piece, La Plante uses a compositional technique reminiscent of the call-and-response character of the traditional square dance or play-party game. In this dynamically challenging section, high and low instruments with *subito piano* and *forte* dynamic markings alternate in one-measure fragments of the main melodies.

Unit 3: Historical Perspective

Most music educators are familiar with African-American spirituals and the American square dance tradition, but less is known about the unique folklore associated with play-party events.

As with most American folk music, the origin of the play-party dates back to the native folk music of the first American settlers' European homelands. The late 1800s marked a distinct movement of songs from the initial American states to the pioneer country of the West. The play-party itself was a rural social gathering usually held in a large front room or yard of the farm or ranch house. Although the entire family was in attendance, the event tended to be an evening affair, and most of the "fun" did not begin until the youngest children had been put to bed. Typically, the "old-timers" provided musical accompaniment while the games were played by high school-aged children, young single adults, and young married couples. The games were accompanied by the folk instruments of the day: fiddle, guitar, banjo, harmonica, and sometimes piano or organ. (Dress varied with the social status of the participants, but spurs were always removed!)

Play-party events may have also included the more familiar square dance, but the play-party was considered less restrictive by virtue of the inclusion of rhythmic movement and dramatic action. It is this combination of song, movement, and drama that gives the play-party its distinctive character compared to other social gatherings such as birthday parties and picnics, where games were also played. *Skip to My Lou* is an example of a popular play-party game involving song, movement, and drama, as dance partners are "stolen" rather than "chosen." Specific instructions for action are provided within the text (for example, "My wife skips and I'll skip too"), but participants would generously supplement the text with spontaneous action and improvisation.

Unit 4: Technical Considerations

In keeping with the Grade 1 designation, instrument ranges have been controlled by the composer. The piece is limited to the notes of the B-flat major scale, and there are no accidentals. There are unison parts for all sections except for the divided trumpet and clarinet parts and occasional *divisi* sections for flute, alto saxophone, and the combined bass part (trombone, baritone, and bassoon). The fastest rhythmic value for the brass and woodwinds is a quarter note, but a few eighth notes are found in the first percussion part. The highest note for first trumpet is written A-natural (second space, treble clef). Both clarinet parts are written below the "break" with the highest note being A-natural (second space, treble clef).

Conductors should take special care to achieve balance in measures 19 and 49 where the melody shifts from the higher first clarinet or trumpet part to the lower second part; the melody may be lost beneath the higher harmony part. With the exception of measures 56 and 62, the low brass and woodwind instruments (trombone, baritone, baritone saxophone, bass clarinet, and bassoon) share the same part to enhance player security and the overall bass sonority. The tuba part is an octave lower than the combined bass line and doubles this material exactly except for four notes in measures 61 and 62. The French horn and alto saxophone parts are functionally independent, although important French horn material is doubled or cued across other sections. While the oboe and tenor saxophone parts contain a functionally independent part at Letter F, this is cued in first clarinet. Eight percussion instruments are required: snare drum, bass drum, suspended cymbal, crash cymbals, orchestra bells, woodblock, cowbell, and xylophone. Temple blocks are optional. A piano reduction is provided in the full score.

Unit 5: Stylistic Considerations

La Plante indicates the tempo as *allegro moderato* with no specific metronome marking. However, the score suggests that the piece be performed with a "boisterous 'down home' feeling" and notes that the tempo may be increased concomitant with the ability of the students to maintain proper control. Given these recommendations, a tempo between 100 and 120 beats per minute is advised.

Regardless of tempo, conductors should guard against acceleration of the beat (or "rushing"). The piece is virtually devoid of articulation markings, and depending on the ability of the beginning ensemble, the conductor may want to add articulation markings to some sections to facilitate a stylistically correct performance. For example, the accompaniment at Letter E (quarter note/quarter note/quarter rest/quarter note) could be marked "*tenuto–staccato–* (rest)–*tenuto*" to add shape and musical interest.

Try to incorporate as many of the "color percussion" instruments as possible. The woodblock and cowbell will add to the feeling of a real hoedown. In keeping with the folk music character of the piece, it is not unreasonable for the creative conductor to add additional percussion instruments (tambourine, shakers, etc.) as available.

Unit 6: Musical Elements
There are numerous musical elements that serve to introduce (or reinforce) important concepts to the beginner ensemble. These include time signature (4/4), key signature (B-flat major), written dynamics (*piano*, *mezzo piano*, *mezzo forte*, and *forte*), phrase markings (breath mark), terminology (*allegro moderato*, *crescendo*, *diminuendo*, unison, *divisi*), and the graphic representation for *crescendo* (expanding lines) and *decrescendo* (contracting lines). There are no articulation markings other than the occasional use of accented (>) notes. The compositional device of fragmentation is also employed.

Unit 7: Form and Structure

SECTION	MEASURES	EVENT AND SCORING
Introduction	1-4	Hand clap/foot stomp (flute, oboe, trumpet, horn, and second percussion) with snare and bass drum (first percussion)
"A" theme	5-12	Letter A; first complete statement of melody in unison by clarinet, alto saxophone, and tenor saxophone; hand clap/foot stomp continues; bass line (bass clarinet, baritone saxophone, bassoon, trombone, baritone, and tuba (enters in m. 12 with descending scale (F to C) to set up tonic in m. 13
"A" theme	13-20	Letter B; second complete statement of melody (flute, oboe, and trumpet); *tutti* scoring
Transition	21-24	Letter C; four-measure transition to new theme; wind instruments sustain final chord from previous section while percussion returns to "clap/stomp" motif
"B" theme	25-32	Letter D; second theme, melody harmonized in thirds (flute with clarinet cues); open fourths and fifths (horn, alto saxophone with tenor saxophone cues) function as accompaniment

148

Section	Measures	Event and Scoring
	33-40	Letter E; second theme, melody again harmonized in thirds (trumpet with alto saxophone cues); sustained dominant tone in oboe and tenor saxophone (cued in clarinet)
"Development"	41-48	Letter F; alternating one-measure fragments from both "A" and "B" themes; high versus low sonorities with *piano* and *forte* dynamic changes; all parts are unison
"Recapitulation"	49-56	Letter G; return of "A" theme in *tutti* orchestration
"Coda"	57-58	Letter H; two-measure fragment of "B" theme (trumpet and horn, cued in clarinet and tenor saxophone)
	59-60	*Tutti*; two-measure fragment of "A" theme in rhythmic augmentation
	61-62	I–V7–I closing cadence

Unit 8: Suggested Listening

James Andrews, *Hill Songs*
Aaron Copland, *Rodeo* (specifically *Hoedown* excerpt)
Donald Grantham, *Southern Harmony*, Movement III
Clare Grundman, *Kentucky 1800*
Pierre La Plante, *American Riversongs*

Conductors might also consider showing students *The Farmer and the Cowman* dance sequence from the musical *Oklahoma* (Rodgers and Hammerstein). The film version of this musical is readily available on VHS and DVD. While it is not suggested here that the musical traditions of *Barn Dance Saturday Night* and *Oklahoma* are in any way related, this wonderfully enthusiastic performance will give young band students a glimpse of the color and energy of a western hoedown.

Unit 9: Additional References and Resources

Botkin, B.A. *The American Play-Party Song*. Lincoln, NE: University of Nebraska, 1937.

Green, H. *Square and Folk Dancing*. New York, NY: Harper & Row Publishers, 1984.

Nevell, R. *A Time to Dance*. New York, NY: St. Martin's Press, 1977.

Ryan, G.L. *Dances of Our Pioneers*. New York, NY: A.S. Barnes & Co., 1924.

Contributed by:
Patrick Dunnigan
Florida State University
Tallahassee, Florida

Teacher Resource Guide

Canterbury Overture

Anne McGinty
(b. 1945)

Unit 1: Composer

Anne McGinty was born on June 29, 1945, in Findlay, Ohio. She received her Bachelor of Music (*summa cum laude*) and Master of Music degrees from Duquesne University, where she concentrated on flute performance and theory/composition. Aside from her compositional career, McGinty has performed as principal flute of the Tucson Symphony Orchestra and was active as a flute teacher. Her compositional accomplishments include a large number of works for various combinations of flutes. It was largely through her efforts in encouraging major publishing companies to publish flute choir music that the flute choir became recognized as a viable ensemble.

With more than 150 works in publication, McGinty is one the most prolific composers in the field of concert band literature. Although her outstanding works for young band may be her best-known works, she is developing an equally strong collection of compositions for advanced bands. In 1988, Women Band Directors National Association (now Women Band Directors International) honored McGinty with its Golden Rose Award for her superior contributions to the field of music. Her *Hall of Heroes* was commissioned by the United States Army Band and Chorus, and was premiered in the spring of 2000 with the composer conducting.

McGinty and her husband, John Edmondson, developed Queenwood Publications, which specializes in music for the young concert band. In addition to her busy schedule as a composer, McGinty is active as a guest conductor and clinician throughout the United States and Canada.

Unit 2: Composition

Canterbury Overture, composed in 1995, is an original work for band from Queenwood Publications' beginning band series. Canterbury is a city in southeast England and is associated with the fourteenth century *Canterbury Tales* by Geoffrey Chaucer (c. 1340-1400). McGinty purposely uses English titles for her overtures (*Cambridge Overture, Foxwood Overture, Oxford Overture, Wellington Overture*). Not only do these titles bring to mind modal harmonies and thoughts of the Old English culture, but these real locations help teachers provide cross-curricular lessons with maps and stories of England while providing a stimulus for students' imaginations. Students often enjoy creating their own stories to fit the music, an activity that McGinty heartily endorses.

This musical work is scored for flute, oboe, first and second clarinet, saxophone, first and second trumpet, low brass, bells, snare drum, tom-tom, and tambourine. Tenor saxophone and horn parts are included but are optional, indicating that these parts are covered elsewhere in the scoring. The bassoon, bass clarinet, baritone saxophone, trombone, baritone, and tuba all play the same part. This conscientious scoring for the beginning band will allow bands of most sizes and instrumentations to present a musical performance of this composition.

The work is sixty-three measures in length and approximately two minutes and thirty seconds in duration.

Unit 3: Historical Perspective

Overtures comprise a significant portion of the repertoire for band and typically make excellent opening works for the concert program. The overture was originally employed as introductory music for an opera, oratorio, ballet, and such. Early overtures consisted of three sections, generally fast–slow–fast. By the nineteenth century, an independent form emerged: the concert overture. This instrumental composition is a single-movement form and is not introductory music. Works such as Brahms's *Academic Festival Overture*, Berlioz's *Roman Carnival Overture*, Copland's *An Outdoor Overture*, and Schuman's *Chester Overture for Band* are all examples of this form. Transcriptions of orchestral overtures are a significant portion of the concert band repertoire, but this malleable form also affords composers a vehicle for exploring their own creative ideas.

Unit 4: Technical Considerations

The key signature for *Canterbury Overture* is d minor with a modal character, but the work includes sections in F major and B-flat major. All key and mode changes are accomplished through the use of accidentals. Because all of these keys are closely related, the number of accidentals is minimized. The first clarinet and second trumpet players will need to know how to finger concert C-sharp. The alto saxophones will need to know how to finger A-sharp. All low brass and woodwind players will need to be reminded that the As are natural.

The ranges of all parts are consistent with the capabilities of the beginning band. The clarinet and bass clarinet parts do not cross the break. The flute part extends from A3 to C5 and is sometimes doubled by the oboe. In measures where the flute part becomes more technical, the oboe player has whole notes. The alto saxophone part extends from D3 to A4 and provides more of a technical challenge for young players. An effective performance of this part is best accomplished by players with good tone quality and the ability to control the dynamic ranges of the instrument. Since many young saxophone players do develop finger dexterity more quickly than their peers, this part will afford such students the opportunity to develop tonal control while providing interesting melodic material. The trumpet parts are well within the range capabilities of the young player, extending from D3 to D4 in the first trumpet and D3 to B3 in the second trumpet. Students should be encouraged to use the third valve extension to lower the pitch of D3. A solid bass line will easily be achieved since the bass part is scored for bassoon, bass clarinet, tenor saxophone, horn, trombone, baritone, and tuba. With such doublings, even bands with limited instrumentation have the opportunity to cover all voicings. Bands with good instrumentation will find that the depth of possibilities offered by the bass part will enhance the overall tone quality of the band.

Canterbury Overture is written in 4/4 meter and has a tempo of quarter note = 100 beats per minute. Its rhythmic structure uses whole notes, dotted-half notes, half notes, quarter notes, and eighth notes in simple rhythmic patterns. Clarinets and trumpets will need to be aware that the second parts do not always have the same rhythm as the first parts. This may cause some confusion in young players. To address this concern, it will be necessary to isolate the individual parts. Use a metronome to provide a steady beat and have the students:

1. Say the rhythm using a counting system.
2. Clap the rhythm while counting aloud.
3. Say the part in rhythm using the note names (do not say the flats or sharps).
4. Finger the part while saying the note names in rhythm.
5. Play the part.
6. If mistakes occur, repeat the procedure more slowly.

Check at each step for understanding by listening to the verbalization of the rhythm and then watching the fingering patterns. Once the individual parts are secure, it will be possible to put the two parts together. The above procedure may also be utilized for this step.

The percussion section includes parts for bells, snare drum, tom-tom, and tambourine. Four players are required, but all parts are well-conceived and easily performed by young players. The snare drum and tom-tom parts do not include rolls, and many of the rhythms are unison. The tambourine and bell parts are the most independent.

Unit 5: Stylistic Considerations

Canterbury Overture is written in eight-measure phrases, but it is possible to retain the integrity of the phrasing while breathing every four measures. Strive for quick breaths so as not to disturb the musical line. The opening section of the music calls for clearly articulated rhythms, but it is not to be played in a *staccato* fashion. The composer suggests using "tum" (rhymes with plum) articulation. The "t" will help to initiate the tone, the "u" will promote duration of the tone, and the "m" will provide an ending to the tone yielding a bit of separation without choppiness. The second section of the work begins at measure 29 and should provide a definite contrast to the opening section. This portion of the overture is *legato* in style but maintains the original tempo. All sustained pitches are held for their full value.

Unit 6: Musical Elements

MELODY:

Although *Canterbury Overture* has a key signature of d minor, the presence of the lowered seventh degree of the scale gives the opening melody a modal quality. Modes, or church modes, were the basis of pitch organization for compositions of the Medieval and Renaissance periods. Each mode is a seven-note scale comprised of two half steps and five whole steps in a variety of combinations. If the basic scale for the construction of modes is based on C major, then the half steps will always occur between E and F, and B and C. The position of these half steps will vary depending on the identity of the first note on which the scale is constructed. Although *Canterbury Overture* is written in d minor, it maintains the modal flavor because of the use of the natural minor scale (D–E–F–B–A–B-flat–C–D). It is the lowered seventh degree that projects the sense of an ancient tonality.

To assist students in hearing and playing the natural minor scale, use a concert F scale as part of the band's warm-up. Explain how the key of d minor is derived from this major scale. Have the students write the F concert scale on a sheet of manuscript paper. Once they have done this, ask them to write a scale starting on the sixth degree of the F scale. It will be beneficial to duplicate this exercise on the dry erase board so that the students may check their work. Remind the students that the starting note will vary depending on the key of their instrument. Place degree numbers under the pitches of the major scale to assist the students in identifying the sixth degree. Once the band members have written the new scale, it will be possible to play the d minor scale. If the band has been taught to identify whole and half steps, it would be appropriate and helpful to have a student come to the board and mark the location of the half steps in the major and minor scales.

HARMONY:

Canterbury Overture mixes elements of music of the Renaissance with modern music. The contrast of old and new is accomplished by the mix of modal, minor, and major harmonies. Students will need to be aware of the various tonal centers within the work and must learn to tune A minor and A major chords. A good way to help students learn to tune major and minor versions of the same chord is to begin by identifying the root, third, and fifth of the chords. The use of an overhead projector, a PowerPoint (or other similar) presentation, or a dry erase chalkboard will help the conductor to clarify these issues. Begin by spelling out the notes in the two chords. Put the two chords next to each other on a visible staff. Label the root, third, and fifth. Have the students indicate which element of the chord is different. Using a keyboard instrument, play the major chord in arpeggiated fashion, then in block form. Do the same with the minor chord. Ask the students to define the difference in the sound of these two chords. Next, have the students play an A major chord by stacking the root, third, and fifth. (The conductor will need to do the transposition if the band members have not yet been taught how to do the transposition.) Help the students identify which parts are playing the third. This can be accomplished in the following way:

1. Play the third on the keyboard.
2. Ask the students to sing the third.
3. Have the students play the chord again.
4. Ask the students who think they just played the third to raise their hands.
5. Visually assess the results.
6. Ask those students who correctly identified the third to play the note.
7. Add any others who may also have the third.

Follow the same or a similar procedure to help students find the root and fifth. Only when the students understand which element of the chord is in their parts will it be possible to accurately tune both A major and A minor chords.

Tuning is vital to fine performances. By teaching the band a tuning procedure and developing listening skills within the ensemble, it will be possible to establish good intonation. To tune a chord, begin by tuning the root of the chord. Once the root is in tune, add the fifth of the chord. To demonstrate the sound of an out-of-tune perfect fifth, use two tuners calibrated to different pitch levels. By gradually bringing the two pitches to the same calibration, the students will aurally identify the difference between in-tune and out-of-tune fifths. Next, use two students to help reinforce the idea of playing fifths in tune. Have students listen for the absence of beats between the two pitches. Once the band can tune the root and fifth of the chord, it will be appropriate to add the major third. To brighten the tone quality of the chord, it will be necessary to raise the third. Encourage the students to listen to the tone quality of the chord. In general, a pleasing tone quality will indicate an in-tune chord. Repeat the procedure to create the minor chord, but now the third will be played on the lower side of the pitch to darken the tone color. Have the band play the major chord and then the minor chord. Singing the two chords will further reinforce the differences in the sound of major and minor chords.

If beginning instrumentalists are allowed to play out of tune, they will begin to accept the resultant intonation as appropriate and correct. Therefore, the earlier students are taught to play in tune, the better the band's tone quality will be.

RHYTHM:

The meter of *Canterbury Overture* is 4/4. Its basic rhythm patterns should be well within the capabilities of the beginning band, but consider using a metronome to establish the initial pulse as the band learns to perform this work. Set the metronome at a slower tempo than the one that is indicated on the score and ask the students to pat their feet in time to the clicks. Make sure their feet are patting in a rhythmic "one-and-two-and," with the "up" stroke occurring on "and." Students will initially snap their feet up in a non-rhythmic fashion.

To assist the students in establishing an even division of the beat, ask them to place the left hand about eighteen inches above the left thigh, palm toward the leg. Place the right hand between the left hand and thigh. Now with the metronome, count "one-and-two-and" and have the right palm slap the left thigh on "one" and the back of the right hand slap the left palm on "and." Using this method, the students will feel the rhythmic division of the beat and will be more likely to establish the same evenness in the foot pat. Using a metronome that will provide two different tones for the beat and the "and" will help students in this endeavor.

It is often beneficial to simplify the rhythmic structure of the piece into a simple series of "down-ups" as the counting system. Students are more inclined to develop a sense of rhythm when the concern is focused on whether the note occurs when the foot is "down" or "up." Always use a metronome to help students develop an internal pulse. The following system has proven to be quite efficient in developing a solid rhythmic foundation:

1. Teach students to pat their feet in time with a metronome. Slightly amplifying the metronomic tone through a small guitar amplifier will help.

2. Develop a consistent and even rhythmic structure with the feet by using the hand/thigh exercise to establish a feeling of "down" and "up."

3. Teach the students to say a concise "down" and "up" as they pat their feet in time with the metronome.

4. Using a method book, rhythm studies book, rhythm slides, PowerPoint (or other similar) display, or any other projection of various rhythmic patterns, teach the students to say each rhythm using a series of "downs" and/or "ups." Make sure the foot pat is constant and even.

5. Teach one rhythmic pattern at a time and then begin to mix patterns into various combinations and in a variety of meters.

6. Have students "down-up" each new rhythm/exercise before it is played on the instruments. (An additional exercise is to ask the students to finger the part as they say the rhythm on "downs" and "ups.")

7. To further improve reading skills, ask the students to say the names of the notes of a melodic line in rhythm with the metronome. Do not say the sharps or flats since this will disrupt the flow of the rhythm. Once the students are comfortable with the names of the notes, ask them to say the names of the notes as they finger the specific passage. The final step is to play the passage. Remember to keep the foot pat going throughout the exercise.

The development of a counting system is essential to rhythmic accuracy and a sound foundation for sight-reading. Students must learn to recognize rhythmic patterns just as they learn that the combination of the letters "c-a-t" when combined spell "cat." The establishment of a counting system provides students with a basis for figuring out new rhythmic patterns on their own. It will eliminate most, if not all, rote teaching of rhythms and ultimately improve the overall quality of the band's performance. So many times the problem is not what to play, but when to play. A counting system coupled with a rhythmic pattern vocabulary will vastly improve performance skills at all levels of experience.

To improve vertical alignment of the rhythms in this work, have the students clap and say their parts while the metronome maintains the steady beat. Reinforce learning by asking the students to say the rhythm while fingering their parts. When this can be accomplished with accuracy, ask the students to finger the part while saying the note names in rhythm. These activities assist students in the cognitive and kinesthetic aspects of making music by reinforcing learning through right and left brain activities.

TIMBRE:

The timbre of *Canterbury Overture* combines elements of Renaissance and modern music. The modal character of the opening melodic material lends itself to the lighter tone quality associated with early instrumental music. Balance is always critical to the fine performance of music. Students will need to be able to identify the melody throughout the work and to then keep accompaniment figures in a subordinate position to the melody. Keep in mind that the countermelodies at rehearsal numbers 17, 29, 37, and 53 will need to be brought out while maintaining proper balance.

Students must be encouraged to develop a characteristic tone in all dynamic ranges. A valuable tool for developing this capacity is the long tone exercise. The students play a tone for twelve beats. The initial dynamic level of *pp* is allowed to *crescendo* to *ff* and then *decrescendo* back to *pp*. Students will need to be taught to gradually increase the tone's volume over the entire number of counts in the *crescendo*. Early trials of this exercise will identify potential concerns such as 1) insufficient intake of air, 2) inadequate control of the exhalation of air, 3) poor tone quality in the extremes of the dynamic range, and 4) poor intonation at the *pp* and *ff* levels. The exercise may be addressed in the following manner:

1. Set the metronome at 60 beats per minute.
2. Ask the students to breathe in on count four and then play a concert F in the instrument's mid-range for six beats.
3. Once this is automatic, ask the students to breathe in on count four and sustain the pitch at *mf*.
4. Repeat at *mp*, then *p*, then *pp*. Students will need to be taught that the softer dynamic levels are executed by using less air that is intensely compressed (more air speed, less air).
5. Draw the following diagram on the chalkboard/dry erase board:

1	2	3	4	5	6
pp	*mp*	*p*	*mf*	*f*	*ff*

6. Tell the students to imagine they are turning up the volume control on a CD player and to increase the volume of the tone a bit on each click of the metronome. To improve the tone quality at the louder dynamic levels, remind the students that their embouchure must not overly tighten or relax. Encourage them to experiment to find the best way to control the tone as the volume increases. Tell the students that flute pitches will tend to go sharp while clarinet pitches will tend to flatten at louder dynamic levels. Use tuners to assist students in their efforts to control the intonation of their instruments. The visual display of pitch variation will help young players to comprehend this acoustical concern.

7. Play the concert F for six beats as described.

8. Repeat the procedure to create a controlled *decrescendo*. Bands tend to decrease the volume too quickly when executing a *decrescendo*. Again, the volume control analogy may assist the students in understanding this concept.

9. Once the students can *crescendo* and *decrescendo* with reasonable success, put the two parts together as a twelve-beat exercise.

10. Use this exercise as a regular component of the band's daily warm-up. Do not attempt to do this exercise for extended periods of time, particularly in the developmental stages, as embouchure strain may occur. Use different pitches and gradually work into different registers.

Modeling is also a valuable tool in the development of good tone. Use recordings of professional artists or ask local professional musicians to demonstrate the characteristic tone. It should be noted that there are various artist-in-residence programs. Explore such possibilities to assist in bringing professional musicians into the classroom.

Unit 7: Form and Structure

Canterbury Overture is written in three-part form, ABA. The contrasting sections are achieved through changes in style and key while the tempo remains constant.

SECTION	MEASURES	EVENT AND SCORING
A	**1-29**	Full band; melody in first trumpet; full percussion supports the harmonic and rhythmic structure; D-natural minor/modal
a theme	1-9	Antecedent: first trumpet
	9-17	Consequent: first trumpet with flute/oboe/bells (4 measures); trumpet (4 measures)
b theme	17-25	Flute with woodwinds and tambourine; F major
a theme	25-29	Full band with melody in first trumpet and first clarinet
B	**29-45**	Texture change, less dense; no trumpets or battery percussion; *legato*; *mezzo piano* dynamic level; B-flat major
	29-37	Flute melody with alto saxophone countermelody; more sustained accompaniment figures than in the A section

SECTION	MEASURES	EVENT AND SCORING
	37-45	Flute melody continues with alto saxophone countermelody; trumpets rejoin the texture; *mezzo forte*
A	**45-end**	Full band; D-natural minor/modal
a	45-53	Melody in first trumpet as in opening
a-b	53-end	Melody in first trumpet; flute plays "b" theme as a countermelody

Unit 8: Suggested Listening

William Byrd/Fenske, *La Volta*

William Byrd/Jacob, *Battell*

Norman Dello Joio, *Variants on a Medieval Tune*

William Dunscombe/arr. Finlayson, *Early English Suite*

Edward Gregson, *The Sword and the Crown*

Gordon Jacob, *William Byrd Suite*

George Kirck, *Renaissance Triptych*

William Latham, *Court Festival.*

Bob Margolis:

    Fanfare

    Ode and Festival

    The Renaissance Fair

    Soldiers' Procession and Sword Dance

Anne McGinty:

    Foxwood Overture

    Windsor Overture

Ron Nelson:

    Courtly Airs and Dances

    Medieval Suite

Michael Praetorius/Margolis, *Terpsichore*

Elliot Del Borgo, *Renaissance Motet*

Henry Purcell/Schaefer, *Battle Symphony*

Tielman Susato/Curnow, *Renaissance Suite*

Tielman Susato/Margolis, *The Battle Pavane*

Fisher Tull, *Sketches on a Tudor Psalm*

Unit 9: Additional References and Resources

Apel, Willi. *Harvard Dictionary of Music*, 2nd edition. Cambridge, MA: The Belknap Press of Harvard University Press, 1970.

Blume, Friedrich. *Renaissance and Baroque Music*. New York, NY: W.W. Norton & Company, 1967.

Bukofzer, Manfred F. *Music in the Baroque Era*. New York, NY: W.W. Norton & Company, 1947.

Creasap, Susan. "American Women Composers of Band Music: A Bibliography and Catalogue of Works." D.A. diss., Ball State University, 1996.

Duckworth, William. *A Creative Approach to Music Fundamentals*, 4th edition. Belmont, CA: Wadsworth Publishing Company, 1992.

Grout, Donald Jay. *A History of Western Music*, 5th edition. New York, NY: W.W. Norton & Company, 1996.

McGinty, Anne. Telephone conversation with Susan Creasap, June 6, 2000.

Perkins, Leeman L. *Music in the Age of the Renaissance*. New York, NY: W.W. Norton & Company, 1998.

Reese, Gustave. *Music in the Renaissance*, revised edition. New York, NY: W.W. Norton & Company, 1959.

Stone, Stuart. "Renaissance Music for Band." *The Instrumentalist*, May 2000, 22-28.

Contributed by:

Susan Creasap
Assistant Director of Bands
Morehead State University
Morehead, Kentucky

Teacher Resource Guide

Celebration for Winds
John Edmondson
(b. 1933)

Unit 1: Composer

John Edmondson was born in 1933 in Toledo, Ohio. A graduate of Sarasota (Florida) High School in 1949, he received a Bachelor of Arts from the University of Florida in 1955, majoring in music theory with minors in English and sociology. After a two-year stint with the U.S. Army Eighth and Ninth Division Bands, he received his Master of Music in composition from the University of Kentucky in 1960, where he studied composition with Kenneth Wright and band scoring with R. Bernard Fitzgerald. He was the first recipient of a graduate degree from the university.

Edmondson taught music for ten years in the Central Kentucky area public schools, where he wrote extensively for his own students. During this same time, he freelanced as a writer for various university and high school marching bands, including seven years as Staff Arranger for the University of Kentucky Wildcat Marching Band. He has over 600 publications in the field of band and educational music. He has been involved in various capacities with Alfred Publications, Hansen Publications, and Jensen Publications. In 1986, he and his wife, Anne McGinty, founded their own publishing company, Queenwood Publications, which is recognized worldwide as one of the leading publishers of quality educational music for school bands.

Edmondson was honored in 1991 as the recipient of the University of Florida, Department of Fine Arts, Music Department Alumni Achievement Award. He is a member of the American Society of Composers, Authors, and Publishers (ASCAP) and is listed in the *International Who's Who of Music*.

Unit 2: Composition

Celebration for Winds is an original composition for band. It was commissioned by the 1993 Samuel L. Wagner Middle School "Clipper" Band, Winterport, Maine, Patrick Michaud, director. This Grade 1 work is approximately two minutes and twenty seconds in length.

Unit 3: Historical Perspective

Although great historical significance is not apparent, one could draw a parallel to the many educational works and composers of substance for band. Other composers of educational music include Anne McGinty, John Kinyon, Pierre La Plante, and James Barnes, to name a few.

Unit 4: Technical Considerations

This piece centers around the key of B-flat major and features contrasting musical styles and instrumental colors. Most students should be familiar with the B-flat concert scale, so performing this work should not be a problem from a tonality standpoint. The piece remains in common time throughout, and the tempo does not vary from the initial marking of "Majestically" with quarter note = 100 beats per minute. There is no syncopation or asymmetrical patterns, and the most difficult rhythm is a group of four eighth notes. Accidentals do occur throughout the piece and are spelled enharmonically to facilitate easier execution. Percussion scoring includes snare drum, bass drum, crash cymbals, bells, and triangle. The composer notes that the piece is playable without bass clef instruments, or with only one flute, two clarinets, one alto saxophone, two cornets/trumpets, and percussion. The clarinet parts stay below the break, and optional French horn and tenor saxophone parts are written in their best ranges.

Unit 5: Stylistic Considerations

Students should approach the piece with energy to give the feeling of a celebration. Although accents appear in the last two measures, most of the quarter notes and half notes need to be articulated in a fanfare manner to produce clarity. Phrasing usually occurs in four-measure patterns, so students should abide by this for breathing purposes. Dynamic contrast is very important and markings include *piano*, *mezzo forte*, and *forte* with several *crescendos* throughout the piece.

Unit 6: Musical Elements

MELODY:
The melody appears exclusively in the treble clef instruments and centers around the tonality of B-flat major. The melody must always predominate over any other element. Players should know that when a half or whole note is tied to an eighth note over the bar line, they should release the note on the

count where the eighth note appears. This appears many times throughout the piece, as in measures 3 and 4, and at the end of the "A" section in measure 12.

HARMONY:

The harmonic framework deals exclusively with B-flat concert and its nearly related chord structures. This can easily be seen by the root movement in the low brass and low reed line, as this part generally moves between I, IV, and V.

RHYTHM:

The meter stays in common time throughout the work. Rhythms are basic in nature, although players should have the feeling of the eighth note subdivision to ensure exactness. There is minimal rhythmic independence, which is not unusual for a Grade 1 band work.

TIMBRE:

As with most Grade 1 works, the tone color does not change substantially during the piece. The melody appears exclusively in the high brass and woodwinds. Occasionally the flutes play the tonic an octave above the melody, so careful attention must be paid to melodic balance in these areas. The "B" and "C" sections of the work present melodic fragmentation between the cornet/trumpet, clarinet, alto saxophone line, and that of the flute and oboe line. Careful attention must also be paid to the moving quarter and eighth note lines, as they are important in regard to harmony and moving from section to section. Do not hesitate to thin out the instrumentation if needed to provide correct balance.

Unit 7: Form and Structure

SECTION	MEASURES	EVENT AND SCORING
Introduction	1-5	Full band introduction leading to main theme in clarinet, alto saxophone, and cornet/trumpet
A	5-13	Melody in clarinet, alto saxophone, and cornet/trumpet; some harmony provided in split writing in these instruments; low voices outline the harmonic progression
B	13-22	New melodic material in fragments in all treble clef instruments; some rhythmic and harmonic independence between upper voices
A	22-30	Complete restatement of mm. 5-13

SECTION	MEASURES	EVENT AND SCORING
C	30-49	New material presented in a four-measure antecedent/consequent manner with a shifting tonal center that eventually arrives on F major (the dominant); tonal center is shifted through the use of accidentals
A´	49-55	A shortened version of "A" leading to a codetta
Codetta	55-end	A four-measure codetta using material from the introduction

Unit 8: Suggested Listening

James Barnes, *Westridge Overture*
John Edmondson:
    Tatum Square Festival
    Windhaven Celebration
Anne McGinty, *Windsor Overture*
Jared Spears, *Star Flight*

Unit 9: Additional References and Resources

Queenwood Publications. "John Edmondson: Composer." Composer Gallery. 1999: photo, 7 paragraphs. On-line: Internet address http://www. queenwood.com/composers.html (April 2, 2000)

Smith, Norman, and Albert Stoutamire. *Band Music Notes*, 3rd edition. Lake Charles, LA: Program Note Press, 1979.

Contributed by:

Rodney C. Schueller
Associate Director of Bands
Western Illinois University
Macomb, Illinois

Teacher Resource Guide

Chant and Canon
John O'Reilly
(b. 1941)

Unit 1: Composer

John O'Reilly is one of the most-performed composers of band music in the world today. He is the recipient of numerous ASCAP awards and has studied composition with Robert Washburn, Arthur Frackenpohl, Charles Walton, and Donald Hunsberger. As co-author of the *Yamaha Band Student*, *Accent on Achievement*, and *Strictly Strings*, O'Reilly has made a major impact on the education of young musicians.

O'Reilly attended the Crane School of Music, State University of New York at Potsdam, receiving a Bachelor of Science degree. In addition, he is the recipient of a Master of Arts in Composition and Theory from Columbia University. His twelve years of teaching experience at elementary through college levels has provided him with insights and sensitivities to the needs of both students and educators. An elected member of the prestigious American Bandmasters Association, O'Reilly is a frequent conductor of honor bands worldwide. He currently resides in Los Angeles, California, where he serves as executive vice president and editor-in-chief of Alfred Publishing.

Unit 2: Composition

Chant and Canon was written in 1995. It is part of the *Yamaha Band Series*, published by Alfred Publishing Company. All of the works in this series correspond with lessons in the *Yamaha Band Student* band class method. *Chant and Canon* correlates with book 1, page 7. The indicated grade level is characterized as "Very Easy."

166

Unit 3: Historical Perspective

Gregorian Chant and *organum*-style singing in the Catholic Church date back almost 1,500 years. The scales used in chant are called *modes*. In the Latin, (Gregorian) chant is written in a free rhythm and is monophonic. The Anglican chants are harmonized and the cadence is in a strict meter.

The term *canon* is a contrapuntal device whereby an extended melody, stated in one part, is imitated strictly and in its entirety in one or more other parts. Usually the imitating part follows at a short distance (one measure). The technique of canonic imitation (canon) was first used in the thirteenth century. The earliest composition consisting exclusively of a canon is *Sumer Is Icumen In*.

Unit 4: Technical Considerations

Since the composition is written to enhance the activities shown in book 1 of *Yamaha Band Student* and corresponds with those skills presented in the earliest stages of beginning instruction, the technical requirements are minimal. The young players should possess basic skills and concepts in tonguing and breath support so that the melodic lines are smooth and connected. They should be able to recognize simple time signatures (in this case, 4/4) and understand duration in notation (whole, half, and quarter notes and rests). The written ranges for each instrument are appropriate for this stage of instruction.

Unit 5: Stylistic Considerations

The basic style in both the *Chant* and *Canon* is smooth and connected. While the melodic lines are simple, they offer the opportunity to continue work on *legato* articulations and to observe the flow and shape of melodic lines. A musical phrase is the natural division of a melodic line. It is demarcated by a cadence. More importantly, it is a musical movement from and to a point of repose. Musical phrases are similar to sentences in language. The language (musical lines) are enhanced by having climactic points and cadences that are similar to punctuation marks.

Unit 6: Musical Elements

There are many opportunities for creative teaching throughout *Chant and Canon*. There are no printed expressive markings, so the conductor could focus on phrase shaping with particular emphasis on releases at the end of a phrase (prior to a rest). Simply stated, the tone ends when the silence begins! There are also opportunities to consider melodic contour through experimenting with various dynamic levels and then, perhaps, writing in dynamic indications that the ensemble has chosen. Other teaching possibilities include working on octave tuning and, with the call-and-response sections, contrasts of timbre. Since both the chant and the canon are in a *legato* style, a review of "D" (dah, doo, duh) articulations would be most helpful.

Unit 7: Form and Structure

Chant and Canon is written in three sections (A, B, C).

As indicated by the title, the A section (measures 1 through 24) is a chant, written in the Dorian mode. The tempo indication is *moderato*. This section features six monophonic chant statements beginning with the upper wood- winds and bells, then alternating between the low woodwinds and brass. The first two statements are four measures in length. The second two statements are two measures long. The melodic motion is conjunct with a very simple rhythmic structure.

The B section, "canon," begins in measure 25. A new tempo indication is shown as *allegro*. The key is now B-flat major, with the melodic line being slightly more disjunct than the opening section. The canon is strict with two voices at the octave and a one-measure delay.

The C section, beginning in measure 42, features expanded harmony (tri- ads) with parallel sixths, somewhat reminiscent of *fauxbourdon*. The canon is now at two-measure intervals until the piece ends on a plagal cadence.

Unit 8: Suggested Listening

Eighteenth Century Miniatures, Stuttgart Chamber Orchestra, London 417
    718-2
Music for Winds and Percussion, Vol. 5, Northern Illinois University Wind
    Ensemble, Stephen E. Squires, Conductor, DR HSB-005

Unit 9: Additional References and Resources

Lisk, Edward S. *The Creative Director; Intangibles of Musical Performance* . Ft.
    Lauderdale, FL: Meredith Music Publications, 1996.

Contributed by:

William A. Gora
Appalachian State University
Boone, North Carolina

Teacher Resource Guide

Chorale Prelude:
All Things Bright and Beautiful
Claude T. Smith
(1932–1987)

Unit 1: Composer

Claude T. Smith was a well-known and respected composer of music for bands. He held degrees from Central Methodist College and University of Kansas. He served in the 371st Army Band and has over twenty years' experience as a public school music educator in Missouri and Nebraska. He served on the faculty of Southwest Missouri State, was elected president of the Missouri Music Educators Association, and enjoyed a productive career as guest clinician and conductor. A recipient of numerous awards, Smith's instrumental and choral compositions have been performed by the world's leading ensembles. Well-known works include *Declaration Overture*, *Variations on an English Folk Song*, *Emperata Overture*, and *Incidental Suite*.

Unit 2: Composition

The subtitle to this work is "An Old English Melody," though the origin and source of the melody is not given. The work is a difficult Grade 1, accessible to advanced second- and third-year players. The scoring is for standard wind band; percussion scoring calls for timpani, bells, snare drum, bass drum, suspended cymbal, and crash cymbal. *Chorale Prelude: All Things Bright and Beautiful* was published in 1985 and is approximately one minute and fifty seconds in duration.

Unit 3: Historical Perspective

Choral preludes grew out of the tradition of playing brief interludes or introductions to chorales sung during the mass or church service. These interludes eventually developed and grew into their own genre; the first great composers of chorale preludes include Pachelbel, Sweelinck, and Schiedt. Several great composers have written fine examples of chorale preludes, most notably J.S. Bach. Examples of chorale preludes for winds include original works by Persichetti and settings of Bach chorale preludes by Reed and Grainger, among others.

Unit 4: Technical Considerations

For the most part, ranges in this work are playable by second-year students. The only range concerns would be in flute (E-flat above the staff), and first clarinet (C above the staff). All parts are amply doubled, and the scoring is full throughout most of the piece. Rhythms are all simple combinations of whole, half, quarter, and eighth notes. There is one key change and minimal use of accidentals and non-chord tones. Students will need to be able to play the concert F and E-flat major scales. The most difficult aspects of this work concern style, balance, and dynamics.

Unit 5: Stylistic Considerations

Most of the interest in this setting is created through contrasts in style and scoring. Students will need to be able to perform *legato*, *staccato*, *marcato*, and accented note styles. There is a wide range of dynamics employed, so there will need to be a distinct difference between all levels of written dynamics. The scoring is full throughout most of the work; therefore, balance becomes an issue so the melody will be heard at all times.

Unit 6: Musical Elements

The chorale is presented twice: once in E-flat major, then again in F major. The form of the chorale is ABA´. Rhythm consists of simple combinations of whole, half, quarter, and eighth notes. There is little use of dotted rhythms, and there are no instances of syncopation. The melody is scalar; students will need to be able to perform the concert E-flat and F major scales. The work is harmonically simple; there are few unexpected or chromatic chords.

This piece would serve as an excellent tool to transfer skills learned in the study of warm-up chorales. Full, singing tones are a must, as are all the wonderful nuances that make a good performance of a chorale exciting for both listeners and players. It would prove beneficial to arrange a simple four-part harmony version of the melody used in this piece and teach the students to sing both the melody and their harmony part. Due to the simplicity of the beat patterns and the clarity of the form of this work, an instructional unit focusing on basic elements of conducting might also prove interesting for the students.

Unit 7: Form and Structure

SECTION	MEASURES	EVENT AND SCORING
Introduction	1-5	
A	6-13	Clarinet and saxophone with melody
B	14-21	Clarinet, horn, and trombone with melody
A´	22-25	Shortened version of A
Transition	26-27	
A	28-35	Key change to F major; low brass and low reeds with melody
B	36-43	Flute *soli* for four measures; full band enters
A´	44-53	Use of extension at end of A; *fermata* in m. 49; final cadence in F major

Unit 8: Suggested Listening

Chorale Preludes by Bach, both original works for organ and those set for
   winds by Reed, Grainger, and others
Vincent Persichetti:
   O God Unseen
   So Pure the Star

Unit 9: Additional References and Resources

Dvorak, Thomas, Cynthia Crump Taggart, and Peter Schmalz. *Best Music for Young Band*. Brooklyn, NY: Manhattan Beach Music, 1986.

Kennedy, Michael, ed. *The Concise Oxford Dictionary of Music*, 3rd edition. Oxford: Oxford University Press, 1980.

Lane, Jeremy. *Teaching Music Through Performance in Band and Texas U.I.L. Grade I Prescribe Music List for Band*. Graduate project. Waco, TX: Baylor University, 1998.

Miles, Richard, ed. *Teaching Music through Performance in Band*. Chicago, IL: GIA Publications, Inc., 1997.

Miles, Richard, ed. *Teaching Music through Performance in Band*, Volume 2. Chicago, IL: GIA Publications, Inc., 1998.

Rehrig, W.H., and P.E. Bierley. *The Heritage Encyclopedia of Band Music*. Westerville, OH: Integrity Press, 1991.

Smith, N., and A. Stoutamire. *Band Music Notes*, revised edition. Lake Charles, LA: Program Note Press, 1979.

Contributed by:
Jeremy S. Lane
Doctoral Graduate Assistant, Music Education
Louisiana State University
Baton Rouge, Louisiana

Teacher Resource Guide

Clouds

Anne McGinty
(b. 1945)

Unit 1: Composer

Anne McGinty received her B.M. and M.M. degrees in Flute and Composition from Duquesne University. She has over 130 published pieces to her credit, ranging in grade levels from 1 to 5. She and her husband, John Edmondson, operate Queenwood Publications, a company devoted to publishing quality music for young bands. Other works by McGinty include *Bach: Chorale and Variation*, *Bartok: Folk Trilogy*, *Chorale Prelude*, *Madrigal for Band*, *Sea Song Trilogy*, *Satie: Three Gymnopedies*, and *The Red Balloon*.

Unit 2: Composition

Clouds is a work in three sections inspired by three different types of clouds: cirrus, thundercloud, and cumulus. The moods of the sections reflect the nature of their namesakes: cirrus are high-altitude, thin, fleecy clouds; thunderclouds are dark, ominous, and result in storms; cumulus are dense, fluffy clouds with well-defined shapes and multiple rounded outlines. Composed in 1994, the work is suitable for second-year players. It is approximately two minutes and thirty seconds in duration.

Unit 3: Historical Perspective

In most every era and genre, there are numerous instances of music inspired by forces of nature. Haydn, Debussy, Robert Schumann, Beethoven, Copland, Brahms, and Strauss are just a few of the many composers who attempted to depict nature in their music. An interesting project for both director and students would be to listen to some of the works by these composers and compare how each one reflected nature in their music. Music for winds inspired by nature include Copland's *Outdoor Overture* and Melillo's *Stormworks*.

Unit 4: Technical Considerations

This piece is accessible to advanced first- and second-year players. Ranges are all within reach for first-year players. Rhythm is not difficult, and all parts are doubled throughout. There is need for independent playing, especially in the clarinet and flute parts. There are several instances of accidentals throughout the work; students will need to pay careful attention to non-key signature notes. Students will also need to be able to play a concert B-flat major scale in eighth notes at quarter note = 100. There are two meter changes (from 3/4 to 4/4 and back) and no key changes.

Unit 5: Stylistic Considerations

This is a great piece for introducing first-year players to style contrasts within a single-movement work. The first section should be light and graceful, with a sort of waltz feel. The second section introduces the students to some modern compositional devices, such as sound events notated by duration in seconds rather than in a measure. The third section should be smooth and seamless, with the individual patterns weaving in and out of the full textures. The only style markings are accents. The dynamics are an important part of the piece and should be given full attention.

Unit 6: Musical Elements

Rhythmically, the individual parts present few difficulties, but the combined effect of the parts played simultaneously may prove challenging. If the students are secure in their individual parts, it will not be difficult to meld the separate parts together. Harmonically, the work is fairly straightforward, with limited use of accidentals. During the "Thundercloud" section, there are some tone clusters and dissonant harmonies used to create the effect of the storm. Melodically, the themes are very scale-oriented, with no wide leaps. The melody in the final section is split into two choirs; these elements must be combined to create a smooth, seamless presentation of the melody.

This piece presents some wonderful opportunities for exploring and learning. Twentieth century music could be introduced and studied through comparison and contrast with the second section of the work ("Thundercloud"). An instructional unit could be structured around the study of various composers' portrayal of events in nature through their music. The piece also provides possibilities for cross-discipline studies with other art forms. A fantastic example of this is described in Mike Pearce's article, "Diving Deep in Quest of 'Atlantis'" (see Unit 9).

Unit 7: Form and Structure

MEASURES	EVENT AND SCORING
1-22	**"Cirrus"**
1-8	Introduction; key of B-flat major; flute, clarinet, saxophone, and percussion
9-16	Cirrus theme; cornet with melody; flute and horn with countermelody; full band accompanies
17-22	Transition; recap of introduction
23-45	**"Thundercloud"**
23-30	Storm effect; change to 4/4 time; full band; *tutti* rhythm; tone clusters
31	Percussion "free time"; percussion creates thunder noises for eight to ten seconds
32-39	Storm effect; *tutti* rhythm; tone clusters
40-46	Transition; flute with melody; all others pedal tones on F major chord
46-68	**"Cumulus"**
46-53	Cumulus theme; theme woven between two groups — group I: flute and oboe; group II: saxophone, horn, low brass, and low woodwinds
54-61	Variation of theme; groups changed slightly — group I: flute, oboe, and cornet; group II: clarinet; all else accompany
62-68	Coda; reprise of introduction to Cumulus theme; piece ends quietly on B-flat major chord

Unit 8: Suggested Listening

Ludwig von Beethoven, *Symphony No. 6, "Pastorale,"* Movements III and IV
Aaron Copland, *Outdoor Overture*
Claude Debussy:
   La Mer
   "Nuages" from *Nocturnes*
Ferde Grofe, *Grand Canyon Suite*
Richard Strauss, *Alpensinfonie*

Unit 9: Additional References and Resources

Dvorak, Thomas, Cynthia Crump Taggart, and Peter Schmalz. *Best Music for Young Band.* Brooklyn, NY: Manhattan Beach Music, 1986.

Kennedy, Michael, ed. *The Concise Oxford Dictionary of Music,* 3rd edition. Oxford: Oxford University Press, 1980.

Lane, Jeremy. *Teaching MusicThrough Performance in Band and Texas U.I.L. Grade I Prescribe Music List for Band*. Graduate project. Waco, TX: Baylor University, 1998.

Miles, Richard, ed. *Teaching Music through Performance in Band*. Chicago, IL: GIA Publications, Inc., 1997.

Miles, Richard, ed. *Teaching Music through Performance in Band*, Volume 2. Chicago, IL: GIA Publications, Inc., 1998.

Pearce, Mike. "Diving Deep in Quest of 'Atlantis'." *Teaching Music* 6:6 (June 1999): 30-32.

Smith, N., and A. Stoutamire. *Band Music Notes*, revised edition. Lake Charles, LA: Program Note Press, 1979.

Contributed by:

Jeremy S. Lane
Doctoral Graduate Assistant, Music Education
Louisiana State University
Baton Rouge, Louisiana

Teacher Resource Guide

Concert Contrasts
Robert Palmer
(b. 1945)

Unit 1: Composer

Robert Palmer received his Bachelor of Arts in English from Davidson College in Davidson, North Carolina, and his Doctor of Music in Composition from Florida State University, where he was a student of Carlisle Floyd and John Boda. Since that time, Palmer has taught in the public schools of Brevard, North Carolina, where his bands and choruses have won many regional and national honors. He has also taught at Brevard College and from 1988 to the present has been on the faculty at the Brevard Music Center as wind ensemble conductor and lecturer in theory and composition. Palmer has received many commissions, including several from the North Carolina Arts Council. Among these was a commission for the creation of a large work for chorus and orchestra for the fiftieth anniversary of the Raleigh Oratorio Society. Many of his band compositions are on festival lists throughout the United States.

Unit 2: Composition

Concert Contrasts was written for the beginning band at Brevard Middle School. The composer writes:

> The motivation for writing this work was that my daughter was in beginning band and I wanted to do something with her musically. The three-note solo in measure twenty (cued in bells) was for her. A secondary motivation was to attempt a more or less abstract piece playable by kids who had been playing not quite a year. I wanted to write good melodies for all instruments and especially give low brass some melodic writing, as so many young band pieces implicitly assume the low

brass can't play, and I knew how frustrated those players can be by that. I also wanted to write independent and musical percussion parts within the narrow range of what is reasonable for beginners.

As the title indicates, *Concert Contrasts* is in two dissimilar sections. The first, "Spiritual," is to be played in a smooth, *cantabile* style with careful attention to balance and blend. The second, "March," is more *marcato* with special attention needed in the area of rhythmic ensemble and dynamics. Published in 1991, *Concert Contrasts* is approximately two minutes and fifteen seconds in length.

Unit 3: Historical Perspective

Concert Contrasts provides an excellent opportunity for the introduction of instructional units on indigenous American music. Historical research into blues, ragtime, jazz, and spirituals will provide young band students with many learning possibilities. Composing and improvising are two of the many creative approaches that may be used to support and enhance performance. In addition, listening to spirituals will assist the students in discovering performance practices that may better inform the rendition of this work.

Unit 4: Technical Considerations

The instrumentation is well suited for beginning band: flute; oboe; first and second B-flat clarinet; B-flat bass clarinet; alto, tenor, and baritone saxophone; first and second B-flat trumpet (cornet); horn; trombone; baritone; bassoon; tuba; percussion I using snare drum, bass drum, suspended cymbal, and triangle; percussion II using bells, tambourine, and suspended cymbal with yarn mallets. The score contains a helpful piano reduction. Ranges for all instruments are very moderate, most not requiring more than a perfect fifth span in the middle *tessitura*. The key signature of F concert is retained throughout. A lowered seventh scale degree, E-flat, is used due to the Mixolydian scale construction that generates the basic melodic and harmonic material. Rhythmic values are basic: whole, half, quarter, and eighth with no dotted rhythms. For young percussionists, the parts are musically challenging, requiring dynamic control and precision. The "March" section features four, one-measure percussion fills. Most melodic material is assigned to the flute, oboe, clarinet, and trumpet parts. However, there is ample opportunity for exposed, expressive playing in the secondary instruments. A one-measure, three-note oboe solo ends the first section and is cued in the flutes and bells.

Unit 5: Stylistic Considerations

Two opposing musical styles challenge the embryonic musician to pay careful attention to characterization: one is *legato/cantabile*, the other *marcato/staccato*. Lyrical, sustained playing with opportunities for careful attention to balance and blend are the main challenges of the first section, "Spiritual." The tempo is indicated as "ca. 80 to the quarter," allowing for some flexibility in performance. Dynamics range from *piano* to *mezzo piano*. The second section, "March," requires a more marked approach with frequent *staccato* indications. Dynamics are generally *forte*. Call-and-response technique is used frequently.

Unit 6: Musical Elements

A tonal center of F major is used throughout. However, frequent use of the flatted seventh (E-flat) often projects a Mixolydian quality both melodically and harmonically. This gives certain passages a blues-like sound, but the blues scale is not used. Several chords often associated with popular music and jazz are employed: Cm7, Cm9, E-flatM9, for example. The texture is primarily melody with accompaniment. Call-and-response technique lends interest, especially in "March." Melodic ideas are developed in interesting ways. The motive of a rising M2, m3, introduced in the second phrase of "Spiritual," is manipulated in "March," using interval expansion and retrograde inversion.

Unit 7: Form and Structure

Section	Measures	Event and Scoring
Section 1: "Spiritual"		
A	1-10	Theme in flute and trumpet after two-measure introduction; phrase is in two parts: antecedent-consequent
B	11-14	New melodic material in flute, answered by other winds; reduced scoring
A	15-20	Return of A with altered harmony; oboe solo last two measures
Section 2: "March"		
Introduction	21-28	Uses motive derived from B section of "Spiritual"; call-and-response, low brass and reeds answered by trumpet; upper winds present motive in retrograde inversion on lowered seventh
A	29-41	Beginning of a three-part section; A theme based on Introduction motive; development of theme
B	42-50	Although based on A, reduced dynamic and scoring make this passage a noticeable contrast; ends with percussion solo and A in augmentation
Coda	51-55	Percussion solo sets up call-and-response imitation

Unit 8: Suggested Listening

Robert Palmer:

 Awake My Soul (chorus and orchestra)
 Celebration for Band
 Ceremonial Music for Band
 Cityscape (band)
 Overture on a Southern Hymn (band)
 Psalm for Band
 Toccata in Dance Rhythm (band)
 Winter Mountainscape (band)

Unit 9: Additional References and Resources

Carl Fischer, 62 Cooper Square, New York, NY, (publisher of *Concert Contrasts* score).

Dvorak, Thomas L., Cynthia Crump Taggart, and Peter Schmalz. *Best Music for Young Band*. Edited by Bob Margolis. Brooklyn, NY: Manhattan Beach Music, 1986.

Gridley, Mark C. *Jazz Styles*. Upper Saddle River, NJ: Prentice Hall, 2000.

Kreines, Joseph. *Music for Concert Band*. Tampa, FL: Florida Music Service, 1989.

Contributed by:

Scott Carter
East Carolina University
Greenville, North Carolina

Teacher Resource Guide

Contredanse

Larry Clark
(b. 1963)

Unit 1: Composer

Larry Clark holds degrees from Florida State University and James Madison University. A native of Florida, he composed *Contredanse* in 1998 while living in Miami. He currently resides in New Jersey. He is the former Director of Bands at Syracuse University in Syracuse, New York, and he has taught at public schools in Florida. He has also worked for Warner Brothers and Carl Fischer. A versatile composer and arranger, Clark has numerous works published for concert band, marching band, and orchestra. Other works for concert band include *Engines of Resistance* and *Bartok Suite*.

Unit 2: Composition

The term "contredanse" is from a popular dance performed during the late eighteenth century, with roots in both England and France. The composer writes that *Contredanse* was written to contain the musical elements of a French contredanse. This type of piece was an extended series of eight-measure phrases to which couples danced. The work is seventy-eight measures in length with a performance time of approximately two minutes and fifteen seconds. It is a lively piece, marked *Allegro con brio*.

There are ten distinct phrases: nine are eight measures in length, one seven-measure phrase serves as a transition, and then there is a seven-measure coda. This is, for the most part, consistent with the original form of a contredanse. Three different themes are presented and developed throughout the composition. The key center is B-flat major, with one brief section in G minor. The indicated level of difficulty is "Easy."

Unit 3: Historical Perspective

Although Clark notes that his idea for *Contredanse* came from this late eighteenth century dance form, no stylistic elements from that time period are incorporated in the piece. The music is in eight-measure phrases for the most part, but this is the only historically consistent musical element. It is quite possible that *Contredanse* (or a similar piece) will be the first dance-style piece a young musician will perform. It is this association of music and dance that is important. Understanding how music and motion can coexist opens many possibilities for instruction.

A dance implies some type of movement for some specific reason. Some dances are slow, some are fast, some are happy, some are comical, and so on. Whatever the dance, it is merely a reaction to the music. How can a musician indicate to a dancer what to do? The answer is through the many variations in tempo, articulation (style), or perhaps even volume that music as an art form contains. Each dance-style composition is different and, therefore, must be performed differently, just as each dance is different.

Unit 4: Technical Considerations

Harmonically, the composition is very basic, with each eight-measure phrase either ending on or leading to B-flat major. Throughout the entire piece, there are no accidentals. The piece is made up of very basic rhythms with simple quarter note and eighth note rhythms in each part. The exception is the snare drum, which has passages that contain eighth and two sixteenth notes. There is no syncopation. There are passages in which groups of instruments are required to alternate parts of a phrase with other sections, requiring rhythmic independence from the ensemble. Ranges for each instrument are well within a beginning band's capabilities. For example, clarinets do not go over the break, and trumpets and horns only go up to D and C in the staff, respectively. The piece is scored in a manner that requires each section of the band to be able to perform independently, as the orchestration constantly changes.

Unit 5: Stylistic Considerations

There are five different articulations in *Contredanse*: notes with no indication, notes with *staccato* markings, notes with *marcato* markings, a written *marcato* marking, and slurs. These appear with a fair amount of independence throughout each of the parts. There are also several places where different articulations occur within the same measure. Dynamic contrast ranges from *piano* to *fortissimo*. There are numerous *crescendos*, from two beats in duration to two measures, but there are no *decrescendos*.

To accurately perform *Contredanse*, students must be able to differentiate between the many articulations and dynamics presented. The style of a dance piece is in many ways determined by the different articulations used by the ensemble. Care must be taken to ensure that these articulations do not promote pedagogically inaccurate types of articulation. An example of this would be stopping a note with the tongue on either a *marcato* or *staccato* marking.

Clark indicates at the beginning of the piece a marking of *Allegro con brio*. A brisk tempo of quarter note = 132-144, along with extensive articulation markings, provide ample indicators of how the piece should be performed. The ability to perform with a high energy level combined with good dynamic control, particularly in the softer markings, is required.

Unit 6: Musical Elements

MELODY:

There are three themes presented in *Contredanse*. The first theme is in B-flat and is eight measures in length. It is almost exclusively the diatonic scale, with only one large interval of a fourth. The second theme is also in B-flat and is eight measures long. It has more jumps but also contains the only slurred passages in the piece. The softer dynamic of the second theme and type of articulation indicate it is a more subtle melody than the first theme. The third theme appears only twice: first in G minor and marked *staccato* and *piano*, then last in E-flat major.

With three distinct themes occurring independently of each other as well as simultaneously, it is important that students are able to identify the three themes. Understanding what parts of a composition are more important than others, such as melody and accompaniment, is one of the critical aspects of ensemble playing.

HARMONY:

A very basic harmonic structure is used in *Contredanse*. The harmonic progression is almost exclusively a I–V–I progression. With only two exceptions—one beginning on the relative minor and one on the subdominant—each phrase begins on a B-flat chord. Seven of the ten phrases end on a B-flat chord. The other three end on the dominant, leading back to a tonic B-flat major. Although the harmonic structure is basic, both major and minor tonalities are present; this provides instructional opportunities relating to tonality.

RHYTHM:

Basic quarter note/eighth note rhythms (with the exception of the snare drum part) are presented throughout. There are no dotted rhythms and no syncopation, but there are several places where the rhythm changes in subtle ways. For example, in phrase seven (measure 49), quarter/two eighths/quarter/two eighths is changed to two eighths/quarter/two eighths/quarter. There are also numerous places where rhythmic independence is required of the players. Clark divides themes between different parts on several occasions, which presents counting and listening challenges for the players.

Instructional opportunities involving rhythm abound in *Contredanse*. The rhythms presented include every possibility using quarter note/eighth note combinations. Although syncopation and dotted rhythms are not part of the rhythmic language found in *Contredanse*, understanding the rhythms in it is a prerequisite to understanding the more complex rhythms. Rhythmic independence is also an important musical concept presented in *Contredanse*. The ability to rest, count, and play in tempo following another section is an important musical element to be explored. Listening to other pieces to identify the four- or eight-measure phrases can reinforce the idea of structure and form in music.

Timbre:
The overall timbre of the piece is bright and energetic based on the orchestration, articulations, harmonic structure, and tempo selected by the composer. The orchestration creates many different timbre changes from the ensemble as the themes are divided between and presented by each section of the band. Care must be taken to ensure that the proper balance is maintained between the melody and the accompaniment throughout each phrase. Although doubling of parts does occur, it is not the type of doubling that is generally seen in music at this level. Doubling of parts is not the same throughout the piece. There are numerous examples where different instruments pair together at different times in the doubling of parts. These textural changes present listening opportunities for the players as the orchestration constantly changes. At no time is there a part that is not doubled. Assuming a full ensemble is used, asking the students to identify and actively listen to the other instruments that are also playing the same part is a worthy instructional objective.

The percussion section provides both melodic and rhythmic support, with parts for bells, timpani, snare drum, bass drum, crash cymbals, tambourine, and triangle. The percussion section, which is used to support the textural changes in each theme, has many independent parts. The entire section is never used simultaneously.

Although related to style, namely the way music is articulated, the way music is performed often affects the way music is perceived. Ask the students to perform any short musical phrase in several different ways, for example, happy, excited, tired, with fire, stately, or funny. Ask them to perform in a way that might encourage a dancer to dance the way they play. Having students attempt to perform in a way that affects the listener is perhaps the first step in the development of an effective musical vocabulary.

Unit 7: Form and Structure

In keeping with the form of a contredanse, a series of ten phrases are used to present three independent themes.

MEASURES	EVENT AND SCORING
1-8	Phrase one; presents theme one in flute and bells
9-18	Phrase two; repeats phrase one with the addition of the full ensemble in a harmonized version of the first theme
17-24	Phrase three; introduces the second theme in a much more sparse orchestration
25-32	Phrase four; a return to the first theme with the full ensemble
33-40	Phrase five; introduces the *staccato* third theme; begins in G minor
41-48	Phrase six; an altered form of the second theme
49-56	Phrase seven; an altered version of the first theme
57-63	Phrase eight; serves as a seven-measure transition; combines the first and third themes
64-71	Phrase nine; a return to the original first theme with the full ensemble
72-78	The final phrase; acts as a seven-measure coda; combines the first and third themes

Unit 8: Suggested Listening

Larry Clark:
   Bartok Suite
   Engines of Resistance
   Excelcia
   Mystic Legacy
   The Torch Burns Bright
Elliot Del Borgo, *Modal Song and Dance*
David Holsinger, *Deerpath Dances*
John Kinyon, *Air and Dance*
Pierre La Plante, *Barn Dance Saturday Night*
Anne McGinty, *Kachina: Chant & Spirit Dance*
John O'Reilly, *Two English Dances*
Leroy Osmon, *Fanfare, Elegy and Dance*
Bruce Pearson:
   Ayre and Dance
   Renaissance Festival and Dances

Unit 9: Additional References and Resources

Bellson, Louis. *Modern Reading Text*. Melville, NY: Belwin Mills, 1963.

Cooper, Grosvenor, and Leonard B. Meyer. *The Rhythmic Structure of Music*. Chicago, IL: The University of Chicago Press, 1960.

Dvorak, Thomas L., Cynthia Crump Taggart, and Peter Schmalz. *Best Music for Young Band*. Edited by Bob Margolis. Brooklyn, NY: Manhattan Beach, 1986.

Froseth, James O. "Individualizing in the beginning instrumental music class." *Journal of Band Research* 6: 11-32, 1971.

Hickman, David R. *Music Speed Reading for Beginners*. Century City, CA: Trigram Music, 1993.

Kreines, Joseph. *Music for Concert Band*. Tampa, FL: Florida Music Service, 1989.

Contributed by:

John M. Laverty
Director of Bands
Syracuse University
Syracuse, New York

Teacher Resource Guide

Country Wildflowers
Larry Daehn
(b. 1939)

Unit 1: Composer

Born in Rosedale, Wisconsin, Larry Daehn received his bachelor's degree from the University of Wisconsin-Oshkosh and his master's degree from the University of Wisconsin-Platteville. As a public school teacher for thirty-five years, he has directed elementary through high school bands, including twenty-seven years at New Glarus High School, New Glarus, Wisconsin. An ardent Grainger scholar, Daehn pursued studies at the Grainger Museum in Melbourne, Australia. Since 1988, he has devoted his career energies to composing/arranging and publishing quality repertoire for wind band as owner of Daehn Publications.

Unit 2: Composition

The following notes accompany the conductor's score:

> This setting for concert band is loosely based on an old Scottish folk song, "In April, When Primroses Paint the Sweet Prairie," also known as "The Yellow-Hair'd Laddie." This song first appeared in *Mrs. Crokat's Manuscript Music Book* in 1709, and later in *The Tea-Table Miscellany* in 1725.

> With deepest affection, admiration and appreciation, Country Wildflowers is dedicated to my dear friends, Sally and Harvey Ott. Like spring and summer wildflowers, they make the world beautiful.

Unit 3: Historical Perspective

The folk song repertoire and traditions of the British Isles continue to be a rich source of engaging melodies destined to be set for wind band. Daehn's interest in the folk song tradition is no exception, and *Country Wildflowers* is one of a growing list of quality arrangements and compositions by Larry Daehn. Daehn's previous editions of Grainger's settings (*I'm Seventeen Come Sunday, Walking Tune,* and *Themes from "Green Bushes"*) were an attempt to "faithfully preserve the voicings and harmonies of the original." Similar in intent, *Country Wildflowers* retains the essence of the tune and harmonic character of the folk song within the musical and technical capabilities of young ensembles.

Unit 4: Technical Considerations

The lack of technical demands belies the simple beauty of this folk song setting. Accessible keys (B-flat and E-flat major), appropriate scoring, and limited range expectations create rewarding opportunities for expressive and artistic music making by inexperienced ensembles; yet this piece is worthy of performance by any musical organization. Except for the occasional dotted-eighth note figure and two *fermatas* with accompanying *caesuras*, there are no complex rhythmic patterns presented throughout the prevailing 3/4 meter.

Unit 5: Stylistic Considerations

The predominant *legato* and slurred articulations reinforce the *sostenuto* character of this work. Whether melody or accompaniment, each voice requires adherence to the singing quality of its line. Although Daehn has clearly marked those cadential points that "cry out" for a slowing of the pace, there remains ample opportunity for expressing the natural elasticity that will enhance the overall shape and direction of each voice.

Unit 6: Musical Elements

Country Wildflowers is scored for full concert band with divided parts in flute, clarinet, alto saxophone, trumpet, and trombone. The limited percussion parts of timpani, bells, triangle, and suspended cymbal are employed sparingly to enhance the altered textures of the ensemble. Daehn's setting explores a variety of timbral possibilities for thematic statements while providing enough contrapuntal interest in supportive voices. Dynamic indications are clearly marked and provide sufficient guidance regarding issues of balance. Replete with warm sonorities and engaging suspensions, *Country Wildflowers* presents excellent opportunities for expressive playing.

Unit 7: Form and Structure

SECTION	MEASURES	EVENT AND SCORING
A	1-8	First statement of Theme I by clarinet and horn supported by remainder of ensemble (except for flute, oboe, and trumpet)
B	9-16	B section begins with Theme II stated by flute and oboe accompanied by clarinet, saxophone, trumpet, and percussion; second half of Theme I returns with original accompaniment
B´	17-24	Exact repetition of B section except for dramatic conclusion that includes first *forte* dynamic with *fermata/caesura* and modulation to E-flat major
A	25-32	*Tutti* scoring with theme stated in flute, oboe, alto saxophone I, and trumpet (partially); overall dynamic level increased to *mezzo forte* and above; percussion voices play throughout
B´´	33-40	*Piano* dynamic returns with new statement of B section but with expanded instrumentation; continuation of previous melodic voice assignments
B´´´	41-48	Final climactic statement of B section, which brings work to peaceful *pianissimo* conclusion on a plagal cadence

Unit 8: Suggested Listening

John Barnes Chance, *Elegy*
Larry Daehn:
    As Summer Was Just Beginning
    Song for Friends
Percy Grainger, *Irish Tune from County Derry*
Clare Grundman:
    A Welsh Rhapsody
    English Suite
David Holsinger:
    On a Hymnsong of Philip Bliss
    On a Hymnsong of Lowell Mason

Pierre La Plante, *English Country Settings*
Ronald Lopresti, *Elegy for a Young American*
Frank Ticheli:
   Amazing Grace
   Shenandoah
Pavel Tschesnokoff/Houseknecht, *Salvation Is Created*

Unit 9: Additional References and Resources

"Basic Band Curriculum: Grades I, II, III." *BD Guide*, September/October 1989, 2-6.

Broadwood, Lucy. *English Traditional Songs and Carols*. London: Boosey & Co., n.d.

Daehn, Larry. Notes taken from conversations during February 2000.

Dvorak, Thomas L., Cynthia Crump Taggart, and Peter Schmalz. *Best Music for Young Band*. Edited by Bob Margolis. Brooklyn, NY: Manhattan Beach Music, 1986.

Randel, Don Michael, ed. *The New Harvard Dictionary of Music*. Cambridge, MA: Harvard University Press, 1996.

Rehrig, William H. Paul E. Bierley, ed. *The Heritage Encyclopedia of Band Music*. Westerville, OH: Integrity Press, 1991.

Slonimsky, Nicolas, ed. *Baker's Biographical Dictionary of Musicians*, 7th edition. New York, NY: Schirmer, 1984.

Contributed by:

Gordon R. Brock
Director of Bands
University of North Dakota
Grand Forks, North Dakota

Teacher Resource Guide

Court Festival

arranged by Bruce Pearson (b. 1942)
after William Byrd (1543–1623)

Unit 1: Composer/Arranger

Bruce Pearson is a world-renowned music educator, composer, and author. He is the author of the best-selling *Standard of Excellence Comprehensive Band Method*, which is regarded as an important contribution to the band music field. In addition, he is the author of the method *Best in Class* and the *Encore!* supplemental band study series. He is also co-author of the *Standard of Excellence Jazz Method* with Dean Sorenson. Pearson is an active composer and arranger, with numerous published works for beginning and intermediate band.

Pearson received his Bachelor of Science degree in Music Education from St. Cloud State University and his Master of Arts degree in Music Education from the University of Northern Colorado. He has over three decades of teaching experience at the elementary, junior high, high school, and college levels. During his 22-year tenure in Elk River, Minnesota, Pearson received numerous honors, including the Wenger's "Most Outstanding in the Field of Music Education" award for the state of Minnesota and two nominations for the prestigious "Excellence in Education" award. Pearson has also served as Director of Bands and Coordinator of Instrumental Studies at Northwestern College in St. Paul, Minnesota.

In addition to his work in the classroom, Pearson is a respected guest conductor, speaker, and adjudicator, having made appearances in Australia,

Canada, Finland, Great Britain, Holland, Hong Kong, Japan, Korea, Mexico, Norway, Singapore, Taiwan, and every state in the United States.

Pearson and his wife, Dee, currently live in Elk River, Minnesota, which is a part of the Minneapolis-St. Paul metropolitan area. A father of three with five grandchildren, he enjoys sports and outdoor activities of all types. He is also an active participant in local school, church, and community affairs.

Unit 2: Composition

Court Festival is an arrangement of the composition "The Earle of Oxford's Marche" by Renaissance composer William Byrd. Written in ABB form, the piece includes an introduction, an interlude, and a coda that features percussion. This composition is included in the *Standard of Excellence in Concert* series.

Unit 3: Historical Perspective

The study and performance of *Court Festival* presents unique teaching opportunities that introduce students to the Renaissance period. Expanded musical forms and harmonies, additional musical instruments, and greater uses of music are topics for study from this period. An introduction to music written for the virginal, which is the instrument William Byrd wrote his "The Earle of Oxford's Marche" for, is also appropriate. Other virginal composers of the Renaissance period who are worthy of study are John Bull and Orlando Gibson. In addition, major historical figures in the areas of the arts, inventions, discoveries, and philosophies flourished during this time, presenting opportunities for integrated arts study. Important figures include Leonardo da Vinci, Christopher Columbus, Queen Elizabeth I, and William Shakespeare.

Unit 4: Technical Considerations

The music is written in the key of E-flat concert. The tempo is to be held steady at approximately quarter note = 84 mm. Clear distinction between the four dynamic markings (*p, mp, mf, f*) should be heard. An unusual number of percussionists are required for performances. The six players are asked to play timpani, bells, finger cymbals, tambourine, hand drum, snare drum, and bass drum. Two snare drums and two bass drums are needed. The rhythmic structure is simple using quarter notes, half notes, and eighth notes. Ranges lend themselves to secure performance as the clarinets do not go above the break and trumpets are written within the staff no higher than C. Students are introduced to the concept of choirs or consorts. Trombones and trumpets are asked to use straight mutes.

Pearson writes of this arrangement:

> It is a wonderful vehicle to teach Renaissance dynamics known as terraced. I also attempted to capture the sounds of the ancient crumhorns and shawms through the use of muted brass. I also wanted

to have the three choirs (brass, woodwind, and percussion) be given the opportunity to perform as isolated choirs.

Unit 5: Stylistic Considerations

Lightness of articulation and exact rhythmic stability are the two most important issues to consider. The students will need a good aural model to grasp this mature, Renaissance keyboard articulation. The students will also need to experience their internal pulse to maintain a steady beat and a clearly defined subdivision of the beat.

Unit 6: Musical Elements

The harmonies are simple and triadic. The chord progression is logical with an occasional secondary dominant included. The prominent musical elements that have the greatest potential to inspire listeners are the style and rhythmic pulse.

Unit 7: Form and Structure

SECTION	MEASURES	EVENT AND SCORING
Introduction	1-4	Percussion only
A	5-8	Woodwinds
	9-12	Woodwinds and brass
	13-16	Woodwinds
	17-20	Woodwinds and brass
B	21-24	Woodwinds and brass
	25-28	Woodwinds
	29-32	Woodwinds and brass
Interlude	33-36	Percussion
	37-40	Muted brass
	41-44	Woodwinds
B	45-48	Muted brass
	49-52	Woodwinds
Coda	53-56	Percussion
	57-60	Woodwinds and brass
	61-64	Woodwinds and brass

Unit 8: Suggested Listening

William Byrd Suite, arranged by Gordon Jacob, British Band Classic CD,
    Tokyo Kosei Wind Orchestra, Frederick Fennell, Conductor
Renaissance Music, any recordings of Renaissance dances
    The pavanne and galliards were popular styles of the virginal composers.
    In addition to William Byrd, John Bull and Orlando Gibson were
    Renaissance composers for the virginal.

Unit 9: Additional References and Resources

Fennell, Frederick. "William Byrd Suite." *The Instrumentalist*, 30 September, 1975.

Fuller, A.J., and William Barclay Squire, eds. *The Fitzwilliam Virginal Book*. Mineola, NY: Dover Publications, Volumes I and II, 1963.

A special "Teacher Resource Guide" is included with the published score and parts. The contributing editor for the Teacher Resource Guide is Wendy Barden. Information in Unit 7 is derived from the Teacher Resource Guide. The Teacher Resource Guide also includes warm-ups appropriate for this composition and lessons that address each of the National Standards.

Contributed by:

Richard Greenwood
Director of Bands
University of Central Florida
Orlando, Florida

Teacher Resource Guide

Glorioso

Robert W. Smith
(b. 1958)

Unit 1: Composer

Robert W. Smith received his Bachelor of Music Education degree from Troy State University and his Master of Music degree from the University of Miami. He is currently Director of Bands at Troy State University. With over 300 publications to his credit, he is one of the most prolific composers of concert band literature today. He has been awarded numerous commissions from ensembles of all levels, including middle school and high school bands, as well as university and professional military bands. His symphony entitled *The Divine Comedy* has received worldwide critical acclaim. As a conductor and clinician, Smith has performed throughout the United States, Canada, Japan, and the United Kingdom. He is an elected member of the American Bandmasters Association.

Unit 2: Composition

Glorioso, subtitled "A Fanfare and Procession for Band," is a single-movement work written specifically for younger bands. The title is derived from the word "glory," which means to rejoice triumphantly or to exult. This exciting and dynamic monothematic piece is fifty-nine measures long and is suitable for the opening of a concert or festive occasion. Further, it would serve as an excellent introduction to the fanfare style. The publisher is Belwin-Mills Publishing Corporation, a division of Warner Brothers Publications, Inc. The piece is approximately one minute and forty-five seconds in length.

Unit 3: Historical Perspective

The word "fanfare" is a French term for a military or civilian brass band or a short tune for trumpet or horn. Historically, fanfares have been used to announce the arrival of royalty or as a signal for ceremonial, military, or hunting purposes. The melodies of fanfares generally consist of a few notes, primarily the tones of the major triad. The early fanfares were originally intended for natural brass instruments on which only a single note and its overtones were available. Numerous composers have used fanfares in program music (music that tells a story), operas, etc.

Unit 4: Technical Considerations

Listed in the publishers' beginning band series, *Glorioso* is scored for standard beginning band instrumentation and offers young players few technical difficulties. The composition employs much doubling of parts, the *tessitura* is appropriate for all instruments, and the clarinet part does not cross the break. Rhythmically, the work includes no rhythm smaller than eighth notes. The main teaching elements are the use of accents, slurs, *staccato* markings, a brisk tempo of quarter note = 152, and the balancing of the *marcato* and lyrical statements. This work, with a single continual thematic idea, is in B-flat major with few accidentals.

The percussion part is active and will offer interest to young percussionists. It includes parts for bells, snare and bass drums, crash and suspended cymbals, triangle, sleigh bells, and timpani.

Unit 5: Stylistic Considerations

Because the work is a fanfare and procession, careful attention should be directed to a unified articulation style. Clarity is essential in the *marcato* style, and all accented half notes should be observed and emphasized with breath and space, not tongue. Dynamic levels range from *mezzo forte* to *fortissimo*, although the lyrical sections marked *mezzo forte* could be performed at *mezzo piano* for greater contrast. The tempo marking of quarter note = 152 may provide young performers with the challenge of maintaining tempo and intensity. The use of a metronome in rehearsal would be helpful. It should be noted that there are no indications for the piece to "slip" into cut time. Providing listening opportunities of other fanfares would be an important element in teaching this style.

Unit 6: Musical Elements

While this composition is a monothematic work, there is much to learn for young players.

MELODY:
The melody is a symmetrical period, which is a combination of phrases that end in a final cadence. There are four phrases in the period and they are presented

three times, joined together by transitional *staccato* material. The melody is firmly in B-flat major with use of an A-flat. The first presentation of the melody is in a fanfare style with brass doubled in saxophones. It is rhythmically augmented from the next two periods. Both the second and third presentations use two lyrical phrases followed by two accented phrases. This variety affords the teacher an opportunity to teach effective contrasts in articulation and dynamics with a beginning discussion of phrase shaping and development.

HARMONY:
Basic harmonic progressions are utilized, enabling the students to firmly identify with the tonic-dominant chordal relationships. As an exercise, have the students listen and sing the tuba part at measure 38, helping them identify the tonic-dominant sound (of which they are well versed by daily pop music). This exercise will enable the students to begin the concept of listening to and for other parts, beginning the process of balance and blend. Discussion should also focus on texture, which in this work is homophonic. Have students collectively play the melody in unison (by memory, *National Standards for Arts Education*, Standard 3A) to demonstrate monophonic versus homophonic sounds.

RHYTHM:
Minimal demands are placed on the students in this work, with no note length smaller than an eighth note. The challenge may be in the brisk tempo. Rehearse with a metronome, insisting upon good tempo integrity. Clarity of articulation will be the key.

TIMBRE:
The focus on timbre in *Glorioso* will center around blend and balance. In the fanfare section, work for good balance between the trumpets, horns, and trombones. At measure 19, the flutes and saxophones will find it necessary to stay below (dynamically) the melodic instruments. Shaping phrases will also help balance. At measure 34, the brass should *diminuendo* to allow the lyrical woodwind melody to soar. With careful instructional techniques, students can learn to blend and balance at an early age.

Unit 7: Form and Structure

PERIOD	MEASURES	EVENT AND SCORING
1	1-8	Introduction; fanfare theme in rhythmic augmentation
	9-14	Woodwinds added to brass fanfare
	15-18	Woodwind transitional material
2	19-26	*Legato* theme in alto voices
	27-33	Accented theme in brass
	34-37	Brass transitional material

PERIOD	MEASURES	EVENT AND SCORING
3	38-45	*Legato* theme in woodwinds
	46-53	Accented theme in brass
	54-59	Coda
ERRATA:		
	33	Trumpet part, quarter note on count four should be B-natural, not B-flat

Unit 8: Suggested Listening

Leo Arnaud, *Three Fanfares*

Aaron Copland, *Fanfare for the Common Man*

Paul Dukas, *Fanfare pour preceder "La peri"*

Morton Gould, *Fanfare for Freedom*

Ron Nelson, *Fanfare for the Hour of Sunrise*

Jack Stamp, *Fanfare for the Great Hall*

Joan Tower, *Fanfare for the Uncommon Woman No. 1*

Clifton Williams, *Fanfare and Allegro*

Ralph Vaughan Williams:
> *Flourish for Glorious John*
> *Flourish for Wind Band*

Unit 9: Additional References and Resources

Ammer, Christine. *Harper's Dictionary of Music*. New York, NY: Barnes & Noble Books. 1972.

Dvorak, Thomas L., Robert Grechesky, and Gary Ciepluch. *Best Music for High School Band*. Bob Margolis, ed. Brooklyn, NY: Manhattan Beach Music, 1993.

Dvorak, Thomas L., Cynthia Crump Taggart, and Peter Schmalz. *Best Music for Young Band*. Bob Margolis, ed. Brooklyn, NY: Manhattan Beach Music, 1986.

Fontaine, Paul. *Basic Formal Structures in Music*. New York, NY: Meredith Corporation, 1967.

Miles, Richard, ed. *Teaching Music through Performance in Band*, Volume 2. Chicago, IL: GIA Publications, Inc., 1998.

Randel, Don Michael, ed. *Harvard Concise Dictionary of Music*. Cambridge, MA: The Belknap Press of Harvard University Press, 1978.

Contributed by:
Richard Anthony Murphy
Director of Bands
Middle Tennessee State University
Murfreesboro, Tennessee

Teacher Resource Guide

Hotaru Koi

arranged by Nancy Fairchild
(b. 1962)

Unit 1: Composer/Arranger

Nancy Fairchild teaches elementary general music and beginning band in the Platteville, Wisconsin public schools. She received a Bachelor of Science from the University of Wisconsin-Platteville and a Master of Science from the University of Illinois at Urbana-Champagne. She is currently President of the Wisconsin Youth Band Directors Association.

In addition to the many demands of elementary school teaching, Fairchild remains active as a composer and arranger of music for young bands. In her work, she often seeks to introduce students to new performance styles or techniques, including chanting, singing, drumming, and poetry recitation. Recent works include the original composition *Brown Sugar* for beginning band and *Obwisana*, a Ghanaian children's game song arranged for band and Orff instruments (and even optional game players).

Unit 2: Composition

This arrangement of *Hotaru Koi* was originally written in 1990 as part of a course in elementary classroom music teaching.[1] Fairchild heard the song presented and sung by the instructor, noted authority on multicultural music teaching Patricia Shehan Campbell, and immediately realized its potential as an instrumental selection. The arrangement was published in 1996.

Hotaru Koi is a short, single-movement piece offering four statements of a simple melody in two contrasting settings. Extensive doubling provides teachers with opportunities to include further contrasts among sections, between instrument families, or between vocal and instrumental presentations. The duration is published as three minutes and ten seconds but may be extended through inclusion of additional repeats.

This piece may be performed successfully by ensembles with limited instrumentation. Most of the arrangement calls for unison wind playing. In the final section, unison melodic duties are assigned to flute, oboe, first and second clarinet, alto saxophone, and first and second trumpet. (First and second clarinet and trumpet parts are identical.) A pedal is provided by bass clarinet, tenor saxophone, and horn. The bass line is carried by the baritone saxophone, trombone, baritone, bassoon, and tuba.

Unit 3: Historical Perspective

The Bon Odori festival, observed in mid-August throughout Japan, celebrates the return of ancestors' souls to earth.[2] It remains one of the few occasions when citizens all across the country don traditional summer dress. Music plays a central role in this festival as clearly evidenced by the prominent Taiko drum commanding the center of each town's festival stage. As evening descends, adults tend to their own music- and merry-making while the children run off in search of their own fun which, on warm summer nights, often includes chasing fireflies.

As its name, "Ho, Firefly," suggests, *Hotaru Koi* is a children's song commonly sung while in pursuit of these twinkling summer visitors. The song is thought to have originated in Akita prefecture in the northern part of Japan. The translation provided by the publisher is given as

> Ho! Ho! Ho, firefly!
> Bitter water you will find on that side.
> Sweet water you will find on this side.
> Ho! Ho! Ho, firefly! Through the mountain road.
> Come, come again with your little lantern bright.

The exclamation "Ho!" is not a laugh. It is a nonsense syllable meant to entice the firefly toward the singer, an enticement further sweetened by the subsequent lyric.

Unit 4: Technical Considerations

Technical challenges are limited in this arrangement, though students will confront several new musical demands. For wind players, the range is well within reach of virtually every beginning player. Only four pitches are used in the wind parts: concert B-flat, D-flat, E-flat, and F. It will probably be necessary to introduce concert D-flat to the wind students. Similarly, the xylophone players may be unfamiliar with the G-flat that appears in their part. Fortunately, the familiar pitches surrounding these new notes along with the very accessible rhythmic context should facilitate quick success. There is little need to wait until these two pitches are introduced in the students' method series before approaching this piece.

Percussionists will be required to play both pitched and non-pitched instruments, including bells, xylophone, high and low tenor drums, triangle, and Japanese gong. Parts are largely independent and include several exposed passages, including an eight-measure percussion interlude mid-way through the piece.

For teachers who choose to include a sung verse, a final technical consideration must be linguistic accuracy. While the syllabic transliteration provided on each of the instrument parts can serve as a helpful guide, it would be important to seek out an aural model to assist with proper pronunciation. A spoken model is available on CD from the publisher. Better yet, involving a Japanese-speaking member of the band, faculty, or community would offer students a valuable educational interaction.

Unit 5: Stylistic Considerations

As with many children's songs, *Hotaru Koi* should reflect both energy and buoyancy. Articulation should be crisp but light. The percussion should keep the momentum pushing ahead. Two particular aspects of this piece make achieving this light style difficult. First, the many sustained pitches that appear in the melody and accompaniment tend to add weight to the performance. Second, the half rests that appear within the melodic subphrases—the "Ho! Ho!" phrase, specifically—tend to interrupt the forward momentum of the song.

These difficulties may be overcome by working for clean releases that lift away from the notes (rather than taper and extend the decay) and by shortening the longer notes—releasing half notes and whole notes on the front side of the second and fourth counts, respectively. A second (and complementary) solution would be to work toward the usual performance tempo of the song. Children tend to sing this song in a cut time feel at approximately half note = 100 rather than the given quarter note = 126.

Unit 6: Musical Elements

MELODY:
The melody is very limited in pitch content, including only concert E-flat, B-flat, D-flat, and F. Nevertheless, it does present several interesting musical challenges to the young performers. First, each large phrase of the melody consists of three subphrases rather than a more familiar two or four. For students who may be expecting a typical western antecedent-consequent (usually dominant-tonic) relationship between phrases, the melody demands that the musical "thought" continue over four additional measures:

phrase 1

subphrases: 1   2   2a

phrase 2

subphrases: 1a   3   4

Second, as seen in the figure above, there is very little repetition across the entire 22-measure melody. Of the six subphrases, only two appear more than once. Given that each melodic segment contains, at most, four different pitches, students' attention will need to be directed to the small but significant differences among the segments.

HARMONY:

The tonal center of this piece is clearly E-flat. While the G-flat in the xylophone part gives the song a distinctly "minor" character, it would not be appropriate to say that the piece is actually in E-flat minor. It is, instead, strictly modal, employing an E-flat–F–G-flat–B-flat–D-flat pentatonic pitch set. Pentatonic modes such as this are a common feature of traditional music throughout much of East and Southeast Asia.

Rather than providing harmonic information, the printed key signature (two flats) is included only to maintain consistency between students' parts and corresponding exercises in their method books.

RHYTHM:

Rhythms in the wind and pitched percussion parts include only whole, half, and quarter notes. The bell and xylophone *ostinatos* (to which are added low woodwinds and low brass in the coda) are, by nature, very repetitive. It will be important to teach the performers strategies for counting repeated measures.

Eighth note patterns are introduced in the percussion interlude, an eight-measure section that layers several challenging rhythm patterns. In the score notes, Fairchild offers a series of spoken syllable patterns (often used by musicians in Japan) to be used as mnemonic aids in performing these more complex passages.

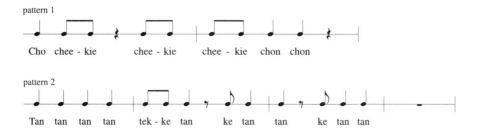

pattern 1

Cho chee - kie   chee - kie   chee - kie   chon chon

pattern 2

Tan   tan   tan   tan   tek - ke tan   ke tan   tan   ke tan tan

pattern 3

To - ro - ro

When teaching the piece to her own students, Fairchild begins by rote-teaching the spoken rhythm patterns to the entire ensemble. Performances would ultimately include these chants along with the percussion playing.

TIMBRE:

The sound of drumming characterizes much Japanese festive music. Where the score calls for high and low tenor drums, it would be appropriate to find instruments that provide a rich, resonant tone rather than the more familiar "tom-tom" character. Similarly, the high, piercing quality of wood on wood is also featured in much of Japan's music making. Even several children's game songs include accompaniment by woodblocks or large pairs of wooden sticks. While this arrangement calls for drumstick clicks, it would be desirable to again feature a deeper wooden timbre.

Unit 7: Form and Structure

The form of this arrangement is generally strophic, with a percussion interlude at the mid-point and a textural variation of the melody in the coda. To increase the challenge for the performers or to highlight particular sections of the ensemble, two alternative performance options are included; others are certainly possible.

			PERFORMANCE OPTIONS		
SECTION	MEASURES	EVENT	OPTION 1	OPTION 2	OPTION 3
A	1-2	Ostinato	Percussion		
	3-14	First phrase	Unison winds	Unison winds	Sung with percussion accompaniment
	15-24	Second phrase	Unison winds	Unison winds	Sung with percussion accompaniment
A	1-2	Ostinato	Percussion		
	3-14	First phrase	Woodwinds	Sung with percussion accompaniment	Unison winds
	15-24	Second phrase	Woodwinds	Sung with percussion accompaniment	Unison winds

SECTION	MEASURES	EVENT	PERFORMANCE OPTIONS		
			OPTION 1	OPTION 2	OPTION 3
B	25-26	Ostinato	Percussion (with ensemble chanting)		
	27-34	Interlude			
A	1-2	Ostinato			
	3-14	First phrase	Brass	Unison winds	Woodwinds
	15-24	Second phrase	Brass	Unison winds	Brass
A′	35-36	Ostinato	Percussion		
	37-48	First phrase	Full ensemble		
	49-58	Second phrase			

Unit 8: Suggested Listening

Libana, "Hotaru Koi." In *The Fire Within*. Ladyslipper LR108CD, 1990. Compact disc.

Ogura, Ro, arr. *Hotaru Koi* (for SSA choir). Bryn Mawr, PA: Theodore Presser, 1987.

Unit 9: Additional References and Resources

Higuchi, Sachiko. *101 Favorite Songs Taught in Japanese Schools*. Essay and translation by Ichiro Nakano. Tokyo: Japan Times, 1983.

Kuo-Huang, Han, Ricardo D. Trimillos, William M. Anderson, and Tatsuko Takizawa. "Music of East Asia." In *Multicultural Perspectives in Music Education*, 2nd edition. ed. William M. Anderson and Patricia Shehan Campbell, 308-348. Reston, VA: MENC, 1996.

Contributed by:

Steven J. Morrison
Assistant Professor of Music
University of Washington
Seattle, Washington

---

1 Nancy Fairchild generously provided information on the development of this arrangement as well as many suggestions regarding the teaching of this piece to young instrumentalists (interview with the author, 26 January 2000).

2 The author gratefully acknowledges Akiko McCartney, a student at the University of Washington, for sharing her knowledge and her own memories of the musical and social traditions of Japan.

Teacher Resource Guide

Hungarian Folkround
Robert Garofalo (b. 1939)
and
Garwood Whaley (b. 1942)

Unit 1: Composers

Robert Garofalo is currently Professor of Music and guides the graduate programs in conducting at Catholic University of America in Washington, DC. A native of Pennsylvania, he holds a Bachelor of Science degree from Mansfield University as well as Master of Music and Doctor of Philosophy degrees from the Catholic University. Originally a trombone major, Garofalo's conducting associations indicate a wide and varied interest in the wind band, its history, and music education. He conducted Heritage Americana from 1978 to 1988 and specialized in recreating authentic Civil War-era brass band music on the original instruments. From 1989 to 1993, Garofalo conducted a professional ensemble, Eternal Winds, which performed music from a broad spectrum of style periods. He is an important author of books and articles concerning instrumental music education, including *Guides to Masterworks and Guide to Score Study* (co-authored with Frank Battisti).

Garwood Whaley is a native of Dobbs Ferry, New York. He received his bachelor's degree from the Juilliard School of Music. He received his Master of Music from the Catholic University of America while serving six years performing in the United States Army (Pershing's Own) Band in Washington, DC. Whaley currently serves as Director of Bands at Bishop Ireton High School in Alexandria, Virginia, working in some capacity with that program since 1966. A percussionist of international note, he joined *Music for*

Percussion, Inc. in 1979 as chief editor, which was the same year he formed Meredith Music Publications, of which he is president and owner.

Unit 2: Composition

Hungarian Folkround, composed in 1981 as a series of creative pieces and published in 1985 by Meredith Music, is an ideal piece for the first-year band. The composers wanted to create teaching works that included a wide variety of learning opportunities for young ensembles. The work, approximately three minutes and thirty seconds in length, includes two Hungarian folk songs from various collections. The inside cover of the score includes suggestions for teaching and performing the work, such as audience participation and multi-cultural ideas such as clapping, singing, and dancing. Interdisciplinary opportunities that enhance this work combine with physical education and social studies. Limited *tessituras* and extensive doubling allow this piece to work for most young ensembles.

Unit 3: Historical Perspective

Eastern European countries, Hungary in particular, provide a wealth of folk song material in the twentieth century based upon harmonic materials and rhythms that are highly dance-oriented. Kodaly, Bartok, and Dvorak are well-known composers who drew from their heritage to write major instrumental works, and this continues as composers find that Eastern European melodies have a certain grasp on the listeners' imagination. As the Eastern Bloc countries gained their independence in the 1980s, students could easily identify compositions with ideals of that period and make the connection between current events and musical ideas. The accessibility of the Hungarian music makes the folk songs used in *Hungarian Folkround* particularly appealing for cross-cultural studies.

Unit 4: Technical Considerations

Hungarian Folkround is programmable for ensembles completing the first method book successfully. Eighth note figures and dotted-quarter/eighth note rhythms are the most complex counting skills required for performance. While the key signature indicates C minor, a great deal of the piece uses accidentals to allow the melodic material to maintain a modal feel indigenous with Eastern European dance music. Accidental recognition is key. In terms of range, the clarinet part is *divisi* in sections, so not all students must play over the break. However, performance does require this in the first part, while the second part must be capable of independent lines, such as at measure 17. Range and instrumentation considerations include flute/oboe (C above the staff/G above the staff), first and second clarinet (fourth line D/second space A), alto saxophone (A above the staff), first and second trumpet (fourth line D/third line B-flat), horn in F (third space C), trombone (C above the staff), and low reed/low brass (heavily doubled and adjusted octaves). A highly active percussion section is a delight. Instrumentation includes bells, triangle, tambourine, snare drum, tenor drum, bass drum, and suspended cymbal. The writing seems to be open to additional instruments (since the winds have clapping parts) that could allow for improvisation. The phrases are fairly short and in 2/4 time, so sustained figures are not a problem. Students should have an understanding of *poco ritardando*, *fermata*, and *Fine*; if not, these are clearly defined by the composers on the inside of the score cover as reminders of discussion topics. The entire second folk melody section is repeated, so repeat sign recognition is also necessary.

Unit 5: Stylistic Considerations

The tempo for *Hungarian Folkround* is marked "*moderato*" with a section that is "a little faster" at rehearsal letter C. Articulations are a major part of this piece, and the composers have included detailed reminders of *legato*, *marcato*, *staccato*, and *tenuto*. This is a wonderful piece for contrasting articulations, as there are situations where more than one articulation is indicated at the same time. Dynamics range from *mezzo piano* to *fortissimo*, and while not marked, there are plenty of opportunities for discussion about reinforcing the contour of both the melodic line and harmonic figures. Contrary to articulations, motion is quite homophonic with very few independent lines. This is countered by the opportunity to perform the folkround melody in its rounded form. There is a glossary of terms, as well as the folkround melody, on each part so students may study and perform all of the important aspects of the work.

Unit 6: Musical Elements

MELODY:

The first of two folk melodies, found in measure 17, has the Phrygian mode as its scale pattern. This is a good opportunity to discuss modes and scales and how these patterns are affected by accidentals. Initially outlining the fifth and first scale degrees, the melody is a good study of jump versus skip in the melodic line and how that may determine air flow and, in turn, dynamics. Of interest is how this line creates harmonic interest against the open fifths in the accompaniment.

The second folk melody is written on all parts, complete with the indication of when entrances should occur. This is the perfect chance to explain and demonstrate how rounds work to create harmonic interest. One suggestion is to have students compose and perform their own rounds, which reinforces that component of the National Standards consisting of improvisation and composition. Written within the framework of one octave, this melody is accessible to young and old voices alike, and incorporating the singing allows the students to adapt that approach to their playing.

HARMONY:

The harmonies are simply orchestrated, and the open fifths and octaves allow for work on tuning issues. Scalar motion often creates the harmonic interest, and this is best demonstrated in measure 101. To reinforce the pedal points and the concept of listening down through the ensemble, consider stopping at cadence points and having the ensemble sing the bass note.

RHYTHM:

Rhythmic issues in the performance of *Hungarian Folkround* will include avoiding the tendency to rush. This piece works very well for teaching young players to identify the eighth note subdivision in the ensemble, and the percussion is highly integrated in this area. Rhythm in the accompaniment creates much of the direction in the low winds, and concentration in this area for those instruments is critical. Students can understand the concept of rhythmic augmentation by comparing measures 37 through 39 with measures 45 through 48, or comparing measures 103 and 104 with the coda.

TIMBRE:

Treble voices usually double in *Hungarian Folkround* on the melody, although at measure 65 there is a chance to allow the students to listen for the change in color when the trumpet has a counterline at that point followed by doubling of the melody at measure 73. The stark parallel fifths in the introduction have as much effect at measure 33 when added voices and lines create new harmonies. Also, compare the dark sounds of the Phrygian mode used in the first melody to the Ionian mode, or major key center, for the second melody.

Unit 7: Form and Structure

SECTION	MEASURES	EVENT AND SCORING
Introduction	1-8	Clarinet and horn establish pedal on the Phrygian fifth degree
	9-16	Trombone and low woodwinds enter to reinforce fifth and add the Phrygian root
Section I	17-32	First clarinet and alto saxophone introduce the first strain of the initial folk melody in the Phrygian mode
	33-48	Second statement of the first strain with trumpet and bells entering on the second count to reinforce the melody
	49-64	Flute enters for the first time to introduce the second strain in Phrygian mode with a countermelody in clarinet

SECTION	MEASURES	EVENT AND SCORING
	65-80	Ensemble continues to add to the second statement of the second strain, building and reinforcing the line
Bridge	81-84	Full ensemble in modal transition to major (this is a good time to introduce the Picardy third)
Introduction	85-92	Entire ensemble performs rhythmic introduction with woodwinds clapping
Section II	93-100	Flute, oboe, first clarinet, and alto saxophone present first strain of the second folk song, reinforcing the singing in the low woodwinds in C major
	101-108	Trumpets perform the second strain melody, reinforcing the singing that now occurs in the woodwinds
	85-108	Ensemble repeats
Coda	109-112	Augmentation of mm. 103-104

Unit 8: Suggested Listening

Bela Bartok, *Dance Suite*

Elliot Del Borgo, *Modal Song and Dance*

Antonin Dvorak, *Slavonic Dances*

Robert Garofalo/Garwood Whaley, *Ahrirang*

Zoltan Kodaly, *Hary Janos Suite*

Bedrich Smetana:

   The Bartered Bride

   The Moldau

Tielman Susato/arr. Bob Margolis, *The Battle Pavane*

Unit 9: Additional References and Resources

"The Basic Band Curriculum: Grades I, II, III." *BD Guide*, September/October 1989, 2-6.

Garafalo, Robert J., and Garwood Whaley. "Hungarian Folkround," Score, 1985, Personal Collection, Rod M. Chesnutt, Mississippi State University, Mississippi State, MS.

Garafalo, Robert J. *Instructional Designs for Middle/Junior High School Band*. Fort Lauderdale, FL: Meredith Publications, 1995.

Kvet, Edward, ed. *Instructional Literature for Middle-Level Band*. Reston, VA: Music Educators National Conference, 1996.

Music Educators National Conference, Committee on Performance Standards. *Performance Standards for Music*. Reston, VA: Music Educators National Conference, 1996.

Pearson, Bruce. *Standard of Excellence*, book 1. San Diego, CA: Neil A. Kjos Music Company, 1993.

Rhodes, Tom C., Donald Bierschenk, and Tim Lautzenheiser. *Essential Elements: A Comprehensive Band Method*. Milwaukee, WI: Hal Leonard Publishing Corporation, 1991.

Whaley, Garwood, composer and owner of Meredith Music Publishers. Interview by author, February 2000, Bishop Ireton High School, Alexandria, Virginia. Phone conversation. Mississippi State University, Mississippi.

Contributed by:
Rod M. Chesnutt
Director of Bands
Mississippi State University
Mississippi State, Mississippi

Teacher Resource Guide

Imaginary Soundscape No. 2
Elliot Del Borgo
(b. 1938)

Unit 1: Composer

Elliot Del Borgo was born in Port Chester, New York, in 1938. He received degrees from the State University of New York, Temple University, and the Philadelphia Conservatory, where he studied theory with Vincent Persichetti and trumpet with Gilbert Johnson. Del Borgo taught instrumental music in the Philadelphia public schools for five years before joining the faculty at the Crane School of Music in Potsdam, New York, from 1965 to 1995.

An award-winning member of ASCAP, Del Borgo is an active consultant, clinician, lecturer, and adjudicator. In addition to his works for band, he also composes extensively for orchestra, chorus, and chamber groups.

It is the sincere desire of the composer that band directors select literature for their bands that will achieve appropriate artistic goals. Del Borgo believes these pieces should contain all the aspects of quality music.

Unit 2: Composition

Imaginary Soundscape No. 2 was composed at the request of Warner Brothers Publications; the only prerequisite was that the piece be written for beginning band. This freed Del Borgo to write a contemporary piece for the young ensemble using his discretion as to style and complexity. The challenges in this piece include the use of polyrhythms in the percussion and non-traditional harmonic language in the winds (described in Unit 6).

The compositional idea stems from a series of paintings based on "Imaginary Landscapes" by early twentieth century painter Paul Klee. Del Borgo felt that a similar contribution could be made to the band medium. His original *Imaginary Soundscape* was composed for percussion ensemble and contains far more technical complexity than its full band sequel. Works also based on this idea are John Cage's *Imaginary Landscape Nos. 1-5* and *An Imaginary Landscape* by Harrison Birtwistle.

Unit 3: Historical Perspective

Paul Klee (1879-1940) was one of the great colorists of the twentieth century. At the age of thirty-four, Klee stopped writing and composing to become an artist. He began studying by himself and working as a graphic artist in Munich. Constantly striving for personal artistic maturity, he explored every medium of the art world, including drawing, sculpturing, and painting. Klee found his greatest success in water colors, where his graphic artistry combined with his stark use of color to earn him acceptance from fellow artists, critics, and the general public.

Unit 4: Technical Considerations

Imaginary Soundscape No. 2 was written and scored for young players. Many of the parts are doubled, and each section is given exposure at some time during the piece. Clarinet and trumpet parts are written independent of the other parts of the ensemble. The bells are paired with the flutes or the trumpets, while the rest of the percussion are used to create a continuous rhythmic texture.

There are eight percussion instruments playing polyrhythms for much of the piece. These parts form *ostinatos* that create interest and give rhythmic stability to the work. Instrumentation is normal for young bands, and if a percussion instrument is missing, timbre should be considered when making a substitution.

The note ranges for each part are flute, oboe, alto saxophone, tenor saxophone, and baritone saxophone from F to F (written pitch) on the staff; clarinet from low E to B-flat on the staff; trumpet and horn from C below the staff to C on the staff; low woodwinds from B-flat (bass clef) on the staff to B-flat above the staff; and tuba from B-flat below the staff to B-flat on the staff.

Unit 5: Stylistic Considerations

The tempo of this piece remains "Moderately," with quarter note = 132 throughout. The composer stresses the importance of treating every phrase with musical integrity while teaching musicianship.

Del Borgo does not write long slur marks in the music to show phrasing. Instead, he gives dynamic markings and writes in *crescendos* and *decrescendos* at specific points. The true phrasing of the composition is easy to recognize in the score and often lies in an eight- or ten-measure format.

Dynamics for each part range from *pianissimo* to *fortissimo*; much of the time they are *mezzo forte* or *forte*. Accents are used in all parts, especially in the percussion. For a few measures, "*marc.*" (*marcato*) is written in the wood-wind parts. This is the only stylistic marking that the composer gives apart from the tempo, dynamics, and notated accents.

Unit 6: Musical Elements

Imaginary Soundscape No. 2 is a rhythmically and harmonically driven piece. Del Borgo's intent was to acclimate young players to the compositional techniques of modern composers. There is a melodic motive that travels through the piece, but the true interest of the composition lies in Del Borgo's use of rhythm and harmony.

The melody, a short motive displayed fully at measure 50, relates to the harmonic minor scale. Del Borgo accommodates young players by writing in the closely related keys of F minor, G minor, D minor, and B-flat major. This piece does not have a key signature; it only has accidentals in each part.

The harmonies to these motives are varied and range from major, triadic harmony to quintal and cluster chords. Del Borgo's harmonic language for this piece incorporates linear chordal writing in the woodwinds and bells over multiple rhythmic devices in the percussion.

Every woodwind part must be counted carefully. Though the woodwind rhythms are written simplistically, there are several *tutti* cluster chords played with quarter note rhythms and rests.

The percussion parts are written using subdivisions down to sixteenth notes while making use of eight different instruments.

At measure 44, the band plays a three-part contrapuntal section. The clarinets, alto saxophones, and horns play unison rhythms on concert E, while the upper and lower woodwinds play a four-note, F minor *ostinato* pattern based on the harmonic minor motive. That *ostinato* is played in half, quarter, and eighth notes until measure 50. The third element, a contrasting G minor motive in the oboe and trumpet, enters above this texture at measure 48.

The final seven measures of this piece are traditionally written with triadic, major harmonies.

Unit 7: Form and Structure

The overall form of *Imaginary Soundscape No. 2* resembles a ternary form with a coda. The *da Capo* is what generates the form of the composition. The piece, approximately three minutes in length, flows from phrase to phrase as a display of textures, rhythms, and harmonies.

FORM	MEASURES	EVENT AND SCORING
A	1-8	Flute and clarinet centered on F minor with percussion accompaniment
	9-16	*Tutti* with melodic fragments in flute and oboe, or trumpet in F minor

FORM	MEASURES	EVENT AND SCORING
	17-20	Four-measure rhythmic transition; winds in cluster harmony (quintal chords)
2 times to coda	21-30	Low woodwinds play G minor melody with rhythmic
B	31-38	Staggered wind entrances with melody in bells
	39-43	*Tutti* rhythm on cluster chord
	44-49	Three-part contrapuntal writing
	50-55	*Tutti* F minor motive with growing dissonance
da Capo coda	56-end	Replaying of melodic motive in traditional harmony

Unit 8: Suggested Listening

For band:
>Elliot Del Borgo:
>>*Adagio for Winds*
>>*Britannic Variants*
>>*Canterbury Overture*
>>*Do Not Go Gentle into that Good Night*
>>*Parable Symphonic Paraphrase*

For orchestra:
>Elliot Del Borgo:
>>*Romany Dances*
>>*Songs Before Sunrise*
>>*Songs of the Sea*

Works by Bela Bartok:
>The composer suggests that his biggest musical influence is Bela Bartok. He admires Bartok's contrapuntal writing, complexity of rhythm, and use of percussion.

Unit 9: Additional References and Resources

Del Borgo, Elliot. "More Views on Choosing Music." *The Instrumentalist*, Volume 52, No. 12 (July 1998): 15.

Klee, Paul. *Paul Klee*. Edited by Caroline Lancher. Boston, MA: Little Brown and Company, 1987.

Rehrig, William H. *The Heritage Encyclopedia of Band Music*. Edited by Paul E. Bierley. Westerville, OH: Integrity Press, 1991.

Also visit the Internet at:
www.curnowmusic.com/elliot.htm
www.meredithmusic.com/bios1.html

Contributed by:
Matthew J. Seifert
Graduate Conducting Intern
Louisiana State University
Baton Rouge, Louisiana

Teacher Resource Guide

Imperium
Michael Sweeney
(b. 1952)

Unit 1: Composer

Michael Sweeney is a graduate of Indiana University at Bloomington, Indiana, where he studied music education. In addition, he studied composition with Bernard Heiden, John Eaton, and Donald Erb. While at Indiana, he contributed compositions and arrangements to the jazz ensembles and marching band. As an arranger, he has written for many top college and high school bands across the country. Sweeney taught five years in the public schools of Ohio and Indiana, where his teaching experience included working with successful concert, jazz, and marching programs at all levels from elementary to high school.

Since 1982, Sweeney has worked full time for Hal Leonard Corporation in Milwaukee, Wisconsin. Hal Leonard is currently the largest publisher of printed music in the world. In his present position as Instrumental Product Manager, Sweeney is directly responsible for development, production, and marketing of new publications for jazz ensemble and marching band. He is particularly known for his writing at the younger levels for concert band and jazz. Since 1982, Hal Leonard has published over 400 of Sweeney's compositions and arrangements for concert, jazz, and marching band. His composition, *Ancient Voices*, is included in *Teaching Music through Performance in Band*, Volume 1.

Unit 2: Composition

This composition was written in 1992 and is built on a three-note melodic motif (concert G, F, and A-flat). The intervals of M2, m3, and m2 make up a majority of the thematic and accompanying materials found in the work. As in most other works by Sweeney, the percussion writing is important and colorful.

Some non-traditional harmonies (dissonances) are found within the chords. This 75-measure work, published by Hal Leonard Corporation, is at the Grade 1 1/2 level and has a performance time of two minutes and thirty seconds.

Unit 3: Historical Perspective

Imperium is a twentieth century educational band work. The work sounds somewhat stereotypical of the static rhythms and harmonies associated with music of the American Indian. Sweeney attributes much of the inspiration of this work to American band composer W. Francis McBeth and his 1968 composition, *Masque*.

Unit 4: Technical Considerations

The greatest technical demands occur in the percussion section, where a variety of instruments are used: snare drum, bass drum, crash cymbals, gong, bells (optional), triangle, and suspended cymbal. A minimum of four players is required (five if the optional bell part is performed). Difficulty will occur in having the snare drum play even sixteenth notes and rolls in tempo. Percussion writing plays a role in the melodic as well as rhythmic framework. Wind players will play some dissonant chords that involve a major or minor second interval. The meter remains in 4/4 time throughout, there are no key changes, there are few accidentals, and there are no range problems for the young players.

Unit 5: Stylistic Considerations

Wind players will need to demonstrate a variety of articulations. Careful attention must be paid to notes that are accented, full value, detached (*staccato*), and slurred. Often a variety of these articulations are found in the same measure. To perform this work effectively, students will need to focus on the contrast found in the attack or length of each note. The work is full of different instrument groups, which provide new colors for the players.

The initial three notes of the work serve as its building block. The melody found in the second section is a variation of this three-note figure. The first eight measures of the middle section of the work (measure 45) has two, three-measure phrases followed by a two-measure phrase. This 3+3+2 division first appears in measure 17 as a two-measure introduction to the second statement of the theme. Alto saxophones, trumpets, and horns have a three-beat rhythm on beat one and again on beat four of measure 17, which is then followed by only the first two beats of the same rhythm before the pattern begins again. This motor rhythm helps to suspend the bar line and provide motion for the musical line. The figure is again repeated in measures 19, 21, 29, and 68. Steady tempo, accurate rhythmic division, and emphasis of contrasts in color and articulation should be continually emphasized.

Unit 6: Musical Elements

MELODY:

The work begins with a unison passage for the woodwinds, and the germ for the composition can be found in the first three notes. Melodically the work is primarily a succession of two- or four-measure modal fragments based on these initial three notes. Each of these fragments is held together with a one- or two-measure rhythmic interlude in the percussion or woodwind sections. There are only a few isolated lyrical passages, none more than two measures in length.

HARMONY:

No formal harmonic structure appears to be in place, and a case can be made for the tonality of the introduction to be in C minor (with an implied tonic). The second section of the work, beginning at measure 11, leans toward F Dorian. Students should not try to associate this work with a specific key but should rather focus on clusters of sounds.

RHYTHM:

Divisions of the beat are duple in nature. The rhythm of the work is based upon the eighth note, and only the snare drum plays sixteenth notes. Eighth notes in the woodwind parts are always found in pairs, and there are only two instances where the woodwind players play two consecutive pairs (beats) of eighth notes. Placement of the paired eighth note is found on both strong and weak beats within the measure. Independent percussion writing requires players to count and play with an accurate division of beat.

TIMBRE:

The introduction of the work is written as two, two-measure unison woodwind motifs bridged by the percussion writing. This is followed by two, two-measure dissonant woodwind motifs again bridged by the percussion section. The second section of the work begins with a two-measure percussion introduction followed by a statement of the four-measure theme by *soli* clarinets accompanied by the triangle to provide a definition of pulse. The percussion introduction is then imitated by the alto saxophones, trumpets, and horns with a *soli* statement of the theme appearing in the low brass and woodwinds. Harmonic block chords also appear in the woodwinds. There are isolated woodwind and brass colors, and the percussion's role serves both melodic and as an accompaniment.

Unit 7: Form and Structure

SECTION	MEASURES	EVENT AND SCORING
Introduction	1-4	Two two-measure unison rhythmic motifs that are connected by the percussion section; tempo is quarter note = 96 beats per minute
	5-9	A one-measure percussion solo leads to the final four measures of the introduction; woodwinds are now written in unfolding dissonance
Theme	11-12	Two-measure percussion introduction at a new tempo of 126 beats per minute
	13-16	Four-measure melody written for *soli* clarinet with triangle accompaniment
	17-18	Two-measure introduction to restatement of melody played by alto saxophone, trumpet, and horn
	19-22	Melody restated in the low brass and woodwinds; alto saxophone, trumpet, horn, and snare drum provide the accompaniment
	23-26	Two two-measure harmonic figures provide a temporary sense of calm
	27-30	Two-measure statement of initial three-note melody (see m. 1) followed by two-measure rhythmic, dissonant accompaniment
	31-34	Two-measure statement of initial three-note melody repeated with slight variation and followed by two-measure lyrical, harmonic passage
	35-36	Two-measure motives in a question-and-answer style
	37-40	Two-measure motive repeated and extended two additional measures into a sense of resolution or half cadence
	41-44	Percussion solo serves as a bridge to "B" section of work

SECTION	MEASURES	EVENT AND SCORING
	45-52	Two three-measure harmonic motives and one two-measure motive written in half and whole notes accompanied by a syncopated bass line consisting of quarter/half/quarter note rhythms; percussion writing is for snare and bass drum and helps to provide energy to an overall static section
	53-60	Two four-measure phrases follow, building intensity
	61-62	Restatement of rhythmic introduction found in m. 11; played by trumpet
	63-66	Snare drum joins trumpet as rhythmic *ostinato* continues over harmonic woodwind writing
	67	Rhythmic *ostinato* shifts to flute and clarinet
	68-71	Instrumentation thickens as *ostinato* and harmonic passages repeat and build intensity
	72	No woodwind writing as snare drum and suspended cymbal rolls add suspense
	73-75	*Fortissimo* block chords augment the composition's initial three-note motif as the work concludes

Unit 8: Suggested Listening

W. Francis McBeth, *Masque*
Michael Sweeney:
   Ancient Voices
   Legends in the Mist

Unit 9: Additional References and Resources

Teaching Aids for the director provided by Michael Sweeney.

Contributed by:

Charles T. Menghini
VanderCook College of Music
Chicago, Illinois

Teacher Resource Guide

In Dulci Jubilo
John Zdechlik
(b. 1937)

Unit 1: Composer

Dr. John P. Zdechlik is a native of Minneapolis, Minnesota. A trumpeter, conductor, and pianist, he received his Bachelor of Music Education degree from the University of Minnesota in 1957. After teaching music for two years in the public schools, he returned to the University of Minnesota where he earned his master's degree in Theory and Composition. He served as Associate Director of Bands while earning his master's. He then taught full time at the same university but soon resumed his studies, this time earning his doctorate in Theory and Composition from the University of Minnesota in 1970, where he studied with Paul Fetler and Frank Bencriscutto. He accepted a position at Lakewood Community College in White Bear Lake teaching theory, where he now serves as Chair of the Department of Music and Band Director.

Since the time he was a high school pianist and trumpeter, Zdechlik has had an interest in jazz, both as a performer and as a composer; in 1981, he founded the Lakewood Community College Jazz Ensemble. He is recognized among the jazz community as a prominent conductor and instigator of jazz music and has gained a reputation throughout the area and nationally for his superb concerts and directorship of the Lakewood Community College Jazz Ensemble. Since 1970, Zdechlik has written numerous commissioned and published works for high school and college concert bands, including *Chorale and Shaker Dance, Chorale and Shaker Dance II, Faces of Kum Ba Yah, Lyric Statement, Psalm 46, Dialogues on "In Dulci Jubilo," Grace Variants, Images of Aura Lee, Intermezzo, Passacaglia, Lake Washington Suite, Romance for Band, Z's Blues, Dance Variations, Meyer March, Prelude and Fugue, Rondo Capriccio, St.*

Croix Suite, Celebrations, Grand Rapids Suite, Hats off to Thee, and *Rondo Jubiloso.* He has received many commissions, including those from Kappa Kappa Psi/Tau Beta Sigma and the Medallist Band of Bloomington, Illinois. His works are frequently performed around the world.

Unit 2: Composition

In Dulci Jubilo is based on the famous fourteenth century German Christmas carol of the same name. The Latin title translates to "in sweet jubilation." Below is one text setting of the carol attributed to John Mason Neale (1818–1866):

> Good Christian friends, rejoice with heart and soul and voice;
> give ye heed to what we say: Jesus Christ is born today;
> ox and ass before him bow, and he is in the manger now.
> Christ is born today! Christ is born today!
>
> Good Christian friends, rejoice with heart and soul and voice;
> now ye hear of endless bliss; Jesus Christ was born for this!
> He hath opened heaven's door, and we are blest forevermore.
> Christ was born for this! Christ was born for this!
>
> Good Christian friends, rejoice with heart and soul and voice;
> now ye need not fear the grave: Jesus Christ was born to save!
> Calls you one and calls you all to gain his everlasting hall.
> Christ was born to save! Christ was born to save!

Zdechlik's music setting is a Grade 1 1/2; it is approximately two minutes and fifty seconds in duration. The three large sections of the piece (*Moderato, Allegro, Maestoso*) seem to match the standard three verses for this carol. The piece is correlated with page 24 of book 1 of the *Best in Class Comprehensive Band Method* series. These volumes are designed to reinforce carefully the musical skills and concepts from *Best in Class*, book 1 and book 2. Learning concepts written in the score and student parts provide valuable teaching ideas and outline the significant characteristics of each piece. These exercises include exercises for scales, rhythms, melodies, phrasing, tuning, and harmony skills. Cross-scoring, singable melodies, contemporary harmonies, and important themes in every part are just a few of the quality musical features found in each of the *Best in Class Performance Selections* published by Neil A. Kjos Music Company (catalog number WB114).

Unit 3: Historical Perspective

Zdechlik is best known for writing music for school band performance. During the 1970s, two trends in band composition emerged: Claude T. Smith, W. Francis McBeth, and Robert Jager were among the best-known composers for school bands, while Karel Husa, Martin Mailman, and Donald Erb saw wind and band music as a new compositional frontier. One general inclination among school band music composers was little emphasis on solo writing with a greater emphasis on full ensemble scoring.

Unit 4: Technical Considerations

This piece is rated Grade 1 1/2. All players are playing all of the time, and there are no solos. All parts are in a very comfortable range for all of the instruments. From measures 47 through 74, *In Dulci Jubilo* features a correlated snare drum/bass drum part and an advanced snare drum/bass drum part. The conductor or performer can select the part (or parts) that best suit the abilities of the percussion section. Both parts can be played simultaneously. The first large section of the piece (*Moderato*) is in 3/4, the second (*Allegro*) is in 2/4, and the third (*Maestoso*) is in 3/4. The concert keys of B-flat major and E-flat major are used. The list of percussion instruments used includes timpani, tambourine, suspended cymbal, crash cymbals, snare drum, bass drum, triangle, sleigh bells, orchestra bells, and chimes. The tambourine part requires a thumb roll, which may be difficult for young players. The timpani part, set to B-flat and E-flat, does not require any pedal changes.

Unit 5: Stylistic Considerations

There are different articulations that students may practice and learn, including *staccato*, *legato*, slurs, and accents. Trombones are never given slurs, presumably to keep them from smearing the notes; instead, they are given *legato* articulations. Dynamics range from *piano* to *forte*. The piece is jocund throughout, matching the merry character of the carol text. The outer two sections of the piece feature longer notes and a chorale style, while the middle section is energetic, faster, and lighter. This provides students with an excellent opportunity to learn about musical contrast and form, and conductors should make the most of this. The performance style of this final *maestoso* should contrast with the light and playful sound of the preceding *allegro* section. Performers should follow the dynamic and articulation markings carefully throughout this selection.

Unit 6: Musical Elements

MELODY:

In Dulci Jubilo uses a diatonic melody in the concert keys of B-flat major and E-flat major; there are no accidentals. There are also no difficult jumps in range; most leaps are no more than a major third. Players should all be proficient playing in the concert keys of B-flat major and E-flat major. Flute players should be prepared to play A-flat major and B-flat major arpeggios for measures 64 and 65; flute players also have several B-flats above the staff. A good way to teach the melody and importance of parts would be to have all of the students sing through the carol either on "la" or using the text; however, the melody is familiar and easy to grasp quickly.

HARMONY:

The harmony is all very lucid and diatonic. Chordal movement is slow, usually by the measure, so young students can have a chance to hear the chord progressions. Because of this slow harmonic movement, this setting differs a bit from standard harmonizations (e.g., Charles Winfred Douglas (1867–1944)). The tonic is firmly established at the beginning and the end of each section. There is frequent use of III, IV, and V (for important cadences). The chord motion is homophonic in the first two sections; in measures 77 through 92 (in the third section), there are several suspensions. Measure 101 contains a bichord with a IV chord in second inversion played by the brass and low woodwinds and a I chord above it in flutes, oboes, and clarinets. This work provides a good occasion for teaching and practicing balancing chords using *Effective Performance of Band Music* by W. Francis McBeth as a paradigm.

RHYTHM:

A festive, *allegro* tempo beginning in measure 39 includes a variation of the melody written in 2/4 meter. In measure 77, the main theme returns in its original 3/4 time signature. Ending the first large section (*Moderato*), there is a three-measure *decrescendo* into a *fermata*, followed by a *caesura*. There is a two-measure *poco ritard.* and *decrescendo* into the *Maestoso* at the end, again with a *fermata* and *caesura*. Most rhythms are homophonic, although the third section features various instruments moving on different beats for suspension effect. There are eighth notes at the ends of the first and third sections and throughout the second section; the only sixteenth notes to be found in the piece are in the snare drum parts. A basic tempo pulse for each section is crucial, and players must especially take care to keep long notes from rushing. Clapping or counting rhythms would also help teach rhythm and tempo fundamentals.

TIMBRE:

In this setting, clarinets and alto saxophones begin the statement of the melody accompanied by open fifths. Low brass and low woodwinds continue the theme in measure 13 against a changing harmonic background. Flutes, clarinets, and alto saxophones take the theme again over a *tutti* long-note accompaniment. Throughout the piece, most of the band is playing with some instruments left out for a few measures, usually before entering with the theme. All parts are in a very comfortable range for all of the instruments; with the exception of flute, bass clarinet, and tuba, there is very little playing above or below the staff. Besides different instruments taking the theme, there is little change in overall timbre throughout the piece, so this work provides an opportunity for teaching concepts of consistency in sound, tone production, and breath support in the context of three different rhythmic frames.

Unit 7: Form and Structure

MEASURES   EVENT AND SCORING

Moderato — quarter note = 100; 3/4; B-flat major (Verse 1)
1   Theme, stanza 1; clarinet, alto saxophone
13   Theme, stanza 2; low brass, low woodwinds
21   Theme, stanza 3; flute, clarinet, alto saxophone
29   Theme, stanza 4; closing

Allegro — quarter note = 116; 2/4; E-flat major (Verse 2)
39   Theme variation, stanza 1; trumpet 1, alto saxophone 2
48   Theme variation, stanza 2; trumpet 1, alto saxophone 1
56   Theme variation, stanza 3; trumpet 1, clarinet 1,
                         alto saxophone 1
64   Theme variation, stanza 4; trumpet 1, clarinet 1,
                         alto saxophone 1

Maestoso — quarter note = 90; 3/4; E-flat major (Verse 3)
77   Theme, stanza 1; flute, oboe, clarinet, trumpet
86   Theme, stanza 2; flute, oboe, clarinet, trumpet
94   Theme, stanza 3; trumpet 1
100   Theme, stanza 4; closing

Unit 8: Suggested Listening
John Zdechlik:
  Celebrations
  Chorale and Shaker Dance
  Dance Variations
  Faces of Kum Ba Yah
  Rondo Jubiloso

Unit 8: Suggested Listening
Battisti, Frank, and Robert Garofalo. *Guide to Score Study for Wind Band Conductors*. Fort Lauderdale, FL: Meredith Music Publications, 1990.

Ewen, David. *A Comprehensive Biographical Dictionary of American Composers*. New York, NY: G.P. Putnam & Sons, 1982.

McBeth, W. Francis. *Effective Performance of Band Music*. San Antonio, TX: Southern Music Company, 1972.

Miles, Richard, ed. "John Zdechlik – *Chorale and Shaker Dance*." *Teaching Music through Performance in Band*, Volume 1. Chicago, IL: GIA Publications, Inc., 1997, pp. 234-237.

National Band Association Selective Music List for Bands.

Neil A. Kjos Music Company website: http://www.kjos.com/

Rehrig, William H. *The Heritage Encyclopedia of Band Music*. Westerville, OH: Integrity Press, 1991.

Smith, Norman, and Albert Stoutamire. *Band Music Notes*. Lake Charles, LA: Program Note Press, 1989.

Zdechlik, John. *Celebrations*. Frank B. Wickes and the Louisiana State University Wind Ensemble. Compact disc "Live from LSU," 1995.

Zdechlik, John. *Chorale and Shaker Dance*. John P. Paynter and the Northshore Concert Band. Compact disc "Stars and Stripes: Music for a Summer Evening," Brewster Records 4-4104-2, 1994.

Zdechlik, John. Personal website: http://www1.minn.net/~johnz/

Contributed by:

Matthew Mailman
Director of Bands and Associate Professor of Conducting
Oklahoma City University
Oklahoma City, Oklahoma

Teacher Resource Guide

Japanese Folk Trilogy

Anne McGinty
(b. 1945)

Unit 1: Composer

Anne McGinty, a native of Findlay, Ohio, received her Bachelor of Music and Master of Music degrees from Duquesne University, with emphases in flute performance and composition. McGinty is a well-known composer and arranger of music for young bands and has been active throughout her career as a teacher and clinician. She has composed over 160 works for band ranging from Grade 1 through Grade 5. Along with her husband, John Edmondson, McGinty operates Queenwood Publications, a publishing company specializing in music for young musicians. Along with *Japanese Folk Trilogy*, other arrangements of world folk music by McGinty include *African Folk Trilogy*, *American Folk Trilogy*, *Bartok: Folk Song and Dance*, *English Folk Trilogy*, and *Kum Ba Yah*.

Unit 2: Composition

Japanese Folk Trilogy is comprised of three authentic Japanese folk tunes: "Moon Song" (Otsukisan), "Festival of the Dolls" (Hinamatsuri), and "Please Come Spring" (Haru Yo Koi). The melodies are based upon both pentatonic and diatonic scales, which occur within five separate tonal centers throughout the piece. McGinty achieves this without changing the concert key signature of three flats. *Japanese Folk Trilogy* is scored for flute, oboe, two clarinets, alto saxophone, tenor saxophone, two cornets, horn, a low brass and woodwind line in octaves, bells, triangle, woodblock, tambourine, snare drum, and bass drum. The oboe, tenor saxophone, horn, and bass line in octaves are all optional in this beginning band series. The total time for performance is approximately two minutes and forty-five seconds.

Unit 3: Historical Perspective

Japanese music has historically been divided into two types: art music and folk music. Both typically included music for voice, flute, drums, cymbals, and bamboo percussive instruments. The folk music reflected day-to-day life, particularly activities related to work, such as rice planting, fishing, and building. In addition, instrumental pieces were usually performed for dances, ceremonies, and celebrations, such as weddings, births, and funerals. Because Japan is an island nation, its music developed without outside influence until the period from approximately 453 A.D. to 701 A.D., when visitors from the mainland brought with them the music of China, India, and Korea. In time, the Japanese absorbed some of this music, as well as the instruments upon which it was played, into their own culture. With the arrival of visitors from the west in the nineteenth century, the Japanese were exposed to the sounds of European music. Emperor Meiji, who reigned from 1868 to 1912, decreed that European music was to be taught in the schools, thereby making it an influence on the twentieth century Japanese culture. While the three folk songs in *Japanese Folk Trilogy* are authentic, the accompaniment style and harmonization are western. This is due primarily to the influence of Luther Whiting Mason who, at the invitation of the Imperial family, went to Japan in the 1880s. While there, he arranged many Japanese folk songs in a western style, and Japanese children have been learning the same hybrid styles ever since. The authentic children's songs and accompaniment patterns were suggested to McGinty by Bryan Burton, Associate Professor of Music Education, West Chester University, West Chester, Pennsylvania; he is an expert in the field of multicultural music.

Unit 4: Technical Considerations

Japanese Folk Trilogy is written throughout in a 4/4 meter and with a concert key signature of three flats. Even though the key signature does not change, the tonal center does through the use of accidentals. Flute and oboe players will need to be familiar with the fingerings for G-flat, D-flat, and B-natural; clarinet players will need to know E-flat and F-sharp; alto saxophone players will need to know B-flat and E-flat; tenor saxophone players will need to know C-sharp; cornet players will need to know C-sharp, E-flat, and A-flat; horn players will need to know F-sharp; low brass and low woodwind players will need to know D-flat and G-flat, and bell players will need to know D-flat.

In addition, it will be important for conductors to teach proper techniques for playing the triangle, tambourine, and woodblock to ensure the best possible tone quality. Special attention should be given the bell player, as the part requires the development of two mallet skills. The tempo gradually increases as the *Trilogy* progresses. The indicated tempo for "Moon Song" is quarter note = 80 beats per minute, "Festival of the Dolls" is quarter note = 88 beats per minute, and "Please Come Spring" is quarter note = 100 beats per minute.

These subtle relationships should be checked regularly with a metronome.

Unit 5: Stylistic Considerations

The three Japanese folk songs included in the *Trilogy* are characteristically light and somewhat delicate. Emphasis will need to be placed upon the well-supported, soft dynamic levels, which never exceed *mf*. Harmonic voices are at times specifically written at softer dynamic levels than melodic voices, a difference that must be brought to the attention of the players. One way to explain this difference is to ask if the students have ever noticed how the principal character on stage in a play is usually in the center or toward the front, with supporting actors "backstage." As roles change, important parts move toward the front/center. This will help students understand how their functions or roles change throughout the composition's development and, as such, why their attention to balance and dynamic changes is important. The light detachment or separation of notes, particularly eighth notes, will be a major ingredient in achieving the desired lightness of style. This will be a particular challenge to low brass and low woodwinds as they play the melodic line at the beginning of "Festival of the Dolls."

Unit 6: Musical Elements

MELODY:

The *Japanese Folk Trilogy* provides the conductor with an opportunity to introduce the pentatonic scale and show students how it differs from major scales they are beginning to learn. Instead of seven notes to the octave, as in major and minor scales, the pentatonic uses only five, a difference easily seen at the keyboard by playing only the black keys. Students may also see how a relationship with both major and minor keys exists by playing only the first, second, third, fifth, and sixth scale steps to get a pentatonic scale. This is the basis for the melodies in each of the three folk songs in the *Trilogy*. A worksheet including all of the pentatonic scales incorporated into the composition might be helpful as students learn to identify each new occurrence.

The melody in "Moon Song" is presented three times, each time within an eight-measure phrase. In addition to giving each of the upper woodwind and brass voices an opportunity to play a portion of the melody, the final phrase shifts from the opening tonal center of C minor to F minor, giving students a new pentatonic scale to play that includes a D-flat concert accidental.

The melody shifts to the alto saxophones and low brass and woodwind voices to begin the second song, "Festival of the Dolls." At this point, two accidentals are added to the melody, D-flat and G-flat, presenting a third pentatonic scale based upon the tonal center of B-flat minor. Attention to articulation and the light separation of the melodic eighth notes will be a challenge for the students with larger instruments. Eighth note patterns occur in both slur two/tongue two patterns as well as groups of four tongued notes.

McGinty often writes repeated tongued notes for beginners in order to develop the concept of blowing through the notes, thereby giving them direction or forward motion. Since beginning musicians tend to make repeated notes sound isolated and separate from the musical line, the conductor will want to give particular attention to using these patterns in the students' development of musical direction. Intervalic skips of thirds and fourths in the flute, oboe, alto saxophone, and cornet melodic lines will provide an opportunity to develop these skills as the preparation of this folk song develops.

The third song, "Please Come Spring," is organized in four-measure phrases and opens in the woodwinds and bells with another new pentatonic melody centered on F major. As with the previous two folk songs, the key signature does not change, rather incorporating concert E-naturals and A-naturals as accidentals. This melody evolves into the fifth and last new tonal center of E-flat major for the final statement of the third melody before a short, four-measure coda in C minor brings back the first tune, "Moon Song," as a familiar conclusion.

HARMONY:

As noted in the section on melody, the key signature remains constant throughout the *Trilogy*; however, five different tonal centers are presented. The work opens in C minor and remains there for the first two phrases until moving into F minor in measure 17 for the final phrase of the first song. The third tonal center, B-flat minor, occurs at measure 25, which is the beginning of the second folk song. Once again, the key center shifts back to the original C minor at measure 34 for the final statement of the second song. The fourth tonal center is introduced in measure 42 at the beginning of the third folk song, with a transition into the final new center of E-flat major at measure 51. The *Trilogy* concludes with the coda restatement of the first folk song in the opening tonal center of C minor. With the exception of the transitional measures used to move from one tonal center to another, all three folk songs are supported by a simple harmonic structure based primarily upon the I, IV, and V chords in each tonal center.

RHYTHM:

The meter is a consistent 4/4 throughout the *Trilogy*, with varying rhythmic patterns comprised of quarter, eighth, and half notes and rests. Most of these patterns place quarter notes on strong beats (one and three) and eighth notes on weaker beats (two and four). These patterns do change occasionally in the accompaniment voices adding variety to the music and, as an extra benefit, providing the conductor with a tool for observing that students are accurately reading their parts. Accompanying voices will also need to pay close attention to the lengths of notes to maintain the clarity of parts exposed by rests, or measured silence. This would be another opportunity to emphasize the concept of music having measured lengths of sound and silence, as well as the importance

of internalizing the subdivided beat to ensure accuracy. Clapping and counting rhythms is extremely effective in the development of this skill.

TIMBRE:

A variety of textural colors is achieved by McGinty through the skillful movement of melodic and harmonic lines between all voices. This will provide the conductor with many opportunities to blend and balance different instrumental combinations in the process of teaching students how to listen for these important ensemble concepts. The transition of the folk songs through five different tonal centers also serves to place both melodic and harmonic lines within a comfortable range and *tessitura* for each instrument, thereby allowing for maximum concentration on tone quality, blend, and balance.

Particularly important to the characteristic eastern sound of this piece is the careful performance of the percussion parts. Correct techniques for holding and striking the triangle, woodblock, and tambourine must be stressed in order to maximize resonance without playing too heavily. Particular attention must be given to the *diminuendo* from *mf* to *p* in the woodblock part. Not only is this critical to the musical effect in measures 2 and 16, but it sets the pattern for the *diminuendo* in the bells, low brass, and low woodwinds in measure 8.

One other critical element is the role the bells play at measure 17 in the first song and in its reprise in the coda. An eighth note pattern of octave Fs supports the light, final statement of the first tune in the flutes, oboes, and cornets. This becomes slightly more challenging in measure 20 as the bells continue the eighth note pattern with octave Cs on beat one, D-flats on beat two, E-flats on beat three, and Gs on beat four before returning to the octave Fs in measure 21. All percussionists must learn to use two mallets, and this part helps develop this skill. The dynamics throughout the *Trilogy* range from *p* to *mf*, giving the entire piece a light, delicate style.

Unit 7: Form and Structure

Japanese Folk Trilogy may best be described as a medley of three songs, each of which makes use of pentatonic and diatonic scalar melodies supported by major and minor harmonic centers.

MEASURES   TONAL CENTER   EVENT AND SCORING

"Moon Song"
(tempo: quarter note = 80 beats per minute)

1-8	C minor	Clarinet melody with triangle and woodblock accompaniment joined by bells and remainder of the ensemble to end the phrase on a half cadence

MEASURES	TONAL CENTER	EVENT AND SCORING
9-16		Optional horn/tenor saxophone line joins clarinet on the melody over pedal point bass line; remainder of the ensemble joins to conclude the phrase on the tonic
17-24	F minor	Flute, oboe, cornet melody accompanied by octave subdivisions in the bells; phrase concludes with open fifths on the tonic F minor, which sets up the dominant transition into B-flat minor

"Festival of the Dolls"
(tempo: quarter note = 88 beats per minute)

25-28	B-flat minor	Alto saxophone, low brass, and low woodwind lines carry the melody with rhythmic, chordal accompaniment in clarinet, horn, and tenor saxophone
29-33		Flute, oboe, cornet, and bells are accompanied by chords in other voices leading to a modulation into C minor
34-37	C minor	Flute, oboe, and bell melodic segment answered by cornet melodic segment; simple chordal accompaniment
38-41		Flute, oboe, and bell melodic segment answered by alto saxophone segment; chordal accompaniment ends on tonic C minor, which also serves as dominant for the next song in F major

"Please Come Spring"
(tempo: quarter note = 100 beats per minute)

| 42-45 | F major | Flute, oboe, and bell melody accompanied by rhythmic chords in clarinet and alto saxophone |
| 46-50 | | Clarinet, tenor saxophone, horn, and bells melodic segment answered by flute, oboe, alto saxophone, and bells; harmonic parts in cornet, low brass, and low woodwinds are added leading to a modulation into E-flat major |

MEASURES	TONAL CENTER	EVENT AND SCORING
51-54	E-flat major	All but flute and oboe restate harmonized melody
55-58		Clarinet, alto saxophone, and cornet share melody accompanied by chords in remaining voices

Coda
(tempo: quarter note = 100 beats per minute)

59-62	C minor	"Moon Song" theme returns in flute, oboe, clarinet, and alto saxophone parts over chords in the brass and low woodwinds; octave subdivisions in the bells and rhythmic woodblock bring the *Trilogy* to its conclusion

Unit 8: Suggested Listening

Toshio Akiyama, *Japanese Songs for Band*
John Barnes Chance, *Variations on a Korean Folk Song*
James Curnow, *Korean Folk Rhapsody*
Clare Grundman, *Japanese Rhapsody*
Soichi Konagaya, *Japanese Tune*
Bernard Rogers, *Three Japanese Dances*

Unit 9: Additional References and Resources

"Anne McGinty: *The Red Balloon*." *Teaching Music through Performance in Band*. Compiled and edited by Richard Miles. Chicago, IL: GIA Publications, Inc., 1997.

Apel, Willi, ed. *Harvard Dictionary of Music*, 2nd edition. Cambridge, MA: Belknap Press, 1972.

Dvorak, Thomas L. *Best Music for Young Band*. Brooklyn, NY: Manhattan Beach Music, 1986.

Kreines, Joseph. *Music for Concert Band*. Tampa, FL: Florida Music Service, 1989.

Miles, Richard, ed. *Teaching Music through Performance in Band*. Chicago, IL: GIA Publications, Inc., 1998.

Randel, Don Michael. *The New Harvard Dictionary of Music*. Cambridge, MA: Harvard University, 1986.

Rasmussen, Richard Michael. *Recorded Concert Band Music, 1950–1987*. Jefferson, NC: McFarland Press, 1988.

Rehrig, William H. *The Heritage Encyclopedia of Band Music*. Westerville, OH: Integrity Press, 1991.

Smith, Norman, and Albert Stoutamire. *Band Music Notes*. Lake Charles, LA: Program Note Press, 1989.

Contributed by:
Robert Spradling
Director of Bands, Professor of Music
Western Michigan University
Kalamazoo, Michigan

Teacher Resource Guide

Jeanette, Isabella

William Ryden
(b. 1939)

Unit 1: Composer

William Ryden was educated at the American Conservatory of Music (Chicago) and at Mannes College, where his primary teacher was Tibor Serly. He has written music for all genres, including film and television—his music has been heard on the popular children's program, *The Electric Company*. He has received numerous ASCAP awards and twenty-five Meet the Composer grants. He currently resides in Forest Hills, New York.

Unit 2: Composition

Jeanette, Isabella is an arrangement of a seventeenth century Christmas carol entitled "Un Flambeau, Jeanette, Isabella." It is a moderately difficult Grade 1, accessible to advanced first- and second-year players. It is scored for standard wind band; percussion scoring calls for timpani, bells, xylophone, chimes, triangle, suspended cymbal, tambourine, crash cymbal, and bass drum. The work was published in 1993 and is approximately two minutes in duration.

Unit 3: Historical Perspective

This carol originates form the Provence region of France. The composer is believed to have been Nicolas Saboly (1614-1675). Music written for Christmas celebrations have long been popular; the best-known example is probably Bach's *Christmas Oratorio*. Holst and Britten wrote fine settings of carols for orchestra and voice. The best-known Christmas music for winds includes Grainger's *Sussex Mummers' Christmas Carol* and Alfred Reed's *Russian Christmas Music*.

Unit 4: Technical Considerations

Technical demands of this work are minimal. Ranges and rhythms are all within the grasp of second-year players. There are few accidentals, and there is no note length shorter than a quarter note. There is some need for independent playing, as the textures and scoring are constantly changing. The percussion scoring is unique for a Grade 1 work: it assumes a role of the same importance as the winds.

Unit 5: Stylistic Considerations

There are no style markings indicated in the score, so the conductor is free to experiment with a variety of styles. The piece works best, however, when a *legato* singing style is used. The pulse is a graceful triple meter; students may encounter some difficulty learning to play in that style. As mentioned before, the scoring and textures are constantly changing, so students will need to maintain the sense of line and phrasing.

Unit 6: Musical Elements

Harmonically, this work is very simple; there are no unexpected chords or tonal centers. All three statements of the melody are in E-flat major, and there is very little use of non-harmonic tones. The familiar melody is scalar and easy to sing. Rhythmically, there is some use of syncopation; however, the syncopated figures are not difficult and are easily negotiable.

A major obstacle for the students to overcome will be the amount of independent playing and shifting textures used throughout the piece. Charles Forque and James Thornton's book, *Harmonized Rhythms*, may prove a useful source in this regard. Possible units of study may include studies of French folk music (Milhaud's *Suite Francaise* would be possible supplemental material) or the study of various ritual or religious music from different parts of the world.

Unit 7: Form and Structure

SECTION	MEASURES	EVENT AND SCORING
Introduction	1-4	Key of E-flat major, cornet, percussion
A	5-12	Upper woodwinds with melody; low woodwinds and percussion accompany
B	13-20	Cornet with melody; clarinet, trombone, low woodwinds accompany
C	21-31	Full scoring; cadence in E-flat major, m. 30
A	32-39	Percussion *soli* section
B	40-47	Brass choir; low reeds
C	48-58	Full scoring; cadence in E-flat major in m. 57

Section	Measures	Event and Scoring
A	59-66	Low brass and percussion *soli*; *fortissimo*
B	67-74	*Tutti* scoring; full dynamics
C	75-85	Full scoring; *piano* dynamics
Coda	86-91	*Piano* dynamics; cadence in E-flat major

Unit 8: Suggested Listening

J.S. Bach, *Christmas Oratorio*

Benjamin Britten, *A Ceremony of Carols*

Percy Grainger, *Sussex Mummers' Christmas Carol*

Alfred Reed, *Russian Christmas Music*

Unit 9: Additional References and Resources

Dvorak, Thomas, Cynthia Crump Taggart, and Peter Schmalz. *Best Music for Young Band*. Brooklyn, NY: Manhattan Beach Music, 1986.

Forque, Charles, and J. Thornton. *Harmonized Rhythms for Band*. San Diego, CA: Neil A. Kjos, Inc., 1994.

Kennedy, Michael, ed. *The Concise Oxford Dictionary of Music*, 3rd edition. Oxford: Oxford University Press, 1980.

Lane, Jeremy. *Teaching MusicThrough Performance in Band and Texas U.I.L. Grade I Prescribe Music List for Band*. Graduate project. Waco, TX: Baylor University, 1998.

Miles, Richard, ed. *Teaching Music through Performance in Band*. Chicago, IL: GIA Publications, Inc., 1997.

Miles, Richard, ed. *Teaching Music through Performance in Band*, Volume 2. Chicago, IL: GIA Publications, Inc., 1998.

Smith, N., and A. Stoutamire. *Band Music Notes*, revised edition. Lake Charles, LA: Program Note Press, 1979.

Information and recordings of works by William Ryden are available on-line at: members.aol.com/mbmband

Contributed by:

Jeremy S. Lane

Doctoral Graduate Assistant, Music Education

Louisiana State University

Baton Rouge, Louisiana

Teacher Resource Guide

La Volta

William Byrd
(1543–1623)

arranged by Katheryn Fenske
(b. 1964)

Unit 1: Composer

William Byrd is considered the greatest English composer of the Renaissance. Although actual evidence is not available, it is likely that Byrd was born in Lincoln, England, in 1543. As a boy, he played organ in his home community and at some point studied music with Thomas Tallis. At the age of twenty, he was still serving as organist at the Lincoln Cathedral, but later he became a member of the Royal Chapel of Queen Elizabeth, where his duties included serving as organist and resident composer. It is indeed interesting to note that despite his Roman Catholic faith, Byrd maintained Royal favor throughout his career in Protestant England. He and Thomas Tallis jointly held publishing rights, but upon Tallis's death, the publishing monopoly was awarded to Byrd. Because of this, Byrd had the means to publish Latin sacred music among his other works. These compositions were probably performed at private functions or in secret religious services since they would have not been sanctioned by the Church of England. No doubt Byrd's unquestionable loyalty to the Crown and his ability to be discreet permitted him to have such freedom.

His musical output includes several hundred works, including motets, three Latin Masses, liturgical music, secular songs, consort music, and keyboard pieces. It is in the compositions for keyboard that Byrd reveals his true genius.

Unit 2: Composition

La Volta is an arrangement of a lively seventeenth century court dance. It was arranged for young band by Katheryn Fenske while she was teaching at Byron Middle School in Byron, Illinois. Of particular interest is the fact that the arranger's students were integrally involved throughout the arranging process. Not only did they provide live-band run-throughs, but each part had to pass the "boring part" test. The students played through their parts and then offered their opinions as to the amount of interest the part held. If something was deemed "boring," the arranger happily restructured the part until it passed the test. *La Volta* was premiered by the Byron Middle School seventh grade band on October 20, 1994, in Byron, Illinois, with the arranger conducting. The work is sixty-five measures in length and has a duration of approximately two minutes.

Unit 3: Historical Perspective

The *La Volta* (also *Lavolta* or *Levalto*) is a Renaissance dance of a somewhat randy reputation due to its athletic nature. The dance partners must execute a series of two hopping steps and a giant airborne leap with the lady supported on the gentleman's thigh. To ensure the success of these nimble moves, the dancers needed to hold tightly to one another. The close proximity of the couple, the unusually large steps required of the female, and the possibility of seeing more than a dainty ankle as the lady was elevated skyward contributed to the dance's questionable nature. Lavoltas were typically composed in dotted 6/8 meter.

This particular *La Volta* is a keyboard work included in *The Fitzwilliam Virginal Book*, a set of keyboard manuscripts composed during the Renaissance period and published as a collection in two volumes (1894–99). The collection of 297 works includes madrigal transcriptions, contrapuntal fantasies, dances, preludes, descriptive pieces, and sets of variations based on familiar songs, slow dance tunes, and folk tunes. The editors, J.A. Maitland and W. Barclay Squire, managed to include works by most of the composers who were associated with virginal writing.

During the early sixteenth century, the term "virginal" referred to a specific instrument of the harpsichord family. This small, rectangular box could be held on the player's lap and had a rather light, delicate sound. By the end of the century, the term referred to any of several types of harpsichords.

Unit 4: Technical Considerations

The work is scored for young band with only the clarinets and trumpets divided into two parts. The tenor saxophone, trombone, and euphonium are unison and are often written at the interval of a fifth above the tubas. The oboe is an octave below the flute. Composed in 3/4 meter, the tempo of *La Volta* is quarter note = 116-126, but this may be altered to accommodate the technical abilities of the band. All rhythms are simple, utilizing only the dotted-half note, half note, dotted-quarter note, quarter note, and eighth note. The rhythmic difficulties lie in the use of the quarter note/quarter note tied to an eighth note/eighth note measures and an occasional tie across the bar line. The percussion section includes xylophone, snare drum (with snare off), tambourine, finger cymbals, bass drum, and timpani (F, C).

Because these parts were student-tested during the creative process, all parts are ideally suited to young musicians. That is not to say that there are no challenges for the performers but rather that each instrument is utilized in a manner consistent with its nature and the abilities of the young instrumentalist. Range does not present any major concerns, although the first trumpets are asked to perform a written E5 and the flutes are scored to a D6. The arranger purposely altered ranges from the original to make this music available to young musicians. However, the form, rhythms, and harmonies are exactly as Byrd composed them.

The major technical consideration of *La Volta* will be performing dotted-quarter note rhythms in 3/4 meter at the indicated *lively* tempo while maintaining a light, bouncing style. Bands should be encouraged to approach this work at a slower speed before attempting the performance tempo. It is advisable to prepare for this piece by using a warm-up in 3/4 meter that employs the dotted-quarter note/eighth note rhythm. Use this pattern during the band's scale warm-up or find an appropriate technical exercise in the band's method book. By establishing a counting system and using a metronome to develop individual and group inner pulse, the band will execute accurate rhythms at any tempo. (See exercise in Unit 6 under "Rhythm" in this Teacher Resource Guide.)

Unit 5: Stylistic Considerations

The style must convey the buoyancy of a lively dance. The original Lavoltas were usually written in an energetic 6/8, so to adequately convey the bouncy, enthusiastic quality of this piece in 3/4, the musicians should be encouraged to play with a lighter style. Avoid heavy articulations and an overzealous approach to the *forte* dynamic markings. Students should articulate with a lighter articulation by using "do" or "dee" syllables rather than the heavier "tah" or "ti." Have the students verbally articulate their parts on an airy "do" or "dee." Use a metronome to keep the vertical alignment of the rhythms accurate and to help maintain the tempo.

Music of the Renaissance is characterized by clarity of texture, balanced voicing, controlled expressiveness, simplicity of style, and generally small melodic ranges. Therefore, the band must always strive for a straightforward approach to this music. Avoid expressive gestures within the individual lines, but rather strive for a happy, lively bounce in the overall effect. Maintain a consistent tempo without a *ritardando* at the end of the work.

Most of today's band instruments did not exist during this period of music history, and those that were present have undergone significant changes over the centuries. Instruments were generally smaller and less capable of bombastic dynamics. Since these movements were originally works for virginal, it will be important that the students understand the capabilities of that instrument. All dynamics are more restrained with the notable lack of *crescendos* and *decrescendos* since these are not characteristic of the Renaissance period.

Unit 6: Musical Elements

MELODY:

Although *La Volta* has a key signature of B-flat, it is actually composed in Mixolydian mode. Modes, or church modes, were the basis of pitch organization for compositions of the Medieval and Renaissance periods. Each mode is a seven-note scale comprised of two half steps and five whole steps in a variety of combinations. The Mixolydian mode is closely related to what we call a major scale but has a lowered seventh degree. It is characterized by half steps between the third and fourth, and sixth and seventh degrees of the scale. The Mixolydian scale in this work is:

Scale pitches:	F	G	A	B-flat	C	D	E-flat
Scale degrees:	1	2	3	4	5	6	7
			half step			half step	

The melody is stated in the upper woodwinds and first trumpets. The melody is clearly defined and frequently doubled by more than one instrument. The accompanying figures are less rhythmically complex, and their sustained qualities help to make them easily identifiable as accompaniment.

In some sections of the piece, the brass and saxophones could easily overpower the melody; therefore, it will be important for the students to understand where the melody is in every measure. In the initial presentation of the work, the conductor may wish to play the melody for the students, starting with the melody in measures 1 through 8. The conductor then may ask the flutes, oboes, first clarinets, and first trumpets to play their parts at the beginning of the piece. Students should recognize this as the melody that was just presented to them. After replaying this portion of the melodic material, the conductor may ask the students to examine their parts between rehearsal letters A and B for any similarities. Students should be able to identify elements of the melody, which is distributed in four-measure segments, first to the upper woodwinds (measures 9 through 13) and then to the first trumpets (measures 13 through 16). This procedure may be repeated throughout the piece to assist the students with melodic recognition.

Another key element of the melodic structure of this work is the use of ornamentation to modify the melody. Students will need to be guided through the analysis of this aspect of the music. The use of an overhead projector or dry erase board will be helpful. Write out the oboe melody in measures 1 through 9. Below this melody write out the oboe's melody at rehearsal letter D. Take care to line up the beats in score fashion. This will help the students to more readily identify common elements in both melodies. The same procedure may be used to clarify the ornamentation of the B theme as initially presented at rehearsal letter B and then modified at rehearsal letter F. Define a passing tone as a tone or tones that are used to diatonically connect two notes of the original melody. Again, a visual representation of this on the chalkboard is suggested.

HARMONY:
The harmonic texture of the work is essentially homophonic with some contrapuntal elements. When a single melodic voice is supported by a harmonic accompaniment, the resultant texture is identified as being homophonic. When two or more melodies simultaneously occur and each is of equal importance, then the texture is described as contrapuntal. Students should become familiar with these terms and be able to identify these textures within the composition. This will be more easily accomplished if the students can recognize the individual melodies. The accompaniment parts will be quickly identified by the presence of more sustained note values scored in open fifths or simple triads. This uncomplicated harmonic structure coupled with appropriate doublings affords students the opportunity to hear within the band. It will be beneficial to have like melodic and harmonic lines play alone. Identify areas where tuning may be a concern within this octave structure and demonstrate to students how an "in tune" octave will generate the sounding of the perfect fifth.

This tuning exercise may be accomplished by first playing an octave on the piano/keyboard and then playing the fifth. Next have the students sing the fifth once you have played the octave. Select two students who are likely to play an octave in tune, then once correct intonation is established, sing the fifth. Repeat this exercise but have the students supply the fifth by singing with the band director. At this point, the students should be ready to listen for that particular overtone. If presented in a supportive manner, this exercise may actually provide a challenging game for pairs of band members. It is possible to make this an assignment for extra credit. Students should be encouraged to play an octave for the band and allow the band to listen for the fifth. By limiting this experience to just a few minutes once or twice a week, students will be motivated to develop this aspect of tuning.

The use of ornamentation was common during the Renaissance as were the prepared cadences that are in evidence throughout *La Volta* and the indication of the appearance of a functional harmonic structure. The well-constructed eight-bar phrases with clearly defined cadence points will assist the students in defining breathing points.

RHYTHM:

The meter of *La Volta* is composed in an uncomplicated 3/4. The students will need to know how to play dotted-half notes, half notes, dotted-quarter notes, quarter notes, and eighth notes. The woodwinds have a limited number of quarter notes tied across the bar line, but ties are more prevalent in the percussion parts. Because this selection is often contrapuntal in harmonic structure, it will be important to develop vertical alignment of the rhythms. Consider using a metronome to establish the initial pulse as the band learns to perform this work. Set the metronome at a slower tempo than the 116-126 that is indicated on the score and ask the students to pat their feet in time to the clicks. Make sure that the foot is patting in a rhythmic "one-and-two-and," with the up stroke occurring on the "and." Students will initially wish to snap the foot up in a non-rhythmic fashion.

An exercise to assist the students in an even division of the beat is to ask them to place the left hand about eighteen inches above the left thigh, palm toward the leg. Place the right hand between the left hand and thigh. Now with the metronome, count "one-and-two-and"; have the right palm slap the left thigh on "one" and the back of the right hand slap the left palm on "and." Using this method, the students will feel the rhythmic division of the beat and will be more likely to establish the same evenness in the foot pat. Using a metronome that will provide two different tones for the beat and the "and" will help students in this endeavor.

It is often beneficial to simplify the rhythmic structure of the piece into a series of "down-ups" as the counting system. Students are more inclined to develop a sense of rhythm when they focus on whether the note occurs when the foot is "down" or "up." Always use a metronome to help students develop an internal pulse. The following system has proven to be quite efficient in developing a solid rhythmic foundation:

1. Teach students to pat their feet in time with a metronome. (Slightly amplifying the metronomic tone through a small guitar amplifier will help.)
2. Develop a consistent and even rhythmic pulse with the feet by using the hand/thigh exercise to establish a feeling of "down" and "up."
3. Teach the students to say a concise "down" and "up" as they pat their feet in time with the metronome.
4. Using a method book, rhythm studies book, rhythm slides, PowerPoint (or other similar) display, or any other projection of various rhythmic patterns, teach the students to say each rhythm using a series of "downs" and/or "ups."

3	↓	↓	↓	↓ ↑	↓ ↑	↓ ↑	↓ ↑	↓
4	down	down	down	down-up	down-up	down-up	down-—-up	down

5. Teach one rhythmic pattern at a time and then begin to mix patterns up into various combinations and in a variety of meters.
6. Have students "down-up" each new exercise before it is played on the instruments. An additional exercise is to ask the students to finger the part as they say the rhythm on "downs" and "ups."
7. To further improve reading skills, ask the students to say the names of the notes of a melodic line in rhythm with the metronome. Do not say the sharps or flats, since this will disrupt the flow of the rhythm. Once the students are comfortable with the names of the notes, ask them to say the names of the notes as they finger the specific passage. The final step is to play the passage. Remember to keep the foot pat going throughout the exercise.

The development of a counting system is essential to rhythmic accuracy and a sound foundation for sight-reading. Students must learn to recognize rhythmic patterns just as they learn that the combination of the letters "c-a-t" when combined will spell "cat." The establishment of a counting system provides students with a basis for figuring out new rhythmic patterns on their own. It will eliminate most, if not all, rote teaching of rhythms and ultimately improve the overall quality of the band's performance. So many times the problem is not *what* to play, but *when* to play. A counting system coupled with a rhythmic pattern vocabulary will vastly improve performance skills at all levels of experience.

TIMBRE:
The timbre of *La Volta* involves a series of color changes as the melody is passed from one voicing combination to another. It is essential to keep the general timbre on the light side. Although a variety of cues are provided, it is important to use only those cues that are necessary for an artistic performance of the work. Utilizing all of the cued parts will not only increase the density of the composition but will mask the intended color changes.

Establish balance and blend by constantly reminding the students that in the homophonic sections there is a primary melody that must be heard. Have the students practice each individual section and identify the texture and the hierarchy of dynamic importance. By making a recording of the band in rehearsal and allowing the students to analyze the balance, students will more easily identify what the balance concerns may be. This self-assessment will also provide the students with a sense of individual and group responsibility for the musical product.

Students may easily be encouraged to develop a characteristic sound by providing them with sound musical examples of each instrument. Local libraries are often a fine source of recordings of professional musicians performing solo works. Provide students with a list of quality performers and ask them to listen to a CD performed by the recognized artist. If there is a professional orchestra or band in the community, invite these musicians to the band room for master classes or mini-performances. Beginner band students can be encouraged to listen to the sound of their chosen instrument before they attempt to produce that first tone. It is extremely important that the students know what kind of sound should come from the instrument. Modeling is a valuable tool in the development of good tone.

It is also noted that there is grant money available for various artist-in-residence programs. Explore such possibilities to assist in bringing professional musicians into the classroom.

Unit 7: Form and Structure

The classification of form is not always a cut-and-dried issue. A prime example of this is the form of *La Volta*. Although the work is essentially a binary form as indicated by the presence of A and B themes, the compositional tactics of the Renaissance may lead one to make a case for labeling the piece as a continuous variation form. The A theme is presented in the upper woodwinds and first trumpets during the first eight measures of the piece. This melody is then repeated at rehearsal letter A, first in the woodwinds and then in the brass. Letter B provides a B theme, again in the upper woodwinds. It is repeated at rehearsal letter C by the first trumpets for four measures, and then the upper woodwinds rejoin the melodic line with the trumpets. However, this repeat of the B theme comes with rhythmic and melodic enhancements, particularly the use of passing tones. Letter D is a variation on the initial A theme, and its repeat at rehearsal letter E is a further embellishment of the opening theme. Letter F is another enhanced version of the B theme. Of particular interest is the development of the melodic material at rehearsal letter G. The B theme is now presented in both augmentation and variation.

Because one has to look carefully to find the theme, students will need a visual display to understand how the theme has been used as a basis for the melodic material. Consider creating a handout or an overhead projection of the themes and their enhanced versions. Notice that subsequent repeats of each theme become more complex. The composer has made extensive use of passing tones to modify the melodies.

Rehearsal letter:		A	B	C	D	E	F	G
Melodic material:	A	A	B	B1	A1	A2	B2	B3

SECTION	MEASURES	EVENT AND SCORING
A theme	1-9	Homophonic presentation of A theme by flute, oboe, clarinet 1, trumpet 1, xylophone; full percussion; *forte*
A theme	9-17	Repeat of A theme; four measures of woodwinds and low brass, then four measures of brass
B theme	17-25	Presentation of B theme by flute, oboe, clarinet 1, xylophone
B1 theme	25-33	Variation of B theme; four measures of trumpet 1 and brass, then full band with upper woodwinds and xylophone on the melody
A1 theme	33-41	Ornamentation of A theme; woodwinds and xylophone
A2 theme	41-49	Second modification of A theme; xylophone solo for four measures, then *tutti*; more extensive use of passing tones
B2 theme	49-57	Second variation of B theme; melody in upper woodwinds for four measures with full band, then trumpet 1
B3 theme	57-end	Third variation of B theme; full band; contrapuntal texture with melodies in (1) flute, oboe, trumpet 1, xylophone; (2) clarinet, bass clarinet, alto saxophone, tenor saxophone; (3) trumpet 2, horn; (4) trombone, euphonium, tuba

Unit 8: Suggested Listening

William Byrd/arr. Jacob:
  Battell
  William Byrd Suite
William Dunscombe/Finlayson, *Early English Suite*
Katheryn Fenske, *Music from the Great Hall*
George Kirck, *Renaissance Triptych*
Bob Margolis, *Fanfare, Ode and Festival*
Ron Nelson:
  Courtly Airs and Dances
  Medieval Suite
Henry Purcell/Schaefer, *Battle Symphony*

Tielman Susato, *The Battle Pavane*
Tielman Susato/Curnow, *Renaissance Suite*

Unit 9: Additional References and Resources

Apel, Willi. *Harvard Dictionary of Music*, 2nd edition. Cambridge, MA: The Belknap Press of Harvard University Press, 1970.

Blume, Friedrich. *Renaissance and Baroque Music*. New York, NY: W.W. Norton & Company, 1967.

Bukofzer, Manfred F. *Music in the Baroque Era*. New York, NY: W.W. Norton & Company, 1947.

Duckworth, William. *A Creative Approach to Music Fundamentals*, 4th edition. Belmont, CA: Wadsworth Publishing Company, 1992.

Fenske, Katheryn. *La Volta*. New Glarus, WI: Daehn Publications, 1998.

Fenske, Katheryn. Telephone conversation with Susan Creasap. April 15, 2000.

Gallaher, Christopher. Conversation with Susan Creasap. May 25, 2000.

Grout, Donald Jay. *A History of Western Music*, 5th edition. New York, NY: W.W. Norton & Company, 1996.

McComb, Todd. www.classical.net/comp.1st/byrd.html

Reese, Gustave. *Music in the Renaissance*, revised edition. New York, NY: W.W. Norton & Company, 1959.

Contributed by:

Susan Creasap
Assistant Director of Bands
Morehead State University
Morehead, Kentucky

Teacher Resource Guide

Liturgical Fanfare

Robert W. Smith
(b. 1958)

Unit 1: Composer

Robert W. Smith received a Bachelor of Music Education degree from Troy State University and a Master of Music degree from the University of Miami. He is currently the Director of Bands at Troy State University. As a conductor and clinician, Smith has performed throughout the United States, Canada, Japan, and Europe.

Unit 2: Composition

Liturgical Fanfare was composed in early 1995 when Smith was living in Harrisonburg, Virginia. A Grade 1 piece, the composition utilizes the first notes learned by beginning instrumentalists. Special consideration should be given to the trumpets who are required to play a written C scale, alto saxophones who are required to play a G scale, and tubas who are required to play low B-flat.

The form of the piece is A–B–A–B–A with the use of bell tones to segment the various sections. The "A" statement is the repeated rhythmic pattern of two quarter notes/two eighth notes/quarter note. The trumpets perform the melody after this opening fanfare. Clarinets join the trumpets in the second half of the "B" theme. In the first presentation of the "B" theme, the flute and oboe add a *legato* line for contrast. The trumpets are combined with the alto saxophone section in the restatement of the "B" theme. In addition, the "B" sections include a countermelody played by the trombone and tenor saxophone sections.

Liturgical Fanfare is published by Belwin-Mills Publishing Corporation with all rights administered by Warner Brothers Publications, Inc.

Unit 3: Historical Perspective

An assignment from the publisher, this piece was composed in 1995 as a concert opener or festival work. *Liturgical Fanfare* may also be considered a concert closer with the optional use of antiphonal brass. This beginning band piece offers a slight variation from most Grade 1 compositions, with independent parts as opposed to strict doubling techniques. This allows the composer to add variations in the overall timbre of the ensemble.

Unit 4: Technical Considerations

The piece is pitched in concert E-flat. Primarily the harmony is I–V–I or I–ii–V–I, utilizing several inversions of the tonic and supertonic chords and the addition of sevenths and ninths. The bell tone section is achieved with the stacking of notes a fourth apart.

Accenting is a primary concern for all instruments. The repeated rhythmic pattern of two quarter notes/two eighth notes/quarter note requires a good accenting on beats one, two, and four of the measure. A difference must be made in the method of attack between *staccato* eighth notes and the accented tones.

Unit 5: Stylistic Considerations

The entire work is based on the opening rhythmic figure of two quarter notes/two eighth notes/quarter note. The articulation of this figure includes *staccato* eighths that lean toward the final accented quarter note. The second major consideration should involve the use of bell tones, with each entrance having more intensity than the previous entrance. The entire piece is an excellent exercise for rhythmic accuracy and consistent articulation. In addition, the balance between melody and the *ostinato* pattern will need to be addressed.

The composer makes a note encouraging the use of antiphonal brass from measure 45 to the conclusion of the composition.

Good communication between the conductor and performers is essential for the optional *rallentando* to be achieved at measure 70 to the end.

Unit 6: Musical Elements

The harmonic texture of the piece thickens with the introduction of each fanfare. Careful consideration should be given to balance between voices as they enter. Balance between melody and the repeated rhythmic pattern of two quarter notes/two eighth notes/quarter note is an important consideration.

The use of percussion instruments adds to the color of the composition. The utilization of a triangle achieves a "lighter" feel in the melodic sections of the piece. Crash cymbals add to the majesty of the fanfare sections.

Unit 7: Form and Structure

SECTION	MEASURES	KEY	EVENT AND SCORING
A	1-13	E-flat	Fanfare
Transition	14-17	Bell tones	Accenting and use of *sfz*
B	18-33	E-flat	Trumpet melody joined by clarinet on second statement; counterline provided by trombone and tenor saxophone
A	34-46	E-flat	Fanfare
B	47-55	E-flat	Melody in trumpet and alto saxophone; counterline provided by trombone and tenor saxophone
Transition	55-64	Bell tones	Accenting and use of *sfz*
A	65-end	E-flat	Fanfare with an optional *rallentando* ending

Unit 8: Suggested Listening

William Gordon, *Fanfare of the Bells*

Robert Smith, *Liturgical Fanfare*, available on Warner Brothers CD "Music for Concert Band Beginning Band Series" (CATCD95-1)

Jack Stamp, *Gavorkna Fanfare*

Unit 9: Additional References and Resources

Casey, Joseph. *Teaching Techniques and Insights for Instrumental Music Educators*, revised edition. Chicago, IL: GIA Publications, Inc., 1993.

Lisk, Edward S. *The Creative Director – Alternative Rehearsal Techniques*. Ft. Lauderdale, FL: Meredith Music Publications, 1987.

Rehrig, William H. *The Heritage Encyclopedia of Band Music*. Edited by Paul E. Bierley. Westerville, OH: Integrity Press, 1991.

Whitwell, David. *A Concise History of the Wind Band*. Northridge, CA: WINDS, 1985.

Contributed by:

John Villella
West Chester University
West Chester, Pennsylvania

Teacher Resource Guide

Madrigal for Band

John Wilbye
(1574–1638)

arranged by Anne McGinty
(b. 1945)

Unit 1: Composer/Arranger

John Wilbye, the third son of a prosperous tanner and landowner, was born at Diss, England, in 1574. In 1595, he became the resident musician, in the service of the Kytson family, at Hengrave Hall near Bury St. Edmunds. He served in that capacity for most of his life. Few examples of Wilbye's church music or instrumental music exist. He is, however, regarded as perhaps the finest of all the late Renaissance, English madrigal composers.

Arranger Anne McGinty, a native of Findlay, Ohio, was born in 1945. She began her higher education at Ohio State University, where she studied flute with Donald McGinnis. She left Ohio State University to pursue a career in flute performance and played principal flute in several ensembles in the Tucson, Arizona area. She later earned her Bachelor of Music and Master of Music degrees at Duquesne University in Pittsburgh, Pennsylvania, where she studied flute and chamber music with Bernard Goldberg and composition with Joseph Willcox Jenkins (*American Overture for Band*).

With over 160 published compositions and arrangements for band, McGinty is the most prolific woman composer of concert band music. Her band works are well represented in many state music lists and selected music lists, and are regularly performed by school bands, especially young bands. She is a member of ASCAP and has received annual composition awards from that organization since 1986. Her band works are recognized for their variety of instrumental textures and colors, and for their fresh harmonic vocabulary. Some of McGinty's well-known band works include *The Red Balloon*, *Foxwood Overture*, *Circles of Stones*, *African Folk Trilogy*, and *Emerald Point Overture*.

Although she is no longer a performing flutist, McGinty is a prominent figure in the contemporary flute world. She taught flute at several colleges in the Midwest, served as a flute clinician for an instrument manufacturer, was the co-founder of the "National Flute Association Newsletter" (now known as "The Flutists' Quarterly"), and has served on the Board of Directors of the National Flute Association. She is well known as a flute choir specialist and is largely responsible for several series of published flute choir repertoire.

McGinty and her husband, composer John Edmondson, are co-owners of Queenwood Publications (www.queenwood.com) in Scottsdale, Arizona. McGinty is active as a guest conductor, clinician, and speaker throughout the United States and Canada. Her other interests include weightlifting, reading murder mysteries, learning to play the bagpipes, and nurturing her two cats, Starz and Stripes.

Unit 2: Composition

Madrigal for Band, published in 1994, is a single-movement work that is approximately two minutes and thirty seconds in length. It is based on John Wilbye's madrigal *As Fair as Morn* from *Second Set of Madrigals*, published in 1609. The *Second Set of Madrigals* consists of thirty-four madrigals composed for three to six voices. *As Fair as Morn* is number six and is composed for three voices. Wilbye's *First Set of Madrigals*, consisting of thirty madrigals, was published in 1598. Among his best-known madrigals are *The Lady Oriana*, *Sweet Honey Sucking Bees*, *Weep O Mine Eyes*, and *Happy, O Happy He*. This late Renaissance work is a fine example of the free imitative counterpoint of the late sixteenth century English madrigal.

Unit 3: Historical Perspective

The sixteenth century English madrigal differs from the fourteenth century Italian madrigal. While based on English lyric poetry rather than Latin or Italian texts, English madrigals are generally less text-bound and more musical in approach than their earlier Italian counterparts. The content of these secular vocal works is often humorous, amorous, or melancholy and often deals with some aspect of nature. The English madrigal also tended to be more homophonic than the Italian madrigal, with emphasis on a more prominent, solo-like voice. These works made extensive use of free imitation rather than the strict imitation of the fugue or canon. They were usually composed for three to six solo voices but were often doubled by available instruments. They also were often through composed, as is *As Fair as Morn*. John Wilbye, along with Thomas Morley (1557–1602) and Thomas Weelkes (1575–1623), are the post-important composers of English madrigal.

The music notation of works from this time period is quite different than current notational practices. Mensural, or measured, notation was used. There were no time signatures, measures, or bar lines, and the notes themselves looked different than current notation. Additionally, there was ambiguity of pitch center and voice assignment. Each part was printed alone in a separate part book. There was no way for the musicians to see the relationship of their part to the other parts in the composition. Examples of mensural notation might be of interest to the band.

Other important composers from this time period include William Byrd (1543–1623), John Dowland (1563–1626), Giles Farnaby (1565–1640), Michael Praetorius (1571–1621), and Claudio Monteverdi (1567–1643). Prominent historical figures from this time period include explorer Captain John Smith (1580–1631), author and playwright William Shakespeare (1564–1616), author and statesman Francis Bacon (1561–1626), scientists and astronomers Johannes Kepler (1571–1630) and Galileo Galilei (1564–1642), and artists El Greco (1541–1614) and Peter Paul Rubens (1577–1640).

Unit 4: Technical Considerations

Madrigal for Band is in the key of concert B-flat. It is in 4/4 and is marked *moderato* at quarter note = 108. As part of the *Queenwood Beginning Band Series*, the work is arranged to be performed by quite limited instrumentation: one flute, two clarinets, one alto saxophone, two trumpets, and percussion. However, parts for all instruments are included. There is ample doubling of parts. In general, flute, oboe, and bells double; all low brass and low woodwinds are doubled in octaves and with one of the trumpet parts; and there is an optional part that doubles tenor saxophone and horn. Percussion instruments include bells, tambourine, high tom-tom (the snare with the snares off), and low tom-tom. The percussion is used to emphasize the different entrances of the free imitation. All ranges are appropriate for first-year players, and clarinets stay below the break.

The integrity of the three parts of the work, often with octave doubling, is maintained throughout. Instruments frequently switch from part to part as range and demand require. Rhythms are simple when played alone, with the most complex figures being paired eighth notes (1+2+), groups of three eighth note pick-ups (+4+), and ties across bar lines.

The technical difficulty of this work rests primarily in the independence required by the rhythmic delays of free imitation and the work's non-standard phrase lengths. The staggering of the entrances varies: two beats and four beats. The phrase lengths also vary throughout: two measures, three measures, four measures, five measures, and six measures. McGinty states in the score:

> Careful attention must be given to individual counting as the imitative counterpoint can interrupt one's concentration, especially when

hearing another voice enter, playing your upcoming phrase, when your part has rests. Attack and enter with great confidence.

Addressing the non-standard phrase lengths and varying time intervals between points of imitation will be the greatest challenge in learning and performing this historically important arrangement for band. Secure counting and rhythmic independence are definitely required for this work.

Almost all notes are tongued, with only a few pairs of slurred eighth notes. While these articulations are generally simple in complexity, they are not stylistically easy for beginners.

Unit 5: Stylistic Considerations

Music from this time period did not include any stylistic or expressive markings. Furthermore, there are no style, phrase, or expressive makings in this arrangement. Since the original work was to be sung, McGinty suggests that the style should be *legato* throughout. The conductor might choose to add additional slurs to the parts to facilitate a smoother sound. McGinty states:

> The dynamic marking is *mf* throughout, but allow the dynamics to rise and fall with the shape of the phrase.

The conductor may also choose to add additional dynamic markings, *crescendos*, *decrescendos*, and breath marks to the parts.

Unit 6: Musical Elements

MELODY:

Familiarity with concert B-flat (tonic), concert E-flat (subdominant), and concert F (dominant) scales will be helpful. In several instances, students must play chromatic intervals in close proximity (concert E and E-flat; A and A-flat). These intervals could be isolated and addressed during the warm-up. The thematic material used in this work is generally simple and short. Most often the motives begin with pick-up notes: 2 3 4 | 1 or 3 4+ | 1 or 3+4+ | 1 or +4+ | 1. Since there are no expressive markings in this arrangement, the conductor might choose to focus the ensemble's attention on these pick-up notes. Rather than *crescendos* when ascending and *decrescendos* when descending, a better choice would be to *crescendo* through these pick-up notes toward their resolution (short notes leading to long notes), often across bar lines. This concept could also be addressed during the warm-up. Careful attention should be paid to all notes that move while others are being held so the counterpoint and polyphony may be heard. Dynamic markings could be added to the parts. A truly smooth, *legato* style of playing is quite difficult for young musicians. Too often this results in a sort of "huff-and-puff" style rather than a sustained and connected sound. To smooth out the sound, the conductor may choose to change the articulations by adding appropriate slurs.

HARMONY:
The harmonic structure of this work is simple. Once the above-mentioned scales are secure, attention could be drawn to the relationships of the first, third, and fifth notes of the scale to the accompanying chords. A simple chord progression in B-flat (I–IV–V–I) could be incorporated into the warm-up.

RHYTHM:
The concepts of imitation could be introduced through call-and-response exercises, playing canons or rounds (such as *Are You Sleeping* or *Row, Row, Row Your Boat*), playing scales or rhythmic exercises with staggered entrances, and listening to examples. Staggering entrances at two beats and four beats could be rehearsed individually. Handouts of the different staggered rhythmic entrances could be developed by the conductor and rehearsed. While this arrangement could probably be learned through rote rehearsal, the development of rhythmic and counting independence will have far more long-term benefits. Having students count their parts and/or sing their parts could be helpful. Additional rehearsal markings could be added to the parts to help guide the students in knowing where each episode of imitation begins.

TIMBRE:
As always, the production of the best possible characteristic tone is desired. For young players, this is best approached by encouraging a big sound first and then working to refine it rather than striving for a small, less offensive sound and hoping to build on it later. The control of embouchure and air is essential in building tone. These areas must be regularly addressed in every rehearsal! For young players, articulation tends to interrupt the smooth flow of air required for a mature tone quality. Singing of scales or exercises, followed by the same passages slurred, can help in internalizing the control of the air, which should still be present when attempting a *legato* articulation. Smooth, not lumpy!

The addition of dynamic markings would help in leading the students toward a proper balance of the three parts of this madrigal. Since this arrangement includes so much doubling of parts, the conductor could choose to thin out the texture at times to provide more contrast or better balance.

Unit 7: Form and Structure

SECTION	MEASURES	EVENT AND SCORING
1	1-19	B-flat major tonal center; two-measure percussion introduction; four-measure episode with four-beat staggered entrances; four-measure episode with four-beat staggered entrances; three-measure episode with two-beat

Section	Measures	Event and Scoring
		staggered entrances; six-measure episode with two-beat staggered entrances
2	20-32	Two-measure episode with two-beat staggered entrances; four-measure episode with four-beat staggered entrances beginning on beat two; the next six measures basically repeat the material of the previous six measures, but beginning on beat four
3	33-51	F major tonal center; six-measure interlude of woodwinds and percussion; five-measure episode with two- and four-beat staggered entrances; nine-measure interlude consisting of three three-measure phrases that sequence F major, E-flat major, C major, and B-flat major
4	52-67	B-flat major tonal center; seven-measure episode with four-beat staggered entrances (the most rhythmic motion with continuous eighth notes); three-measure phrase and six-measure phrase (the least rhythmic motion with whole notes and half notes)

Unit 8: Suggested Listening

A full performance recording of this arrangement is available from
   Queenwood Publications.
Recorded excerpts from many of Anne McGinty's compositions (but not
   Madrigal for Band) may be found at the website of J.W. Pepper
   (www.jwpepper.com).
Recordings of madrigals by John Wilbye (but not *As Fair as Morn*), Thomas
   Morley, and Thomas Weelkes are commercially available.
J. S. Bach, *The Well-Tempered Clavier*, Books I and II
William Byrd/arr. Jacob, *William Byrd Suite*
Frescobaldi/Cassado/Kindler/arr. Earl Slocum, *Toccata*
Gordon Jacob: *Giles Farnaby Suite*
William Latham:
   Court Festival
   Three Chorale Preludes

Bob Margolis:
   Soldiers Procession and Sword Dance after Susato
   Terpsichore after Michael Praetorius
Ron Nelson, *Courtly Airs and Dances*
Tielman Susato/arr. Margolis, *The Battle Pavane*
Tielman Susato/arr. Curnow, *Renaissance Suite*

Unit 9: Additional References and Resources

"The Basic Band Curriculum: Grades I, II, III." *BD Guide*, September/October 1989, 2-6.

Battisti, Frank, and R. Garofalo. *Guide to Score Study for the Wind Band Conductor*. Fort Lauderdale, FL: Meredith Music Publications, 1990.

Casey, Joseph. *Teaching Techniques and Insights for Instrumental Music Educators*. Chicago, IL: GIA Publications, 1993.

Dvorak, Thomas L. *Best Music for Young Band*. Brooklyn, NY: Manhattan Beach Music, 1986.

Garofalo, Robert J. *Instructional Designs for Middle/Junior High School Band*. Fort Lauderdale, FL: Meredith Music Publications, 1995.

Hovey, Nilo. *Efficient Rehearsal Procedures for School Bands*. Elkhart, IN: The Selmer Company, 1976.

Kreines, Joseph. *Music for Concert Band*. Tampa, FL: Florida Music Service, 1989.

Lisk, Edward S. *Intangibles of Musical Performance*. Fort Lauderdale, FL: Meredith Music Publications, 1996.

McBeth, W. Francis. *Effective Performance of Band Music*. San Antonio, TX: Southern Music, 1972.

Middleton, James, and G. Garner. *The Symphonic Band Winds*. San Antonio, TX: Southern Music Company, 1986.

Miles, Richard. *Teaching Music through Performance in Band*, Volume 1. Chicago, IL: GIA Publications, 1997.

Miles, Richard. *Teaching Music through Performance in Band*, Volume 2. Chicago, IL: GIA Publications, 1998.

Miles, Richard. *Teaching Music through Performance in Band*, Volume 3. Chicago, IL: GIA Publications, 2000.

Rehrig, William H. *The Heritage Encyclopedia of Band Music*. Westerville, OH: Integrity Press, 1991.

Smith, Norman. *March Music Notes*. Lake Charles, LA: Program Note Press, 1986.

Smith, Norman, and A. Stoutamire. *Band Music Notes*. San Diego, CA: Neil A. Kjos Publisher, 1979.

Strange, Richard E. *Selective Music List for Bands*. Nashville, TN: National Band Association, 1997.

VanderCook, H.A. *Expression in Music*. Miami, FL: Rubank, 1942.

Contributed by:

Wayne F. Dorothy
Kansas State University
Manhattan, Kansas

Teacher Resource Guide

The Minute Arachnida

Robert Jordan
(b. 1929)

Unit 1: Composer

Robert M. Jordan was born on August 4, 1929, in Little Rock, Arkansas. A graduate of Little Rock High School, he studied at Hendrix College, where he received a Bachelor of Arts in Music Education (1951) and a Bachelor of Science in Chemistry (1953). During 1954, Jordan studied at the University of Arkansas Medical School. He received his Master of Music from North Texas State University in 1960.

Jordan taught in the public schools for over forty years in such places as Rison, Arkansas; Texarkana, Arkansas; Texarkana, Texas; Atlanta, Texas; Dallas, Texas; and Hamshire-Fannett, Texas. Known works for wind band by Jordan include *Canto Capers* (unpublished), *Declaration and Song* (1987), *Imperium* (unpublished), *The Minute Arachnida* (1987), *Quest* (unpublished), *Repartee* (unpublished), *Rush Hour Rock* (1988), *Super Solis* (1988), and *Trionfonte* (unpublished).

Unit 2: Composition

The Minute Arachnida (Itsy Bitsy Spider) is pronounced "Men-oot Uh-rack-ni-duh." *Minute* means "small" and *Arachnida* means "spider," which is a fancy name for "Itsy Bitsy Spider." This work is a simple, yet effective, sounding arrangement of a familiar children's song. Approximately two minutes and forty seconds in duration, *The Minute Arachnida* is sixty-five measures long and is in common time. Although marked as "optional," the inventive use of percussion (bells, snare drum, bass drum, triangle, suspended cymbal, and tambourine) adds interest and variety to this one-movement work for young band. The main theme is stated twice followed by a canon voiced as follows: first statement equals upper woodwinds; second statement equals trumpets; third statement equals horns, trombones, and tenor saxophones; fourth statement equals baritone, tuba, and low reeds. The work closes with a partial statement of the main theme in the upper woodwinds and trumpets interrupted by a *fermata*, and it ends on a tonic chord.

Unit 3: Historical Perspective

Children's songs have been a resource for many compositions throughout the history of music. Although the exact source of "Itsy Bitsy Spider" is unknown, it has been a part of children's songs since colonial times. This recognizable tune also has a few other titles and text, such as "Little Spider" and "Tommy's Pet Spider" to name a few. Whatever the text or title, audiences and performers alike will all know this popular children's tune.

Unit 4: Technical Considerations

As mentioned above, this work makes use of six different percussion instruments. Although marked as "optional," they add greatly to the composition. The piece begins and ends in the key of E-flat major. There are no significantly difficult rhythms throughout; however, balance between the melodic line and the accompaniment might prove to be a challenge. The two trumpet parts never extend above a written third-space C. The two clarinet parts do not go above the break; they explore the rich sounds of the lower register.

Unit 5: Stylistic Considerations

The Minute Arachnida contains a moderate use of dynamics ranging from *piano* to *forte*. There are no specific articulation markings used. There are, however, ample breath markings throughout. A tempo marking of *moderato* begins the work, with no indication of tempo change throughout.

Unit 6: Musical Elements

MELODY:
The familiar diatonic melody of this work is passed through the entire ensemble. There are no accidentals and no intervals larger than a major sixth.

HARMONY:
The harmonic accompaniment is in the traditional homophonic style. The tonality of the work is E-flat major throughout.

RHYTHM:
The rhythms used in this work are somewhat basic, making use of half notes, quarter notes, and eighth notes.

TIMBRE:
The opening sixteen measures are for percussion only; the melody is in the bells and is accompanied by snare drum, bass drum, triangle, and suspended cymbal scrapes. After this unusual opening, the composer uses varying combinations of woodwinds, brass, and percussion to create interesting tone colors. As with many Grade 1 and 2 pieces where range is a technical consideration, the melody and its harmonic accompaniment are often scored in the same *tessitura*, thus causing a potential balance problem. The dynamic markings provide a clear view into balance considerations.

Unit 7: Form and Structure

SECTION	MEASURES	EVENT AND SCORING
A (main theme)	1-16	Key: E-flat major Orchestration: percussion only
B (restatement of main theme)	17-32	Key: E-flat major Orchestration: *tutti*; melody in upper woodwinds/brass
C (canon)	33-60	Key: E-flat major Orchestration: first statement = upper woodwinds; second statement = trumpet; third statement = horn, trombone, and tenor saxophone; fourth statement = baritone, tuba, and low reeds
D (coda containing melodic fragments)	61-65	Key: E-flat major Orchestration: *tutti*; melody in upper woodwinds/brass

Unit 8: Suggested Listening
Eugene Bozza, *Children's Overture*
Norman Dello Joio, *Scenes from "The Louvre,"* Movement II ("Children's Gallery")
Percy Grainger, *Children's March*
Charles Ives, *Old Home Days*, Movement V ("London Bridge Has Fallen Down!")
Sammy Nestico, *A Tribute to Stephen Foster*

Unit 9: Additional References and Resources
Rehrig, William H. *The Heritage Encyclopedia of Band Music.* Edited by Paul Bierley. Westerville, OH: Integrity Press, 1991.

Contributed by:
Roy M. King
Assistant Director of Bands
Louisiana State University
Baton Rouge, Louisiana

Teacher Resource Guide

Modal Song and Dance
Elliot Del Borgo
(b. 1938)

Unit 1: Composer

Elliot Del Borgo was born in 1938 in the city of Port Chester, New York. He earned his B.S. degree from State University of New York, his Ed.M. from Temple University, and his M.M. from the Philadelphia Conservatory, where he studied composition with Vincent Persichetti. He taught music in the Philadelphia public schools before returning as a teacher to his *alma mater*, the Crane School of Music at State University of New York, Potsdam (1965). He was awarded a doctoral equivalency by State University of New York in 1973. At Crane, he was a teacher and administrator, earning the rank of Professor of Music prior to his retirement in 1995. Del Borgo wrote music for the 1980 Olympics and has published many compositions for band, orchestra, and other media. In 1993, he was elected to membership in the American Bandmasters Association.

Unit 2: Composition

Modal Song and Dance was written expressly for young players. It consists of two movements: "Song" (approximately one minute in length) and "Dance" (approximately one minute and forty-five seconds in length). Total performance time is almost three minutes. Written in minor modes with limited rhythm and range demands, the piece has become a favorite of students and conductors alike.

264

Unit 3: Historical Perspective

"Mode" is a musical term denoting a system of organizing musical elements. Early in the history of written music, it was used for both rhythms and scale formation, the latter being the most common. In this sense, a mode refers to a group of notes arranged to form a scale. Much of the earliest written music did not indicate the absolute pitch but instead provided a rhythmic and melodic guideline for the musicians. To accommodate different scale patterns (where whole steps and half steps occur), musicians used modes. Eventually a system of notating exact pitch was developed and modes gave way to the different forms of scales we use today. The title of this work, *Modal Song and Dance*, refers to the scale patterns (modes) that the composer used when writing the piece.

Unit 4: Technical Considerations

Because of the modal construction, players should be aware of the scale forms used. Ranges for all woodwinds are moderate except for flute and trombone/euphonium playing a single occurrence of E-flat above the staff. There is also a low B written for the baritone saxophone. The percussion requirements include snare drum, bass drum, cymbals (both suspended and crash), and bells. In the first movement, the snare drum player must be capable of sustaining a buzz roll at a soft dynamic. Other than a few flams and three short rolls, the percussion demands are very simple. The conductor's score consists of twelve staves (two for percussion) and indicates transposed pitches for each instrument except for the combined bass line (bassoon, baritone saxophone, and tuba), which is in concert pitch, bass clef.

Unit 5: Stylistic Considerations

Phrasing is an important aspect of proper performance; players should know where and where not to breathe. In the opening movement, each four-measure phrase should have a tapered release, followed by a full, yet rapid breath. The moving bass line in measures 12 and 16 should be brought forward. A slight *rubato* before the Picardy third in measure 23 will help the cadence settle in. Movement two begins immediately thereafter, although a slight silence (two or three seconds) between the movements would also be appropriate. Care should be taken that the two quarter notes (measures 37, 38, 40, 49, 50, 76, 77) are played with even lengths, not cutting short the second note.

Unit 6: Musical Elements

MELODY:

Movement one makes use of the Aeolian mode (built on the sixth scale degree). The band can play this mode by choosing an easy scale such as B-flat concert, play down two notes to G, then play from G to G using the key of B-flat. This particular mode eventually became known as the natural minor scale. First clarinet and alto saxophone are first to play the theme in measures 1 through 4. If possible, all four measures are best played in a single breath, with *legato*, yet clean articulations. Since the first three notes are the same pitch, musical nuance would imply a slight increase in the intensity of sound for each recurring pitch while the overall arc of the melodic phrase apexes on beat one of the second measure. The same pattern should be used for measures 3 and 4. When the trumpets take the theme at measure 9, the line increases in tension over three measures until measure 12, where the dynamic pulls back. In measure 16, an anacrusis (pick-up) is added to the theme restatement; all parts with a dotted-half note should breathe prior to beat four. The last measure of the movement has a *fermata*, which should be held at least four beats in length.

Movement two uses the Dorian mode (built on the second scale degree), performed by starting on a B-flat concert and playing up one note to C, then playing up an octave in the key of B-flat. The second movement contrasts horizontal melodic material (measures 28 through 35, etc.) with vertical rhythmic material (measures 36 and 37, etc.). It begins with a rhythmic motive played by the snare drum (snares off), later imitated by the winds in measures 36 and 78. Phrases are four measures long except where fragmented among sections (measures 37 through 40, 49 through 52, 68, 76 to the end).

HARMONY:
The opening chordal accompaniment must be played smoothly and well balanced. The use of open fifths and parallel movement adds to the "old" sound of the minor/modal nature. A small amount of *crescendo* may be used to create tension as the first half note in measure 2 moves toward beat three. This dynamic would then recede when moving to the next measure. It would not be inappropriate to completely release all sound between measures 4 and 5, taking care that the rhythmic pulse is not too greatly delayed. The same pattern should repeat itself for measures 5 through 8. The last chord of the first movement uses a Picardy third (in the flutes) to create a D major triad for the cadence. Around 1500, most music composers were employed as church musicians and were required to follow certain rules when composing music for the service. Up until this time, the final chord of a piece could not use the third. When this rule was relaxed, it became popular to add the third and raise it by a half step. This alteration, named a Picardy third, changes the final chord from a minor to a major sonority. The practice became quite popular for the next several hundred years.

RHYTHM:
The work remains in 4/4 meter through both movements and uses only simple rhythms (whole, dotted-half, half, quarter, and eighth notes). Movement two is structurally unified through the use of a simple, two-measure rhythmic motif introduced by the snare drum at the beginning of the movement.

TIMBRE:

The composer chooses to open the work with dark colors by using low voices for sustained notes and the rich registers of clarinet and alto saxophone for the melody. It is important that the clarinets produce a full, warm sound when playing the notes that extend into the throat register (G and A). Alto saxophones must work to match the tone quality when switching registers between notes C and D (measure 2) while trying to match the darkness of sound being produced by the clarinets. When the flutes enter in measure 5, the low A must be played in tune and with full body. As the line rises, the flutes must blend as a section, sounding as one player. Trumpets entering at measure 7 should play strong enough to be the dominant voice but without being too bright or strident. As first clarinet crosses into the clarion register (measure 9), tone must remain blended and not overpower the trumpets. In measure 16, the low voices finally begin to come to the front with their sound so that the descending quarter notes in measure 17 are easily heard. The final cadence of movement one in measure 23 must be played in tune and with a full sound prior to execution of the *decrescendo*.

The snare drum player (with strainer turned off) begins the second movement as a solo player. A better tone might result if this rhythm were played with a single stick so that all notes sound identical. The new theme is first heard by a woodwind choir (measures 28 through 31), then the brass are added to bring more power and drama to the piece. At measure 55, the theme is reiterated in block scoring for all woodwinds. The sound should be full, dark, continuous, and well balanced; care must also be taken to ensure accurate rhythmic alignment with the percussion. The style changes to a more *marcato* articulation in measure 63 as the music progresses to a restatement of the fragmented second theme in measure 66. The addition of a *crescendo* in measure 81 along with the *ritardando* will bring the piece to a powerful conclusion. The numerous unison lines that appear in the woodwinds throughout both movements can be improved by careful pitch matching using long tones, chorales, and unison etude studies.

Unit 7: Form and Structure

SECTION	MEASURES	EVENT AND SCORING
Song:		
A	1-4	Theme in clarinet 1 and alto saxophone
A´	5-8	Literal repeat of A theme with addition of contrapuntal flute line
B	9-16	Contrapuntal line continues in flute and clarinet 1 while trumpets play the B theme

SECTION	MEASURES	EVENT AND SCORING
A	17-20	Return of A theme with addition of a descending sequence in low voices
Coda	21-23	Rhythmic augmentation of last half of A theme in flute, ending with Picardy third
Dance:		
A	24-36	Percussion introduction, then A theme in upper woodwinds; repeated with addition of contrapuntal trumpet line at m. 32
B	37-54	New theme given in call-and-response manner between low voices and upper woodwinds
A	55-63	Return of A theme in block scoring
	63-75	Bridge using parts of A and B themes
B	76-82	Return of B theme; with codetta

Unit 8: Suggested Listening

Thoinot Arbeau/arr. Margolis, *Belle Qui Tiens Ma Vie*
John Cacavas, *Danse Pavane*
Larry Daehn, *Nottingham Castle*
Dmitri Kabalevsky/arr. Seikmann and Oliver, *Suite in Minor Mode*
John Kinyon, *Air and Dance*
W. Francis McBeth, *Chant and Jubilo*
John O'Reilly, *Modal Overture*
Robert Sheldon, *Pevensey Castle*
Jared Spears, *A Furious Fable*

Unit 9: Additional References and Resources

Apel, Willi, ed. *Harvard Dictionary of Music*. Cambridge, MA: Belknap Press, 1970.

Grout, Donald J. *A History of Western Music*, 3rd edition. New York, NY: W.W. Norton & Company, 1980.

Harris, Brian. *Young Band Repertoire Project Website*. San Antonio, TX: Institute for Music Research, The University of Texas at San Antonio, 1999–. <http://imr.uts.edu/ybrp>

William Allen Music, Incorporated, Newington, VA.

Young Band Repertoire Project, Volume 1. San Antonio, TX: Institute for Music Research, The University of Texas at San Antonio, 1996.

Young Band Repertoire Project, Volume 2. San Antonio, TX: Institute for Music Research, The University of Texas at San Antonio, 1999.

Young Band Repertoire Project, Volume 3. San Antonio, TX: Institute for Music Research, The University of Texas at San Antonio, 2000.

Contributed by:
Brian Harris
Associate Professor
University of Texas at San Antonio
San Antonio, Texas

Teacher Resource Guide

Music from the Great Hall

arranged by Katheryn Fenske
(b. 1964)

Unit 1: Composer/Arranger

Katheryn Fenske was born in Milwaukee, Wisconsin, on June 27, 1964. She was valedictorian of her high school graduating class and later graduated *summa cum laude* from Luther College with a Bachelor of Arts in Music and a minor in Mathematics. She obtained her Master of Music degree from Northwestern University, where she worked as a graduate assistant for John Paynter (1928–1996).

Fenske is an active music educator and clarinetist. She is active on the regional and national levels as a panelist and presenter with a focus on issues surrounding the middle school band. Fenske is an experienced band director and has taught at the elementary, junior and senior high school levels. She is in demand as a clinician and guest conductor.

Unit 2: Composition

Music from the Great Hall is an arrangement of two seventeenth century keyboard compositions, a toye and a morisco. Fenske's desire to teach music of the Renaissance to her young band students led her to arrange these two movements for band. As with an earlier arrangement (*La Volta*), Fenske consulted the *Fitzwilliam Virginal Book* for material. This collection of 297 early keyboard pieces, published in two volumes in 1894–99, contains a wealth of potential works for transcription. Fenske sought compositions that could be directly transcribed for young students. It was important that the works could be arranged in a manner that would retain their original flavor and structure. Once the compositions were selected, the arranger's students became integrally involved. Not only did they provide live-band run-throughs, but each part had to pass the "boring part" test. The students played through their respective parts and then offered opinions as to the amount of interest the part offered. If something was deemed "boring," the arranger happily restructured the part until it passed the test. In addition to testing the parts, the students assisted with the title of the piece and its movements. *Music from the Great Hall* was premiered by the New Glarus Middle School Band on May 13, 1998, with the arranger conducting. Publisher Larry Daehn was in the audience for the performance and upon hearing the arrangement approached Fenske with an offer to publish the work. The work is eighty-two measures in length and has a duration of approximately three minutes.

Unit 3: Historical Perspective

Music from the Great Hall is comprised of two movements: "A Toye" and "The King's Morisco." Anonymous selections from the *Fitzwilliam Virginal Book*, the two works are arranged virtually intact for young band. A toye is a composition for the virginal or lute and is typically short in duration and light in character. Although only about fifty toyes are extant, one may surmise from these that the genre is generally uncomplicated in both form and texture. Their contrapuntal melodies lack complexity and are presented with minimal adornment.

In contrast to the simplicity of the toye is the rather fascinating morisco (morisca, moresca), a Renaissance dance that was quite popular in the fifteenth and sixteenth centuries. By examining sculptures and paintings of the period, it has been surmised that the dancers blackened their faces, employed various grotesque disguises and costumes, and wore bells on their legs. These same sources indicate that the actual dance incorporated a rather dramatic whirling movement into its choreography. There is also evidence to support the theory that the dance may have been a pantomime of a battle between the Moors and Christians. In England, this dance was known as the Morris dance. Renditions of the morisco may still be found in Spain, Corsica, and Guatemala. There is also a vocal *moresca*, and although it is associated with the Moors, it is not connected in any way to the dance, moresca. It should be noted that "morisco," "morisca," and "moresca" all refer to the same dance.

Unit 4: Technical Considerations

Each movement of *Music from the Great Hall* presents its own unique challenges for the young musician. The first movement, "A Toye," is written in cut-time, but the tempo marking indicates quarter note = 116-144 (or as fast as possible). Young band students will need to be familiar with a variety of rhythmic patterns, including eighth notes, dotted-quarter notes, and an eighth rest followed by three eighth notes. Because of the complexity of the rhythmic structure and the necessity of textural clarity, it is advisable that this movement initially be presented in 4/4 meter. Once the band has a firm understanding of the rhythms and can maintain the vertical alignment of these rhythms, it will be possible to increase the tempo. The 2/2 meter may be employed once the band has attained a tempo that warrants a conducting pattern of two beats per measure. However it must be reiterated that the arranger's intent in offering a wide range of potential tempi is to allow for the performance of this work by bands at a variety of levels. Clarity of the musical lines is the ultimate goal.

Parts for bells, snare drum, triangle, finger cymbals, suspended cymbal, and tambourine add interest to the work and demand varying degrees of proficiency from the young band percussion section. The bell part has a single-measure solo of a series of diatonic sixteenth notes with an octave eighth note leap on the fourth count. A marking of "freely" may make this solo more accessible, while a cross-cue in the first clarinet presents another option. However, the complexity of the solo line may be equally problematic for a young clarinetist. The snare drum part is moderately complex with many eighth note rolls, but an optional simplified version of the part without the rolls is included (ossia). This easier version of the snare drum part is also more appropriate to the faster tempi. The suspended cymbal part alternates coin scrapes with the stick on the crown of the cymbal. A well-coordinated player will not have any problems with this effect; however, two players could be used if needed.

The ranges of all parts are consistent with the capabilities of a Grade 2 band. During the first movement, the second clarinet and bass clarinet parts do not cross the break. Neither the horn nor trombone parts are divided. The presence of unison parts in these two sections allows for more security among the players while creating a texture that is less dense and more characteristic of music from the Renaissance. Because the arranger's students were involved in the creation of this work, all parts are fun to play and well suited to each instrument. These "kid-tested" parts are interesting, idiomatic, and well-constructed.

Although the movement is actually written in the Mixolydian mode, the key signature of E-flat provides a familiar frame of reference. The use of occasional accidentals takes the players out of the major scale and into the modal scale. Second clarinets, bass clarinets, bassoons, trumpets, horns, trombones, euphoniums, and tubas will need to know how to finger concert D-flat.

The second movement of Music from the Great Hall is "The King's Morisco." It contains two sections: the first has a meter signature of 4/4; the second is in 3/4 with the quarter note remaining constant at a tempo of 108-126. Again, the broad range of tempo possibilities allows this piece to be performed by bands of varying technical abilities. More advanced ensembles may wish to push the limits of the tempo markings. However, it is important to note that the morisco is a dance. To retain the work's historical integrity, remember that the presence of dancers would have placed certain limitations on the tempo.

The opening four-measure introduction to this second movement provides a bit of fun for both audience and performers. Since the early morisco entailed the usage of bells attached to the performers' legs, the clarinet section is required to play jingle bells while the rest of the winds supply footstomps. The arranger has even provided some semblance of choreography by indicating a left-right stomping pattern on the parts. The creation of enough jingle bells for the clarinet section provides an opportunity for some cross-curricular activities. The school's art teacher is an excellent source of information on how to create these sets of jingle bells by attaching different sizes and types of bells to cloth, wristbands, a wooden stick, or other materials. The resulting instruments could be quite unique and colorful, while the construction process would provide an opportunity for developing yet another aspect of artistic self-expression.

The percussion section is required to play two tom-toms, snare drum, suspended cymbal, tambourine, jingle bells, gong, bass drum, crash cymbals, and triangle. Six players will be required. Rolls are included for the snare drum, tom-toms, and bass drum. The tom-tom part will provide an opportunity for young players to develop skills in playing on multiple drums. Students should be encouraged to establish an efficient and fundamentally sound sticking pattern. This topic is addressed in most beginning band methods.

The rhythmic structure of the movement involves quarter notes, eighth notes, a dotted-eighth/sixteenth note pattern, syncopation (eighth/quarter/eighth), ties across the bar line, ties within a measure, and dotted-quarter notes. Although this movement will reinforce rhythmic reading, all necessary rhythmic patterns will need to be a part of the students' vocabulary before the ensemble undertakes this section. Students will be required to tongue eighth notes and the dotted-eighth/sixteenth while reading occasional accidentals. The trombones have diatonic eighth note patterns from the E-flat scale. Use E-flat and B-flat scale exercises during the band's warm-up to prepare the group for these technical demands.

All woodwind ranges are extended in this second movement, while the brass ranges are quite conservative. Two flute parts are now provided, with the range of the upper flute part extending to E-flat5. All clarinet and bass clarinet parts require the students to cross the break, and the baritone saxophone will need to use the octave key. The bass clarinet part includes a C5 to C4 eighth note leap. The euphonium part extends from G2 to B-flat3. The trumpets play from C4 to E5 (D5 in the second part).

Unit 5: Stylistic Considerations

Music of the Renaissance is characterized by clarity of texture, balanced voicing, controlled expressiveness, simplicity of style, and generally small melodic ranges. Dissonances occur as the result of passing tones on weak beats or on a strong beat in a suspension. Most of today's band instruments did not exist during this period of music history, and those that were present have undergone significant changes over the centuries. Instruments were generally smaller and less capable of bombastic dynamics. Since these movements were originally works for virginal, it will be important that the students understand the capabilities of that instrument. During the early sixteenth century, the term "virginal" referred to an instrument of the harpsichord family. This small, rectangular box could be held on the player's lap and had a rather light, delicate sound. By the end of the century, the term referred to any of several types of harpsichords so the characteristic timbre remained on the lighter side. To convey the style of this virginal music, the band must develop a lighter tone and more delicate articulations.

The style of "A Toye" must convey a tinkling quality. The notes need to lift in order to create a very light texture. Have the students listen to the bell part and match that bell-like quality. The bell player will need to use brass mallets. If mallets with small brass tips are available, they would establish the best model for the desired effect. While a brighter, lighter texture will be easily developed in the opening eight measures, the *tutti* sections of the movement will present more of a challenge. Encourage the students to use a more delicate approach to tonguing through the use of softer articulations and by avoiding accents. All *fortes* should be on the softer side. Play a recording of sixteenth century harpsichord music for the students to help them understand the style of that period.

"The King's Morisco" should convey more energy and spirit in keeping with its dance origins. This movement is marked "boldly" by the arranger, indicating a slightly heavier style than the first movement. The sense of rollicking, whirling movements may be conveyed by a slight emphasis on counts one and three while projecting the air stream forward at all times. Articulations and dynamics should remain on the lighter side. The basic articulations should allow for a slight separation between notes, enough to create a bounce without making a noticeable *staccato*. By using a "do" or "dee" stroke with the tongue, students are more likely to get the proper note lengths. Execute this articulation without the instruments by having the students say their parts on these syllables with an airy sound. To help them develop breath support, have the students hold a strip of paper eight inches long and one inch wide about eight inches from their mouths. Have them blow air against the paper using the prescribed articulation. The movement of the strip of paper will allow students to determine whether or not the air is stopping between notes. A continuous air stream will keep the paper in a position away from the face. This exercise is also excellent for teaching beginners how to tongue and blow air at the same time.

Unit 6: Musical Elements

MELODY:

Although the piece has a key signature of E-flat, it is actually written in Mixolydian and Dorian modes. Modes, or church modes, were the basis of pitch organization for compositions of the Medieval and Renaissance periods. Each mode is a seven-note scale comprised of two half steps and five whole steps in a variety of combinations. If the basic scale for the construction of modes is based on C major, then the half steps will always occur between E and F, and B and C. The position of these half steps will vary depending on the identity of the first note on which the scale is constructed.

The Mixolydian mode is constructed on the fifth degree of a major scale, thereby placing the resultant half steps between the third and fourth, and sixth and seventh degrees of the scale. By utilizing the E-flat key signature and basing the scale on B-flat, the melody naturally falls into the Mixolydian mode. Students may construct a Mixolydian scale by simply lowering the seventh degree of any major scale by a half step. The Dorian mode is constructed on the second degree of a major scale, and its half steps are located between the second and third, and sixth and seventh degrees of the scale.

The first movement, "A Toye," is scored with a key signature of E-flat major, but the melodic material predominantly lies in the Mixolydian mode (B-flat–C–D–E-flat–F–G–A-flat). It is important to note that a mode is identified within its horizontal structure not its vertical structure. Therefore, the identification of the mode lies within each individual melodic line. Although early modal compositions did not employ tones outside the mode, it was not uncommon for works composed after 1300 to frequently use accidentals. In addition, composers often mixed modes within a melodic line. This is exemplified in the melodic lines of "A Toye" by the usage of A-flat and A-natural, effectively creating areas of B-flat major and B-flat Mixolydian. To assist the students in identifying the sound of these two tonal areas, consider having them play a B-flat major scale and then a B-flat Mixolydian scale (A-natural versus A-flat). One could also make a case for the use of an F Mixolydian tonal area in the melodic framework of this movement. This is particularly possible in the opening four measures when the melody employs F–G–A–B-flat–C–D–E-flat, an F Mixolydian scale.

"A Toye" is comprised of a series of four eight-measure phrases, each with a four-measure antecedent and four-measure consequent. While the location of breath marks is not in the parts, breathing every four measures will work well with most lines in this movement. When a dotted-half note followed by a quarter note is present at a cadence point, take the breath after the dotted-half note.

After the initial four-measure rhythmic introduction to "The King's Morisco," the twelve-bar melody is broken into three, four-bar phrases. The first segment is stated in the upper woodwinds and first trumpet and is easily identified. The second phrase proceeds for two measures in clarinet and horn before being passed on to the lower woodwinds, alto saxophone, trombone, and euphonium. The third phrase of the melody is found in the first flute, alto saxophone, trumpet, and horn. Because of the contrapuntal nature of this work, excellent balance within the ensemble is a necessity. Always define any primary and secondary melodies. Measure sixteen is the statement of the B theme. This melodic material is readily apparent in the flute part and is eight measures in length. The third section of melody occurs at rehearsal number 24 and is comprised of combinations and juxtapositions of previous material. These bits of melody are found in (a/measure 24) flute and clarinet, (b/measure 25) oboe and alto saxophone, (c/measures 26 and 27) trumpet, (d/measures 28 through 31) flute, oboe, clarinet, first trumpet, and trombone. This section is clearly four-part polyphony, so all parts share equal importance and must balance accordingly.

The mode changes to D Dorian at rehearsal number 32. This section is in 3/4 meter and contains four independent lines. Most of these are paired: flute and second trumpet, horn and trombone, euphonium and tuba. The first trumpet part is not doubled. All parts are marked *piano* so as to convey a balanced voicing. Allow the students to hear each of the four parts independent of the other voices. Then pair the voices in any combination, again asking the students to listen to the sound of two parts. Consider having small groups or a solo from each voicing play this section in pairs or trios. The addition of the fourth voice will complete this process. Students will have learned how the four independent voices work together to create polyphony.

HARMONY:

The texture of the first movement of the work is homophonic. There is a melody that is accompanied by more sustained rhythmic figures. The second movement is polyphonic in texture. Polyphony occurs when two or more independent melodies with different rhythmic structures are generated at the same time. The terms "polyphony" and "counterpoint" are interchangeable; however, it should be noted that the term "counterpoint" is usually used in reference to music composed from the sixteenth to the eighteenth centuries. "Polyphony" is the earlier terminology referring to music written prior to the sixteenth century. The use of counterpoint is easily identified in "The King's Morisco."

To properly balance the contrapuntal texture, students will need to become familiar with the individual melodic line. Any sustained harmonies beneath these voices tend to be open fifths or simple triads. This uncomplicated harmonic structure coupled with appropriate doublings affords students the opportunity to hear within the band. It will be beneficial to have like lines independently performed. Identify areas where tuning may be a concern within this structure and demonstrate to students how an "in tune" unison will generate beatless tones.

This tuning exercise may be accomplished by the use of two alto saxophone players or two tuners that can generate a tone. Deliberately mis-tune the instruments by having one player pull the mouthpiece out almost to the end of the cork and the other player push the mouthpiece further onto the cork. Ask the students to play concert B-flat (their G5) with the octave key. The resultant cacophony should be quite unpleasant, with rapid and obvious "beats" in the sound. Now direct the students to begin moving the mouthpieces either further onto the cork or further out on the cork. Have the students play the tone again and ask the band to determine if the sound is better or worse. Define better or worse by telling the students to identify whether the "beats" are faster or slower than the previous example. Continue this procedure until the beats disappear and the alto saxophones sound as if only one of the two players is playing. Students should be encouraged to experiment with this procedure with a friend who plays the same instrument. Plan to use a few minutes in subsequent rehearsals to allow pairs of students to demonstrate their "beatless" tuning. Students may be given extra credit or some other award for achieving this goal. By limiting this experience to just a few minutes once or twice a week, students may be motivated to improve their tuning. Continue to stop in rehearsal and ask students to determine if something is "in" or "out" of tune. This exercise should be introduced as soon as students are producing a characteristic tone. If beginning instrumentalists are allowed to play out of tune, they will begin to accept the resultant intonation as appropriate and correct. Therefore, the earlier the students are taught to play in tune, the better the band's tone quality will be.

RHYTHM:

The meter of *Music from the Great Hall* is composed in 2/2, 4/4, and 3/4. The students will need to know how to play dotted-half notes, half notes, dotted-quarter notes, quarter notes, eighth notes, dotted-eighth note/sixteenth note, and simple syncopation (eighth/quarter/eighth). There are a limited number of quarter notes tied across the bar line in the winds, and more frequent examples are found in the percussion parts. Because this music is contrapuntal in harmonic structure, it will be important to develop vertical alignment of the rhythms. Consider using a metronome to establish the initial pulse as the band learns to perform this work. Set the metronome at a slower tempo than the slowest one that is indicated in the score and ask the students to pat their feet in time to the clicks. Make sure the foot is patting in a rhythmic "one-and-two-and," with the "up" stroke occurring on the "and." Students will initially snap the foot up in a non-rhythmic fashion.

An exercise to assist the students in establishing an even division of the beat is to ask them to place the left hand about eighteen inches above the left thigh, palm toward the leg. Place the right hand between the left hand and thigh. Now with the metronome, count "one-and-two-and" and have the right palm slap the left thigh on "one" and the back of the right hand slap the left palm on "and." Using this method, the students will feel the rhythmic division of the beat and will be more likely to establish the same evenness in the foot pat. Using a metronome that will provide two different tones for the beat and the "and" will help students in this endeavor.

It is often beneficial to simplify the rhythmic structure of the piece into a simple series of "down-ups" as the counting system. Students are more inclined to develop a sense of rhythm when the concern is focused on whether the note occurs when the foot is "down" or "up." Always use a metronome to help students develop an internal pulse. The following system has proven to be quite efficient in developing a solid rhythmic foundation:

1. Teach students to pat their feet in time with a metronome. Slightly amplifying the metronomic tone through a small guitar amplifier will help.
2. Develop a consistent and even rhythmic structure with the feet by using the hand/thigh exercise to establish a feeling of "down" and "up."
3. Teach the students to say a concise "down" and "up" as they pat their feet in time with the metronome.
4. Using a method book, rhythm studies book, rhythm slides, PowerPoint (or other similar) display, or any other projection of various rhythmic patterns, teach the students to say each rhythm using a series of "downs" and/or "ups." Make sure the foot pat is constant and even.

| ↓ | ↓ | ↓ | ↓ | ↓ ↑ | ↓ ↑ | ↓ ↑ | ↓ ↑ |
| down | down | down | down | down-up | down-up | down-up | down-up |

5. Teach one rhythmic pattern at a time and then begin to mix patterns into various combinations and in a variety of meters.
6. Have students "down-up" each new rhythm/exercise before it is played on the instruments. An additional exercise is to ask the students to finger the part as they say the rhythm on "downs" and "ups."
7. To further improve reading skills, ask the students to say the names of the notes of a melodic line in rhythm with the metronome. Do not say the sharps or flats since this will disrupt the flow of the rhythm. Once the students are comfortable with the names of the notes, ask them to say the names of the notes as they finger the specific passage. The final step is to play the passage. Remember to keep the foot pat going throughout the exercise.

The development of a counting system is essential to rhythmic accuracy and a sound foundation for sight-reading. Students must learn to recognize rhythmic patterns just as they learn that the combination of the letters "c-a-t" when combined will spell "cat." The establishment of a counting system provides students with a basis for figuring out new rhythmic patterns on their own. It will eliminate most, if not all, rote teaching of rhythms and ultimately improve the overall quality of the band's performance. So many times the problem is not what to play, but when to play. A counting system coupled with a rhythmic pattern vocabulary will vastly improve performance skills at all levels of experience.

TIMBRE:

The timbre of *Music from the Great Hall* involves a series of color changes as the melody is passed from one voicing combination to another. It is essential to keep the general timbre on the light side. Although a variety of cues are provided, it is important to use only those cues that are necessary for an artistic performance of the work. Utilizing all of the cued parts will not only increase the density of the composition but will mask the intended color changes.

"A Toye" will require the band to maintain a light, tinkling tone quality. Even the *tutti fortes* should remain on the delicate side in texture. The listener should always be able to hear into the band and find each musical line. In *piano* sections where the melody is in the flute, be sure to keep the accompanying figure well-balanced. Balance this underlying figure from the bass clarinet up to the first clarinet. Strive for beautiful tone in this softer section by compressing the air stream so there is adequate air pressure to fill the instrument. The clarinet embouchure should remain firm so as to support the tone.

Establish balance and blend in "The King's Morisco" by reminding the students that, unlike more contemporary works, contrapuntal music requires that many voices be equally balanced. Have the students practice individual parts and gradually put the pieces together. By making a recording of the band in rehearsal and allowing the students to analyze the balance, they will more easily identify what the balance concerns may be. This self-assessment will also provide the students with a sense of individual and group responsibility for the musical product. The basic texture of the work will be more transparent, allowing the listener to hear all of the contrapuntal lines in a more even distribution.

Students must be encouraged to develop a characteristic tone in all dynamic ranges. A valuable tool for developing this capacity is the long-tone exercise. The students play a tone for twelve beats. The initial dynamic level of *pp* is allowed to *crescendo* to *ff* and then *decrescendo* back to the *pp* level. Students will need to be taught to gradually increase the tone's volume over the entire number of counts in the *crescendo*. Early trials of this exercise will identify potential concerns such as (a) insufficient intake of air, (b) inadequate control of the exhalation of air, (c) poor tone quality in the extremes of the dynamic range, and (d) poor intonation at the *pp* and *ff* levels. The exercise may be addressed in the following manner:

1. Set the metronome at 60 beats per minute.
2. Ask the students to breathe in on count four and then play a concert F in the instrument's mid-range for six beats.
3. Once this is automatic, ask the students to breathe in on count four and to sustain the pitch at *mf*.
4. Repeat at *mp*, then *p*, then *pp*. Students will need to be taught that the softer dynamic levels are executed by using less air that is intensely compressed. (More air speed, less air.)
5. Draw the following diagram on the chalkboard/dry erase board:

1	2	3	4	5	6
pp	*mp*	*p*	*mf*	*f*	*ff*

6. Tell the students to imagine they are turning up the volume control on a CD player and to increase the volume of the tone a bit on each click of the metronome. To improve the tone quality at the louder dynamic levels, remind the students that the embouchure must not overly tighten or relax. Encourage them to experiment to find the best way to control the tone as the volume increases. Tell the students that flute pitches will tend to go sharp while clarinet pitches will tend to flatten at louder dynamic levels. Use tuners to assist students in their efforts to control the intonation of their instruments. The visual display of pitch variation will help young players to comprehend this acoustical concern.
7. Play the concert F for six beats as described.
8. Repeat the procedure to create a controlled *decrescendo*. Bands tend to decrease the volume too quickly when executing a *decrescendo*. Again, the volume control analogy may assist the students in understanding this concept.
9. Once the students can *crescendo* and *decrescendo* with reasonable success, put the two parts together as a twelve-beat exercise.
10. Use this exercise as a regular component of the band's daily warm-up. Do not attempt to do this exercise for extended periods of time, particularly in the developmental stages, as embouchure strain may occur. Use different pitches and gradually work into different registers.

Modeling is also a valuable tool in the development of good tone. Use recordings of professional artists or ask local professional musicians to demonstrate the characteristic tone. It should be noted that there are various artist-in-residence programs. Explore such possibilities to assist in bringing professional musicians into the classroom.

Unit 7: Form and Structure

Music from the Great Hall is an example of through-composed music. It comprises elements of homophony and polyphony (counterpoint).

Section	Measures	Event and Scoring
I — "A Toye"		
Phrase 1	1-9	Mixolydian flute melody; simple accompaniment; *piano*
Phrase 2	9-17	*Tutti*; flute, oboe, clarinet 1, trumpet melody; *forte*
Phrase 3	17-25	Open texture; flute melody; *piano*
Phrase 4	25-end	*Tutti*; moving eighth notes over sustained half and whole notes; *mezzo piano-forte* Bell solo in penultimate measure
II — "The King's Morisco"		
I.	**1-32**	4/4 meter
Introduction	1-5	Percussion, jingle bells, and footstompers
Phrase 1	5-9	*Tutti*; contrapuntal; *forte*
	9-13	Open texture; *mezzo piano*
	13-16	*Tutti*; three distinct melodic lines: (1) flute 1, alto saxophone, horn, trumpet; (2) flute 2, oboe, clarinet; (3) bass clarinet, bassoon, tenor saxophone, baritone saxophone, trombone, euphonium, tuba
Phrase 2	16-24	Open texture; flute melody with clarinet and bass clarinet; *piano*
Phrase 3	24-28	Two choirs; woodwinds with trombone and euphonium; brass with clarinet and low woodwinds; *mezzo piano*
	28-32	*Tutti*; complex melodic rhythm over two simple accompaniment rhythms; *forte*
II.	**32-end**	3/4 meter
Phrase 1	32-39	Four-part polyphony: (1) flute and trumpet 2; (2) trumpet 1; (3) horn and trombone; (4) euphonium and tuba; *piano*

SECTION	MEASURES	EVENT AND SCORING
Phrase 2	39-44	Four-part polyphony: (1) flute and oboe; (2) alto saxophone, tenor saxophone, and horn; (3) trumpet; (4) low woodwinds and low brass; jingle bells; *mezzo forte*
	44-end	Three-part polyphony: (1) flute, oboe, and trumpet; (2) alto saxophone, tenor saxophone, and horn; (3) low woodwinds and low brass; *forte*

Unit 8: Suggested Listening

William Byrd/Fenske, *La Volta*
William Byrd/Jacob:
    Battell
    William Byrd Suite
William Dunscombe/Finlayson, *Early English Suite*
George Kirck, *Renaissance Triptych*
Bob Margolis, *Fanfare, Ode and Festival*
Ron Nelson:
    Courtly Airs and Dances
    Medieval Suite
Henry Purcell/Schaefer, *Battle Symphony*
Tielman Susato, *The Battle Pavane*
Tielman Susato/Curnow, *Renaissance Suite*

Unit 9: Additional References and Resources

Apel, Willi. *Harvard Dictionary of Music*, 2nd edition. Cambridge, MA: The Belknap Press of Harvard University Press, 1970.

Blume, Friedrich. *Renaissance and Baroque Music*. New York, NY: W.W. Norton & Company, 1967.

Bukofzer, Manfred F. *Music in the Baroque Era*. New York, NY: W.W. Norton & Company, 1947.

Duckworth, William. *A Creative Approach to Music Fundamentals*, 4th edition. Belmont, CA: Wadsworth Publishing Company, 1992.

Fenske, Katheryn. *Music from the Great Hall*. New Glarus, WI: Daehn Publications, 1998.

Fenske, Katheryn. Telephone conversation with Susan Creasap, April 15, 2000.

Grout, Donald Jay. *A History of Western Music*, 5th edition. New York, NY: W.W. Norton & Company, 1996.

Reese, Gustave. *Music in the Renaissance*, revised edition. New York, NY: W.W. Norton & Company, 1959.

Smith, Norman, and Albert Stoutamire. *Band Music Notes*. Lake Charles, LA: Program Note Press, 1989.

Contributed by:
Susan Creasap
Assistant Director of Bands
Morehead State University
Morehead, Kentucky

Teacher Resource Guide

Nottingham Castle
Larry D. Daehn
(b. 1939)

Unit 1: Composer

According to a biography provided by Larry Daehn, he was born in 1939 and grew up on a farm near Rosendale, Wisconsin. He received his bachelor's degree from the University of Wisconsin at Oshkosh and his master's degree from the University of Wisconsin at Platteville. He taught vocal and instrumental music at various Wisconsin schools over a distinguished 35-year career. The New Glarus High School Band, which was under Daehn's direction for twenty-seven years, received many state and national honors.

As an extension of his considerable experience as an instrumental music educator, Daehn became a composer, arranger, and publisher of many works for the concert band medium. He is also widely recognized as a leading scholar on the life and music of Percy A. Grainger, and has edited and published numerous selections of Grainger's compositions. He has been honored by inclusion in the 1971 edition of *Leaders in American Education* and by being named the Outstanding Bandmaster by Phi Beta Mu, Pi Chapter, in 1988.

Daehn has been the owner and operator of Daehn Publications since 1988. In addition to his numerous original compositions, he has arranged music by Grainger, Bach, Fauré, Scheidt, Vecchi, and Shostakovich.

Unit 2: Composition

There was no specific motive behind the composition of *Nottingham Castle* other than the composer's intention to provide quality music for young band. It is a single-movement work with several contrasting melodic ideals. In terms of difficulty, *Nottingham Castle* is appropriate for players who have completed their first year of instrumental music instruction (Grade 1). Its form is derived from alternating original melodic material that is presented in a truncated rondo form. Even though it is not a theme and variations, study of that form might provide some insight into how Daehn made adjustments on repeats of sections to achieve variety. There is a simple snare drum introduction and a coda section that make up the "B" section. *Nottingham Castle* is tonal, but some of the parallel harmonizations utilized are representative of either pre- or post-common practice harmonic techniques.

This original work was written with the intention of stimulating students' impressions of England at the time of Robin Hood (who died in 1247). No period folk song material is quoted in this work, but folk-like tunes are suggested. According to the program notes provided,

> Nottingham Castle was built by William the Conqueror in the eleventh century. The town of Nottingham and the county of Nottinghamshire grew up around the castle. In the Middle Ages, some 200 square miles of Nottinghamshire were covered by Sherwood Forest, famous for its oak trees (many fine specimens still survive) and the exploits of the legendary outlaw, Robin Hood.
>
> Only the gateway of the original castle remains today. The site is now occupied by the palace of the duke of Newcastle, which has been turned into a museum and an art gallery. A statue of Robin Hood stands in front of the castle, on Castle Green.

Unit 3: Historical Perspective

Although this is an original composition, the melodies and the compositional techniques utilized would make it quite beneficial to study not only the music of early England but also some basic considerations of music writing. One discussion topic might be, "What makes a melody sound like British folk music?" Comparison between genuine British folk music and the original melodies of *Nottingham Castle* could provide interesting insights for the younger player. Furthermore, because of the attached imagery, there are sociological and historical connections to the life and times of Robin Hood that could be explored. One simple exercise might be to view any of a number of movie representations of the famous bandit and discuss whether or not the background music seems authentic for the time period. If not, then does it represent the spirit of the scene it accompanies?

Unit 4: Technical Considerations

As the grade level would indicate, the technical demands of this work are very few. All ranges have been restricted to facilitate the best possible tone production by players who have had approximately one year of instruction. There are sufficient doublings to allow omission of certain parts if needed for range considerations (principally, the first trombone). The first trumpet and trombone parts go up to a fifth partial, concert C, while the clarinet does not go over the break. Carry-through accidentals must be observed between measures 53 and 66. There are no dotted rhythms, and the smallest note values are sixteenths, which may be found only in the snare drum part. Rhythmic demands are minimal overall.

Unit 5: Stylistic Considerations

Nottingham Castle makes several articulation requests that are basic to good performance practice and that should be reinforced correctly from the very beginning of a player's training. The sections of the work that are written in natural minor keys contain melodies that are slurred by measure, requiring the player to begin each slur with a *legato* tongue. The accompaniments in those sections are to be *legato* tongued. For an authentic performance, the issue of *legato*-style articulation will need to be fully addressed in rehearsal and fundamental training. The section that represents Robin Hood (measure 19) must be played in a more lifted, detached style. Proper use of air and tongue must be addressed away from the work to develop the necessary skill to perform that style. The conductor must also be careful to present excellent models of the articulative style desired through the use of recordings.

Dynamic contrast is clearly indicated throughout the composition, with only three distinct levels requested: *piano, mezzo piano,* and *forte.* There is only one *crescendo* indicated, occurring at measure 61. The music does allow the creative conductor a number of opportunities to move melody, harmony, and rhythm with subtle adjustments to dynamic level. Without further dynamic "tweaking," the best a conductor will achieve is a rather academic reading of *Nottingham Castle,* lacking the optimal vitality.

Unit 6: Musical Elements

MELODY:

All melodies are related to the home key of concert F major. The concept of mode formation may be taught to explain the relationship between the minor-sounding themes and the major Robin Hood theme. By having players start on either the sixth or second step of the F major scale and playing an octave in the key of F major, they can form the Aeolian or Dorian modes, respectively. To be sure they have learned the concept, transfer the procedure to several other keys (B-flat major or C major). This will also set the groundwork for discussion on relative major and minor keys, along with the development of equal-tempered tuning. Singing should also be used for the development of concept and for improving aural acuity.

HARMONY:

Harmonic movement is uncomplicated and tends to follow common practice progressions as might be expected with folk song material. Cadences are traditional. *Nottingham Castle* might be effectively used to demonstrate the dominant-tonic progression of a full cadence.

RHYTHM:
Students will need to be proficient at dividing a beat equally into two parts. This skill may be reinforced through regular use of a dividing metronome in fundamental training and by regularly using a system of counting. Half notes, quarter notes, and eighth notes are the only note values present. The most demanding rhythmic concerns are the eighth notes that follow eighth rests in the percussion parts and the beginning of all melodic ideas on an anacrusis.

TIMBRE:
The coloration of *Nottingham Castle* is achieved through instrumentation additions and variations on repeats of melodic material. The minor-keyed sections are more dominantly (and thinly) scored with woodwinds, while the major melodic material is generally represented by brass with *tutti* ensemble. Generally, the introduction of melodic material is more transparently scored than subsequent presentations. Percussion parts are nicely orchestrated to create timbre and rhythmic variation.

Unit 7: Form and Structure

SECTION	MEASURES	EVENT AND SCORING
Introduction	1-8	Scored for snare drum; *moderato* (quarter note = 88); establishes tempo and division
Theme A	9-16	Melody in woodwinds; Aeolian mode of F major (A minor); slurred and *legato* style; soft, monophonic texture
Theme A (repeat)	9-14, 17-18	Harmonization and accompaniment added
Theme B	19-26	More detached style depicting Robin Hood and his merry men; F major; full ensemble
Theme B (repeat)	19-25, 27	Literal repeat; no variation
Theme A	28-43	Varied instrumentation; bells added; brighter timbre; cornet added at m. 36; theme stated in full twice; *legato*; soft
Theme B	44-51	Theme is more thickly doubled than in original statement; no sustained notes
Theme B (repeat)	44-50, 52	Literal repeat; no variation

SECTION	MEASURES	EVENT AND SCORING
Theme A	53-66	Theme in Dorian mode (F major) and harmonized in parallel thirds; soft; triangle added; at m. 61, all instruments play same rhythm in parallel harmony and *crescendo*
Transition	67-70	Theme A is augmented by a factor of four and turned into a cadence: D minor (second inversion), D minor, G minor (second inversion with an added sixth); C major, setting up a return to F major
Coda	71-80	The first two measures of Theme B are repeated three times and then augmented to create an effective coda in F major

Unit 8: Suggested Listening

The following is a listing of works that contain either traditional British folk songs or original melodies written in British folk-song style. Several of the selections refer to imagery related to *Nottingham Castle*.

Calvin Custer, *A Renaissance Fair*
Gordon Jacob, *An Original Suite*
William Latham, *Court Festival*
Ron Nelson, *Courtly Airs and Dances*
James Ployhar, *Castle Loch and Heath*
Hugh Stuart, *Three Ayres from Gloucester*

Unit 9: Additional References and Resources

Band Music of Distinction, Volume II. New Glarus, WI: Daehn Publications, 1997.

Bellamy, John C. *Robin Hood: An Historical Inquiry*. London: Croom Helm, 1985.

Daehn Publications, P.O. Box 175, New Glarus, WI, 53574, 608-527-2923.

Holt, J.C. *Robin Hood*, 2nd edition. London: Thames and Hudson, 1989.

Rehrig, William H. *The Heritage Encyclopedia of Band Music*. Edited by Paul E. Bierley. Westerville, OH: Integrity Press, 1991.

There are numerous references to Robin Hood on the Internet, including a number of interactive sites.

Contributed by:
John C. Carmichael
Director of Bands
Western Kentucky University
Department of Music
Bowling Green, Kentucky

Teacher Resource Guide

A Prehistoric Suite

Paul Jennings
(b. 1948)

Unit 1: Composer

Paul and Teresa Jennings have worked together musically throughout the twenty-five years of their married life, which started in Huntington, West Virginia, where the two met while at Marshall University. It continues to this day as they run Plank Road Publishing, an educational music company they have owned since they founded it in 1990.

Paul was born in 1948 in Portsmouth, Ohio, and went on to major in bassoon at Marshall. For his graduate work, he studied theory and composition under Dr. Paul Whear. He eventually joined the staff, where he wrote for the band program and directed the jazz bands. In 1979, he moved to Milwaukee, Wisconsin, to join the trend-setting Jenson Publications. While there, he came to control all music published by the company as Vice President of Product Development. Along the way, he also started Dark Orchid Records, where he won a Grammy in 1983 with the Rob McConnell Big Band from Canada. When Jenson was sold to Hal Leonard in 1989, Paul wrote full-time as a freelance arranger while he and Teresa prepared to start their own company. He has published more than 500 works over the years for band, jazz ensemble, orchestra, and choir.

Born in Toledo, Ohio, in 1956, Teresa grew up in West Virginia where her parents, Donald and Suzanne Riggio, taught college while they pursued their musical ambitions as performers, conductors, and composers. In college, Teresa was an accomplished oboist and played many other instruments as well. For the past fifteen years, her primary focus has been her compositions and the world of music publishing. She is most interested in writing music for children to sing, and her extensive work with jazz and rock has helped her develop a unique style. Beyond her wide vocabulary of musical styles, Teresa fills her music with emotion and strong values, though she always tries to remember that music should be fun to perform if it is going to affect the performer. Her music comes alive in the recordings she produces because she has the rare ability to get exciting performances from her young performers and professionals alike.

Teresa has also become one of the most innovative publishers working in the field of music education. Her work as publisher and primary writer for *MUSIC K-8* magazine has had a profound effect on many thousands of schools and millions of children, and the company she manages has grown steadily into a wonderful place for her employees and their families.

Together, the Jennings are enjoying the independence of publishing their own music and the gratification that comes from helping children, teachers, friends, and family achieve their goals in life.

Unit 2: Composition

A *Prehistoric Suite*, published in 1987, is aptly titled as it is a programmatic work, divided into four brief movements, each capturing the personality of different dinosaurs. Jennings suggests performing the first movement, "Stegosaurus (The Gladiator)," in a majestic march style. The deliberate tempo, use of heavily stressed quarter and eighth notes, and modal structure help students to achieve the desired expressive effect. The second movement, "Brontosaurus (Gentle Giant)," requires that students use quick dynamic shifts and *glissandi* to demonstrate a lumbering effect, indicating the physical movement of the dinosaur. In the 3/4 movement, "Pterodactyls (Graceful Giants of the Sky)," students experience a lilting, melodic line focused in the upper woodwinds and bells with thinner texture in the accompaniment voices. The final movement, "The Battle (Tyrannosaurus and Triceratops)," begins with a sixteen- to twenty-second unmeasured segment that calls for students to perform notes at random that "start low and soft; get louder, faster, and higher." The unmeasured chaotic opening resolves on measure 2 with a piercing G-flat/A-flat tone dissonance. Conflict is created through dissonances and programmatic use of dynamics and articulations. The brief aleotoric segment returns and resolves to a heavy, thunderous conclusion.

Unit 3: Historical Perspective

This original composition uses both traditional and a few contemporary techniques. Its expressive content renders it highly programmatic with each of the four movements suggesting a different style portraying dinosaurs.

Unit 4: Technical Considerations

At first, young players may not be accustomed to the modality of the first movement, but good use of repetition will help the students become comfortable with this different sound. The Mixolydian quality could be approached using B-flat major as the springboard and simply adding the flat seventh. Continuing to use B-flat major as familiar ground for learning new musical concepts, the key of G minor should be introduced for the second movement, although the movement reflects G Dorian as well. The dissonant interval of a second dominates the final section.

Rhythmically, the work has few challenges, but it solidifies certain rhythmic concepts. The smallest unit of rhythmic subdivision being the eighth note, its simplicity affords students a chance to focus on expressive elements used in the work.

The range requirements are very accessible in all voices, with most instruments playing in the middle range. The break is not crossed in the clarinet part. Most parts lie within the span of a ninth.

The work is energized with the correct performance of a variety of articulations. The first movement relies on heavy accent. The second movement requires students to make a good distinction between notes held full value followed by crisp *staccatos* at the end of a rhythmic unit. Two-measure swells in the dynamic structure help students to make sense of the *staccato* articulation as it assists phrasing. The third movement calls for another change of style as the flowing melody utilizes slurring and *tenuto* on articulated notes. A return to the heavy accent found in the beginning is noted in the last movement. This articulation is offset with intermittent measures of *staccato* eighths, recalling articulations used in the second movement.

There is periodic use of accidentals throughout the first and fourth movements. In the first, the A-flat provides a modal quality, and its repetition will help students remember the accidental over time. The G-flat/A-flat and E-flat/D-flat clashes in the final movement will need attention. The motives are not fast-moving, however, offering students a good opportunity for success in this unusual piece.

While most of the work is relatively straightforward, instructors will spend extra time teaching a few parts of the piece where non-traditional methods are necessary. Trombones have a *glissando* written in movement two. The score indicates that the *glissando* is optional; it's desirable to use the *glissando* if the students are able to control the rise and fall over three beats and are able to complete the *glissando* on the correct pitch. Intonation work will be essential. Attention to the composer's score marking in the brief aleatoric section that opens the final movement is critical for the effect to be successful. Students should begin softly and in a low range on the instrument. As the score icon indicates, the band should progress through the sixteen- to twenty-second segment with a measured *crescendo*, which is achieved by gaining intensity of sound in addition to more notes being played while climbing in range. Help students avoid getting too loud too soon.

Unit 5: Stylistic Considerations

This work is a study in changing style. Because it was written in four distinct sections, students are given the opportunity to practice each style without the challenge of the transition. Heavy accent and broad playing characterize the first movement, marked *majestically*. In contrast are the supporting voices, which perform undulated, *legato* eighths in the opening segment. Marked *ponderous*, creative use of clearly defined dynamic changes shape the entire second movement. Smooth, *legato* melody and long-tone supporting voices are found in the *gentle, flowing* third movement. A combination of full value accents and pointed *staccato* articulation complete the final movement, marked *dramatically*. A great deal of *tutti* performance is found in this movement, so balance will become a focus. A fair amount of repetition in each movement reinforces the style changes as the work is being rehearsed.

Unit 6: Musical Elements

MELODY:

Movement 1 — The melodic movement is largely stepwise, with a reinforcement of tonic-dominant relationship in the leap that opens the melody (see the trumpet line, measures 13 through 28) and its answer (measures 29 to the end). The material from measures 13 through 28 should be phrased in no less than four-measure segments, lifting from beat one of measure 16, for example, to replenish breath and complete the phrase. It will be important to guard students against taking a breath too soon in the answer portion of the movement. There will be a tendency for students to want to breathe on the first beat of measure 30, for example, rather than sustain at least through the first beat of measure 32. If students are able, an eight-bar phrase (measures 29 through 36) is preferable. Articulation gives the melody a decidedly fanfarish, triumphant flavor and should be performed with full breath support with no break in intensity.

Movement 2 — The two-part melody in this movement is completely stated twice. It is supported throughout with blocked harmony and a contrasting rhythmic line underneath. Open harmonies (such as those found in measures 4 through 8, for example) will be quite effective when played well in tune. The melody in measures 5 through 12 and 21 through 28 moves by small steps, so accuracy will be at issue with brass voices. Consider a slight *crescendo* for first trumpets in measures 9 through 10 so the D is reached with support and good tone quality. This section should be performed as two four-measure phrases. The melody in measures 13 through 18 and 29 through 34, characterized by half note movement, leads to the minor third material found in the introduction and completes the statement of the theme. Open fourths and fifths give way to closer harmonies as blocked chords supporting the melody here.

Movement 3 — The most singable melody is heard in this movement, rendered principally by flute and first clarinet. Its lilting quality is retained by maintaining the suggested tempo; any less will cause the melody to bog down. It will be necessary for players to pay close attention to *legato* and articulated tonguing in this diatonic melody to shape phrases correctly. Work to improve breath support through a long, eight-measure phrase (measures 5 through 12, for example). An instruction to stagger-breathe may help to achieve an uninterrupted effect but will avoid the greater issues of sustained air over greater periods of time. If the phrase must be broken, try using beat three of the middle measure as a pick-up to the second half of the statement. For example, in measure 8, a quick breath might be taken between beats two and three, with *legato* tongue emphasis on beat four as a pick-up into the next portion of the phrase. If this option is taken, students should be instructed to avoid clipping beat two. As with the previous sections, this movement uses two full statements of the two-part melody with just a few adjustments during the second statement. At measure 31, the melody takes on a slight embellishment with the addition of the brief, ascending scalar pattern as opposed to the sustained tonic half note found in the first statement. Melodic movement in the closing six measures repeats as well, giving students ample opportunity for practice.

Movement 4 — This movement relies on harmonic and rhythmic clashes as its main focus rather than identifiable melodic material.

HARMONY:

Movement 1 — As suggested earlier, the Mixolydian quality is easily approached using B-flat major with the addition of the flat seventh. It is likely that by the second year, students will be quite familiar with the B-flat major scale. Adding the flat seventh constitutes one small change from a familiar activity and will reinforce the modal sound.

Movement 2 — Using B-flat major as "home base," both G minor and G Dorian tonalities are heard, so it is a good time to introduce at least one of these scales. After playing B-flat major, move the starting pitch of the scale to G, retaining B-flat and E-flat. Have students perform the scale from G to G instead of B-flat to B-flat. Try this exercise in a few other keys to reinforce the concept. Fortify aural discrimination between major and minor by assigning students to scale degrees that comprise the tonic chord. Modify chord quality by alternately performing with M3 and flatted third scale degrees and label. In addition to the minor tonality, students may be struck by the wanting sound of open intervals such as fourths and fifths. These intervals must be performed in tune, so warm-up activities could include such open intervals.

Movement 3 — The only movement using a major tonality, the harmonic structure will be quite familiar to students. Focusing on the close harmonies found in the lower voices (for example, measures 5 through 17), however, will be necessary. In this range with inexperienced players, these harmonies will tend to become muddy if played tentatively. Be sure to bring the descending scalar pattern found in the bass voices to the attention of the ensemble (measures 5 through 11, 13 through 19, 21 through 25). Anchoring harmonies on this line will help lock intonation.

Movement 4 — Major and minor second dissonances are ubiquitous in the final movement. A deliberate approach is vital. Tentative performance will result in the dissonances sounding more like a mistake than anything else. Again, intonation accuracy is critical. Students have the opportunity to rehearse this interval in both blocked and broken style (compare measures 8 and 9 to 10 and 11).

RHYTHM:
Rhythmic challenges in this work are few. Without rhythmic obstacles, students are free to spend more energy focusing on expressive issues. However, certain rhythmic motives are characteristic of each movement and should be addressed in instruction.

Movement 1 — Accompaniment voices in this movement often use a repeated pattern. A variation of this accompaniment is used in the melodic material. Instructors may reinforce differentiation between quarter notes and eighth notes with clapping or chanting, performing warm-up scales or exercises with like patterns, and using counting or syllables (for example, 1 2+ | 1 2 or Du du-day | Du du). It is likely that the biggest rhythmic challenge in this movement will be tied half notes (measures 26 through 28). Students will want to release this tied note too soon, leaving obvious gaps in sound. Long-tone work and measured breathing exercises will help.

Movement 2 — This movement utilizes whole notes, half notes, and quarter notes in familiar ways. Similar to the previous movement, students may be tempted to release long tones too soon (measures 11 and 12). Instructors should be diligent to the length given to quarter rests (measures 1 through 3, for example). Some students may lengthen the rest and others may shorten it. Exercises and playing games that incorporate internalizing beat may be used to reinforce rests played in time.

Movement 3 — A quarter rest on the downbeat in this 3/4 movement may be confusing at first to trumpets. Have them listen to those who enter on beat one. Instructing trumpets to breathe in time on beat one will avoid early entrances. Dotted-half notes are heard in the accompanying voices and should be given full value. The use of the dotted-half note lends itself to instruction in modification of time value when dots are added or deleted. The *fermata* in the last measure provides an opportunity to teach the concept of phrase endings and closure in music, watching the conductor, and making quality choices about what sounds good. Instructors might consider allowing student conductors to try the *fermata*, using different note lengths and asking the ensemble or the individual to discuss why the length was effective or ineffective.

Movement 4 — As is the case in all four movements, rhythmic motives consist of previously studied note values. The half/quarter/quarter rest motive appears in repetition in several voices, while accompanying voices may be challenged by having to count rests. In measures 2 through 4, for example, a large portion of the ensemble must perform only after a two-beat rest, entering on beat three. Accuracy is reinforced by having the students listen to those performing on beat one and watching the conductor for a solid cue on the third beat, all the while internalizing the quarter note. Rhythmic unity in *tutti* performance is also achieved through constant attention to articulations.

TIMBRE:

Movement 1 — Because of the deliberate nature of the accents used in this section, there may be a tendency for woodwind players to either overblow or use blasts of air rather than sustaining good tone quality throughout. The result will be a spread and unfocused sound. A gradual approach to accented lines may help students to maintain good breath support and to avoid punching each articulation. For example, the ensemble may play at measure 29 using steady air stream and *legato* tongue at first. Work to ensure that the air stream does not stop; allow the tongue to interrupt in order to accomplish *legato* articulation. Once students are able to perform using this technique, isolate one note, perhaps the first note of the phrase at measure 29, and have students repeat this note using more emphasis (and, therefore, more air) when attempting to accent. Listening should focus on maintaining characteristic tone quality, particularly at the outset of the note. Once this has been achieved, use this technique to rehearse the section at measure 29.

Movement 2 — An area of concern in this movement is the *staccato* quarter that concludes the three-beat introductory material found in measures 1 through 3. Students may "choke" off this note, particularly trombones. Articulation exercises for the students should include attention to the final note having the same tone quality as the preceding long tone. In addition to techniques mentioned in the previous paragraph, it may be beneficial to have students sing their parts in these measures using appropriate vocal syllables to reinforce articulation as well as compel continual breath support. Many syllabic choices may be used; be sure to be consistent in their use. For example, a long syllable such as "doo" may be used for the half note, followed by "daht" to assist the *staccato*. Young players may tend to "chew" the *staccato* in order to give the sound closure. Watch embouchures and jaws carefully for too much movement.

Movement 3 — The uplifting melody in this movement is performed primarily by upper woodwinds. Instructors will need to give emphasis to clear, resonant sound as opposed to spread and fuzzy. In addition to this focus, gentle entrances should be stressed because of the expressive nature of the movement. It will be easy to overlook long tones in accompaniment voices since there is little technical difficulty for these players. However, these voices provide a chordal blanket for the moving voices. Balance and blend are extremely important, particularly because of the accompaniment role at a generally soft dynamic level. Warm-up exercises derived from the music are appropriate and may include chord building on these long tones. Work to shift balance from one voice to another to allow students a chance to hear differences between good and bad blend.

Movement 4 — Although the opening sixteen to twenty seconds of this movement are to be played somewhat freely, rules of good performance still apply. This will be a challenge since this brief section is not entirely prescriptive. Conductors will need to focus on helping students make decisions about how to play this section tastefully and within boundaries of good style and performance practice. It may be appropriate to have students explore extremes of the instrument in areas of range, key/valve/mallet movement, and dynamics. There will be points in the range of the extremes where the ensemble simply does not sound good, even for this raucous moment in the movement. By finding and listening to extremes, students will be able to compare these sounds to those that are more pleasant and appropriate in this measure.

Another area to cover in terms of tone quality, blend, and timbre is the second intervals dominating the movement. Students should perform these confidently with good breath support in order for the interval to achieve the desired effect. An example of an exercise that could help students is to assign certain voices to a note that remains constant and other voices to notes that are consonant with the constant tone. Once the ensemble is able to perform the consonant chord or interval at a strong dynamic level with good tone quality, alter the changeable note (maintaining the constant) to create a dissonance. Reinforce breath support and good embouchure so that the dissonance is not performed tentatively.

Unit 7: Form and Structure

SECTION	MEASURES	EVENT AND SCORING
Movement 1: Introduction	1-12	Melodic motives are heard in the introduction that appear in full form in the first statement of the theme; G Mixolydian outlined within first four measures and maintained throughout the movement; trumpets open with two-measure fanfare, answered in mm.

SECTION	MEASURES	EVENT AND SCORING
		3-4 in alto saxophone, low woodwinds and brass, horn; this figure is repeated and followed with a rhythmic *ostinato* that leads to the first statement of the theme
Section A	13-28	In mm. 13-20, the melody, which is stated first in the trumpet line, is echoed by the upper woodwinds while low voices perform a supporting rhythm; this segment is repeated in mm. 21-28
Section B	29-44	The second theme is now voiced in upper woodwinds, trumpet, and bells in mm. 29-36 while other voices support, followed by an eight-measure ending (mm. 37-44) that uses fragments of the first theme
Movement 2: Introduction	1-4	These opening measures reveal the lumbering quality of the title dinosaur, "Brontosaurus," with ascending and descending minor third *glissandi* in trombone (with similar movement in low winds) and punctuated with a gong strike at the conclusion of each *glissando*; a *diminuendo* on a whole note in m. 4 ushers in the first section
Section A	5-12	The main melodic material is stated in alto saxophone, trumpet, and horn with light accompaniment in supporting voices
Section B	13-20	Melody evolves in same voicing while accompaniment is reduced to long tones with suspended cymbal in mm. 13-16; mm. 17-20 is a repeat of introductory material
Section A´	21-28	Repetition of main melody; texture thickens with the addition of flute, oboe, and clarinet doubling melody voices

Section	Measures	Event and Scoring
Section B′	29-37	Repetition of B material with addition of flute, oboe, and clarinet in mm. 29-32; the last five measures revive introductory material and add a *crescendo* on a whole note leading to an accented quarter note at the conclusion
Movement 3:		
Introduction	1-4	Gently, flowing score instructions are depicted in fragments of melody played by flute, oboe, clarinet, and bells
Section A	5-20	The eight-measure theme is introduced then repeated. In the second statement of the theme, a simple countermelody is performed by solo trumpet with optional section performance; remaining voices provide chordal accompaniment
Section B	21-42	This section is very similar to mm. 5-20 with the exception of expanded texture in the melodic line and greater use of moving inner voices; a *ritardando* over a thematic fragment concludes the section
Movement 4:		
Introduction	1	Sixteen to twenty seconds of random notes played by full ensemble gain in intensity, number of notes, and range
Section A	2-9	Heavy use of major second dissonances through this section and the rest of the movement; opening G-flat/A-flat cluster in woodwinds and trumpet answered with full ensemble descending by tritone to C/D; snare punctuates and links the first four measures of the phrase to the second four; the second half of the phrase is a direct reiteration of the first
Section B	10-23	The major second cluster gives way to a minor second performed as separate

SECTION	MEASURES	EVENT AND SCORING
		quarter notes in low woodwinds and leads to D–E-flat–G–A chord cluster answer by upper winds; percussion continues punctuation; as with Section A, percussion links the first and second parts of the phrase; Section B material repeats at measure 16; an ascending half note figure builds in intensity over the two measures that lead to a return to the A section material at m. 24
Section A′	24-36	Material from mm. 2-9 is reiterated in mm. 24-31; a return to the introductory aleotoric measure follows, and the piece concludes with *tutti* ensemble performing descending minor second quarters interspersed with percussion punctuation

Unit 8: Suggested Listening

Hector Berlioz, *Symphonie Fantastique*
Johann De Meij, *Lord of the Rings Symphony*
Gustav Holst, *The Planets*
Stephen Melillo, *Escape from Plato's Cave*
Igor Stravinsky, *The Rite of Spring*
Eric Whitacre, *Ghost Train*
John Williams:
    Jurassic Park
    Star Wars

Unit 9: Additional References and Resources

Battisti, Frank, and Robert Garofalo. 1990. *Guide to score study for the wind band conductor*. Ft. Lauderdale, FL: Meredith Music.

Creasap, Susan D. 1996. "American women composers of band music: A biographical dictionary and catalogue of works." DMA diss., Ball State University.

Gaines, David Alan. 1996. "A core repertoire of concert music for high school band." Ed.D. diss., Columbia University.

Garofalo, Robert. 1992. *Guides to band masterworks*. Ft. Lauderdale, FL: Meredith Music.

Lenzini, Catherine. (1996). "Emerging band classics." *Instrumentalist* 51(4) November: 17-22, 27.

Sheldon, Deborah A. (in press). "Pre-service and in-service teachers' perceptions of band music content and quality using self-report and behavioral measures." *Journal of Research in Music Education.*

Sheldon, Deborah A. 1999. "Exciting works for young bands." *Instrumentalist* 54(1) August: 26-28.

Sheldon, Deborah A. 1999. "Great works for young bands." *Instrumentalist* 53(11) June: 18-21.

Wallace, David, and Eugene Corporon. 1984. *Wind ensemble/band repertoire.* Greeley, CO: University of Northern Colorado School of Music.

Contributed by:

Deborah A. Sheldon
University of Illinois at Urbana-Champaign
Urbana, Illinois

Teacher Resource Guide

Primordium

Mark Williams
(b. 1955)

Unit 1: Composer

Mark Williams was born in Chicago, Illinois, and grew up in Spokane, Washington. He earned both a Bachelor of Arts degree and a Master of Education degree from Eastern Washington University. Williams has toured Europe and the Pacific as a woodwind performer and was chief arranger with the 560th Air Force Band. He has taught band in public schools for well over a decade, focusing primarily on the elementary level. During that time, he was also director of the Spokane All-City Band program. Co-author of the new *Accent on Achievement* band method, Williams also has many published compositions for band, orchestra, and choir. He has earned several awards, including the Western International Band Clinic's Gralia Competition for best new composition for junior high band and an ASCAP special award. He currently performs cornet in a British brass band in the Spokane area.

Unit 2: Composition

A work for very young band, *Primordium* is a single-movement composition at a Grade 1 1/2 level of difficulty. It correlates with the band method book *Accent on Achievement*, book 2, page 29. The title is descriptive of the earliest beginnings of time, when earth was in its primeval stages. With quartal harmonies and modal idioms, this unusual elementary wind band work is sixty measures long and would be an excellent concert festival selection. The publisher is Alfred Publishing, and the work is approximately two minutes in duration.

Unit 3: Historical Perspective

Primordium is a descriptive work about the beginning of time. By definition, music that is inspired by a nonmusical idea is program music. Examples of program music are found in all periods of music from the fourteenth century, and program music attained its greatest prominence in the nineteenth century. During the Romantic and Impressionistic periods of music, one-movement orchestral compositions based upon a nonmusical idea became known as symphonic poems (or tone poems). Contributors to this genre were Franz Liszt, Bedrich Smetana, Alexander Borodin, Jean Sibelius, Ottorino Respighi, Peter Tchaikovsky, Richard Strauss, Claude Debussy, and Igor Stravinsky.

Unit 4: Technical Considerations

Listed by the publisher as a Grade 1 1/2 (easy), the technical and harmonic considerations are great for young instrumentalists. Although the work is centered tonally around D major, which is unusual for compositions for elementary bands, there is much tonal shifting, use of the Phrygian mode, quartal harmonies, occasional dissonances, parallel major chord shifts, and the use of tritones. Accidentals abound in this work. The key signature indicating B-flat is a matter of practicality and has no significant relationship to the actual tonal center.

Orchestrated for the usual beginning band instrumentation, the *tessitura* is appropriate for all instruments, and the usual doublings exist. Rhythmically, the work employs a variety of rhythmic devices, including triplets, dotted-eighth patterns, and grace notes in the flute/oboe part. Dynamics range from *mezzo piano* to *fortissimo* and are used to great effect. Articulation markings include slurs, accents, *staccato*, and *marcato*.

The percussion writing is active and includes parts for xylophone, snare and bass drums, crash cymbals, suspended cymbal, and timpani. There is a piano accompaniment included with the score.

Unit 5: Stylistic Considerations

This composition presents students with a unique opportunity to experience non-tertian harmonies. An explanation of the church modes, prevalent from 800 to 1500, would be helpful. Further, students should learn the Phrygian mode (in this case, D–E-flat–F–G–A–B-flat–C–D). Quartal harmonies, which are harmonies based on fourths instead of the more common tertian harmonies based on thirds, are widely used by the composer. These harmonies are found in slurred eighth note, undulating passages requiring controlled fingers and exact precision. Ed Lisk discusses pulse, time, and rhythm in his book, *Intangibles of Musical Performance*. One can hear the harmonic influences of Holst, Shostakovich, Stravinsky, and contemporary film scores.

The fanfare motif requires good clarity of articulation. At times, the melody is written in a *tessitura* below the accompanying lines, requiring proper balance and dynamics. W. Francis McBeth discusses how to teach pyramid dynamics in his book, *Effective Performance of Band Music*. While parts of the work are slurred, the majority of articulations deal with the tongue, and a clear understanding of accent, *staccato*, and *marcato* is necessary. The melody at measure 13 should be aggressive, thus indicating a more forceful approach to tonguing. This should be accomplished with intensity of air, space, and breath—not tongue. The challenge is to convey the unique oozing character of this excellently crafted educational material.

Unit 6: Musical Elements

MELODY:

The main melody first appears at measure 13 in the clarinets in the *chalumeau* register and doubled in the horns. Only two phrases long, this melody reappears once again at measure 42. The melodic line contains no slurs and should be played aggressively, in part because it lies in a range below the accompanying half note, somewhat scalar pattern. A fanfare-like section appears twice, first at measure 27 and again at measure 52. These block brass chords must be appropriately accented. A rhythmic motif, reminiscent of "Mars, the Bringer of War" from *The Planets* by Gustav Holst is found throughout the work and serves to unify the melody and fanfare.

HARMONY:

Harmonic devices found in *Primordium* are very advanced for a work composed for young band. While the work is tonally centered around D major, the composer uses non-tertian harmonies, dissonances, and moving parallel chords to suggest an eerie aesthetic. Hints of several modes are utilized, harmonic and melodic minor scales are present, and tritones are utilized. Careful attention to these unique harmonies will be necessary for young players. The texture is primarily polyphonic. To acquaint students with quartal harmonies, build fourths off of the B-flat concert scale, ascending and descending.

RHYTHM:

A variety of rhythms are used by the composer. Undulating perfect fourths are found in the beginning, evoking a bizarre scene from the primordial swamp. Triplets are found in the rhythmic motif, occurring throughout the work in a unifying manner. Some syncopated accents are found in the chordal fanfare, along with dotted-eighth followed by sixteenth note patterns. These rhythmic patterns must be performed accurately, without any rushing, to ensure proper placement within the beat. Subdivision of the beat is also imperative on several entrances.

TIMBRE:

Great concern must be placed on proper balance and blend to achieve the eerie and unsettled characteristics of the primordial swamp. The undulating

perfect fourths in the clarinets and saxophones must be balanced, with neither note being more prominent than the other. Rehearse this slowly. The
clarinets and horns at measure 13 must play *forte* and must not be covered by
the alto saxophone half notes. The low brass line at measure 22 must project
itself against the rhythmic motif happening in the ensemble. The chordal fanfare at measure 27 must be appropriately balanced. Emphasize these concepts
to the players for greater effect.

Unit 7: Form and Structure

Measures	Event and Scoring
1-8	Introduction, clarinet and alto saxophone in eighth note patterns; brass added in chordal shifts
9-12	Rhythmic motif in low brass and percussion
13-16	Melody in clarinet and horn
17-20	Saxophone to melody; trumpet enters
21-24	Rhythmic motif expanded
25-32	Chordal brass fanfare
33-39	Return to beginning patterns
40-49	Melody in clarinet and horn; flute, saxophone added to melody
50-60	Restatement of chordal brass fanfare

Unit 8: Suggested Listening

Gustav Holst, *The Planets*
Dmitri Shostakovich, *Symphony No. 5*
Igor Stravinsky, *The Rite of Spring*
John Williams, *Music from Star Wars*

Unit 9: Additional References and Resources

Dvorak, Thomas L., Robert Grechesky, and Gary Ciepluch. *Best Music for
    High School Band.* Bob Margolis, ed. Brooklyn, NY: Manhattan Beach
    Music, 1993.

Dvorak, Thomas L., Cynthia Crump Taggart, and Peter Schmalz. *Best Music
    for Young Band.* Bob Margolis, ed. Brooklyn, NY: Manhattan Beach
    Music, 1986.

Lisk, Edward S. *The Creative Director: Intangibles of Musical Performance.* Fort
    Lauderdale, FL: Meredith Music Publications, 1996.

McBeth, W. Francis. *Effective Performance of Band Music.* San Antonio, TX:
    Southern Music, 1972.

Miles, Richard, ed. *Teaching Music through Performance in Band*, Volume 2. Chicago, IL: GIA Publications, Inc., 1998.

Randel, Don Michael, ed. *Harvard Concise Dictionary of Music*. Cambridge, MA: The Belknap Press of Harvard University Press, 1978.

Contributed by:

Richard Anthony Murphy
Director of Bands
Middle Tennessee State University
Murfreesboro, Tennessee

Teacher Resource Guide

A Quiet Rain

Walter Cummings
(b. 1953)

Unit 1: Composer

Walter Cummings grew up in Mississippi, where he took piano from his mother, sang in the church choir, and played trombone in the school band. He graduated from the University of Southern Mississippi in 1975 with a bachelor's degree in Music Education. He received a Master of Music Education degree from the University of Colorado in 1977, a Master of Music degree in Conducting from the University of Mississippi in 1981, and a Doctor of Arts in Conducting from the University of Northern Colorado in 1994. Cummings has held band director positions at the middle school, high school, and college levels in Mississippi, New Hampshire, and Colorado. His first work for young band was *Gamelan*, which was based on the music of the Gamelan percussion orchestras in Bali and Java. Since then, he has written over thirty compositions for band and orchestra, most of which have been published. Largely self-taught as a composer, Cummings draws his inspiration from an eclectic variety of music from around the world, as well as the magical landscape of the Rocky Mountains and Colorado Plateau. He founded Grand Mesa Music Publishers with his wife, Janet, in 1992 and serves as its president. Presently, Cummings is the low brass instructor at Mesa State College in Grand Junction, Colorado, and plays trombone and tuba with the Grand Junction Symphony Orchestra.

Unit 2: Composition

A Quiet Rain was originally published in 1993. The version reviewed is a re-issue with some minor edits by the composer. No program notes were provided with the score, but the publisher's website indicates that the work is intended to be an introspective work for young band. In addition to the utilization of "new directions" in band scoring, *A Quiet Rain* features opportunities for most sections to perform lyrical melodies. It is in an A–B–A form and includes some harmonic devices not typically found in the more usual young band fare. Because of its unusual harmonic and rhythmic texture, this is an outstanding composition to use to introduce young musicians to certain contemporary music writing techniques. The result of the creative use of percussion and the textural patterns employed in the accompaniment is an effective representation of the gentle precipitation described by the title.

Unit 3: Historical Perspective

The composer has written a work that is somewhat influenced by the textural and harmonic characteristic of the minimalist school, as indicated by the rhythmic texture, the long segments of static harmony, and the use of more popular-oriented harmonies, particularly in the A sections. The conveyance of imagery by the title and musical effects could relate to any number of moments in music history, although a clear connection to impressionism could be drawn. Harmonies, particularly moments of bitonality, are drawn more from twentieth century convention. In terms of difficulty, this work possesses interesting challenges for the young band in general, not only for the ear (as bitonality would indicate) but also for specific players in the ensemble. The bell part is essential for establishing the correct color and atmosphere, but the demand of playing eighth notes in a repetitious pattern over a relatively long period of time might be taxing for the first-year player. Also, the use of concert D-flat several times in the B section could be outside the comfort zone of a Grade 1 performer. Even though the composer/publisher lists this as a Grade 1+, a more successful performance should be obtained by young players well into their second year of instruction.

Unit 4: Technical Considerations

As noted, *A Quiet Rain* is listed as a Grade 1+ by the composer. A syncopated, *ostinato* figure in flute and oboe will require a secure ability to divide the beat, along with enough maturity to sustain the pattern accurately over time. The percussion section must have a minimum of four players to cover the parts. The timpanist will need three pitches (B-flat, E-flat, and F), but there are no changes during the work. Of all the requests made of the performers, the bell part is the most demanding. Not only does it require a sustained, even eighth note pattern while changing notes, but the note patterns themselves change both in pitch and direction. Overall, percussionists will be exposed to a number of performance techniques outside of the typical young band work. Percussion instrumentation requires a rain stick, triangle, wind chimes, and suspended cymbal in addition to three timpani. Alto saxophone and bass clarinet are required to leap across the break in places, while first clarinet must move across the break stepwise. Most brass players have reasonable range demand, with nothing exceeding a fourth partial concert B-flat. Horns, however, must play in unison up to an E-flat at the top of their staff (a concert A-flat), which might tax their range. The melodic line contains dotted rhythms, although only occurring on the first beat of a measure.

Unit 5: Stylistic Considerations

Two basic articulation demands are made in *A Quiet Rain*. First, players must possess the ability to play a smooth *legato*. Raindrop effects are achieved through the use of light accents, which must be made by volume/air alteration as opposed to a percussive tongue. *Legato* concept and the approach to making accents must be addressed separately to facilitate better control when attempting this work. Otherwise, the effect may be more akin to hail on a tin roof.

Dynamically, one would expect a relative softness throughout. This is indeed the case, but the range of volume contrast requested does move from *piano* to *forte* with several notated *crescendos* and *diminuendos*. Control of softer dynamic ranges is essential for the successful performance of this composition.

Unit 6: Musical Elements

MELODY:

Although the melody is diatonic, it contains leaps as large as a major sixth in places, which will challenge performers to maintain connection between the notes with the air stream. Melodic interest is heightened through the use of color notes at moments of repose. Perhaps the most interesting melody moment occurs at measure 36, where the low voices of the ensemble are featured in the key area of A-flat in octaves. When the A section returns, the original theme is harmonized in thirds. For a successful performance of this composition, students will need to be able to play a concert A-flat major scale with fluidity. Furthermore, much work will have to be done on air movement to obtain smooth leaps without disconnection. Isolate the skill and focus on interval playing away from the composition. Short *caesura* have been provided with the melodic line to help players make good breathing choices.

HARMONY:

The harmonies of *A Quiet Rain* are a focal point for listener interest. Although centered around the keys of B-flat and A-flat concert, in sections A and B, respectively, notes more commonly considered as passing tones in traditional harmony have important coloristic function in this composition. Moreover, there are moments, such as at measure 25, where a clear bitonal relationship has been established as a transition between sections. Because of missing thirds in several structures, the bitonal figures may be reconfigured as quartal harmonies. It would be a helpful exercise for the band to learn to form major triads, adding sixths and ninths so that members become familiar with the sound and the structure of such harmonies away from the composition. Another possible strategy would be to interpose open fifths to emulate the bitonal constructions in the work. For example, have low voices play an A-flat/E-flat and high voices play a B-flat/F.

RHYTHM:
Dotted rhythms in the melodic line may prove to be challenging for young players, especially in the midst of the rhythmic texture in the accompaniment, which is fairly complicated for this grade level. Percussionists will have to count rests within measures and read split parts on the same staff. The smallest division of the beat present is an eighth note, with the quarter note receiving the beat (quarter note = 88). Syncopated figures constructed with ties exist as *ostinatos* in the flute and oboe parts. Tied notes that cross bar lines may also provide some challenge in the accompaniment figures as well as for those playing melody. Not only should students be able to count using a system, but they should practice specific rhythms extracted from the work against a source of perfect external time (like a dividing metronome). The only tempo change is a *ritardando* at the end.

TIMBRE:
A *Quiet Rain* is an unusually colorful work, obtaining much of its effect from the percussion section. Variation in timbre is achieved as much with accompaniment texture as through changes in instrumentation. The melody is never presented with the same instrumentation twice, nor is it ever accompanied in the same manner. Something is always altered. To achieve correct coloration, however, harmony parts must be properly balanced. Performers on second parts must be encouraged to project for a more sonorous presentation.

Unit 7: Form and Structure
The overall structure of A *Quiet Rain* is A–B–A, with no variation in tempo. Sectionalization is achieved through change of key center and texture.

SECTION	MEASURES	EVENT AND SCORING
Introduction	1-8	B-flat center established; texture is layered by entrance
Section A a	9-16	Principal theme introduced in trumpet and alto saxophone; *mf*; *crescendo* into m. 17
b	17-24	Second half of theme; first major harmonic change to E-flat; *forte* dynamic for melody

SECTION	MEASURES	EVENT AND SCORING
Transition	25-35	Bitonal figure at m. 25 in anticipation of tonality shift to A-flat; texture thins to just percussion at m. 31; harmonic transition at mm. 34-35
Section B		
a	36-43	New theme in low voices; *legato*, chant-like but lyrical; in A-flat; dominant-seven chord at m. 42; melodic shape clearly defined; simple accompaniment with cross rhythm for texture
b	44-52	Second half of new theme, now in upper woodwinds; some minor tonality; *crescendo* to *forte*, then *diminuendo*
Transition	53-58	Texture similar to composition introduction; moves from A-flat, to bitonal B-flat over A-flat, to B-flat at m. 56 (similar to m. 6)
Section A		
a	59-66	Theme one harmonized in thirds by upper voices; accompaniment similar to m. 9 except for a brief countermelodic figure in tenor voices; *crescendo* into m. 67
b	67-82	Second half of theme (in E-flat) is extended by eight measures beginning at m. 75; tenor voices have a new countermelodic figure that is expanded at m. 75 rather than just repeated; mm. 79-82 cadence back to B-flat and *diminuendo* into the coda
Coda or closing passage	83-88	Texture thins, stays in B-flat; *ritardando* in m. 85; slight swell to fragmentary quote of initial theme; *diminuendo* and *fermata* on B-flat major chord

Unit 8: Suggested Listening

John Adams:

The Chairman Dances, Foxtrot for Orchestra

Harmonielehre, Part III, Meister Echkardt and Quackie

Andrew Boysen, *Tricycle*
Walter Cummings, *The Richness of the Earth*
Claude Debussy, "Images" pour Orchestra, 2. Les parfums de la nuit–
Nancy Galbraith, *with brightness round about it*
Anthony Iannaccone, *After a Gentle Rain*
David Maslanka, *Golden Light*

Unit 9: Additional References and Resources

Gann, Kyle. "A Forest from the Seeds of Minimalism." Music after Minimalism. © 1998. http://home.earthlink.net/~kgann/postminimalism.html

Grand Mesa Music Publishers, Grand Junction, CO (Website: www.gj.net/~gmmusic)

Grand Mesa Music Publishers Compact Disk #4, New Concert Band Music for 2000-2001, University of Northern Colorado Wind Ensemble.

Schwarz, Robert. *Minimalists*. London: Phaidon Press Limited, 1996.

Contributed by:
John C. Carmichael
Director of Bands
Western Kentucky University
Department of Music
Bowling Green, Kentucky

Teacher Resource Guide

Rainbow Bridge

Anne McGinty
(b. 1945)

Unit 1: Composer

Anne McGinty is one of the most prolific female composers in the field of concert band literature. Her many compositions and arrangements (over 150 titles), all of which have been published, extend from the elementary through the college levels. She and her husband, John Edmondson, are co-owners of Queenwood Publications and are responsible for the creation, production, promotion, and international sales and distribution of Queenwood's catalog of concert band music.

McGinty has served as principal flute with the Tucson (Arizona) Symphony Orchestra, Tucson Pops Orchestra, and Tucson Symphony Orchestra Woodwind Quintet. She received her Bachelor of Music, *summa cum laude*, and her Master of Music from Duquesne University, Pittsburgh, Pennsylvania, where she concentrated on flute performance, music theory, and composition. She is a member of the American Society of Composers, Authors, and Publishers (ASCAP), and she has received annual composition awards since 1986. She received the Golden Rose Award from the Women Band Directors National Association and the Outstanding Service to Music Award from Tau Beta Sigma, a national honorary band sorority.

McGinty is also active as a guest conductor, clinician, and speaker throughout the United States and Canada. She has conducted regional and all-state bands; she has given clinics at many state conventions and universities on band performance, literature, and emotions in music; and she has given speeches at state and national conventions, covering many diverse topics, all of which are related to the performance and enjoyment of music and the values of music education.

Unit 2: Composition

Rainbow Bridge is an original Grade 1 1/2 composition for band and is approximately three minutes and forty-five seconds in length. From a conceptual standpoint, the piece is based on the journey across a bridge to heaven taken by pets after their death. It is in heaven where pets await the joyous reunion with their devoted human companions. This work is very emotional, especially considering the age group for which it is written. The composer aims to musically express the emotions attached to death when words are difficult to speak. The death of a pet is a difficult situation for young people and is often their first experience with the loss of life. With this in mind, this piece may serve as a good introduction to programmatic music.

Unit 3: Historical Perspective

Instrumental program music aims to describe, characterize, or interpret a non-musical subject or idea. This is usually done through the title of the piece and the use of certain musical elements, such as melody, tonality, and harmonic language. In this instance, the composer is trying to characterize the often close relationship between humans and their pets and the sorrow felt by people of all ages when a pet dies. The Romantic period is most closely associated with programmatic music with composers such as Richard Strauss, Hector Berlioz, and Modest Mussorgsky. In regard to band literature, programmatic works include *I Am* by Andrew Boysen, *A Movement for Rosa* by Mark Camphouse, *George Washington Bridge* by William Schuman, and *Trail of Tears* by James Barnes.

Unit 4: Technical Considerations

As with all of the works offered by Queenwood Publications, the instrumentation is well suited for a young, developing band. The wind parts include flute, oboe, alto saxophone, two cornets/trumpets, optional French horn/tenor saxophone, low brass/low woodwinds. Percussion includes bells, wind chimes, snare drum, bass drum, tambourine, woodblock, and suspended cymbal. The piece is playable with only one flute, two clarinets, one alto saxophone, two cornets/trumpets and one bass-line instrument, all the way up to full band instrumentation. The second clarinet part stays below the break, and the optional French horn/tenor saxophone line is written in the best playing ranges for this level. Rhythmic values are basic in nature (dotted-half, half, quarter, eighth, sixteenth), with dotted-quarter notes appearing in various lines. The snare drum part calls for rolls and the execution of sixteenth note patterns. Players should be alert, as their parts are written in C with liberal use of accidentals throughout.

Unit 5: Stylistic Considerations

To have the music meet the emotion, students will need to play with a full, sustained sound in the slurred phrases. Close attention must be paid to the varying dynamic markings, *crescendos*, and *diminuendos* to ensure proper balance and blend. The use of wind chimes and the independent bell part provide an interesting ensemble color.

Unit 6: Musical Elements

The composition is primarily grounded in C major but also incorporates B-flat major, E-flat major, and G major in various places throughout the piece. Every instrument in the ensemble has a line that features both chromatic movement as well as skips or leaps that are often slurred, making execution more difficult. Most of the composition is in 3/4 time, with the section marked "playfully" in common time. Various articulations appear throughout the work, including slurs and *staccatos*. Most of the work is lyrical and should be flowing in nature with a sonorous tone.

Unit 7: Form and Structure

SECTION	MEASURES	EVENT AND SCORING
A	1-19	Melody primarily in upper woodwinds; excellent scoring with several lines of interest, including a counterline by the trumpets that uses melodic material from the B section; C major, ending in B-flat major
B	19-30	New melodic material in cornet/trumpet, accompanied by clarinet; this gives way to the upper woodwinds in m. 27; B-flat major
Transition	30-31	Transition that uses material from the upcoming section
C	32-41	The tempo slows in this sorrowful section that incorporates some colorful harmonic language
B´	41-54	Playful section with a faster tempo; uses the material from the B section in light, *staccato* feel; this section represents the fun and playful nature of pets

SECTION	MEASURES	EVENT AND SCORING
A´	54-65	This section is very similar to the original "A" only with slightly different harmonic language; a transition with a *molto ritardando* in m. 64
Codetta	65-end	A codetta, which features elements from each previous section; ends in C major

Unit 8: Suggested Listening

James Barnes, *Trail of Tears*
Mark Camphouse, *A Movement for Rosa*
John Edmondson:
    Two Songs of Nova Scotia
    Windhaven Celebration
Anne McGinty:
    Triton
    Circles of Stones

Unit 9: Additional References and Resources

Miles, Richard B., ed. *Teaching Music through Performance in Band*. Chicago, IL: GIA Publications, Inc., 1997.

Queenwood Publications. "Anne McGinty: Composer." Composer Gallery. 1999: photo, 6 paragraphs. On-line: Internet address http://www. queenwood.com/composers.html (April 2, 2000)

Smith, Norman, and Albert Stoutamire. *Band Music Notes*, 3rd edition. Lake Charles, LA: Program Note Press, 1979.

Contributed by:

Rodney C. Schueller
Associate Director of Bands
Western Illinois University
Macomb, Illinois

Teacher Resource Guide

Sakura (Cherry Blossoms)
Mike Story
(b. 1956)

Unit 1: Composer

Mike Story is a native of Philadelphia, Pennsylvania. He pursued his musical training at the University of Houston, where he earned his Bachelor of Music and Master of Education degrees. Having taught briefly at the University of Houston School of Music, he currently devotes his full attention to composing and arranging. Story has over 500 published original works and arrangements, including works for concert band, jazz ensemble, and marching band. The majority of his published works are available through Warner Brothers/CPP Belwin Publications, Inc.

Unit 2: Composition

The setting of folk melodies from around the world has provided a wealth of literature for the concert band medium, particularly for young bands. The Japanese folk song, "Sakura," which pays tribute to the national flower of Japan, the cherry blossom, has been used in a variety of settings for band, including *Fantasy on "Sakura, Sakura"* by Ray Cramer, *Japanese Tune* by Soichi Konagaya, and Alfred Reed's *Fifth Symphony (Sakura)*. Mike Story's arrangement of *Sakura* utilizes limited ranges and technical demands to provide an opportunity for the young band to study and explore the native music of Japan. Published in 1995 by CPP/Belwin, the piece is approximately two minutes and thirty seconds in duration.

Unit 3: Historical Perspective

The cherry blossom tree is Japan's most beloved and celebrated flower, as evidenced by its prominence in Japanese art, clothing, and other items. During the second week of April, the Japanese people celebrate the blooming of the cherry blossom tree, signifying the arrival of spring. Following is a free translation of the Japanese folk song, "Sakura":

> The sky in springtime
> Is filled with fragrance
> From the cherry blossoms
> As far as we can see.
> Is it haze or is it clouds?
> I can feel the fragrance.
> From where does it come?
> Let's go see.

Unit 4: Technical Considerations

The scoring for *Sakura* follows a basic band instrumentation: flute, oboe, clarinet, bass clarinet, alto saxophone, tenor saxophone, baritone saxophone, trumpet, horn, trombone/baritone/bassoon, baritone (treble clef), and tuba, with no divided parts. All low reed and low brass parts are scored together on a unison bass line, and alto saxophones double the horns throughout the piece. Percussion scoring is for the following instruments: bells, temple blocks, triangle, gong, snare drum, and bass drum. Four players may cover all percussion parts.

Ranges for each instrument cover slightly more than an octave and are within the normal playing range for first-year players. The clarinet part covers the range from *chalumeau* G to throat tone B-flat, so players do not have to execute crossing the break. With the exception of the clarinet part, all parts stay within the key signature (g minor, two flats in concert pitch). Rhythmic values are limited to whole, half, quarter, and eighth notes and rests, and dynamics cover the range from *piano* to *forte*.

Unit 5: Stylistic Considerations

The nature of the melody suggests a flowing, connected style, with expressive shaping that should follow the contour of the melody. Even though only the pairs of eighth notes are slurred, emphasize the connected style of the melody by having the students sing the melody, giving special attention to "letting the notes touch," separated only by a light, quick articulation.

The basic shape of *Sakura* is one that builds gradually from the beginning, through the first two statements of the theme. The music reaches its peak at measure 26 with the *forte* section of full scoring, then quickly returns to the simple, quiet statement of the theme to finish the piece.

Unit 6: Musical Elements

MELODY:

As is frequently found in traditional oriental melodies, *Sakura* is based on a pentatonic (five-tone) scale. The study of this music offers the teacher and students the opportunity to identify the structure of pentatonic scales. The folk song melody is presented four times, each in a straightforward manner. After a brief introduction, the piece opens with unison clarinets accompanied by percussion alone (measures 3 through 12), followed by a second statement of the theme by flutes and oboes in octaves (measures 13 through 25). The third statement of the melody groups the flutes, trumpets, and bells over full band accompaniment (measures 26 through 41), and the piece closes with a final presentation of the theme by unison clarinets accompanied by percussion (measures 42 through 53).

HARMONY:

Although the key signature indicates G minor, the first presentation of the melody by the clarinets is in F minor. This allows the clarinet section to avoid the technical problem caused by crossing the break. The second presentation of the theme by the flutes and oboes shifts to G minor and is accompanied by a single countermelody in the clarinets and a "G" pedal point in the horns and alto saxophones. The third section is the only part of the arrangement scored for the full ensemble; it presents a setting of the theme that is harmonized by traditional minor triadic chords and accompanied by a bass line, thus creating a homophonic texture. The final section returns to F minor for a final monophonic statement of the melody by the clarinets.

RHYTHM:

The meter of *Sakura* is 4/4 throughout, and the basic rhythms of whole, half, quarter, and eighth notes, as well as whole, half, and quarter rests, provide a rhythmic level well within the reach of first-year players. All pairs of eighth notes within the wind parts are slurred, so special attention must be given to the length of the first note of each pair so that the eighth note groupings do not rush. Students should practice the eighth note groupings both tongued and slurred in order to attain evenness of the eighth notes. Percussionists and low brass and reed players must give special attention to rests, noting that the rests are as equally important to the music as the notes and must be accurately placed in order to achieve proper performance.

TIMBRE:

One of the strongest features of *Sakura* is that each instrument is scored for only one part, thus allowing the players to develop confidence in their playing while training their ears to match pitch and tone quality with other players in their section. The piece opens with a combination of clarinet and percussion colors, which expands to a three-voice texture of primarily woodwinds (melody, countermelody, and pedal point). The clarinets playing the countermelody and the horns and saxophones playing the pedal point must carefully consider the *mf* dynamic level so as not to overbalance the melodic line of the flutes and oboes. The third section of the piece marks the climax of the music, with all instruments playing with a rich *forte* sound. All players with harmony to the melody and the bass line must focus their listening toward the flutes, trumpets, and bells to ensure that the melody maintains its prominence above the secondary parts. After a quick *decrescendo* to *piano*, the music closes with a return to the combination of clarinet and percussion colors that begins the piece.

Unit 7: Form and Structure

SECTION	MEASURES	EVENT AND SCORING
Introduction	1-2	Percussion: gong/temple blocks
Section A	3-12	Phrase 1; unison clarinet melody (F minor) with percussion accompaniment (triangle/temple blocks)
Section B	13-25	Phrase 2; flute/oboe melody (G minor) with clarinet countermelody; horn/alto saxophone on "g" pedal tone; addition of bells and snare drum (snares off)
Section C	26-41	Phrase 3; full band scoring with flute/trumpet/bells melody (G minor); oboe/clarinet/alto saxophone/horn with harmonized melody; low reeds/low brass bass line; addition of bass drum
Section D	42-53	Phrase 4; same as Section A; low reeds/brass on unison "f" on final cadence

Unit 8: Suggested Listening

Toshio Akiyama, *Japanese Songs for Band*
James Barnes, *Impressions of Japan*
John Barnes Chance, *Variations on a Korean Folk Song*
Ray Cramer, *Fantasy on "Sakura, Sakura"*
Clare Grundman, *Japanese Rhapsody*
Robert Jager, *Japanese Prints*
Soichi Konagaya, *Japanese Tune*
Alfred Reed, *Fifth Symphony (Sakura)*
Bernard Rogers, *Three Japanese Dances*

Unit 9: Additional References and Resources

Belwin-Mills Publishing Corp., Miami, FL.

Dvorak, Thomas L., Cynthia Crump Taggart, and Peter Schmalz. *Best Music for Young Band*. Edited by Bob Margolis. Brooklyn, NY: Manhattan Beach Music, 1986.

Garofalo, Robert J. *Instructional Designs for Middle/Junior High School Band*. Fort Lauderdale, FL: Meredith Music Publications, 1995.

Kreines, Joseph. *Music for Concert Band*. Tampa, FL: Florida Music Service, 1989.

Randel, Don Michael, ed. *The New Harvard Dictionary of Music*. Cambridge, MA: The Belknap Press of Harvard University Press, 1986.

Rehrig, William H. *Supplement to The Heritage Encyclopedia of Band Music*. Edited by Paul E. Bierley. Westerville, OH: Integrity Press, 1996.

Contributed by:

C. Kevin Bowen
Wake Forest University
Winston-Salem, North Carolina

Teacher Resource Guide

A Shaker Hymn

John O'Reilly
(b. 1941)

Unit 1: Composer

John O'Reilly is one of the most-performed composers of band music in the world today. He is the recipient of numerous ASCAP awards and has studied composition with Robert Washburn, Arthur Frackenpohl, Charles Walton, and Donald Hunsberger. As co-author of *Yamaha Band Student*, *Accent on Achievement*, and *Strictly Strings*, O'Reilly has made a major impact on the education of young musicians.

O'Reilly attended the Crane School of Music, State University of New York at Potsdam, receiving a Bachelor of Science degree. In addition, he is the recipient of a Master of Arts in Composition and Theory from Columbia University. His twelve years of teaching experience at elementary through college levels has provided him with insights and sensitivities to the needs of both students and educators. An elected member of the prestigious American Bandmasters Association, O'Reilly is a frequent conductor of honor bands worldwide. He currently resides in Los Angeles, California, where he serves as executive vice president and editor-in-chief of Alfred Publishing.

Unit 2: Composition

A Shaker Hymn, based upon the traditional melody, "Simple Gifts," was written in 1995. It is part of the *Yamaha Band Series*, published by Alfred Publishing Company. All of the works in this series correspond with lessons in the *Yamaha Band Student* band class method. *A Shaker Hymn* correlates with book 1, page 18. The indicated grade level is characterized as "Very Easy."

Unit 3: Historical Perspective

The Shaker melody, "Simple Gifts," has been arranged for numerous ensembles and uses for many years. Perhaps the most notable setting was composed by Aaron Copland for his ballet, "Appalachian Spring." Its first performance took place on October 30, 1945. Since that time, Copland's ballet music has stood alone, both as a staple for chamber orchestra and in his transcription for the concert band, "Variations on a Shaker Melody."

Unit 4: Technical Considerations

This composition is written to enhance the instructional activities in book 1 of the *Yamaha Band Student* (page 18). At this point in the book, the dotted-quarter followed by an eighth note is introduced for the first time. At this point, the young players should have a basic understanding of the *legato* style of articulation and breath support so that the melodic lines are smooth and connected. The students should be technically proficient in the keys of F and B-flat major. The written ranges for each instrument are appropriate for this stage of technical development.

Unit 5: Stylistic Considerations

The overriding style in *A Shaker Hymn* is smooth and connected, with an indicated tempo of *Andante*. The *andante* tempo does not change throughout the piece, yet the style of articulation will require a light, slightly separated approach in the slur-two/tongue-two eighth note lines. As in most pieces for this level, one should consider the organization of the melodic line and basic phrasing (logical *sounding* "beginnings" and "endings"). The printed score and parts indicate only a very few expressive markings (*mf* and *f*).

Unit 6: Musical Elements

The hymn style requires continued instruction in the *legato* style of articulation. The addition of new dynamic markings will enhance the students' expressive playing and melodic tendencies, such as contour, low to high, high to low, short seeks long, etc. The introduction of a broader array of harmony (chords) requires that balance must now become a major consideration along with the brief contrapuntal statements. These offer an opportunity for lessons regarding listening to each other (for example, "if you have a sustained part, are you able to *hear* those parts that are moving?" or "will the brasses have to make any adjustments so that the woodwinds will be heard easily?"). Point out that listening is a skill in ensemble playing, and demonstrate the difference between "listening" and "hearing"! There are several dotted-quarter followed by eighth note figures. Young players have a strong tendency to rush dotted rhythms. (Example: "How many eighth-notes are equal to a dotted-quarter note?")

Unit 7: Form and Structure

The tune is written in rounded binary form. It is stated twice in the piece, giving the composition an A–A′ structure. The opening section (A) is written in a *tutti* chorale style. The A′ section begins in measure 30. At this point, the melody is stated in diminution with two-voice counterpoint between the woodwinds and the brass following. The brass take the lead five measures prior to the end.

Unit 8: Suggested Listening

Celebration!, The Tokyo Kosei Wind Orchestra, KOCD-3571, Frederick
   Fennell, Conductor

Instrumental Music Selections, Orpheus Chamber Orchestra, Deutsche
   Grammophon, 427, 335-2

Unit 9: Additional References and Resources

Copland, Aaron. *What to Listen for in Music*. New York, NY: McGraw-Hill
   Book Company, Inc., 1939.

Lisk, Edward S. *The Creative Director: Intangibles of Musical Performance*. Ft.
   Lauderdale, FL: Meredith Music Publications, 1996.

Contributed by:

William A. Gora
Appalachian State University
Boone, North Carolina

Teacher Resource Guide

Song for Friends
Larry D. Daehn
(b. 1939)

Unit 1: Composer

Larry D. Daehn was born in 1939 on a farm near Rosendale, Wisconsin. He received his bachelor's degree from the University of Wisconsin-Oshkosh and his master's degree from the University of Wisconsin-Platteville. His 35-year teaching career consisted of teaching vocal and instrumental music in various Wisconsin schools, including New Glarus High School, where he directed for twenty-seven years and won numerous state and national awards. Currently, Daehn is a member of several music organizations, including MENC, Wisconsin Bandmasters Association, ASBDA, Phi Beta Mu, and the Percy Grainger Society. He was also chosen for *Leaders of American Education* in 1971 and was named *Outstanding Bandmaster* by Phi Beta Mu, Pi Chapter, in 1988. In addition to his composing and arranging projects for concert band, Daehn maintains extensive research on the life and music of Percy Grainger. He is also the owner and operator of Daehn Publications, a company special-izing in concert band music since 1988.

Unit 2: Composition

Song for Friends is a piece written especially for seventh and eighth grade bands. The modest instrumental ranges and easy phrasing allow the individ-ual players the opportunity to produce their finest tone quality. Furthermore, the relatively short length of the work will help retain the focus of younger students in rehearsal as well as provide the option of using the work as a part of the daily warm-up routine. The compositional style and aesthetics of *Song for Friends* can best be compared with another composition by the same composer, *As Summer Was Just Beginning*. The melodic phrasing, *legato* style, contrary motion between the melody and countermelody, and extensive use of softer dynamics provides younger students with a solid foundation for the more difficult music they will encounter later in their musical development.

Unit 3: Historical Perspective

During the twentieth century, music written for elementary or middle school bands has followed a basic pattern, which includes block scoring, formula percussion writing, and a lack of musicality expectation; however, *Song for Friends* stands as a wonderful example of how that trend is ending. Daehn has composed a piece that, while retaining the difficulty level required for younger players, gives players the experience of a contemporary piece of music written in what is essentially the ballad song form. Percy Grainger, an early twentieth century Australian composer, essentially pioneered this compositional form/style through works such as *Irish Tune from County Derry*, *Ye Banks and Braes O' Bonnie Doon*, and *Colonial Song*. Therefore, it is easy to make the correlation between Daehn's research into the music of Percy Grainger, his passion for quality music for younger bands, and the compositional style used in *Song for Friends*.

Unit 4: Technical Considerations

The composer has made a very conscious effort to remove all technical difficulties from *Song for Friends*. The piece is written in a basic triple meter, uses only the scales of E-flat and B-flat, and keeps all instruments within a range adequate for any second- or third-year performer. The clarinet part does not approach the "break"(highest note is G_4), and brass parts are well within reason for developing embouchures (the highest note in the trumpet part is C_5, A-flat$_3$ for trombones). Rhythmically, the piece uses nothing more complex than a half note followed by two eighth notes, thereby making the composition a great introduction to sight-reading for younger players.

Unit 5: Stylistic Considerations

Song for Friends should be considered a primary instructional tool for teaching musicality and stylistic instrumental performing. Although the piece is technically easy, the stylistic demands on the performers will provide an excellent challenge and help students grow in one of the most eluding of developmental categories: musical maturity. In this piece, performers are asked to play in a *legato* style throughout, maintain four-measure phrases, be sensitive to the audibility of the melody and countermelody, and consistently perform at the lower dynamic ranges. Moreover, the piece ends with a short, five-measure coda in which the tempo slows, and the dynamics fall even softer. These two factors, combined with the final two *fermatas*, will provide an excellent opportunity for stylistic growth.

Unit 6: Musical Elements

MELODY:

The primary melodic material used in *Song for Friends* consists of a rhythmical motif that can be found in measure 1, a half note followed by two eighth notes. This reoccurring melodic fragment should be addressed early in the rehearsal schedule so as to avoid developing bad habits throughout the entire work. Fortunately, teaching and performing this fragment with the utmost musicality is not difficult. Furthermore, it provides the opportunity to explain the concept of *tenuto* if it has not already been addressed.

First, have the students put a *tenuto* marking underneath the first eighth note. Explain to them that not only should they think of elongating the note, they should also think of playing it with a certain amount of "weight" (defined as *slightly louder, not accented!*). Although something as simple as adding these two concepts to one note may seem trivial, the end result will certainly be indicative of other notes/beats in the piece that might provoke a more musical response through the same method. Certainly, explaining to younger players the difference between an "accent" and "weight" will be challenging; however, this obstacle can be easily traversed by an audible example from the teacher or an advanced student.

Second, continually reinforce the concept of four-measure phrases. Students will have a tendency to breathe after the half note in the melodic motif addressed earlier, as well as after every two measures; both of these tendencies are detrimental to the work and should be avoided. Perhaps an exercise (or game) in which the conductor starts at the beginning of the piece, stops every time he/she sees a breath in the wrong place, and starts again would prove to be a great learning tool. Students will feel an incredible rush of accomplishment after making it through the entire piece without stopping, and they will be eager for another challenge.

HARMONY:

Although the harmonic structure throughout *Song for Friends* is very simple and straightforward, it provides an excellent way to introduce basic music theory.

One area of music theory that can be easily learned from this piece is major and minor chords. Throughout almost the entire work, the root of each chord used is in the tuba or lowest-sounding brass instrument, with the third of the chord being played in the melody (almost all chords are in root position). Play a sequence of major chords on the piano and explain to the students visually how they look on the piano. Then, play a sequence of minor chords and explain how those chords were built by only changing one note. Ask the students how each type of chord sounds (e.g., "happy" or "sad"). Then ask them which type of chords they believe *Song for Friends* is based upon and why. Finally, have the band play the first note of the piece and then show them on the piano how it relates to the chords you were playing earlier. Change the chord to minor on the piano and then instruct the horns, clarinets, and tenor saxophones to lower their note by a half step. Ask the students how they think the piece would be changed if it were based on minor chords instead of major chords. The realization of the correlation between major and minor chords and the overall aesthetics of a piece of music are the first step in the path of learning and appreciating music theory.

RHYTHM:

Rhythmically, *Song for Friends* provides few challenges for even the youngest performers. However, the last five measures of the piece provide a nice exercise for *ritardando* and *fermata*, both of which fall into the category of rhythmic elements.

At some point, take the rehearsal time to explore in-depth the music behind the last five measures of this piece. Conduct this section with the students watching but not playing, then quiz them on gestures used and what they meant (e.g., Was there a break between *fermatas*? Did it "look" as though the music was getting slower and softer?). Then have the students play the last five measures and quiz them on what they believe was done well and what might need improvement to make the ending as musical as possible. Also, this might be the best opportunity to play listening examples of great endings to music similar to *Song for Friends* and ask the students to explain what they believe they did similar to the recording and what they should improve upon. The important concept here is that the students understand how vital these issues are and how important the ending of a piece is to the overall impression of the work.

TIMBRE:

The overall timbre of *Song for Friends* is dictated by three primary factors: the low *tessitura* of the wind instruments, the use of high-pitched percussion instruments, and the relatively soft dynamics used throughout.

The best use of this piece as an educational tool might simply be providing students with a practical example of what timbre means. First, have the clarinets play the first eight measures of the piece and stop. Then, have the percussion and flutes perform measures 17 through 24. Ask the students what the most striking difference is between these two musical examples and then take the time to define timbre and relate it to those two examples. Next, have the mallet percussion play their part at measure 17 down an octave and ask the students if they notice a significant difference. Ask the students how they believe the piece would be changed if the clarinets played their parts "higher" like the flutes and mallet percussion.

Unit 7: Form and Structure

SECTION	MEASURES	EVENT AND SCORING
A	1-16	The piece begins in E-flat major; repeats two eight-measure phrases that are almost identical in the melodic material used
B	17-24	This short B section does not change in its tonal center from E-flat; however, it does revolve around the IV (A-flat) chord, alluding to the plagal cadence at the end of the work
A	25-53	The final A section consists of three of the eight-measure phrases already established; followed by a short five-measure coda
	25-32	Original eight-measure phrase performed in the key of E-flat
	33-48	A modulation to the key of B-flat occurs; again, two eight-measure phrases similar to mm. 1-16 are performed, this time in B-flat
	49-53	This five-measure coda ends the piece gracefully with two *fermatas* creating a plagal cadence

Unit 8: Suggested Listening

Aaron Copland/arr. Patterson, *Down a Country Lane*
Larry Daehn, *As Summer Was Just Beginning*
Frank Erickson, *Balladair*
Percy Grainger, *Irish Tune from County Derry*
Brian Hogg, *Llwyn Onn*
David Holsinger, *A Childhood Hymn*
Frank Ticheli, *Amazing Grace*
Pavel Tschesnokoff/arr. Houseknecht, *Salvation Is Created*

Unit 9: Additional References and Resources

Battisti, Frank, and Robert Garofalo. *Guide to Score Study for the Wind Band Conductor*. Fort Lauderdale, FL: Meredith Music Publications, 1990.

Casey, Joseph L. *Teaching Techniques and Insights for Instrumental Music Educators*. Chicago, IL: GIA Publications, 1991.

Daehn Publications, New Glarus, WI (publisher of *Song for Friends*).

Dvorak, Thomas L., Cynthia Taggart, and Peter Schmalz. *Best Music for Young Band*. Edited by Bob Margolis. Brooklyn, NY: Manhattan Beach Music, 1986.

Garofalo, Robert J. *Instructional Designs for Middle/Junior High School Band*. Fort Lauderdale, FL: Meredith Music Publications, 1995.

Goldman, Richard Franko. *The Wind Band*. Boston: Allyn and Bacon, Inc., 1961.

The World of Wind Ensembles – Online & BandChat Mailing List. http://bandchat.schoolmusic.com/winds

Contributed by:

Andy McMahan
Nicolet High School
Glendale, Wisconsin

Teacher Resource Guide

Song for the Winter Moon
Walter Cummings
(b. 1953)

Unit 1: Composer

Walter Cummings is a native of Greenville, Mississippi. He attended the University of Southern Mississippi, where he received a bachelor's degree in Music Education and a Master of Music in Conducting. He also earned a Master of Music in Music Education from the University of Colorado and a Doctor of Arts in Conducting from the University of Northern Colorado. Cummings taught middle school and high school band in Mississippi and at Plymouth State College during his teaching career, which spanned fourteen years. He currently freelances as a composer and a trombone and tuba performer, and he is the adjunct instrumental instructor at Mesa State College in Grand Junction, Colorado. The recipient of three ASCAP awards for excellence, Cummings won the 1990 Colorado Music Educators Association Band Composition Contest. He is the owner of Grand Mesa Music.

Unit 2: Composition

Published in 1998, *Song for the Winter Moon* is intended for the very young band and incorporates elements of the Native American folk song style. Inspiration for the work came from observing a gorgeous, large December moon during an evening walk that the composer believed deserved a commemorative piece of music. A member of the Sierra Club, Cummings acknowledges an influence of nature upon his life and his music that leads to a spontaneous stream of conscience reflected in the piece. This three-minute work allows every section of the ensemble to have melodic prominence which, the composer relates, reflects his desire to play the melody when he

was a young player. Every line is cross-cued with the exception of the saxophone line that is often independent.

Unit 3: Historical Perspective

Contemporary compositional styles are eclectic, reflecting the composer's desire to grow and explore as a musician. This "post-modern" style includes elements of several time periods, and *Song for the Winter Moon* allows young performers to experience a combination of folk song, medieval modes, and modern harmonies. Michael Sweeney's *Ancient Voices* incorporates many similar compositional techniques. Cummings often listens to Native American music, but the melodic material is entirely original. The composer enjoys experimenting with sounds and phrase length. His *Balinese Gamelan* is another work for young band using unusual harmonies and lines.

Unit 4: Technical Considerations

Ensemble members successfully completing their first method book should be capable of performing *Song for the Winter Moon*. With the exception of sixteenth note figures in the snare drum part (Percussion I), students need eighth note counting skills. Dotted-quarter/eighth figures are the most complex subdivision requirements. Students perform within the E-flat and B-flat concert key signatures and, although the work uses modes, need to be able to perform those concert scales. The score calls for half of the clarinet section to have the ability to play over the break. Range and instrumentation considerations are as follows: flute/oboe/bells (C above the staff/A above the staff), clarinet (third space C), alto saxophone (A above the staff), first and second trumpet (fourth line D/third space C), horn in F (third space C), trombone/baritone/bassoon/tenor saxophone (B-flat top of the staff), and bass.

Performers do have extended *legato* lines that are five measures in 4/4 time, which may push young students and should be a consideration. The independent alto saxophone line requires confident performers; it is not cross-cued in other instruments. The horn part is cross-cued throughout, usually in the clarinet part. Four percussionists need a triangle, suspended cymbal, snare drum, and bass drum. Students should understand breath marks, *ritardando*, and *fermata*.

Unit 5: Stylistic Considerations

Song for the Winter Moon provides a good opportunity to discuss the terms *Andante* and *Piu mosso*, particularly within the framework of tempo, and how these terms do not necessarily mean "slow" and "fast." With the term *legato* specified over the initial melodic statements that include slurs, students learn the difference between *legato* style and *tenuto* and slurred articulations. While the introduction is quite specific about *crescendos* and *diminuendos* that follow the line, the composer tends to use general phrase dynamics in the rest of the piece, requiring students to transfer the line approach to their moving line throughout. Measure 9 is a good time to introduce dynamic reinforcement to repeated figures and continuation of countermelody between sections. The initial melodic idea is a five-measure phrase, and since this high point of that line is the only occurrence of a dotted-quarter note, it is a terrific example of using rhythm to create emphasis in the line. Lines overlap, so students must learn to recognize the end of one phrase and the beginning of the new phrase, while sustained harmonic figures should understand their roles as they relate to the melody and countermelodic motives.

The change of tempo relates to the change of melodic and harmonic material so students recognize these potential relationships. A singing style provides a true interpretation, and a folk song style applies in this case. Having students sing lines at a young age is possible in this piece due to the limited range demands, thus allowing the performers the opportunity to relate singing to performing on their instruments.

Unit 6: Musical Elements

MELODY:

The folk song melody initially revolves around the Dorian mode. To familiarize the ensemble with the concept of modes aurally and technically, consider having the students listen to recordings of medieval chants to develop an aural sense of the modal line and then work tetrachords, adding the lower leading tone. This nearly replicates the melodies as found in the piece. Start on the root and identify it as Ionian mode, the second as Dorian mode, and the third with the Phrygian designation. This is a particularly good opportunity to discuss the role of the modes as defined by the church and how the church affected western music composition. The conductor should allow the ensemble to discover how the same melody, with the same pitch relationships, changes aurally when placed in a different mode, such as the Dorian mode found at measure 9 and the Phrygian mode at measure 47.

When performing the melodies, the ensemble should follow the line dynamically as indicated in the stylistic consideration section, although there are no indications on the page. Similarly, the simple sequence found in the clarinet/horn part in measures 9 through 12 is a good time to introduce development sequences through dynamics and intensity.

HARMONY:

The composer intends the vertical harmonies to be a form of polychords, with ninth chords such as those created by melodic instruments in measure 9 resulting in extended chords. These chords may be difficult to discuss with young students, but there are some harmonic, compositional techniques found in *Song of the Winter Moon* that help develop young ears. The entrance at measure 9 in the trumpets at the ninth, when isolated with the low winds, is a good place to demonstrate the difference between a ninth and a second, and how that changes the sound. Also, consider slowly performing the clarinet/horn line to demonstrate the fifth/fourth vertical relationships in terms of aural interest. Measure 40 represents an easily accessible introduction to double pedal points, with the woodwind line added to provide harmonic interest. Students can discuss how each half note changes the quality of sound.

RHYTHM:

Measure 6 contains the most difficult rhythm found in this piece; it will require some work while perhaps introducing pyramids. Otherwise, the eighth note lines provide momentum throughout and offer a discussion about listening to the subdivision to provide rhythmic security. Conductors might consider having the ensemble play without a pattern, allowing students to identify the moving line and permitting that line to define the subdivision. Discuss how this relates to chamber music performance.

TIMBRE:

Cummings uses a variety of doublings presenting a study of how instrument combinations create different timbres. One set of comparisons of particular interest are those involving the flute/oboe, alto saxophone, clarinet, horn, and trumpet. Measure 40 combines the clarinets with the trumpets, while the alto saxophones are combined with the flute/oboe line. Have students compare that sound to measure 47, where the clarinets combine with the alto saxophones while the trumpets and horns combine to perform the melodic line. Students can discover the difference between various colors based upon instrument combinations.

Unit 7: Form and Structure

SECTION	MEASURES	EVENT AND SCORING
Introduction	1-8	Motives create Dorian modal center
Section I (A)	1-13	Trumpet introduces the primary melodic strain in Dorian mode
	13-17	Flute/oboe part answers with counter melody divided between clarinet and alto saxophone in Dorian mode
	18-20	Bridge back to trumpet statement with motivic material derived from introduction; in Dorian mode
	21-25	Trumpet restates the primary melodic strain in Dorian mode
Transition I	25-30	Transition using augmentation of the clarinet line in m. 21 and motives from the introduction, setting up modal modulation

SECTION	MEASURES	EVENT AND SCORING
Section II (B)	31-34	Treble winds and alto saxophone introduces the secondary melodic strain in E-flat major
	34-37	Low winds answer with rhythmically altered secondary strain in E-flat major
	37-39	Bridge back to second statement with motivic material from m. 35; in E-flat major
	40-43	Final statement of the secondary melodic strain in clarinet (*divisi*) and trumpet; in E-flat major
Transition II	44-46	Modal modulation
Section III (A)	47-51	Trumpet and horn return to primary melodic strain in Phrygian mode
	51-54	Horn, alto saxophone, and clarinet restate strain, with flute and oboe using material from the introduction for countermelody
	55-58	Trumpet makes final complete statement of melodic strain
Coda	59-65	Build to conclusion using the first two measures of the primary melody combined with the introductory material; concluding in B-flat major

Unit 8: Suggested Listening

Douglas Akey, *A Tallis Prelude*
Walter Cummings, *Balinese Gamelan*
Larry Daehn, *As Summer Was Just Beginning*
Norman Dello Joio, *Variants on a Medieval Tune*
Ron Nelson, *Medieval Suite*
Douglas Nott, *The Kalama*
Tielman Susato/arr. Bob Margolis, *The Battle Pavane*
Michael Sweeney, *Ancient Voices*

Unit 9: Additional References and Resources

"The Basic Band Curriculum: Grades I, II, III." *BD Guide*,
   September/October 1989, 2-6.

Cummings, Walter, composer and owner of Grand Mesa Music. Interview by
   author, January 2000, Grand Junction, CO. Phone conversation.
   Mississippi State University, Mississippi.

Cummings, Walter. "Song for the Winter Moon." Score, 1998, Personal Collection, Rod M. Chesnutt, Mississippi State University, Mississippi State, Mississippi.

Garofalo, Robert J. *Instructional Designs for Middle/Junior High School Band.* Fort Lauderdale, FL: Meredith Publications, 1995.

Kvet, Edward, ed. *Instructional Literature for Middle-Level Band.* Reston, VA: Music Educators National Conference, 1996.

Music Educators National Conference, Committee on Performance Standards. *Performance Standards for Music.* Reston, VA: Music Educators National Conference, 1996.

Pearson, Bruce. *Standard of Excellence,* book 1. San Diego, CA: Neil A. Kjos Music Company, 1993.

Rhodes, Tom C., Donald Bierschenk, and Tim Lautzenheiser. *Essential Elements: A Comprehensive Band Method.* Milwaukee, WI: Hal Leonard Publishing Corporation, 1991.

Contributed by:

Rod M. Chesnutt
Director of Bands
Mississippi State University
Mississippi State, Mississippi

Teacher Resource Guide

Space Echoes
John Visconti
(b. 1938)

Unit 1: Composer

John Visconti is a pen name for the award-winning ASCAP composer, Elliot Del Borgo. Born in Port Chester, New York, on October 27, 1938, Del Borgo earned a Bachelor of Science degree from Temple University in Philadelphia and a Master of Music degree from the Philadelphia Conservatory, where one of his composition teachers was Vincent Persichetti. He taught instrumental music in the Philadelphia public schools early in his career. Since 1965, he has been associated with the State University of New York in Potsdam, where he served as a teacher and administrator. He currently holds the title of Professor Emeritus.

In addition to writing over 300 works for band, Del Borgo has composed material for orchestra, chorus, chamber groups, and method books. He wrote music for the 1980 Winter Olympics in Lake Placid, New York, and is presently involved with his own company, Cape Music Enterprises. In addition, he is active as a clinician, conductor, and consultant. Other band compositions under the pen name of John Visconti include *Arioso*, a Warner Brothers Music publication.

Unit 2: Composition

This young band work employs elements of twentieth century compositional technique. With no written key signature and without a prevalent harmonic center, the composer uses musical "cells," or recurring groups of pitches, to create harmonic and melodic interest. Del Borgo's musical cells consist of half steps, augmented seconds, and augmented fourths/diminished fifths (tri-tones).

Canonic writing is evident, along with diminution and augmentation. Musical drama is heightened by the use of dissonance at impact points.

Refreshing for this grade level are the interesting timbres, the use of keyboard instruments, and the percussion writing. Del Borgo treats the three-part percussion block as an independent "third choir." Percussion instruments include bells, woodblock, snare drum, field drum, bass drum, triangle, suspended cymbal, and tom-tom (one). In addition to using straight mutes (trumpets), *Space Echoes* calls for a synthesizer with a "string" sound and a piano. Although the synthesizer duplicates the low woodwind and brass lines, it adds a unique effect. The piano part is minimal, but important; it consists of two elements: 1) a two-hand chord cluster and 2) a one-octave *glissando* played on the piano strings with a triangle beater. The work begins quietly with a suspended cymbal roll, expands to *tutti* impact points, and closes quietly with a single finger snap. Published in 1995 by Warner Brothers, *Space Echoes* is part of the *Belwin Beginning Band* series. It is fifty-seven measures in length, is in 4/4 meter, and is approximately three minutes and thirty seconds in duration.

Unit 3: Historical Perspective

Throughout history, the stars and planets have provided many composers limitless inspiration for their works. Del Borgo's image of space sound (or echoes) is portrayed through clusters of specific pitches or musical cells. Their unique combination and arrangement of dissonant material forms the atonal framework of this piece. In a great deal of twentieth century music, many works that are categorized as atonal do, in fact, treat pitches in a hierarchical fashion, where one or a few pitches play a central part.

For many centuries, certain intervals were regarded as "consonant" (peaceful, pleasant-sounding, orderly, restful), while others were viewed as "dissonant" (wild, harsh, uneasy, needing resolution). In ancient Greece, only the unison, fourth, fifth, and octave intervals were considered perfectly consonant. The half step and the tri-tone relationships in *Space Echoes* would be considered dissonant intervals. Early music dictated that the tri-tone was evil, and it was sometimes called the "devil's interval." During the medieval period, the tri-tone was outlawed as it was considered a threatening, sinister interval.

In contemporary music, however, half steps and tri-tones occur with much more frequency and are even considered interesting. An example of this is heard in Leonard Bernstein's modern opera, *West Side Story* (based on Shakespeare's *Romeo and Juliet*). The tri-tone interval is a necessary component in each of the melodies of the popular songs "Cool" and "Maria."

Unit 4: Technical Considerations

The technical demands of *Space Echoes* are not extreme. Ranges are accessible to less-experienced players; the highest note in the trumpet part is a written third space C, and clarinets do not cross the break. The work is written with one part per instrument, although the flute part utilizes a few *divisi* measures. Adequate doublings are written for those bands with limited instrumentation. The composer suggests that pitches be well centered (played "in tune"), as melodies are generally duplicated at the unison or octave. Rhythms are all simple combinations of whole, half, dotted-half, quarter, and eighth notes. Sixteenth notes are used briefly in the percussion parts. Although there are few exposed lines and no meter changes, the rhythm continually changes from measure to measure. This, and numerous ties across bar lines, may present a challenge for less-experienced players.

The polyphonic texture (two or more melodies simultaneously occurring) requires students to play independent lines with confidence. At one point, five independent layers of rhythms occur. With no written key signature, there is considerable use of accidentals in all of the parts.

The percussion writing, far from generic, is quite detailed with a good deal of information on each part. Percussionists must possess good rhythm, counting skills, and a sense of nuance and style.

Unit 5: Stylistic Considerations

Outer space can be classified as mysterious, boundless, enchanting, ominous, quiet, vast, random, and even eerie. With images in mind, students should be encouraged to play long, expansive phrases in a *sostenuto* (connected) style. Note lengths should be held for full values and sounds should disappear into rests. The challenge for young students lies in making this happen at a very soft dynamic level (*piano*) in a slow tempo (quarter note = 66). Soft, tongued passages require a "du" or "da" articulation, rather than the harsher "tu" or "ta" attack. Ask students to use a light, quick tongue stroke over a very fast, warm air stream. For those passages that require more presence (muted trumpet phrase at measure 11), the "tu" or "ta" syllable may work better. The conductor will want to contour the longer phrases, adding additional dynamics plus expressive markings, such as *crescendos* and *diminuendos*.

The work explores a full dynamic range, from *piano* to *fortissimo*. For young students, two formidable tasks will arise: 1) to distinguish between each of the varying dynamics levels and 2) to control individual timbres in those specified volumes. Extreme dynamic levels, like *piano*, will offer the greatest challenge. The composer's specific dynamic markings (even in the percussion) are helpful in identifying important passages and should be observed. They are a guide for balance and line direction.

Unit 6: Musical Elements

MELODY:

While the melodies in *Space Echoes* are constructed by grouping together smaller motivic ideas, the composer is specific in how these ideas are to be phrased. When notes are slurred together in *legato* passages, students should avoid "clipping" or cutting short those notes at the end of the slur mark. (For example, in measure 13, the D concert should connect to the A-flat concert in the upper woodwind and bell voices.) The avoidance of clipped sounds is required especially at the ends of phrases, or when a leap of some kind is involved (measures 14 and 15, same instruments, same pitches).

A canon is a contrapuntal form that uses imitation of basic melodic material. The opening motive is used as a canon in its basic original form, at the fifth, and at the minor second. Since these types of phrases overlap, students will need to develop a good sense of phrasing. They should have an understanding of the hierarchy of phrases, especially the point where each phrase begins and ends. Isolating individual passages in rehearsal is suggested.

In *tutti* passages, students should work to develop similar articulation and musical expression. The use of a metronome set on eighth notes is recommended to keep subdivision "honest" for those phrases that have multiple lines (measures 41 through 45). To identify each line, passages should be isolated, played in different combinations, and then put back together. In phrases where the melody is in the same register as the accompaniment, the conductor and students will need to adjust balances accordingly.

While the trumpet melody at measure 11 is not doubled, trumpets should be made aware that their pitch will rise when using mutes. This is a good place to talk about the different physical adjustments that can be made when using a mute. Also, it would be appropriate to teach where (or where not) to place the mute when not in use, as they are easy to kick or drop from a chair.

Teaching strategy — To teach sustained tones in a canonic setting, choose any scale. Using half notes and a "du" articulation, play the scale one octave up and down with no tonic repeat at the top. Divide the band into three or more groups. Play the scale in a "round" or "canon." (You may want to sing a few bars of "Row, Row, Row Your Boat" as an example.) Begin each new group on the first (tonic) scale degree. Once finished with the scale, each group holds out the tonic until the last group reaches the end. Students should refrain from taking a breath until the third half note (or longer) and should not breathe when their stand partner breathes.

HARMONY:

Although *Space Echoes* has no prevalent tonal center, harmonic interest is created through the linear activity of melodic cells or motivic ideas. When no tonal center is prevalent, it is difficult for students to have an awareness of "where they are going." Some intervalic relationships used in contemporary music are not easily heard (tri-tones). In order for students to be required to comprehend contemporary music, they need a basic understanding of unusual intervalic relationships.

Teaching strategy — Have students play a B-flat chromatic scale, one octave, in quarter notes, repeating the tonic B-flat before progressing to the next scale degree (B-flat/B, B-flat/C, B-flat/D-flat, B-flat/D, B-flat/E-flat, B-flat/E, B-flat/F, B-flat/G-flat, B-flat/G, B-flat/A-flat, B-flat/A, B-flat/B-flat). Play and sing the passage. You can divide the band in half: one-half of the band can play; one-half can sing. Keep the instruments close to the embouchures while singing so as not to lose time putting down/picking up instruments. One variation would be to play the B-flat concert every time and sing the other notes. Play the entire exercise "backwards." Start on the upper B-flat and proceed chromatically to the low B-flat repeating the upper B-flat concert (B-flat/A, B-flat/A-flat, B-flat/G, B-flat/G-flat, B-flat/F, B-flat/E, B-flat/E-flat, B-flat/D, B-flat/D-flat, B-flat/C, B-flat/B, B-flat/B-flat). Once students are able to sing and play with ease, without "bumping" notes, have them isolate selected intervals. For study in this work, isolate the minor second, augmented second, and tri-tone, to name a few.

RHYTHM:

The basic rhythmic structure of *Space Echoes* is not difficult. An understanding of whole, half, quarter, eighth, and sixteenth note subdivision is required. Because the music is contrapuntal, it will be important for students to develop an awareness of horizontal independence and rhythmic alignment. This can be practiced outside the music with various scale warm-ups. Scales work well for this exercise, as students can memorize them fairly quickly.

Teaching strategy — Divide the band into five sections and assign each group a rhythm to play (whole note, half note, quarter note, eighth note, sixteenth note). Ask students to play a B-flat concert scale (in 4/4 time at quarter note = 60-72) using their prescribed rhythms to fill out each measure (one whole note, eight eighth notes, two half notes, four quarter notes, etc.). Play the chosen scale up and down one octave without repeating the tonic. You can divide individual sections into different rhythmic groupings or keep instrument families together. (Note: For every measure there is one pitch.) Sixteenth notes may be a challenge to some students at this level. Work for a clear, *similar* articulation; tell students what articulation to play ("du," "tu," "da," etc.). Encourage full sounds and a sense of subdivision. Switch rhythms. Use different scales, and assign different dynamics to various rhythms once students are comfortable with all aspects of subdividing.

TIMBRE:

A blended tone quality relies on timbre (tone), dynamics (volume), and pitch (intonation). In this composition, fusion of tone (blending) is essential for performance effect. While the synthesizer adds a unique sound color, avoid having this particular sound dominate; it should combine with the wind timbres. For young players, pitch distortion may be more apparent in the softer dynamic levels (clarinets will go sharp, brass flat, etc.). By using the synthesizer as a pitch reference, students can gain valuable experience in discriminating listening. The art of being "in tune" is really a never-ending listening exercise. The ultimate goal is to play "in tune" together *all the time*.

When playing *crescendos*, lower sounds should lead. Distortion of sound at the extreme dynamic levels can be avoided with a strong air stream and firm embouchure support. Oftentimes, lack of air, or air speed, will be the major cause of tone, pitch, and technique problems. Good tone utilizes fast, *warm* air. This is especially true in the softer dynamic levels where students must use less, but more compressed air.

Teaching strategy — To work for tone fusion, choose any slow *tutti* exercise. Isolate students by instrument, in pairs, to match tone and pitch (students should sound as one player). Then, have all students in the section do the same thing (work for "one" sound). To help facilitate this activity, tell students they should be able to hear their "neighbors." If they can't, they are playing too loud. The goal is to play *inside* the sound of the group. After this exercise, have sections that are in the same register (alto saxophone and French horn/trumpet and oboe) try the same exercise. The goal is to "lose" the section sound and create one blended, homogenous sound. This "fusion" of tones is aided through critical listening and choice: darker/ brighter (timbre), louder/softer (dynamics), and higher/lower (pitch).

Unit 7: Form and Structure

Space Echoes is a contrapuntal work.

MEASURES	EVENT AND SCORING
1	Suspended cymbal roll; *p, crescendo*
2-7	Theme 1 unison *legato* melody in clarinet, tenor saxophone, trombone/baritone/bassoon, and synthesizer; woodblock, tom-tom, and suspended cymbal interjections; *p, mp*
5	Flutes enter with Theme 1A fragment (imitation a fifth higher); *mp*
8-10	Theme 1 fragment in bassoon, bass clarinet, tenor and baritone saxophone, horn, trombone, baritone, and tuba; clarinet and alto saxophone join flute in Motive 1A; *p, mp*
11-18	Theme 1B (a half step higher than Theme 1) in muted trumpet; two secondary lines 1) low brass, French horn, low saxophone, bass clarinet, baritone, synthesizer and 2) flute, oboe, clarinet, bells (half steps and diminished fifths); percussion interjections; *mf, crescendo, pp*
17-18	*Fortissimo tutti* quarter notes over sustained rolls in snare drum, field drum, and suspended cymbal; diminished tonality; *ff*

MEASURES	EVENT AND SCORING
19-23	Sparse, open texture; woodblock; staggered long note entrances; eighth and quarter note motive in trumpet; dissonant texture; *p, mp, crescendo, f, ff*
24-28	*Piano* chord cluster chord (C7/d); repeat of staggered long-note material from mm. 19-23; *f, p, mp, crescendo, f, ff*
29-31	*Piano* chord cluster; percussion interlude; *f, mp, mf, mp*
32-37	B-flat pedal; thematic material in flute, oboe, clarinet, also saxophone, and trumpet (material first used in m. 13); percussion interjections; builds to *tutti* eighth note motive in m. 37; *mp, mf, p, ff, crescendo*
38-40	Eighth note *ostinato* pattern in flute and bells (half step and diminished fifths); return of eighth note/quarter note motive on unison G in trumpets; beginning of half note tri-tone pattern in oboe and alto saxophone; *piano* chord cluster; percussion interjections; *fp, mp, f, crescendo*
41-45	Return of Motive 1 in low brass, low woodwinds, and synthesizer; continuation of flute and bell half note *ostinato*; continuation of oboe and alto saxophone tri-tone half notes; percussion interjections; *ff, p*
46-48	Transitional material; *fp* E pedal in low brass, low winds, and synthesizer over an eighth note half step *ostinato* in bells; percussion interjections; *fp, mp, mf, f*
49-54	*Glissando* on piano strings; continuation of second bell *ostinato*; repeat of staggered long-note dissonant texture from mm. 19-23; this time trumpet motive is muted; *p, mp, crescendo, ff*
55-57	Continuation of half step *ostinato* in bells; *forte piano* chord cluster; sounds disappear into m. 56; a single *forte* finger snap ends the work in m. 57; *f, mf, decrescendo, f*

ERRATA:

Conductor's score, mm. 42-43:

A tie should be added to connect the half note on beat three in m. 42 to the beginning quarter note in m. 43 in the following parts: bass clarinet, tenor saxophone, baritone saxophone, bassoon/trombone/baritone, tuba, and synthesizer.

Unit 8: Suggested Listening

Leonard Bernstein, "Maria" and "Cool" from *West Side Story*

George Crumb, *Ancient Voices of Children*

Elliot Del Borgo, *Distant Voices*

Donald Erb:
   Space Music
   Stargazing

Gustav Holst, *The Planets*

John Visconti, *Arioso*

Unit 9: Additional References and Resources

Dallin, Leon. *Twentieth Century Composition*, 3rd edition. Dubuque, IA: William C. Brown Company Publishers, 1974.

Del Borgo, Elliot. *Contemporary Rhythm and Meter Duets for Bass and Treble Clef Instruments*. Ft. Lauderdale, FL: Meredith Music Publications (reprinted by Hal Leonard, 2000).

Del Borgo, Elliot. *Contemporary Rhythm and Meter Studies for Bass and Treble Clef Instruments*. Ft. Lauderdale, FL: Meredith Music Publications (Hal Leonard, 2000).

Del Borgo, Elliot. Telephone conversation, April 17, 2000.

Dvorak, Thomas L., Peter Schmalz, and Cynthia Taggart. *Best Music for Young Band*. Brooklyn, NY: Manhattan Beach Music, 1986.

Garofalo, Robert. *Rounds, Catches, and Canons for String Orchestras and Ensembles*, Ft. Lauderdale, FL: Meredith Music Publications (Hal Leonard, 2000).

Grout, Donald Jay. *A History of Western Music*, 3rd edition. New York, NY: W.W. Norton & Company, 1980.

Miller, William. *Band Director Secrets of Success*. Edited by N. Alan Clark. Lakeland, FL: Aiton Publishing, 1997.

Rehrig, William H. *The Heritage Encyclopedia of Band Music*. Edited by Paul Bierley. Westerville, OH: Integrity Press, 1991.

Schoenberg, Arnold. *Structural Function of Harmony*. Edited by Leonard Stein. Revised edition. New York, NY: W.W. Norton & Company, 1969.

Westrup, Jack Allan. *The New College Encyclopedia of Music*, revised edition. New York, NY: W.W. Norton & Company, 1976.

Contributed by:
Linda R. Moorhouse
Associate Director of Bands
Louisiana State University
Baton Rouge, Louisiana

Teacher Resource Guide

The Stars Asleep, the Break of Day

Bob Margolis
(b. 1949)

Unit 1: Composer

Bob Margolis, composer and publisher, is well known for his many fine compositions and arrangements for band as well as his publishing efforts dedicated to producing quality educational band music and band resource guides. A resident of New York, Margolis received his education at Brooklyn College and University of California. He founded Manhattan Beach Music in 1981, and his publications have received high praise and recommendations by many state music associations. Several of his own compositions have been recommended as significant literature by the Florida Bandmasters Association, including *Fanfare, Ode, & Festival*; *Color*; and *Terpsichore*. Two of his arrangements that have received this rating are *Belle Qui Tiens Ma Vie* and *The Battle Pavane*. Other titles by Margolis include *Prelude and March*; *Soldier's Procession and Sword Dance*; and *The Renaissance Fair*.

Unit 2: Composition

In the program notes to the score, Margolis says of this work,

> *The Stars Asleep, the Break of Day* is my most instrumentally colorful Grade 1 work...the musical content greatly exceeds "Grade 1" expectations. Beginning band students have something to study here that presents opportunity for real musical development.

Indeed, through the course of this charming two-movement work, many of the various timbrel combinations available to a beginning band are employed. Additionally, the simple yet highly musical thematic material provides a fruitful learning experience in the areas of expressive interpretation and phrasing. Movement one is slow and lyrical, almost reverent, while movement two is fast and light. The music attempts to evoke the images suggested in the title.

Unit 3: Historical Perspective

The Stars Asleep, the Break of Day was published in 1995 by Manhattan Beach Music. While the musical material is all-original, it harkens to different eras. The melody for movement one was written in the tradition of American folk song and popular melody that produced *Shenandoah* and *Stars of the Summer Night*. These songs arose out of more innocent times in American history, when gentleness and sentimentality were common expressions in popular culture.

The material for movement two, with its fast 3/4 rhythmic structure and its modal melodic material, recollects the much older musical tradition of medieval court dances.

In spite of these stylistically historical references, both of these movements demonstrate their late twentieth century origin in their non-repetitive formal designs.

Unit 4: Technical Considerations

Technical demands are easily within the reach of a mature Grade 1 band. Ranges are very accessible and extremely idiomatic for young players. Rhythmic materials for the wind players are comprised solely of whole, dotted-half, half, and quarter notes and rests. The percussion parts in the second movement contain some eighth notes within repetitive passages, but these should come easily to even beginning players. The timpani part is extremely important, as it frequently is the sole generator of rhythmic impulse.

In the first movement, the most challenging task for the wind players will be the production of sustained, expressive melodic lines while maintaining good tone quality without forcing the sounds. This movement will provide an excellent opportunity to discuss the topics of phrase shaping and how dynamic continuity between phrases functions to generate the overall shape of the piece. The short length of both movements should make the concept of overall musical shape more readily apparent to young players and the execution of that shape an achievable goal.

Light, quick, and fluid playing will be the players' biggest challenge in the second movement. The composer has assisted in this task by restricting the material to four- and eight-measure segments, so fatigue should not become a factor. Close attention to dynamic markings and articulations will be crucial to performing this movement with maximum efficacy.

Unit 5: Stylistic Considerations

The slow, *legato* first movement, almost hymn-like in its singing, open sonorities and reverent mood, requires stylistic unity from all players. Melodic lines must be executed with a true *legato* technique, while accompaniment players must be careful to play their notes for full value, continuing to the next beat with a relaxed ending to their sounds.

The stylistic requirements of movement two are slightly more complex. Players are required to perform *marcato, staccato, tenuto,* and *legato* articulations as well as accents and many other dynamic nuances. Care must be taken to ensure that the *staccato* concept is established uniformly across the ensemble. Players must listen to ensure that they are performing their *staccato* quarter notes, and particularly *staccato* half notes, with the exact same length and shape as other players with the same rhythmic material.

Additionally, this work utilizes several Italian terms, which may be new to some players, including *dolce, secco, tenuto, sostenuto, poco, più,* and *meno.*

Unit 6: Musical Elements

The melodic and harmonic material for movement one is in the key of F major, with very few chromatic alterations. The harmonic structure, which analyzes easily, clearly delineates the phrasal structure and convincingly generates the climactic moment of the movement. As the dynamic markings are sparse in this movement, it provides an excellent opportunity to teach expressive interpretation. Rhythmically, this movement displays two basic patterns:

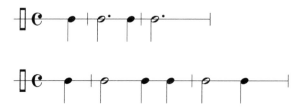

This often occurs over a sustained whole note backdrop.

While retaining the F tonal center, movement two contrasts movement one by shifting to a modal scale structure, specifically F lydian. The lydian mode is characterized by a raised fourth scale degree. In the key of F, this produces a B-natural on C instruments. This may present some tuning challenges for a beginning band. The composer has avoided the B-natural in the low brass, particularly the trombones, where this note would present the most difficulty. The solution to this problem is the occasional mixture of the lydian and major modes. The occasional temporal proximity of B-flats and B-naturals results in dissonances that require resolution. The conflict between the B-naturals and B-flats is resolved in the final measures, with the B-natural prevailing and resolving to a final C major triad.

Rhythmically, this movement is a study of the variations possible using quarter notes and half notes in 3/4 time. Because the phrases are short and vividly contrast one another in terms of rhythm, texture, and timbrel combinations or color, this movement may be an ideal vehicle to develop critical listening exercises. Players could be asked to describe the rhythmic difference between two adjoining four-measure phrases. Musical texture and musical color could be introduced with this movement; players could be asked to describe the sounds they hear and produce using metaphoric adjectives that they may not have yet associated with sounds (e.g., crisp, light, dark, bright, bouncing, warm). Of course there are many others; encourage players to come up with their own before making suggestions.

Unit 7: Form and Structure

Movement one, "The Stars Asleep," is a modified ternary song form composed of three non-repeating phrases with a briefly extended final cadence: A (measures 1–8), B (measures 9–16), C (measures 17–24). A ternary song form usually implies a repetition of the A section after the B section, with a melodically and harmonically contrasting B section. Each phrase in this movement, however, begins on the I chord and returns to the I chord, and there is no repetition of previously heard material. This through-composed quality keeps the material from the squareness often associated with simple music.

Movement two, "The Beak of Day," shares this through-composed quality. Consisting of two eight-measure phrases and then a series of four-measure segments, there are no melodic repetitions. This movement is not as melodically oriented as the first movement, but rather generates its musical vitality through a series of contrasting textures and rhythmic variations. The phrase structure is:

a	a₁	b	c	d	e	f	g	h	i
mm. 1-8	9-16	17-20	21-24	25-28	29-32	33-37	38-41	42-45	46-50

MEASURES	EVENT AND SCORING

Movement 1: "The Stars Asleep"

1-8	Phrase A: melody in French horn and euphonium; trombone and tuba accompaniment
9-11	Phrase B: alto saxophone joins euphonium and French horn on melody; bass clarinet, tenor and baritone saxophone added to accompaniment
12-16	Trumpet joins melody for the second semi-phrase of phrase B; euphonium, bassoon, and clarinet join accompaniment

349

MEASURES	EVENT AND SCORING
16	Written and orchestrated *crescendo* (flute and oboe join accompaniment), plus *allargando* sets up climax in m. 17
17	Climax and beginning of phrase C
17-21	Trumpet on melody; all other instruments accompany
21-24	Consequent semi-phrase of C fragmented between alto saxophone, clarinet, trumpet, and flute
25-26	Final cadence; oboe and alto saxophone with moving quarter notes

Movement 2: "The Break of Day"

1-8	Melody in flute, oboe; alto saxophone and percussion accompany
9-16	Melody in flute, flute 2, oboe; clarinet, bass clarinet, French horn, and percussion accompany
17-20	Melody in trumpet, saxophone; low brass and percussion accompany
21-24	Melody in trumpet and French horn; saxophone, bassoon, and clarinet accompany
25-28	Melody in flute, oboe, clarinet, trumpet, and French horn; bass clarinet, saxophone, and low brass accompany
29-32	Melody in clarinet and bassoon; saxophone, trombone, euphonium, and percussion accompany
33-37	Melody in tuba, euphonium, trumpet, alto saxophone, French horn, and clarinet on shifting pedal points; *ritardando* mm. 36-37
38-41	*A tempo*; melody passes from alto saxophone and trombone to trumpet and clarinet; tenor and baritone saxophone, euphonium, tuba, and percussion accompany
42-46	Melody in flute, oboe, and trumpet; saxophone, low brass, and percussion accompany
47-50	Melody in flute, oboe, and trumpet; all other instruments accompany; m. 49 *tutti crescendo* and cadence

Unit 8: Suggested Listening

Frank Ticheli, *Shenandoah*
Pierre La Plante, *In the Forest of the King*
Bob Margolis/Susato, *The Battle Pavane*
Bob Margolis, *Royal Coronation Dances*

Unit 9: Additional References and Resources

Dvorak, Thomas L. *Best Music for Young Band*. Brooklyn, NY: Manhattan Beach Music, 1986.

Margolis, Bob. *The Stars Asleep, the Break of Day*. Brooklyn, NY: Manhattan Beach Music, 1995.

Miles, Richard. *Teaching Music through Performance in Band*. Volume 1. Chicago, IL: GIA Publications, 1997.

Miles, Richard. *Teaching Music through Performance in Band*. Volume 2. Chicago, IL: GIA Publications, 1998.

Miles, Richard. *Teaching Music through Performance in Band*. Volume 3. Chicago, IL: GIA Publications, 2000.

Randel, Don Michael. *The New Harvard Dictionary of Music*. Cambridge, MA: The Belknap Press of Harvard University Press, 1986.

Stein, Leon. *Structure & Style: The Study and Analysis of Musical Forms*. Secaucus, NJ: Summy-Birchard Inc., 1979.

Contributed by:

Maxon Day
Graduate Teaching Assistant
University of Wisconsin-Milwaukee
Milwaukee, Wisconsin

Teacher Resource Guide

The Tempest
Robert W. Smith
(b. 1958)

Unit 1: Composer

Robert W. Smith (b. 1958) is recognized as one of the most prolific composers of concert band literature in America today, with over 300 publications to his credit. His original compositions for winds and percussion have been programmed by countless military, university, high school, and middle school bands throughout the United States, Europe, and Japan. Among his works meriting worldwide critical acclaim are "The Inferno" and "The Ascension" from his symphony entitled *The Divine Comedy*, and *Africa: Ceremony, Song and Ritual*. Recent commissions include The United States Air Force Band of Flight, the Gemeinhardt Flute Company, the Phi Mu Alpha Foundation, the University of Alabama, George Mason University, James Madison University, East Tennessee State University, and the University of Alabama-Birmingham.

Smith received a Bachelor of Music Education from Troy State University, Alabama, and a Master of Music from the University of Miami, Florida. He is currently Director of Bands at Troy State University in Troy, Alabama. In addition to his administrative duties, he is the conductor of the Troy State University Symphony Band and director of the "Sound of the South" Marching Band. His recent CD, entitled *The Divine Comedy: The Symphonic Music of Robert W. Smith*, is available through Warner Brothers Publications.

Unit 2: Composition

The Tempest was conceived and written as an educational work for the developing young band. It serves as an educational vehicle to address the concepts of phrasing, articulation, musical texture (timbre), tone production,

352

intonation, dynamic contrast, and tonality (major vs. minor). As the title suggests, the work seeks to portray the violent nature of the tempest with its high winds, hail, and rain. Young students can identify with this programmatic imagery and are encouraged to use their imaginations in conjuring the storm with sound. The work is approximately two minutes and fifteen seconds in length.

Unit 3: Historical Perspective

Because of its referential nature, *The Tempest* can provide young band students an introduction to program music. Program music can be introduced and defined as music that describes, characterizes, presents, interprets, or is inspired by a nonmusical subject or idea that the composer indicates by title, explanatory remarks, or prefatory material. This information, in turn, serves to enhance the meaning and performance of the work. Class discussions or projects can revolve around the differences between referential (program music) and absolute music, with examples being provided for each, how composers portray ideas and images through sound (in program music), and how the students themselves can portray thoughts, ideas, and images through their individual instruments.

As the concept of program music originated in the Romantic era, an introduction into this genre is warranted. Exploring program music can begin with some of the first programmatic works of the nineteenth century (e.g., Beethoven's *Pastorale Symphony*) and expand to include more recent works. Significant works with programmatic themes include Berlioz, *Symphonie Fantastique*; Tchaikovsky, *1812 Overture* and *Romeo and Juliet*; Mussorgsky, *Pictures at an Exhibition*; Dukas, *The Sorcerer's Apprentice*; Schuman, *George Washington Bridge*; Benson, *The Leaves Are Falling* and *The Solitary Dancer*; Husa, *Music for Prague 1968*; and Dello Joio, *Scenes from the Louvre*. Some programmatic works for young band include Ticheli, *Portrait of a Clown*; McGinty, *The Red Balloon*; Duffy, *Snakes*; and Broege, *The Headless Horseman*.

Unit 4: Technical Considerations

The tonal center of *The Tempest* is G-natural minor. However, Smith manipulates the leading tone often to create V-i chordal progressions. Smith also utilizes a Picardy third three measures from the end to conclude the work in its parallel major tonality. Because of these chromatic alterations, students must be familiar with reading accidentals. For the most part, *tessitura* is appropriate for young players, with no extreme ranges required (with the exception of trumpet high Ds and Es in measures 41 through 58 and 77, and horn high Ds and Es in measure 73). Technical demands are also at a minimum, with all passages being relatively scalewise. For young trombonists, however, the fifth position F-sharp may prove somewhat difficult. Fortunately, this interval is always approached from fourth position G above. Drilling aurally and physically the interval of the minor second will assist these players greatly. Rhythmic difficulty is appropriate for young band, with the smallest subdivision being the eighth note. Although there are many whole notes, the tempo of the piece should alleviate any sustaining problems young players may have.

A mastery of slurring, accent, *staccato*, and *legato* articulations is necessary for a successful performance. In addition to articulation, a control of dynamic range must be mastered. Smith assists the players in this regard by thinly scoring softer passages and thickly scoring fuller passages. *Crescendos* and *decrescendos* also should be rehearsed for smoothness.

The work is scored wisely for young band. Parts are kept interesting by judiciously partitioning motives, melodies, and countermelodies to various sections. Many parts are reinforced through doubling, allowing the work to be performed by bands with limited instrumentation. A bare minimum of six percussionists are required to cover orchestral bells, xylophone, timpani, snare drum, bass drum, triangle, wind chimes, suspended cymbal, and tambourine. It is also important to note that oboe is not doubled in any other voice in measures 7 and 8. A possible solution for ensembles without oboes would be to rescore these measures for second flute to preserve the seventh of the Cm7 chord resolving to the fifth of the D major triad.

Unit 5: Stylistic Considerations

Careful attention to proper balancing, variation of articulations, and dynamic contrast are paramount to the success of *The Tempest*. *Legato* lines must be sustained, supported, and given shape in order to portray the wind-like rise and fall of the tempest, while accented passages must be given weight and precise articulation to signify the sheer force of the storm. *Forte* passages must be performed with a rich, beautiful tone quality that is full but not strained. The *ostinato* appearing between flute, clarinet, and keyboard percussion must be rhythmically solid and intense, yet soft enough to allow the contrasting, *legato* melody in horn and saxophone to come to the forefront (measures 22 through 36). Similarly, in passages where more than one motive appears, players must be sensitive enough to allow melodic material to dominate. Furthermore, entrances into growing *crescendos* must be rehearsed to ensure smoothness and evenness of sound (measures 5 through 9, 69 through 73).

Unit 6: Musical Elements

MELODY:

As *The Tempest* is composed by using both G-natural minor and G harmonic minor, warm-up material should be based on these scales. Students not only should be able to perform these scales, but they also should be able to discriminate aurally between them. Repetition and modeling are excellent ways of reinforcing this concept. It is suggested that the relationship between G minor and its relative major, B-flat, is used to ease young players into the new scale. By beginning with a scale that is already familiar (B-flat major) and "walking down" to its sixth degree (concert G), students can be asked to perform a scale from concert G to concert G with the same key signature as B-flat major. After this is done, students might be asked to comment on the different sonorities heard. The concept of minor mode can then be introduced.

The Tempest provides ample opportunity to address various articulations. For example, Theme 1 requires mastery over accented passages. Accents should be performed here as full-value quarter and eighth notes with appropriate weight and gravity and a precise beginning that is not overly harsh or too heavily tongued. On the other hand, Theme 2 requires that students master slurring and *legato* tonguing. Each new phrase should begin with a *legato* tongue (e.g., "du" syllable) and move flowingly under the slur marking. The rhythmic *ostinato* requires that students grasp *staccato* tonguing. *Staccato* here should be light in character in order to contrast with the accents (full value) that are interspersed throughout this passage. Accents appear again in the minor second motive at measure 69. These accents, however, are located under a slur marking, and students should be able to give weight to these notes without rearticulating.

Conductors are encouraged to address each articulation in scale and arpeggio warm-up exercises. By addressing each articulation, students can focus on the sound quality of each articulation and begin to discriminate both aurally and mechanically between each. Encouraging students to speak each articulation will also assist in solidifying their interpretation.

Theme 2 provides an excellent opportunity for students to play expressively. An introduction into expressive playing can be presented by the teacher, modeling expressive versus non-expressive playing. Subsequent group warm-ups utilizing scales and arpeggios can be used as a vehicle for exploring various ways of expressing the same material. Returning to Theme 2, students can be shown how music contains areas of repose and unrest, and how they can intensify these moments as musicians by speeding or slowing tempo, or increasing or decreasing volume. Students might be asked to explain where they think the areas of rest and unrest are within this theme and how they might highlight these areas. Students also can be encouraged as individuals to perform their "personalized" interpretations of scales, thematic material from *The Tempest*, or originally composed/improvised work.

Additionally, the melodies presented in Theme 1 and Theme 2 can be compared to teach students how a composer can maintain interest in a work by writing contrasting themes/melodies. This can be referred to in class listenings to further familiarize students with this concept.

HARMONY:
Harmonically, *The Tempest* provides opportunities for exploring major-minor tonalities. As most harmonic structure hinges on major dominant-minor

tonic progressions, these passages can be isolated and performed or sung to develop aural skills in young players. Measures 7 through 9 (Cm7-V-i) can also be isolated to assist students' ear training. Instructors can manipulate the third degree within these triads to illustrate the basic construction of major and minor triads. After carefully studying *The Tempest*, students should be able to discriminate aurally between major and minor chord qualities and key centers. Students should also be able to construct basic major and minor chords by manipulating the major and minor third.

The Tempest also provides examples of homophonic writing. Theme 1 is presented in a homophonic setting with chordal accompaniment. Students can be introduced to this concept and then asked to give examples of other music they know that contains a single, clearly defined melody with chordal accompaniment (e.g., most popular songs, Mozart minuets, a Strauss waltz, etc.). Theme 2, however, is presented throughout the work with an accompanying *ostinato* figure. This *ostinato* figure can be defined to students as a short musical pattern that is repeated throughout a given passage, which acts as supporting or accompanying material. Students might be asked why the composer chose to use an *ostinato* to accompany Theme 2 rather than continuing in the chordal style.

RHYTHM:

Although rhythms in *The Tempest* are appropriate for young bands, rhythmic independence is essential. The *ostinato* presents an interesting challenge in that two independent rhythms are occurring simultaneously to form a composite rhythm of eight eighth notes per measure. Several strategies for building independence can be used to ensure success. One strategy here is to rehearse each line separately, allowing players to concentrate on mastering their line. Another strategy would be to write each rhythm on the board (or a handout) and rehearse each rhythm in scalar warm-up passages (one measure per pitch), then combine the rhythms by dividing the ensemble into two sections (one on rhythm A; one on rhythm B) and performing scales as a group. Battery percussion can be used to supply the eighth note pulse to ensure that there is no rushing through the quarter notes. Returning to the *ostinato* in the piece, players should be reminded to subdivide eighths throughout and to listen to the tambourine for metronomic security. Students can also be encouraged to speak their rhythms or "tizzle" (hiss while articulating the rhythm) while fingering the notes to solidify the passage.

To address the rhythmic independence of Theme 2 superimposed over the *ostinato*, similar strategies can be employed. Warm-up scales can be constructed to keep *ostinato* players on the first degree of the scale repeating the *ostinato* rhythm while other players ascend and descend the scale in various rhythms (e.g., half notes on first and eighth degrees, quarter notes elsewhere; quarter notes on first and eighth degrees, eighth notes elsewhere; etc.). Bass players, who have whole notes through this passage, can be instructed to play repeated whole notes on the first degree of the scale to build independence. In addition, counting and clapping is encouraged throughout, especially when rests are involved (measures 45 through 60, 73 through 75).

Further class activities could revolve around student-composed *ostinato* passages. These *ostinatos* could be composed within certain instructor-given parameters (e.g., compose an *ostinato* utilizing the first three notes of the G minor scale) to facilitate students' work. Theme 2 could then be superimposed over these student-composed *ostinato* passages to demonstrate how different *ostinatos* create different textures. Hearing their work combined with that of a master composer will encourage creative thinking and hopefully invite students to explore further the rewards of composing on their own.

TIMBRE:

The aspect of timbre can be presented to young students in an effort to demonstrate how a composer uses the various colors of an ensemble to convey the character of the music. For example, the character of the introduction is dark and mysterious. The composer chooses to orchestrate this in darker-sounding instruments (*chalumeau* register of B-flat clarinet, bass clarinet, and bassoon). Consequently, each musician should strive to play with dark sonorities reflecting the overall timbre of the introduction even when additional instruments enter. By analyzing each section in this manner, students and instructors should be able to portray the character of each element of the storm through sound/timbre.

Unit 7: Form and Structure

SECTION	MEASURES	EVENT AND SCORING
Introduction	1-4	Soft passage alluding to Theme 2 is introduced by clarinet and bassoon; passage *crescendos* and *decrescendos* reflecting "wind"
	5-8	Flute, oboe, and saxophone add to clarinet and bassoon and begin statement again; full band enters *piano* (m. 7) and *crescendos* to downbeat of m. 9; chordal progression from mm. 7-9 is Cm7–DM–G, respectively
Theme 1	9-12	Theme 1 is presented in clarinet, alto saxophone, and horn; all other instruments reinforce concert G in octaves, either on the downbeat of each measure or following the same

SECTION	MEASURES	EVENT AND SCORING
		rhythmic pattern of the theme; chordal progression is i (mm. 9-11) — V (m. 12)
	13-17	Theme 1 is restated by flute, oboe, alto saxophone, trumpet, and horn; accompaniment is as before; clarinet and xylophone lead transition to next section (m. 17)
Ostinato/Theme 2	18-21	Ostinato is created between flute, clarinet, and keyboard percussion; tambourine and triangle create texture
	22-29	Theme 2 is presented in horn, alto and tenor saxophone; rhythmic ostinato and percussion texture continue
	30-35	Bass voices are added (tuba, baritone saxophone, and bass clarinet), moving from tonic to dominant; Theme 2 repeats but is altered in m. 33 to begin transition back to Theme 1; ostinato and percussion continue
Theme 1 repeat	36-44	Exact repeat of Theme 1 (mm. 9-17)
Ostinato/Theme 2 repeat	45-58	Repeat of Theme 2 (mm. 22-35); the rhythmic ostinato is recreated by clarinet, trumpet, and keyboard percussion; Theme 2 is presented by flute, oboe, alto saxophone, and horn; bass voices reinforce tonic-dominant relationships; percussion provides rhythmic drive
	59-62	Theme 2 extension in low voices
Theme 1 repeat	63-68	Theme 1 is repeated exactly with the exception of the last two measures, which are omitted
Coda	69-72	Minor second motive begins in clarinet, trumpet, and xylophone; the rest of the ensemble is added gradually to the crescendo poco a poco
	73-75	Crescendo climaxes
	76-79	Theme 1 fragment resolves to G major in flute, oboe, clarinet, and trumpet; work concludes on concert G in octaves

Unit 8: Suggested Listening
Ludwig van Beethoven, *Symphony No. 6, "Pastorale"*
Hector Berlioz, *Symphonie Fantastique*
Timothy Broege, *The Headless Horseman*
Paul Dukas, *The Sorcerer's Apprentice*
Robert W. Smith:
   The Ascension
   The Inferno
Frank Ticheli, *Portrait of a Clown*

Unit 9: Additional References and Resources

Apel, Willi, ed. *Harvard Dictionary of Music*, 2nd edition. Cambridge, MA: Belknap Press, 1970.

Duarte, Leonard, P., Daniel S. Hiestand, Carol Ann Prater, and Doy E. Prater. *Band Music That Works*, Volume 1. Burlingame, CA: Contrapuntal Publications, 1987.

Duarte, Leonard, P., Daniel S. Hiestand, Carol Ann Prater, and Doy E. Prater. *Band Music That Works*, Volume 2. Burlingame, CA: Contrapuntal Publications, 1988.

Dvorak, Thomas L., Cynthia Crump Taggart, and Peter Schmalz. *Best Music for Young Band*. Edited by Bob Margolis. Brooklyn, NY: Manhattan Beach Music, 1986.

Garofalo, Robert J. *Instructional Designs for Middle/Junior High School Band*. Fort Lauderdale, FL: Meredith Music Publications, 1995.

Grout, Donald J. *A History of Western Music*, 3rd edition. New York, NY: W.W. Norton & Company, 1979.

Lisk, Edward S. *The Creative Director: Alternative Rehearsal Techniques*, 3rd edition. Fort Lauderdale, FL: Meredith Music Publications, 1991.

Lisk, Edward S. *The Creative Director: Intangibles of Musical Performance*. Fort Lauderdale, FL: Meredith Music Publications, 1996.

Randel, Don Michael. *The New Harvard Dictionary of Music*. Cambridge, MA: The Belknap Press of Harvard University Press, 1986.

Stolba, K Marie. *The Development of Western Music*. Dubuque, IA: William C. Brown Publishers, 1990.

Contributed by:
Daryl W. Kinney
Ohio State University
Columbus, Ohio

Teacher Resource Guide

Theme and Variations
Timothy Broege
(b. 1947)

Unit 1: Composer

Timothy Broege is a respected composer of educational music for young bands. He received his education at Northwestern University, and he has taught at both the public school and university levels. Currently Broege serves on the faculty of Monmouth Conservatory, Red Bank, New Jersey, and also works as Director of Music for the First Presbyterian Church in Belmar, New Jersey. He has over thirty published band compositions to his credit, as well as music for voice, guitar, and piano. Other well-known works for band by Broege include *Dreams and Fancies, The Headless Horseman, Rhythm Machine, Sinfonia VI: The Four Elements,* and *Sinfonia V: Sacred et Profana.*

Unit 2: Composition

This piece is designed to introduce young players to theme and variations. The work is technically very simple and allows the players to concentrate on musical events happening in the music. The melody is clearly stated at the beginning, and the variations are simple enough for students to see and hear the composer's manipulations. Scoring is for standard wind band; percussion scoring calls for bells, triangle, snare drum, and bass drum. The work was composed in 1993 for the North Courtland School Band of East Stroudsberg, Pennsylvania, Melodie A. Shamp, Director; it is approximately two minutes in duration.

Unit 3: Historical Perspective

Theme and variations is a classic compositional device that has been used since the earliest of musical times. In Beethoven's day, a popular concert attraction was the improvised variations on a given theme. Most every major composer has written some type of theme and variations; well-known examples include Beethoven's *Diabelli Variations*, Brahms's *Variation on a Theme by Haydn*, and Britten's "Variations and Fugue on a Theme of Purcell" from *A Young Person's Guide to the Orchestra*. In the history of band literature, well-known compositions in this manner include *Variations on a Korean Folk Song* by John Barnes Chance, *Variants on a Medieval Tune* by Norman Dello Joio, *Theme and Variations, Opus 43a* by Arnold Schoenberg, and William Rhodes's arrangement of Charles Ives's *Variations on "America."*

Unit 4: Technical Considerations

This piece is accessible to first-year players. Ranges are not a problem; neither are the rhythms, which are basic combinations of whole, half, quarter, and eighth notes. The melody is based on the D Dorian mode (white notes of the keyboard starting on D). The key signature indicates C minor, there are very few instances of accidentals, and the final cadence is in C major. The technical demands are intentionally kept to a minimum to allow the players to focus on broader issues of the composition and musical style.

Unit 5: Stylistic Considerations

Students will need to understand and be able to perform *legato* and *staccato* styles, as they play a major role in the variations of the melody. Balance is an important issue, especially in the first variation (canonic imitation). Students will need to be fully aware of the melody and each of the manipulations of that melody. Most of the piece is written with block (terraced) dynamics, so students will need to be able to make sudden changes between *piano* and *forte*, and vice versa.

Unit 6: Musical Elements

The melody used in this piece is eight measures in length, with two two-measure call-and-response patterns. The work opens with a presentation of the theme in Dorian mode, followed by four sets of variations: canonic imitation, rhythmic variation, harmonic variation, and retrograde. In variation one, the melody begins in the clarinets and saxophones, is passed on to the flutes, oboes, cornets, and horns, and is then passed on to low brass and woodwinds. The second variation brings a style change from *legato* to *staccato*, as well as rhythmic variance. The third variation is clearly in major mode, while the fourth and final variation is both melodic and rhythmic retrograde. Tempo is constant throughout at quarter note = 92.

An instructional unit could be structured to focus on the compositional technique of theme and variations. Students could be assigned to take a simple theme from their method book and manipulate it in simple ways (such as rhythm, articulation, style, etc.). Another focus might be on learning different styles of articulation: *legato, staccato, marcato*. There are numerous issues pertaining to balance and blend that could be pursued. Due to the technical ease of this work, the possibilities of exploration of the various aspects of composition and style are virtually endless.

Unit 7: Form and Structure

MEASURES	EVENT AND SCORING
1-8	Presentation of main theme; low voices call, high voices respond
9-16	Variation I: canonic imitation; Group 1 includes clarinet, saxophone; Group 2 includes flute, oboe, cornet, horn; Group 3 includes low brass and reeds
17-18	Transition
19-26	Variation II: rhythmic variation; first clarinet and flute with melody; all others accompany; first cornet joins melody in m. 23
27-35	Variation III: harmonic variation; flute, oboe, alto saxophone, cornet, and horn with melody; all others accompany
35-36	Transition (percussion *soli*)
37-45	Variation IV: retrograde; low brass and reeds with melody; all others accompany; cadence in m. 45 in C major

Unit 8: Suggested Listening

Johannes Brahms, *Variations on a Theme of Haydn*
John Barnes Chance, *Variations on a Korean Folk Song*
Aaron Copland, *Variations on a Shaker Melody*
Charles Ives/Rhodes, *Variations on "America"*

Unit 9: Additional References and Resources

Dvorak, Thomas, Cynthia Crump Taggart, and Peter Schmalz. *Best Music for Young Band*. Brooklyn, NY: Manhattan Beach Music, 1986.

Kennedy, Michael, ed. *The Concise Oxford Dictionary of Music*, 3rd edition. Oxford: Oxford University Press, 1980.

Lane, Jeremy. *Teaching Music Through Performance in Band and Texas U.I.L. Grade I Prescribe Music List for Band*. Graduate project. Waco, TX: Baylor University, 1998.

Miles, Richard, ed. *Teaching Music through Performance in Band*. Chicago, IL: GIA Publications, Inc., 1997.

Miles, Richard, ed. *Teaching Music through Performance in Band,* Volume 2. Chicago, IL: GIA Publications, Inc., 1998.

Recordings of works by Broege are available on-line at: www.members.aol.com/mbmband

Contributed by:
Jeremy S. Lane
Doctoral Graduate Assistant, Music Education
Louisiana State University
Baton Rouge, Louisiana

Teacher Resource Guide

Train Heading West and Other Outdoor Scenes

Timothy Broege
(b. 1947)

Unit 1: Composer

Timothy Broege was born in Belmar, New Jersey, on November 6, 1947. Following early studies in piano and music theory with Helen Antonides, he earned a Bachelor of Music degree at Northwestern University (with highest honors) in 1969, where he studied composition with M. William Karlins, Alan Stout, and Anthony Donato. Broege taught in the public schools of Chicago and taught elementary school music in Manasquan, New Jersey. He is currently Organist and Director of Music at First Presbyterian Church in Belmar, New Jersey, and teaches at the Monmouth Conservatory of Music in Red Bank, New Jersey. He has composed over forty original works for band, including several *Sinfonia*, concertos for piano and marimba, *Peace Song*, *Dreams and Fancies*, and *Three Pieces for American Band*.

Unit 2: Composition

Train Heading West and Other Outdoor Scenes is a three-movement work portraying various outdoor scenes in late nineteenth and early twentieth century America. It was originally composed as a set of three sketches for beginning band in the mid-1970s, and was revised and expanded in 1997. It is approximately four minutes and thirty seconds in length.

Unit 3: Historical Perspective

Programmatic music, which evokes pictorial images or narrates a story, has been an important component of western art music since the early nineteenth century. Works such as Berlioz's *Symphonie Fantastique*, Smetana's *The Moldau*,

Tchaikovsky's *Romeo and Juliet*, and Strauss's *Also Sprach Zarathustra* are significant nineteenth century programmatic works. American composers have a rich tradition of program music depicting folklore and images of the great outdoors. Prominent American programmatic works include Grofé's *Grand Canyon Suite*, Copland's *Appalachian Spring* and *Rodeo*, and Reed's *La Fiesta Mexicana*. *Train Heading West and Other Outdoor Scenes* is conceived in the great American tradition of programmatic music describing outdoor images. In his preface to the score, Broege cites the music of Copland as an outstanding example of American "outdoor" music, and states his hope that band conductors will use *Train Heading West and Other Outdoor Scenes* as an introduction to the music of Copland and other American composers.

Unit 4: Technical Considerations

The first movement is primarily in the key of C minor, and the second and third movements make extensive use of the key of D minor. There is no rapid figuration, but mastery of these scales will be necessary by the entire ensemble. All three movements are in common time throughout. The tempo of the first movement is quarter note = 92, and the tempo of the second movement is quarter note = 72. The third movement has several tempo changes and a gradual *accelerando*. It begins at quarter note = 66, accelerating to quarter note = 176 at measure 17. The movement continues at this tempo until measure 31, where it abruptly shifts to quarter note = 108 and slows for two measures before quarter note = 176 resumes. The rhythmic writing is very accessible for young bands, using whole, half, quarter, and eighth notes. The eighth/quarter/eighth note syncopation figure at the beginning of the third movement is the most challenging rhythm pattern.

Instrumental ranges are conservative, and there are no solo passages. The bassoon part is doubled in the bass clarinet throughout, and a passage in the third movement requiring the baritone saxophone to play repeated Bs below the staff also has an optional higher part for younger players. The percussion section includes timpani, xylophone, bells, maracas, cymbals, tambourine, triangle, suspended cymbal, tom-tom, bass drum, snare drum, and optional train whistle. The bass drum plays rolls with timpani mallets in the second movement, and the snare drum is played with brushes in the third movement. The percussion parts can be covered by five players.

Unit 5: Stylistic Considerations

The primary challenge in this area will be to effectively communicate the programmatic content of *Train Heading West and Other Outdoor Scenes*. In addition to the overall conception of the work as an "outdoor" suite, the composer had specific imagery in mind for each movement. The first movement, "Solemn Ceremony," portrays a Native American dance around a blazing fire on the great plains of the Midwest. The second movement, "Rain on the

Mountains," is self-descriptive, and the third movement, "Train Heading West," describes a great steam locomotive slowly accelerating out of a Midwestern train station. The conductor is encouraged to discuss the programmatic content of *Train Heading West and Other Outdoor Scenes* with students, asking for verbal and written responses on their personal ideas about each movement. Additionally, students should be encouraged to create visual images of each movement. While technical and rhythmic demands are modest, the composer uses a rich variety of articulations, dynamics, and timbres in creating brilliantly expressive portraits of the three outdoor scenes.

Unit 6: Musical Elements

MELODY:

The melodic material of *Train Heading West and Other Outdoor Scenes* frequently uses perfect fifths and minor thirds. Students should be asked to identify these intervals as they appear in context. The primary melodies of the first and second movements provide opportunities to develop skills in phrasing and melodic playing. These melodies are presented in Example 1 (first movement) and Example 2 (second movement).

EXAMPLE 1

EXAMPLE 2

In both melodies, the long tones must not be allowed to stagnate in terms of melodic direction, tone quality, and pitch. The conductor is encouraged to demonstrate appropriate phrasing by playing the melodies on his/her principal instrument. Additionally, since the ranges of both melodies are relatively narrow, the conductor may wish to have students sing both melodies to develop a lyrical style. A new melody is introduced in measure 11 of the second movement in the piccolo, flute, oboe, and first clarinet, which the composer wishes to predominate over the repetition of the primary melody. The new melody is seen in Example 3.

EXAMPLE 3

The primary melody of the third movement is shown in Example 4.

EXAMPLE 4

This movement is a series of rhythmic and timbral variations of the primary melody. The melody does not appear in its original form and is frequently presented in the manner of a tone color melody, with different instruments playing a portion of the melody as it progresses. Students should sing and play the original form of the melody so they can recognize it in the context of a series of variations.

HARMONY:

The piece provides many opportunities to expand young players' knowledge of triads, seventh chords, and quintal harmony. All three movements make extensive use of parallel fifths in vertical sonorities. This interval is a hallmark of the "American" sound and serves as an important unifying element throughout. Instances of parallel fifths may be introduced at the keyboard. The second movement contains an excellent vehicle for introducing the relationship between melody and harmony in the formation of cadences and phrases. The main melody and accompanying harmony make up the chord progression seen in Example 5.

EXAMPLE 5

The final chord coincides with a point of repose in the melody and clearly represents a significant point of arrival because the harmonic progression moves from a series of seventh chords to triads at the conclusion of the phrase. The conductor should consider introducing this progression at the keyboard prior to rehearsing. The vertical sonorities of the third movement frequently involve chords constructed in fifths and seventh chords constructed from two sets of perfect fifths, which also can be introduced at the keyboard.

RHYTHM:
Rhythmic demands are well within the grasp of young players. The conductor should present the primary rhythms of the piece and ask students to identify them in context. Students should be encouraged to find rhythmic relationships between movements. The drum rhythm of the first movement is the same as the second train rhythm of the third movement, and the beginning of the first train rhythm is the rhythm of the second movement's primary melody in diminution. These rhythms are shown in Example 6 (first movement—drum rhythm), Example 7 (second movement—raindrop rhythm), and Examples 8a and 8b (third movement—train rhythms).

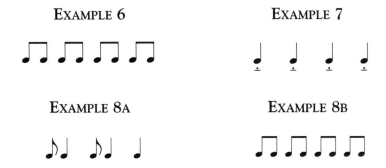

EXAMPLE 6   EXAMPLE 7

EXAMPLE 8A   EXAMPLE 8B

The major rhythmic objective of the first movement will be to maintain consistent performance of the eighth notes in the drum rhythm. Clapping exercises and the use of subdivision syllables can serve as aids in attaining consistent tempo. The second movement is the most straightforward of the three from a rhythmic standpoint, using whole, half, and quarter notes exclusively. The third movement is the most challenging, including an extended *accelerando*, a *caesura* followed by an immediate shift to a slower tempo, and a return to the primary, fast tempo. The conductor will undoubtedly wish to introduce the idea of *accelerando* without the music, starting with various clapping and playing exercises that incorporate flexibility of tempo. It will be very helpful to explain that the increase in tempo from the opening to "full speed" at measure 17 underscores the programmatic idea of a steam train accelerating away from the station. Consistent, accurate execution of eighth notes by the entire ensemble will be necessary for a successful performance of this movement.

TIMBRE:
Tone color is a very important component in all three movements. One of the most important tasks in this area will be to provide a thorough explanation of which instruments are assigned primary melodies and rhythms in order to

realize the textures intended by the composer. To this end, the conductor may consider creating a "flow chart" of each movement, with the assistance of students, that diagrams where important melodies and rhythms are found, which instruments are playing them, and which instruments are assigned accompanying material. This kind of teaching aid, developed in a collaborative setting, may help to achieve a more insightful performance.

The primary melody of the first movement is presented in two distinct timbral settings. It appears in the opening measures in piccolo, flute, oboe, alto saxophone, and trumpet, and is repeated at measure 10 by clarinet, bass clarinet, bassoon, tenor and baritone saxophone, trombone, euphonium, and tuba. The conductor and players should strive for appropriate balance and blend within the sections presenting the theme, as well as emphasizing the contrast between the bright sound of the initial presentation and the dark sound of the repetition. The instruments playing the raindrop rhythm of the second movement (flute, second clarinet, bells) must blend to form a distinct tone color so this important unifying element is heard in a consistent manner.

The main melody of this movement presents several challenges in terms of balance. It is first played by oboe, first clarinet, and alto saxophone in a fully harmonized texture. These instruments must not be dominated by the low woodwinds, horns, and low brass. The secondary melody shown in Example 3 (played by flute, piccolo, oboe, and first clarinet) must be heard over the repetition of the primary melody when it is introduced at measure 11. As stated earlier, the third movement is a set of variations in which the main thematic material is presented in the manner of a tone color melody. The primary objective in terms of timbre will be to achieve a seamless connection between sections of instruments playing fragments of the melody. The ensemble will certainly benefit from playing or singing the original form of this melody as shown in Example 4.

Unit 7: Form and Structure

MEASURES   EVENT AND SCORING

Movement I: "Solemn Ceremony"

1-9   Primary melody (C minor) in piccolo, flute, alto saxophone, trumpet; drum rhythm in parallel fifths in clarinet, bass clarinet and bassoon, tenor and baritone saxophone, horn, trombone, euphonium, tuba, tom-tom

10-15   Primary melody (C minor) in clarinet, bass clarinet, tenor and baritone saxophone, trombone, euphonium, tuba; drum rhythm in piccolo, flute, alto saxophone, trumpet, horn, timpani, xylophone, tom-tom

MEASURES	EVENT AND SCORING
16-18	Secondary theme in piccolo, flute, oboe, clarinet 1, alto saxophone, trumpet, xylophone; cadence at m. 18 reinforces C as tonal center
19-22	Closing section; secondary theme in clarinet, alto saxophone, horn, trumpet, piccolo, flute, oboe; movement concludes with cadence to open fifths (C, G)

Movement II: "Rain on the Mountains"

1-2	Introduction; raindrop rhythm in piccolo, flute, clarinet 2, bells
3-10	Primary melody (D minor) in oboe, clarinet 1, alto saxophone 1; melody is fully harmonized; raindrop rhythm continues in piccolo, flute, clarinet 2, bells
11-18	Primary melody (D minor) in alto saxophone, trumpet 1; secondary melody in piccolo, flute, oboe, clarinet 1; raindrop rhythm continues in clarinet 2, bells
19-22	Primary melody fragment; raindrop rhythm ceases
23-26	Closing section; closing melody in trumpet 1; raindrop rhythm resumes in piccolo, flute, bells; movement concludes with cadence to open fifths (D, A)

Movement III: "Train Heading West"

1-16	Presentation of primary melody in four variations (four measures each); *accelerando* from opening tempo (quarter note = 66)
17-18	Arrival at "full speed" tempo (quarter note = 176)
19-30	Three variations of main melody (four measures each); *caesura* at conclusion of m. 30
31	"Hold back"; tempo abruptly slows to quarter note = 108; new melody in bass clarinet, bassoon, baritone saxophone, trombone, euphonium
33	A *tempo* (quarter note = 176); two variations of main melody (four measures each)
41-42	Closing section begins "off into the distance"
43	Optional vamp measure (players may imitate train sounds)
44	Snare drum with brushes and tambourine conclude movement playing train rhythm *ppp*

Unit 8: Suggested Listening

John Adams:
    Common Tones in Simple Time
    Shaker Loops
Timothy Broege:
    America Verses
    Peace Song
    Sinfonia IV
    Sinfonia V: Symphonia Sacra et Profana
    Sinfonia VI: The Four Elements
    Sinfonia XVI: Transcendental Vienna
    Streets and Inroads
    Three Pieces for American Band
    Train Heading West and Other Outdoor Scenes
Aaron Copland:
    Billy the Kid
    John Henry
    Lincoln Portrait
    Rodeo
    Symphony No. 3
    The Tender Land
Ferde Grofe, *Grand Canyon Suite*
Roy Harris, *Symphony No. 3*
David Holsinger, *On the Grand Prairie Texas*
Douglas Nott, *The Kalama*
Steve Reich:
    Different Trains
    It's Gonna Rain
Toru Takemitsu:
    Rain Spell
    Toward the Sea
Dan Welcher:
    Arches
    The Yellowstone Fires
    Zion

Unit 9: Additional References and Resources

Broege, Timothy. "The Listener as Citizen." In *Thoughts* (collection of essays on the website of the Composers Guild of New Jersey, http://www.cgnj.org). Volume 1, Number 2 (July, 1999).

Delaney, Jack. "Timothy Broege: His Contributions to the Wind Band Repertory with an Emphasis on Sinfonia III and Sinfonia V." D.M.A. Thesis, University of Cincinnati College-Conservatory of Music, 1986.

Dvorak, Thomas L., Cynthia Crump Taggart, and Peter Schmalz. *Best Music for Young Band*. Edited by Bob Margolis. Brooklyn, NY: Manhattan Beach Music, 1986.

Dvorak, Thomas L., Robert Greschesky, and Gary Ciepluch. *Best Music for High School Band*. Edited by Bob Margolis. Brooklyn, NY: Manhattan Beach Music, 1993.

Fullmer, David. "The Contemporary Wind Composers: Timothy Broege." Graduate Thesis, University of Washington, 1997.

Groeling, Charles. Review of *Procession and Torch Dance* by Timothy Broege. *The Instrumentalist* 53 (February 1999): 75.

Lambert, James. Review of *Theme and Variations* by Timothy Broege. *The Instrumentalist* 51 (August 1996): 68.

_____. Review of *Sinfonia IX—A Concert in the Park* by Timothy Broege. *The Instrumentalist* 53 (June 1999): 60.

Manhattan Beach Music website, http://members.aol.com/mbmband (includes catalog, price list, and complete on-line recordings).

Moss, Bruce. Review of *Train Heading West and other Outdoor Scenes* by Timothy Broege. *The Instrumentalist* 53 (February 1999): 76.

_____. Review of *Jody* by Timothy Broege. *The Instrumentalist* 54 (October 1999): 70.

Sheldon, Deborah. "Exciting Works for Young Bands." *The Instrumentalist* 54 (August 1999): 26.

Sindberg, Laura Kautz. "Concerts that Teach." *Teaching Music* 5 (June 1998): 36.

_____. "CMP (Comprehensive Musicianship through Performance) Teaching Plan Using Sinfonia VI." *Music Educators Journal* 85 (November 1998): 40.

Thomson, John. Review of *Sonata for Wind Band* by Carl Phillip Emanuel Bach, arranged by Timothy Broege. *The Instrumentalist* 49 (April 1995): 62.

_____. Review of *Concert Piece for Trumpet and Band* by Timothy Broege. *The Instrumentalist* 50 (June 1996): 53.

_____. Review of *Three Preludes* by Anton Bruckner, arranged by Timothy Broege. *The Instrumentalist* 51 (April 1997): 44.

Contributed by:
John Bleuel
Assistant Professor of Music,
University of West Georgia
Carrollton, Georgia

Musical examples generated by:
Thomas George Caracas Garcia
Assistant Professor
University of West Georgia
Carrollton, Georgia

Musical examples used by permission of Manhattan Beach Music, Brooklyn,
New York.

Teacher Resource Guide

Two English Dances

arranged by John O'Reilly
(b. 1941)

Unit 1: Composer
John O'Reilly has been active as a composer and arranger for more than twenty-five years. He has written original works for bands, choirs, and orchestras, and has been involved in developing the *Accent on Achievement* method books for beginning bands. Other titles to his credit include *Northwest Suite*.

Unit 2: Composition
Two English Dances is accessible to advanced first- and second-year players, and serves as an excellent introduction of young musicians to the British band tradition. The two tunes set in this arrangement are "Shepherd's Hey" and "Country Gardens." Both settings are very short; the entire duration of the work is two minutes. Scoring is for standard wind band; percussion scoring calls for bells, woodblock, and tambourine. The arrangement was published in 1992.

Unit 3: Historical Perspective
During the early years of this century, Ralph Vaughan Williams and Gustav Holst laid the foundations for the British band tradition. Relying heavily on English folk songs they had discovered and collected, they produced the earliest masterworks for band, including Vaughan Williams's *Folk Song Suite* and *Sea Songs*, and Holst's two suites for military band. Other major composers who were influenced by British folk music and wrote masterpieces for band include Percy Grainger, Gordon Jacob, and Malcolm Arnold.

Unit 4: Technical Considerations

The technical demands of this work are not extreme; the only range consideration is the use of high E-flat in the flute part. The scoring is full throughout most of the work, and parts are sufficiently doubled. There are some exposed sections in the upper woodwind parts; however, they are short and not too difficult. The work presents some rhythmic problems; there are several instances of dotted-quarter/eighth note patterns, as well as dotted-eighth/sixteenth note rhythms. The true difficulty in this piece lies in matching styles and note lengths throughout the ensemble.

Unit 5: Stylistic Considerations

Students will need to know the styles of *staccato*, *marcato*, and *tenuto*. Matching note lengths and styles between instrument groups will prove challenging, as will making the style changes from one measure or note to the next. There are few dynamic markings in the score, which gives the students and conductor considerable freedom to experiment with various dynamic schemes.

Unit 6: Musical Elements

Both of the melodies used in this setting are very scalar with few wide skips. The harmonic motion is traditional, with little use of non-harmonic tones. The first movement is in E-flat major, and the second movement is in B-flat major. As mentioned before, the rhythm is of a primary concern; students must play together in matching styles for a successful performance of this work.

The unison rhythms in the first movement present some challenges that will need to be isolated. Combining the rhythm patterns with scales would prove helpful. This piece is also a great introduction to the British band tradition as exemplified in the works of Holst, Vaughan Williams and, particularly, Grainger. Study of settings of the melodies used in this work could also be a unit of further study.

Unit 7: Form and Structure

SECTION	MEASURES	EVENT AND SCORING
Movement I: "Shepherd's Hey"		
A	1-8	Flute, clarinet *soli*
B	9-16	Full scoring; cornet with melody; cadence in E-flat major in m. 16
A´	17-24	Flute, clarinet *soli*; slight variation of A
A´´	25-33	Full band; cornet and flute with melody; final cadence in E-flat major

SECTION	MEASURES	EVENT AND SCORING
Movement II: "Country Gardens"		
A	1-8	Full band; cadence in B-flat major in m. 8
B	9-16	Flute, clarinet, percussion; full band enters m. 13; section repeats
C	17-24	Brass choir, saxophone call for two measures; full band answers; cadence in B-flat major in m. 24
B	25-32	Woodwind *soli* for four measures; full band enters m. 29; final cadence in B-flat major in m. 32

Unit 8: Suggested Listening

Percy A. Grainger:
   Country Gardens (arrangement for string choir)
   Shepherd's Hey
Gustav Holst:
   First Suite in E-flat for Military Band
   Second Suite in F for Military Band
Ralph Vaughan Williams:
   Folk Song Suite
   Sea Songs

Unit 9: Additional References and Resources

Dvorak, Thomas, Cynthia Crump Taggart, and Peter Schmalz. *Best Music for Young Band*. Brooklyn, NY: Manhattan Beach Music, 1986.

Kennedy, Michael, ed. *The Concise Oxford Dictionary of Music*, 3rd edition. Oxford: Oxford University Press, 1980.

Lane, Jeremy. *Teaching Music through Performance in Band and Texas U.I.L. Grade I Prescribe Music List for Band*. Graduate project. Waco, TX: Baylor University, 1998.

Miles, Richard, ed. *Teaching Music through Performance in Band*. Chicago, IL: GIA Publications, Inc., 1997.

Miles, Richard, ed. *Teaching Music through Performance in Band*, Volume 2. Chicago, IL: GIA Publications, Inc., 1998.

Smith, N., and A. Stoutamire. *Band Music Notes*, revised edition. Lake Charles, LA: Program Note Press, 1979.

Contributed by:
Jeremy S. Lane
Doctoral Graduate Assistant, Music Education
Louisiana State University
Baton Rouge, Louisiana

Teacher Resource Guide

The Two Minute Symphony
Bob Margolis
(b. 1949)

Unit 1: Composer

Bob Margolis is a well-known and highly respected composer and arranger of quality music for bands. Founder of Manhattan Beach Music, a publishing company devoted to promoting fine band music, Margolis has many arrangements and original band works to his credit. Several of these works are settings of Renaissance music by such composers as Gervaise, Susato, and Praetorius.

Margolis was educated at Brooklyn College and University of California, and has been active in the publishing field since 1981. His works include *Prelude and March*; *Soldier's Procession and Sword Dance*; *The Stars Asleep, the Break of Day*; *Fanfare, Ode & Festival*; *The Renaissance Fair*; *Color*; and *Terpsichore*. Margolis has also published arrangements of Susato's *Battle Pavane*, Arbeau's *Belle Qui Tiens Ma Vie*, Gabrieli's *Canzona No. 1*, and Gervaise's *Royal Coronation Dances*.

Unit 2: Composition

The Two Minute Symphony is a work that is designed to increase ensemble awareness of musical events in a composition. The work is not a true symphony in form or structure, although it does contain symphonic-style manipulation of melodic material—fragmentation, development, extension, and tonal center changes are all used to demonstrate to students the various methods a composer may use to enliven a composition. As Margolis writes in the notes to the score:

> The purpose is not so much to teach your class symphonic form...but rather to get them to listen to what is happening in the music.

This piece is an original composition written in 1988. As the title indicates, it is approximately two minutes in duration.

Unit 3: Historical Perspective

The symphony as an art form has a long, rich tradition of development, innovation, and musical quality. Most every great master of music from the Classical era to the present has contributed to this genre. The history of the symphony follows the clean, elegant lines of Haydn and Mozart, to the expanded forms of Beethoven, Berlioz, Liszt, and Brahms, to the monumental works of Mahler, Bruckner, and Shostakovich. Symphonies for bands have a much more condensed history, but there is still a great deal of quality symphonic music for winds. The earliest examples of a "symphony" for band are the masterpieces by Persichetti, Giannini, and Hindemith. Other composers who have contributed to the "band symphony" include Robert Jager, Timothy Broege, Morton Gould, and Johann De Mej.

Unit 4: Technical Considerations

Technical demands on the players in this piece are minimal. The ranges are well within a first-year player's capabilities: the clarinet parts do not cross the break, the highest note for the flutes is D above the staff, and the highest note for the first trumpet part is D in the staff. Rhythm is very simple; there is some use of dotted-quarter/eighth patterns. Students will need to be able to play a concert B-flat major scale at quarter note = 120. There are some sixteenth notes in the percussion, but they are used in simple combinations with eighth notes. The composer has intentionally made the parts simple so the players can learn to listen across the group and hear other musical events happening throughout the ensemble. This piece is accessible to advanced first- and second-year players.

Unit 5: Stylistic Considerations

A wide variety of style markings are used in this piece. Players will need to understand how accents, *staccato* accents, *legato* accents, rooftop accents, *legato*, and *staccato* markings are performed. There is a great deal of dynamic contrast, from the softest *pianissimo* to a nice, full *fortissimo*. Students will need to be able to match styles, both playing in unison and when the theme is broken up between instrument groups. They will also need to exaggerate each articulation and dynamic change so as to provide the maximum amount of contrast between sections.

Unit 6: Musical Elements

The title of this work may be somewhat misleading. This piece was not conceived as a model of symphonic form and structure. It was designed to demonstrate to young musicians how a composer manipulates a musical idea.

There is only one primary theme that undergoes numerous changes, both melodic and motivic. The melody is based on four notes: the first four notes of the B-flat major scale. Harmonically, the work is firmly in B-flat major, with no use of non-harmonic tones. The rhythm is manipulated constantly, but in simple manners so as not to increase the difficulty level.

The Two-Minute Symphony would be an excellent choice to help students transfer and synthesize previously taught skills into a single piece. There is a great deal of contrast between the three sections; short instructional units could be devised to focus on each section individually, then the piece as a whole. Other instructional units might focus on historical aspects of the symphony or on the compositional techniques used to manipulate the melody.

Unit 7: Form and Structure

SECTION	MEASURES	EVENT AND SCORING
Introduction	1-8	Percussion only; no woodwinds
A	9-16	Trombone, baritone, saxophone, clarinet, and flute
A	17-24	Full band; *tutti* scoring
Transition	25-26	Low brass and woodwinds
Development	27-30	Full band; tuba, bass voices on pedal G beneath development
A´	31-38	All woodwinds except flute; no percussion
Transition	39-47	Low brass and woodwinds
A´´	48-55	Split choirs; woodwinds call, brass respond; key of B-flat major
Development	56-72	Motive passed around instrument groups; cadence on G minor chord
Transition	73-74	Flute, clarinet, oboe
Recapitulation	75-92	Full band; *tutti* scoring
Coda	92-103	Establishment of B-flat major as final tonality; full band; piece ends on B-flat major chord

Unit 8: Suggested Listening

Wolfgang A. Mozart, *Symphony No. 40*, Movement I
Antonin Dvorak, *Symphony No. 9 "New World,"* Movement I
Sergei Prokofiev, *Symphony No. 5, "Classical,"* Movement I
Any piece in which a theme can be easily detected and followed through a movement while it is manipulated and developed

Unit 9: Additional References and Resources

Dvorak, Thomas, Cynthia Crump Taggart, and Peter Schmalz. *Best Music for Young Band*. Brooklyn, NY: Manhattan Beach Music, 1986.

Kennedy, Michael, ed. *The Concise Oxford Dictionary of Music*, 3rd edition. Oxford: Oxford University Press, 1980.

Lane, Jeremy. *Teaching Music through Performance in Band and Texas U.I.L. Grade I Prescribe Music List for Band*. Graduate project. Waco, TX: Baylor University, 1998.

Mahr, Timothy. "An Interpretive Analysis of Color." *The Instrumentalist* 51:2 (October, 1996): 26-32.

Miles, Richard, ed. *Teaching Music through Performance in Band*. Chicago, IL: GIA Publications, Inc., 1997.

Miles, Richard, ed. *Teaching Music through Performance in Band*, Volume 2. Chicago, IL: GIA Publications, Inc., 1998.

Smith, N., and A. Stoutamire. *Band Music Notes*, revised edition. Lake Charles, LA: Program Note Press, 1979.

Information and recordings of music by Bob Margolis are available on-line at: members.aol.com/mbmband

Contributed by:

Jeremy S. Lane
Doctoral Graduate Assistant, Music Education
Louisiana State University
Baton Rouge, Louisiana

Teacher Resource Guide

Two Russian Folksongs

arranged by Ralph Gingery
(b. 1945)

Unit 1: Composer/Arranger

Ralph Gingery has composed and arranged numerous works for concert band and jazz ensemble. He received his bachelor's degree in Theory/Composition from Indiana University and did graduate work at the University of Wisconsin. He is a former staff arranger with the United States Navy Band in Washington, DC, and co-founder of William Allen Music Company.

Unit 2: Composition

Two Russian Folksongs is a setting of two contrasting Russian songs. The opening section is a lyrical song, which gives the band the opportunity to play in a lyrical, expressive style. The second section is a slower, march-like song, providing ample opportunity to work on the elements of good march style.

Unit 3: Historical Perspective

The two folk songs used in the work, "Stenka Razin" and "Varshavyanka," are characteristic of the rich folk tradition of old Russia yet remain popular today. Many composers have used Russian folk music in their works for orchestra and band, including Tchaikovsky, Rimsky-Korsakov, Glazunov, Moussorgsky, Stravinsky, Prokofiev, and Shostakovich.

Unit 4: Technical Considerations

The work has limited technical demands. The keys of E-flat major and G minor should be well within the educational goals of young bands. The trumpet parts remain in the staff, and the horns do not play above D in the staff. The principal rhythmic demands are the dotted-eighth/sixteenth note rhythm in the march section and the sixteenth note figures in the trumpets after rehearsal number 41.

Unit 5: Stylistic Considerations

A sustained *legato* style must be achieved in the opening section with emphasis on a full, rich sonority. The second section must be in good march style with the appropriate space and accent. The section beginning at rehearsal number 41 ("slower") should have a "grandioso" feel, with a full, balanced sound from the ensemble.

Unit 6: Musical Elements

MELODY:

The melodic lines must be as song-like as possible. The eight-measure principal melody in the first clarinet provides an excellent opportunity to work on melodic shape and phrasing. (A possible dynamic shape is shown in Example 1.) Students should strive to play four-measure phrases and follow the contour of the line.

EXAMPLE 1

Ex. 1 Clarinet 1 (mm. 1-8)

HARMONY:

The harmony is triadic and functional. The opening section is in E-flat major and the second (march) section in G minor. The texture is homophonic throughout. Students must listen carefully to ensure that all chords are balanced equally. The chordal accompaniment must not overpower the melodic line.

RHYTHM:

The opening section is in a slow 3/4 meter. Students should work to mentally pulse eighth notes to ensure the accuracy of the dotted-quarter/eighth note rhythm. The march section is in 4/4 meter. The accuracy of the dotted-eighth/sixteenth note rhythm is extremely important in the march section (Example 2). Students should be encouraged to mentally pulse sixteenth notes to aid the proper placement of the sixteenth.

EXAMPLE 2

Ex.2 Flute 1 (mm. 24-27)

An effective teaching method is to have a student play sixteenth notes on the snare drum (snares off for clarity) while the band plays the dotted-eighth/sixteenth note rhythm. This allows them to hear exactly where the sixteenth note is placed in the rhythmic structure. They should play this rhythm with a slight space after the dotted-eighth note, ensuring good march style. The trumpet sixteenth notes must be cleanly articulated with space (Example 3).

EXAMPLE 3

Ex.3 Trumpets (mm. 41-44)

TIMBRE:

The woodwinds must work to produce a beautiful, sustained tone in the opening section. In the second section, students should work for a dark, well-focused tone, portraying the character of the G minor march. Blend and balance are of the utmost importance. The players must be aware of which instruments carry the melodic line and which are accompanimental. They must listen carefully to achieve the proper balance.

Unit 7: Form and Structure

SECTION		MEASURES	EVENT AND SCORING
Song 1:			
A	a	1-4	Principal melody in clarinet; key of E-flat major; clarinet 2/alto saxophone thickens the texture beginning in m. 3
	a′	5-8	Consequent phrase; bass line enters; full triadic harmony
A′	a	9-12	Repeat of opening phrase; full band with *obligato* in flute
	a′	13-16	Consequent phrase
	a′	17-21	Repeat of consequent phrase with increased rhythmic activity; one-measure harmonic transition to prepare new key of G minor

SECTION	MEASURES	EVENT AND SCORING
Song 2:		
B b	22-27	Slow march; two-measure introduction followed by antecedent phrase; principal melody in flute; key of G minor
b´	28-31	Consequent phrase; flute/oboe harmonized in rhythmic unison
c	32-35	New phrase in B-flat major; trumpet and horn enter, full texture
b´	36-40	Return of opening phrase (G minor); final measure prepares new key
Coda	c 41-44	Final section begins with return of B-flat major phrase in a slower, more stately manner
b´	45-50	Consequent phrase followed by a two-measure restatement of the final cadence

Unit 8: Suggested Listening

For band:

    Aram Khatchaturian, *Armenian Dances*
    Boris Kozhevnikov, *Symphony No. 3, "Slavyanskaya"*
    Nicolai Miaskovsky, *Symphony No. 19*
    Sergei Prokofiev, *Marches, Op. 69, Nos. 1-4*

For orchestra:

    Modest Moussorgsky (orch. Maurice Ravel), *Pictures at an Exhibition*
    Nicolai Rimsky-Korsakov, *Scheherezade*
    Igor Stravinsky, *Petrouchka*
    Piotr Tchaikovsky, *Marche Slav*

Unit 9: Additional References and Resources

Grout, Donald Jay, and Claude V. Palisca. *A History of Western Music*, 5th edition. New York, NY: W.W. Norton & Company, 1996.

Rehrig, William H. *The Heritage Encyclopedia of Band Music*. Edited by Paul E. Bierley. Westerville, OH: Integrity Press, 1991.

Sadie, Stanley, ed. *The New Grove Dictionary of Music and Musicians*. London: Macmillan Publishers, Ltd., 1986.

Swan, Alfred Julius. *Russian Music and Its Sources in Chant and Folk-song.*
New York, NY: W.W. Norton & Company, 1973.

Contributed by:

Bradley P. Ethington
Associate Director of Bands
Syracuse University
Syracuse, New York

Teacher Resource Guide

Visions on an
Old American Tune

Wayne Pegram
(b. 1938)

Unit 1: Composer

Wayne Pegram was born in Nashville, Tennessee, in 1938. Currently serving as Professor of Music and Coordinator of Music Education at Tennessee Technological University, he has been a career educator, composer, and woodwind performer. With sixty published compositions to his credit, Pegram has been a strong contributor to the educational repertoire. He received degrees from Tennessee Technological University (B.M.E.), University of Tennessee at Knoxville (M.M.), and University of Northern Colorado (D.A. in Composition and Conducting).

Unit 2: Composition

Pegram's musical setting is based on the hymn tune *Happy Land*. Its bright, cheerful melody was first published in *Southern Harmony and Musical Companion*. This famous tunebook, compiled by William Walker (1809–75), has had a unique longevity, which continues to gain the attention of composers in search of the attractive simplicity of the melodies and harmonies that are embodied in its songs. The beginning of the text of *Happy Land* reveals its buoyant, joyful spirit in the opening words:

> There is a happy land,
> Far, far away,
> Where saints in glory stand,
> Bright, bright as day.

After a simple, homophonic introduction that establishes each choir of the ensemble, Pegram builds a set of variations that gains weight as the texture builds toward an eventual *tutti*. A special feature of the music is the framework for improvisation that is presented in variation two.

Unit 3: Historical Perspective
The source of the tune itself provides ample historical significance for this piece. *Southern Harmony*, *Kentucky Harmony*, and subsequent collections in this lineage can be viewed as among the first music series designed to cultivate music reading in the United States. The *fasola* notation, which is based on *solfeggio*, was set as shape notes (triangular, oval, square, or diamond noteheads) that helped the singers recognize the pitches that were to be sung.

Unit 4: Technical Considerations
The scales of B-flat major and E-flat major are required of all woodwind and brass parts. While the tempo is marked "moderately fast" (quarter note = 120-132), the rhythmic demands are elementary. Note values fall consistently into the categories of half, dotted-quarter, quarter, and eighth notes. With each variation the texture thickens, moving from simple homophonic texture at the beginning of the work to simple contrapuntal writing near the climax. A special quality and technical consideration of the work is found at measures 43 through 50. This section is devised to facilitate both solo and accompaniment improvisation, and may be repeated as desired. Each player will see a four-measure sample solo on each part, with four more measures left open for improvisation.

Unit 5: Stylistic Considerations
The prevailing style of the music is lyrical. Though marked to be performed at a moderately fast tempo, a *legato* that imitates vocal character should be employed throughout. Care should be taken so that each four-measure phrase speaks as a unified, flowing statement. It is also important that performers hide the breath marks from phrase to phrase. An important aspect of this piece is that it provides the opportunity for improvisation in a non-jazz context. Performers will be challenged to create improvisations that speak in a manner that is consistent with the context set up earlier in the piece.

Unit 6: Musical Elements
MELODY:
A diatonic melody is one of the key features of this work, as the main sixteen-measure tune is repeated three times. With each variation, there is either melodic ornamentation or textural variation. Performers will be challenged to present lines that flow without choppiness.

HARMONY:

With the exception of a modulatory moment in measure 58, the harmony is diatonic. The prevalence of root position tonic and dominant chords contributes to the direct, rough-hewn character of the music.

RHYTHM:

Though the original setting of *Happy Land* was in 2/4 meter, Pegram has chosen to set *Visions on an Old American Tune* in 4/4. By doing so, all note values are doubled, making it more easily understandable for beginning players. In addition, seeing the music in 4/4 might aid the performer in thinking of the melody in a more lyrical way.

TIMBRE:

The composer has been attentive to characteristic ranges for quality tone production among young players. Nevertheless, there are intervalic challenges, especially in the trombone, baritone, and tuba parts. Warm-up studies provided as a part of the publication can help serve as a preparatory study for performing the piece.

Unit 7: Form and Structure

After a ten-measure introduction that establishes the key of B-flat major and features the main melodic motive in each choir of the ensemble, the entire sixteen-measure statement of *Happy Land* is made. A simple aabb´ form, the tune and accompaniment are stated in alternating phrases between the woodwinds and brass. These statements are made over an ongoing percussion texture that supports rhythm with the cymbals, triangle, snare drum, and bass drum; and melody and harmony with the bells and timpani. Measures 27 through 42 present a variation of the initial statement featuring a more decorative version of the "a" phrases in the woodwinds. The second variation begins at measure 43, continuing through measure 58. It is in this section that the "a" phrases provide an opportunity for ensemble improvisation. Variation two concludes with a modulation to the key of E-flat major. The final variation is heard from measure 59 through measure 74.

Marked "somewhat slower," the "a" phrases are set majestically, brass against woodwinds, followed by woodwind statements of the "b" phrases against the brass. There is a four-measure coda that reinforces the conclusion of the work.

SECTION	MEASURES
1-10	Introduction
11-26	Theme
27-42	Variation 1
43-58	Variation 2
59-74	Variation 3
75-78	Coda

Unit 8: Suggested Listening
Frank Ticheli, *Amazing Grace*
David Holsinger, *On a Hymnsong of Philip Bliss*

Unit 9: Additional References and Resources
Walker, William. *The Southern Harmony and Musical Companion,*
  4th edition, Edited by Glenn C. Wilcox. Lexington, KY: University Press
  of Kentucky, 1987.

Contributed by:
Frederick Speck
Director of Bands
University of Louisville
Louisville, Kentucky

Index by Difficulty Level
for
Teaching Music through
Performance in Beginning Band

Index by Publisher
for
Teaching Music through
Performance in Beginning Band

Index by Composer
for
Teaching Music through
Performance in Beginning Band

Index by Title
for
Teaching Music through
Performance in Beginning Band